The
Red Roots
of
Terrorism

THE RED ROOTS OF TERRORISM

Symptoms of a critical illness of civilization, and ways to remedy it.

Copyright 2002 by Christian Hartwright

ISBN 1-880177-07-2

CUI BONO BOOKS
PAN-TECH INTERNATIONAL, INC.
P. O. Bos 4548
McAllen TX 78502

Printed in the United States of America

PREFACE

Since September 11, 2001, government officials and the media have strongly emphasized the dangers of terrorism, but the tactic, or strategy, of terrorism is not a new arrival on the world's stage. Throughout history it has played a long and uninterrupted role as a major factor in the decline and disappearance of many governments and cultural groups. It has had far more influence on government policies in the US during past decades than most people realize.

There has been a tendency of government agencies, politicians, academia, and ethnic pressure groups to focus our attention on the Islamic connections of some of the most spectacular terroristic acts, meanwhile ignoring or downplaying dangers arising from other sources which may constitute more serious threats to our country.

For over a hundred years, America has been under continuous terrorist attack by individuals and groups which could be described as Reds, or Soviet agents, and which had little or no connection with Arab countries. Dangers from such sources still exist, though their actions may be less organized and not as well coordinated as they were during the heyday of the Soviet Union.

Terrorists operate under many disguises: the hammer-and-sickle flag was never their only ensign. So, when the Marxist or fellow traveler found his preferred lode star had vanished from the political horizon, he was able to select a substitute from a large number of alternatives. He could choose feminism, liberation theology, animal rights, environmentalism, black power, or whatever other movement promised the most excitement and debauchery and provided the most opportunities to injure persons or groups.

Presumably, seekers for a new spiritual nest will be strongly attracted to organizations emphasizing in their mission statements (or equivalents) a justification or goal that the seeker has already found to be appealing as a result of his prior indoctrination by teachers, parents, or the media. The primary inducement will always be their opportunity to maim, kill, and destroy.

In this connection, we learn from Bennett (1994B), " . . . a professor at Wellesley College, says that while Marx focused on workers, today's Marxists are concerned with 'analysis of how institutions are oppressive based on gender, race, and sexuality' " (Bennett 1994B). "Still, some people pine for the fervor of the late '60s and early '70s, when Marxist economics courses were routinely packed with idealistic students . . . a Marxist economist at U of MA Boston, felt a twinge of nostalgia during the debate over the North American Free Trade Agreement . . . 'Without a strong movement, it's hard to feel really relevant and positive about what you are doing,' he says . . . [a professor] who teaches economics at the U MA Boston, turned to Marxism because she feels it's a 'paradigm that explains inequality . . . Her specialty — and her passion — is the economics of gender, but she does much of her research in state and local finance'."

The ultimate, but usually hidden, purpose behind all red causes is the gaining of power and privileges for the controllers by exploiting persons attracted to the putative programs of the organizations. The basic operations involved in this exploitation are (1) the obtaining of money from donations and extortions, (2) the gaining of political power through blackmail and votes, (3) the gratification obtained from exerting control over enthusiasts, (4) the experiencing of pleasure from sexual relations with unsophisticated members, and (5) the destruction of envied persons and segments of society.

The Author's Purpose

A major goal of the author was to provide readers with an analysis of the true motivations of persons who commit terrorist acts with the professed intention of furthering a Communist cause. He presents for the readers' consideration a hypothesis that such terrorists are afflicted with a deeply embedded maliferous suite of behaviorisms, a syndrome which we can describe as a manifestation of a psychopathic hatred of humanity, perhaps combined with elements of sadism and envy.

Another objective of the author was to examine and attempt to explain the effects on American culture of the new or refurbished organizations which appropriated much of the Red agenda after the more blatant Red front groups lost their funding, direction, and international linkages when the Russian-centered espionage, disinformation, and dirty tricks agencies collapsed in the 1990s.

The USSR represented the peak of liberal/radical aspirations. It was an ideal and perfect state for the sadistic nonconformer — in fact the embodiment of every hope of the true believers. The stated goals of the Bolsheviks were the perceived goals of virtually every leftist in the world. For this reason, none of the excesses of the Soviet government could be regarded as errors by Reds — since the system was perfect, how could its practitioners make errors? And, the further away one stood, the better the picture.

None of the Communists' tactics were new. Most of them were at least as old as recorded history, but the relatively high level of incompetence and ennui in the staffs of their enemies, plus the Reds' single-minded program of assassinations, theft, espionage, and the like, which were applied with a brutality seldom seen at any other time, made Soviet Russia the most murderous and destructive despotism ever seen.

When the "mother country" imploded, a large number of its trained operatives were left out in the cold. No doubt some of them remained faithful, in their fashion, to the old familiar philosophy, but many agents recognized that intriguing and profitable programs weren't going to be forthcoming; that their connections within the Red network could not give them any assurance of promotion or other reward. Furthermore, they no longer had the tools or money needed to control the assassins and other operatives of Russian covert agencies. And, they stood a much greater chance of suffering retaliation for their crimes. So, there was a gradual drifting away from acceptance of Communism as the major thread governing their thoughts and lifestyle. Never mind — there were other decadent and destructive philosophies to rally around.

Scope of the Book

Much of the text concerns activities that either have had a direct effect on persons in the US or are essential to understanding the development of the Red programs attributed to Marx, Lenin, Stalin, and Trotsky. An occasional departure from this tendency was inevitable because of the interlacing threads of this old and pervasive philosophy.

The author has included in the category of "terror" those activities which, through some covert means, kill or injure numerous persons in a random manner, even though it may not be obvious to the general public that a terroristic act has occurred. In some cases, it may appear that the event was an accident or even a freak of nature — such things as a disease epidemic or a plane crash.

Our attention will be focused on the larger picture. Almost every nation of any size has been plagued by a communist-type underground at some time, but often the movements were small, inept, and temporary. Such groups left only faint footprints on the sands of time and, generally, will be ignored by the author. For example, the communist governments in Africa and Asia have received very little attention in this volume, even though they might provide worthwhile information for diligent students.

Events in modern times have received the greatest emphasis. Ancient and medieval accounts of real and imaginary socialist and nihilistic communities could not be left out of the picture entirely, but the information we have about them is of doubtful validity and is fragmentary, so they receive only a small amount of space.

Organization of the Text

In addition to this Preface, the book includes a table of contents positioned as usual at the front of the book, and a glossary, bibliography, and index placed at the end of the volume. The author has an ingrained aversion to footnotes and the minimum possible number have been used.

The text is organized into seven sections, each of which is comprised of either three or four chapters. Every section is devoted to some large part of the book's theme, such as the definitions and histories of red movements, methods by which democratic institutions have been infiltrated by reds, destructive effects of econuts, the role of zoophilism and its cognates, methods by which existing governments are destabilized, and use of deviant sexuality as a weapon against humanity. The concluding section contains both the author's overview of the present world situation (with emphasis on conditions in the US) and his recommendations for measures that might correct threatened usurpations of every citizen's constitutional and natural rights.

Terminology and Style

Most of the non-specialized terms used in this book conform to the definitions found in Webster's New International Dictionary, Second Edition, Unabridged, which was published in 1961 by G. & C. Merriam & Co. There are some exceptions — these are mainly words, phrases, and abbreviations having specialized meanings appropriate to the book's subject. Also in the Glossary are terms which have been coined or which came into common usage subsequent to the printing of the dictionary. All of these exceptions, and others, are explained in detail in the Glossary.

In a few matters of rhetoric, the author's practice differs slightly from the most common American usage and/or from the conventions recommended by many supposedly authoritative reference works on style and grammar. These peculiarities should not interfere with the reader's understanding of the author's meaning or of the logic used to support his theories. Readers who are interested in this sort of thing should consult the Glossary for further details.

Matters of Nomenclature

A detailed analysis of the names that have been applied to philosophies of the communist and socialist types throughout historical times will be found in the first few chapters of this book, but it is important for readers to understand at the outset the conventions which the author will use to identify various subsets of the more inclusive term, "Communist." In general, these usages conform to common practices, but in a few cases they have been modified in relatively minor ways in order to increase clarity and avoid confusion.

Throughout the following text, "Reds" (the word being distinguished by capitalization) is intended to identify persons who call themselves Communists and openly acknowledge their faith in the principles and doctrines enunciated by the founders of Bolshevism, Stalinism, Leninism, or Trotskyism (roughly equivalent to official Soviet-directed activities), while "reds" (no capitalization) are persons who do not belong, and may never have belonged, to any organization of extreme left-wing orientation but whose actions (or some of them) are driven by the person's sadistic and malevolent desires to destroy or appropriate property and to enslave, maim, and kill persons under the pretense of promoting the common good or for some other "compassionate" reason. Of course, the dividing line between "Reds" and "reds" can be rather murky.

Both logical concerns and editorial convenience suggest that the category, "reds," should be considered as consisting of two groups:

(a) Persons who are enemies of humanity as a result of either learned behavioral patterns or their ingenerate disposition, and who are willing or even eager to humiliate, wound, kill, and destroy in an almost random manner, regardless of the effect their actions have on their own personal advancement or profit. In extreme cases they will risk their their lives or even seek their own death in the process. In Biblical terms, these might be regarded as disciples of Molech (Milcom). In psychological terms, perhaps they could be described as sadists or as motivated by an extreme form of envy. Most, if not all, terrorists come from this group.

(b) Those persons who are almost totally indifferent to the sufferings of others but who will not devote any time or effort to acts of destruction and mayhem if the acts do not yield material benefits or temporal power to themselves. But, when it seems necessary for their own profit and advancement, they will mercilessly exploit humanity to the fullest extent. Biblically, these persons might be regarded as disciples of Mammon. Psychologists might define them as psychopaths. They seldom become personally involved in the action, but they may assist in planning if they expect to profit from the event.

Sources

As a basis for statements in this book, the author relied to a limited extent on personal observations but based most of his conclusions on a vast amount of reference material including government documents, legal records, academic theses, scientific journals, news reports, and many other sources of information thought to be, if not totally reliable, at least fairly representative of a specific viewpoint.

Excerpts from TV programs, news broadcasts, and the like were seldom used, and then never as a source of factual information — they have no value for that purpose. Extracts from websites are also cited in the text, usually with a reminder that these postings are ephemeral in the extreme, and in general are more useful as curiosities than as data.

This book is presented as a scholarly historical publication, and so the author includes many exact quotations (sometimes these are fairly extensive) to get across certain points, but easily recognized text may not show specifics of the source. For example, there is no need to tell the reader what edition or publisher the author used when Marx's *Communist Manifesto* is cited. Except in such instances, the author and date of publication are given adjacent to the quotation. This information will allow readers to find a complete identification of the source in the bibliography. See the introductory paragraphs in the Bibliography for further details.

The Question of Objectivity

The book you are reading is a scholarly study of a difficult and controversial subject. The author *does* have a point of view, but he attempted to be objective when evaluating "data" that could not reasonably be regarded as fully supported by the available evidence. Decisions as to the trustworthiness or pertinency of information were not in any way related to the decision's possible effect on financial or career betterment of the author, but were based on the moral, ethical, and spiritual guidelines adopted by him. If the reader decides to evaluate the evidence in relation to another set of spiritual guidelines, and as a result reaches a different conclusion from that of the author, so be it.

In the limited space available in a book such as this one, it is not possible to cover all viewpoints on our subject, and the author would not wish to do so even if space were available. There are literally thousands of research papers, books, articles, audio and video tapes, films, and other forms of disinformation which can be consulted by the reader who wants to get the establishment's view of "scientific socialism." This book is not one of them.

The Cover Art

The cover illustration shows a stage conjuror performing the well-known "handkerchief color change" illusion. In this case, the magician is transmuting communist flags into anarchist ensigns and banners of other organizations by drawing them through the "magic" tube. Symbolically, the fabric remains the same while the outward appearance turns into something quite different and, usually, of more innocent connotation. It would be reasonable to regard the "magician" as a personification of the establishment news media and all the other whitewashing and disinformation groups operating in the US.

TABLE OF CONTENTS

section 1
THE RED ROOTS OF TERRORISM

The chapters in this section contain discussions of the background, origin, development, and current status of several of the most important ancient, medieval, and modern varieties of political systems ranging from nihilism through anarchism to socialism-communism-Bolshevism. The author provides evidence which indicates there is an inherent connection between these leftist philosophies and the use of terrorism to destabilize democratic nations.

Although Communism and closely related philosophies of social interactions which preceded, accompanied, and followed it have little credibility today because of their functional failures on a massive scale, we still hear about diehard proponents of the original doctrines who are mooching about in the nooks and crannies of the world. Even today, these dinosaurs of the left regard Marx as the true prophet, Lenin as his Aaron, and Stalin as his David. And, they invariably consider terrorism to be an acceptable and effective tactic for influencing historical trends.

More important than the few remaining Red despots, and having more sinister long-term implications for humanity, are the individuals and groups for whom the Communist/Bolshevist type of ideology has a strong appeal as a tool for enhancing their own power and prestige. They occupy positions of prestige and influence in nearly every non-communist country.

For example, Communism remains a dominant influence in many, if not most, of the universities throughout the free world, including virtually all large institutions of higher education in the US. And, small pockets of professed or concealed socialists, Marxists, and anarchists can be found in the government, in religious organizations, in charitable groups and foundations, in the entertainment industry, in news gathering and distributing corporations, etc. These people have one all-encompassing goal: gaining power by converting as many persons as possible to their way of thinking.

chapter one

ANCIENT AND MEDIEVAL ROOTS

The basic ideas of communism have been around for a very long time, and they have been put into effect (in more or less modified forms) many times. The concept that people would be better off and more contented if they commingled their goods and services is certainly ancient: something of the sort undoubtedly occurred to the first human who noticed his neighbor had more food than he did, or whose mate smelled better than his own.

Ancient Speculations

Many ancient and medieval philosophers were attracted to the concept of common ownership of, and universal access to, all the land and goods existing in a community or nation, and, of course, eventually in the world. It looked good on paper. This primitive idea has been greatly elaborated and modified by thinkers and doers who expected to benefit in some way, not necessarily in a material way, from their "improved" forms of communism.

The ancient Greek philosophers seemed to be fascinated by the concept of the perfect government. These intellectuals, like those of every other age, believed that collections of humans would be happiest when most of them were deprived of their belongings, families, and freedom, and put to work at menial tasks while the philosophers and poets lounged around the pool and talked about important things.

Plato (flor. 400 BC) had a great deal to say about the ideal society. Two of his works, *The Republic* and *Laws*, describe his conception of the perfect community. It bears startling similarities to an ant hill, according to one commentator. Another authority wrote, "Plato's entire program is founded on the denial of personality." Both admirers and denigrators of his ideas describe the Platonic nation as a form of chiliastic socialism.

Two of the surviving comedies of Aristophanes (flor. 400 BC), *Ecclesiazume* and *Plutus*, include socialist themes.

The *Historical Library* of Diodorus, an author living in the first century BC, describes mythical socialist communes located in sunny islands somewhere in the Indian ocean. All citizens must work and the tasks are rotated. The food is provided by the state according to a menu established by law. The men enjoy communal wives, and children are brought up apart from their parents. Wet nurses exchange babies they are feeding so the children do not become attached to a particular woman, and vice versa. Everyone who was incurably ill or suffered from a physical defect was supposed to commit suicide, as were those who reached the maximum age prescribed by law.

From the earliest centuries of the Christian religion, its authorities or would-be authorities were writing about the ideal community, and their concepts frequently took the form of a socialist group in which all property was shared. In many of these paper paradises, the family unit was also abolished.

Terrorism, as a separate feature of the founding or conduct of socialist nations, does not seem to form a part of the imaginary utopias dreamed up by the ancient poets and philosophers. It does come into the picture, however, when actual communities of the socialist type began to appear in the historical record.

Early Experiments

In the first century AD, the Nicolaites sect advocated shared wives and property. In the second century AD, the gnostic sect of Carpocratians appeared in Egypt. They followed principles of complete communality, including sharing of all women without restriction. Among the writings attributed to them, is "God made everything common for man; according to the principles of commonality, he joins man and woman. In the same way, he links all living beings; in this he has revealed justice demanding communality in conjunction with equality."

The following descriptions are taken from the very detailed study of the history of socialism compiled by Shafarevich (1980). He said, "The appearance of Manicheism gave rise to a great number of sects that professed doctrines of a socialist character. St. Augustine wrote about the existence of such sects at the end of the third and the beginning of the fourth centuries AD.

A heresy attributed to a Persian named Mazdak, gained considerable acceptance at the beginning of the fifth century. It was based on Manichean doctrines, and taught that contradictions, anger, and violence are related to dissensions over women and material things. "Therefore," in the words of a Persian historian, "he made all women accessible and all material wealth common and prescribed that everyone had an equal share of water, fire and pastures." The breakdown in family relations and in the economy which resulted from instituting these practices was such that, "Frequently, a man did not know his son nor the son his own father, and no one possessed enough to be guaranteed life and livelihood. In the disturbances which subsequently arose, the followers of Mazdak were defeated."

Medieval Communism

The word "Utopia" was first coined by Sir Thomas Moore and used as the title for his book of the same name, which described an "ideal" community. The Latin version of this work appeared in 1516 and the English translation became available about 1551. Utopia was represented as being an imaginary island, the inhabitants of which had formed a government, or society, which was nearly perfect. Moore's concept has such a strong appeal that the word "utopian" has been used since Moore's time to designate proposals for governance that are, or that are advocated as potentially being, the closest possible approach to perfection in human communities.

However, "Utopian" is often regarded as a term of ridicule or disparagement when attached to an imaginary, or proposed, scheme of government, especially when the system is obviously impractical.

The historical record indicates that there were strong socialistic currents circulating in Europe during the Middle Ages, and many of the communities or groups which were formed as a result of these trends showed tendencies toward violence in propagating their doctrines or in obtaining their freedom from control by traditional religious organizations (e.g., the Roman Catholic Church) and even from kings. In fact, many of their tactics are strongly reminiscent of terrorism as we know it today.

Shafarevich (1980), in his review of socialist movements through the ages, says that it is possible to divide the "heresies" of the Middle Ages into three groups:

(1) Manichean heresies: the Cathars, Albigenses, Petrobrusians — from the eleventh to the fourteenth centuries.

(2) Pantheistic heresies: Amalricians, Orliebarians, Brethren and Sisters of the Free Spirit, Adamites, the Apostolic Brethren and the related groups of Beghards and Beguines — from the thirteenth to the fifteenth centuries).

(3) Heresies which, long before the Reformation, developed ideas that were close to Protestantism: Waldensians, Anabaptists, Moravian Brethren — from the twelfth to the seventeenth centuries.

The aforementioned historian believes that most of these "heresies" were based on the same source — the gnostic and Manichean heresies which, as early as the second century AD, spread through the Roman Empire and beyond, even as far as Persia. They all had one feature in common: they eventually came into armed conflict with both the Catholic Church and the nobility of the countries they evangelized, with the inevitable result that they were crushed, most of their leaders were tortured and executed, and the lay members were killed or dispersed.

A fairly common feature of these rebellions was the condemnation of property rights and the praising of poverty during the early part of the movement and the use of confiscated property (and women) to provide an extravagant lifestyle for the leaders after full control of the masses was achieved. In any case, it was customary to divide the congregation into two parts: the greater number of converts were expected to contribute their property and labor to the good of the movement, while a few persons who were closely associated with the founder and/or figurehead made use of the general fund for their own purposes and served as priests or administrators for the community.

As we examine these movements in greater detail, we find that communality of goods was a predominant feature, the devoting of labor and the harvest (or handicraft product) to a central authority was very common, and the elimination of the normal family unit was frequent. Celibacy was sometimes advocated, and celebrated by its avoidance. Terrorism was extremely common, with destruction of whole villages, and the murder of hundreds of enemies (or people who had goods or lands that were coveted by members) was not unusual. Most of these outrages were justified as having been demanded by God, or Christ, or some other supernatural being.

The groups known as Cathars were fairly representative of the common pattern, although they did have some unusual features. Since their doctrines spread over wide areas during a long period of time, temporal and geographical differences in their practices developed.

The name "Cathars" was given to several different communist-like groups in Central Europe who apparently first appeared in the eleventh century. They were all heretical in terms of Catholic doctrine, but varied considerably in the specifics. There seemed to be no single doctrinal point common to them all, although some writers say they were all gnostic or Manichean heretics. In a general way, they did, however, share a belief in the irreconcilable contradiction between the evil physical world and totally good spiritual world. Some Cathars believed there were two Gods, a good one who created the spirit world and an evil one who created the earth and its creatures. A connected doctrine said that the evil god (perhaps Satan or Lucifer) gave us the Old Testament while the beneficient creator was responsible for the New Testament.

Cathars were basically socialists, and members of the select group ("perfecti") were forbidden to have any personal belongings, although collectively they controlled the possessions of the sect. Marriage was considered sinful, but in some cases it appears that sexual acts outside of marriage were regarded as acceptable. Their enemies said the Cathars practiced free love and had wives in common. The perfecti were supposed to be celibate. In spite of variations in details, the general principle governing the relations of men and women seemed to be the destruction of family bonds.

The Cathars hated the Catholic Church, and they were occasionally responsible for outbreaks of violence and the committing of terroristic acts directed at priests and church buildings.

It is quite apparent that the Cathars preached the same three principles common to so many communistic societies:

1. Family ties were discouraged or forbidden.
2. Property was held in common.
3. Terrorism was practiced.

For more than 200 years, Cathars were a powerful force in several countries in southern Europe in spite of strong efforts by the Catholic church to destroy them. Several "Crusades" were organized to exterminate them, but the survivors continued their activities in isolated parts of the continent for a long time.

Intensive Applications

Readers for whom socialism is a religious imperative may claim that some specialized features were responsible for the downfall of the Soviet Union, and, if the Bolsheviki had only been left to develop their society for a few more years, or if the leaders had only been a bit more committed to the Communist doctrine, everything would have come out all right. They should examine the historical record. There are clear examples that it is the principle of rigid state control and lack of individual incentives that are the overriding problems in all the variations of socialism, and that no amount of tinkering, no extent of duration, can remedy these and other defects. Two examples of long-term application of communal principles will be described in the following paragraphs.

The Inca Empire — When the invading Spanish discovered what is now called Peru in 1531, they found a tightly controlled civilization that had existed for about 200 years. It covered a large area, including all or part of the present-day countries of Ecuador, Bolivia, Chile, and Argentina as well as Peru. The Spaniards estimated the total population to be about 12 million people.

This culture was ruled by a totalitarian emperor called the Inca. The capital was Cuzco, which had a population estimated by the Spaniards at about 200,000. This city had large temples and palaces, aqueducts, and paved streets. It was connected to other parts of the empire by fine roads which were said by the invaders to be the equal of highways built by the Romans.

From a technical standpoint, however, the Incas were not much advanced from stone age practices. Tools and weapons (lances, maces, bows and arrows, etc.) were made of wood and stone, although the making of gold and silver vessels and ornaments was highly developed. The llama was the Inca's only domestic animal: it was a source of meat and wool, but was not used for transportation. They had no writing system, but used a complex method of knotted strings as an aid to memory.

Many interesting aspects of Incan culture are not connected (at least, not directly) to the subject of state socialism and terrorism and so the preceding short introduction should suffice as a basis for the discussion of their economic and administrative systems.

There were three classes of persons in the Incan empire: the ruling class, the bulk of the population (e.g., peasants, herdsmen, artisans, and soldiers), and the slaves (herdsmen, farmers, and servants). This is not far different from the situation existing elsewhere in the world during the feudal period, but in the Incan culture there were greater controls and a distinct flavor of socialism was involved. According to contemporary accounts quoted by Shafarevich (1980), "Not only work but the whole life of the citizenry was controlled by officials. Special inspectors continuously traveled about the country observing the inhabitants. To facilitate supervision, peasants were obliged to keep their doors open during meals (the law prescribed the time of meals and restricted the menu)." Clothing issued by the state had features peculiar to the area lived in by the wearer.

"Socialist principles were clearly expressed in the structure of the Inca state: the almost complete absence of private property, in particular of private land; absence of money and trade; the complete elimination of private initiative from all economic activities; detailed regulation of private life; marriage by official decree; state distribution of wives and concubines."

These details are strongly reminiscent of an ideal worker/peasant state as envisioned by Marx or Lenin, or a Utopia dreamed up by a Middle Ages philosopher. But, the "utopian" image of the Inca empire is somewhat marred by the undoubted existence of human sacrifice (on a large and systematic scale) and cannibalism as embedded practices in the community.

This large and highly regulated, and apparently prosperous, empire was rapidly conquered by less than two hundred Spanish invaders. Shafarevich suggests that this remarkable outcome was the result of " . . . the complete atrophy of individual initiative, in the ingrained habit of acting only at the direction of officials, [and] in the spirit of stagnation and apathy."

Chinese tyrannies — According to Shafarevich (1980), "The history of China is an extraordinarily interesting example of how the tendencies of state socialism find expression in a multitude of forms over a tremendous span of time." He cites some historical examples, of which the following is typical. It is based on a translation of *The Book of the Ruler of Shang*, supposedly written by the ruler of Shang province in the fourth century BC. He thought the ideal state must concentrate its effort on agriculture and war. All economic activity was based on agriculture, which was to be the sole interest of the peasants. The nobility must look for success in the military, as a preparation for government appointments. All other occupations were to be suppressed. Private traders were to be forced to work the land. "When gold appears, grain disappears — and when grain appears, gold disappears," the author wrote. Such industries as mining and water transportation were to become state monopolies. "That is why a wise ruler makes laws eliminating private interests, thereby delivering the state from worms and cracks."

Enemies of the state were said to include the traditional books of artistic and historical education, music, virtue, veneration of old customs, love of mankind, selflessness, eloquence, wit, knowledge, talent, and learning. And, Shang wrote, "... the art of ruling well consists precisely in the ability of removing the clever and the gifted." No doubt Pol Pot, that typical red genocidist, had studied Shang — he, too, killed the clever and gifted first.

Lessons and Excuses

The failed forms of state socialism, especially those in the Far East, were troubling to Marx, Engels, and other Communist icons. These concrete examples of the theoretical endpoints of economic development in a worker/peasant state could not be explained by Communist theory, which promised wonderful living conditions at the end of their expected development. So, communists relegated these cultures to the category of "Asiatic modes of production," considering them to be aberrant branches of economic development (principally because of the slavery aspect) and thereafter tried to forget about them.

What is the one unifying feature in all of these experiments, including that of the Soviet Union?

THEY ALL FAILED

To prevent a truly socialist state from rapidly declining into chaos, it must be ruled by a dictatorship that relies on force and intimidation to coerce the workers. And dictatorships bear within their souls a weakness that inevitably leads to destruction, either from internal collapse or invasion by a more vigorous nation. Would-be socialist dictators never seem to learn that individual enthusiasm and diligence are the ultimate causes of the creation of goods and services over and above the amount needed to sustain the workers at a bare subsistence level, and this enthusiasm and diligence will *never* exist in an environment where the possibility of individual enrichment by a person's own efforts is eliminated by confiscation and where the instituting of improved methods yields no benefits to the innovator.

chapter two

NIHILISM AND ANARCHISM

> There lives no greater fiend than Anarchy,
> She ruins states, turns families out of doors,
> Breaks up in rout the embattled soldiery.
> Sophocles: *Antigone*

Anarchy and communism are but two sides of the same counterfeit coin. The meanings of these two words have been blurred so much and used so indiscriminately over the years that the doctrines they are supposed to identify often overlap to a considerable degree. No doubt part of this confusion is the result of deliberate efforts by red sympathizers in the publishing business, including the compilers of dictionaries, who have encouraged changes in the traditional definitions so as to to make anarchy and communism seem less destructive than they actually are. We will attempt to be more precise in our usage of the terms.

For reasons which will be explained in greater detail in the appropriate place, anarchism (or an alleged form of anarchism) is one of the philosophies most favored by disgruntled teenagers and their mental equivalents of all ages. Like, you know, cool guys.

Classical Definitions

If we resort to the dictionary used as a guide by the writer of this book (see the Glossary for further information) in an attempt to understand the significant differences between anarchism and communism, we find the following.

anarchism — 1. The theory that all government is an evil. At its best it stands for a society in which each person produces according to his powers and receives according to his needs. At its worst it stands for a terroristic resistance to all present government and social order — a phase which is said to have originated with the Russian revolutionist Mikhail Bakunin (1814-1876). 2. Advocacy or practice of anarchistic principles, especially anarchistic revolution; nihilism; terrorism.

communism — 1. Any system of social organization in which goods are held in common. 2. [often capitalized] A doctrine and program based upon revolutionary Marxian socialism as developed by N. Lenin and the Bolshevik party, which interprets history as a relentless class war eventually to result everywhere in the victory of the proletariat and establishment of the dictatorship of the proletariat, and which calls for regulation of all social, economic, and cultural activities through the agency of a single authoritarian party as the leader of the proletariat in all countries so as to achieve its ultimate objectives, a classless society and establishment of a world union of socialist soviet republics.

Problems with the Standard Definitions

The preceding definitions imply that the goals of advocates of Communism and Anarchism are poles apart. In practice, this does not seem to be the case. When there were opportunities for the followers of communism or anarchy to put their principles into practice, both Communists and Anarchists quickly developed authoritarian societies of the worst type, and eventually destroyed the moral and physical well-being of all persons coming under their jurisdiction, and they ruined for years to come the economies of the areas they had controlled.

The real goal of leaders advocating communism or anarchism was the achieving of absolute power over their followers, and the utopian philosophy of communism (and, perhaps, of anarchy) was merely one of the tools used to keep the unilluminated in a state of confusion or complacency until the leaders' power could be consolidated. That is not to say that all of the persons taking leading roles in the cadre initially formed to overthrow an existing government were aware of the covert motives of their more realistic comrades.

History of Anarchical Movements

James J. Martin, in his book *Men Against the State* (1970) gives an extensive review and analysis of the history of anarchical movements (as well as what appear to be, in some cases, nihilistic activities) in an attempt to prove his contention that violence and terrorism were only accidental, or perhaps incidental, accompaniments of what was at its base a peace-loving, non-authoritarian philosophy. However true this might be in theory, it is very clear that any anarchist who was able to gather together a large enough group of people became either (1) a petty tyrant wielding unlimited power over his disciples or (2) a hatcher of terroristic plots involving death and destruction to everyone he considered an enemy.

On the other hand, the isolated anarchist (or nihilist), who operated, for example, while ensconced in a protected enclave such as a university campus, and who appeared to have no interest in personally commanding a group, can be considered a mere cynical dilettante with no doctrinal commitments. He would have just as willingly embraced witchcraft or animal liberation in order to gain notoriety and, perhaps, the sexual favors of some of the academic thrill seekers who attended his pot and coke parties.

Mikhail Aleksandrovich Bakunin (1814-1876), a Russian writer and all-around troublemaker, could probably be considered the prototypical Anarchist. He and Marx collaborated to a minor extent for a rather brief time, but then became bitter enemies.

For the purposes of improving the readers' understanding of points to be made in the following chapters, the author will define a few terms descriptive of the types of social systems (or anti-systems) which seem to be related in some way to communism and anarchism. These are "libertarianism," "nihilism," and "syndicalism."

nihilism — 1. This is a doctrine which proclaims that conditions in the social establichment are so bad that destruction is desirable for its own sake independent of any constructive program or development; especially (when capitalized) the program or doctrine of a Russian party, or succession of parties, of the 19th and 20th centuries, which proposed various schemes of revolutionary reform, and resorted to assassination and terrorism to achieve its goals. The term seems to have been derived from Turgenev's novel, *Fathers and Sons.*. 2. In loose usage, the term may mean revolutionary propaganda or terrorism.

syndicalism — This is the theory, plan, or practice of trade-union activity originally advocated and practiced by the French organization "Confédération Générale du Travail." They aimed to establish control over all means of production by using the general strike and direct action tactics of the worker organizations called "Syndicats." The ultimate goal was, apparently, to bring each factory under the control of its workers and then to control groups of factories by some sort of council, the ultimate super council to be dominated, of course, by the intellectuals and terrorists who developed this philosophy and who, probably, never produced a usable article in their entire life.

libertarianism — We are told by the usual authorities that a libertarian is a person who holds to the doctrine of free will; also, one who upholds the principles of liberty, especially, individual liberty of thought and action. But, in fact, "libertarian" and "libertarianism" are two words that have been adopted by at least three groups having substantially different goals and beliefs.

One group, whose members sometimes choose to call themselves "classical" libertarians, announces much the same goals as the Russian anarchists, and in particular, they aim for the complete abolishment of all property rights and all (or almost all) restraints on behavior. As the reader might have guessed, most of these people will be found permanently ensconced in institutions of higher education or residing for indefinite periods of time in other institutions.

The second group of "libertarians" includes persons who seem to be preoccupied mostly with the loosening or abolishing of restraints on drug use and sexual behavior, but who are vehemently opposed to any socialistic type of economic system. Some of these people may go so far as to say they are basically conservative in their *political* outlook. Leaders calling themselves "Libertarians," in this sense, are found in the Economics departments of some major institutions of higher education and heading nonprofit organizations. Members will also be found among the intelligentsia and in academic departments other than Economics.

Homosexuals, all manner of artists (especially performers), abortion rights advocates, and narcotics users have prominent places in formal associations of Libertarians or as self-proclaimed advocates of Libertarianism.

A third group which may, or may not, be properly described as "libertarians" (depending mostly upon the person who is doing the classifying) consists of the followers of Ayn Rand. This famous author and philosopher, now deceased, did not agree that her ideas fell under the libertarian umbrella, but she was adopted as a sort of unwilling godmother by many Libertarians. She evidently preferred the term "objectivism," which has the following standard definitions:

(*Philosophy*) — (1) Any theory that stresses the objective, or external, elements of reality to the relative neglect of subjective, or mental elements. (2) A theory asserting that human knowledge has objective reality.

(*Ethics*) — A theory considering the moral good to be objective and independent of personal or merely human feelings.

(*Aesthetics*) — Theory or practice of objective art or literature.

The hero of *Atlas Shrugged*, perhaps Rand's best known novel, is presented as an extremely self-reliant person with a willingness to disregard manmade laws and superstitions in order to live on his own terms. This man, John Galt, said, "Man's life, as required by his nature, is not the life of a mindless brute, of a looting thug or a mooching mystic, but the life of a thinking being — not life by means of force or fraud, but life by means of achievement."

One admirer of Rand (Adalja 1998), puts it this way: "Ms. Rand was not a libertarian — she referred to them as 'hippies of the right.' She believed in a limited government, and was a radical for capitalism, not anarchy. Her political philosophy, if implemented, would result in a government limited to the police, armed forces and courts."

In summary, the most vociferous and probably the most politically powerful Libertarians are those persons who seek to justify their pursuit of asocial and perverted pleasures by claiming they are advocates of

"Liberty," a concept which has a strong emotional appeal to many people. These Libertarians are much closer in life style and personal goals to the anarchists of old than they are to the standards of social conservatives, and, in the interests of accuracy, they should not call themselves "Conservatives."

Perhaps to be regarded as a fourth group, are members of The Libertarian Party. This political organization was formed in 1972, and it is said to be the third largest US political party. Its candidates have been on the ballots in most states since then, and Libertarians have been elected to a few hundred relatively minor state and county offices.

Some persons have suggested that the main reason for the formation of the Libertarian Party was to drain votes away from conservative Republican candidates, and it has had this effect in numerous races — it served as a Ross Perot type of party. It is a fact, confirmed by the author's observations, that many people who intended to vote for Libertarian candidates were not aware of the hidden agenda of this organization. The Cato Institute, an influential think tank, propagandizes continually for decreased law enforcement, particularly in drug control, and for wider social acceptance of certain kinds of abnormal social behavior, particularly homosexual activity.

A Brief History of Anarchism

The concept of anarchy seems to be very old, going back at least to classical times. To the ancient Greeks and Romans, it meant a very bad state of affairs, a collapse of everything that was good, with the consequent supervening of ubiquitous evil. The word is derived from the Greek *an archos*, i.e., "without a ruler" — thus, it is the condition of chaos or the personification of chaos.

In the English language, "anarchism" evidently first appeared as a demeaning description applied to the Levellers of the English Civil War and the *Enragés* of the French Revolution.

An anonymously authored pamphlet (*Tyranipocrit Discovered*), printed in the Netherlands in 1649, recommended that the property of the rich be shared among the poor, and redivided at least once a year, so as to give "every man with discretion so near as may be an equal share of earthly goods" (Hill 1972). This comes very close to anarchical dogma. No action resulted, and the pamphlet remains merely a literary curiosity.

William Godwin, an English writer, is said to have been the first to publish (in 1793) many of the anarchist axioms, although his "An Enquiry Concerning Political Justice" did not in fact use the word "anarchism." He said human beings were naturally benevolent and, if they could be removed from the influence of government, all would be well. He advocated the progressive removal of all institutions that contributed to coercion and inequality. Even marriage was to be abolished, this being a point also insisted upon by a number of different political movements of the extreme left, such as Leninist Communism. Government institutions would be replaced by voluntary associations and other loose groups.

Proudhon first advocated the word *anarchism* as a favorable description in 1840. Although Karl Marx initially praised Proudhon's theories, he later viciously attacked him for his principle of giving a considerable degree of autonomy to local communities. Marx also fell out with Mikhail Bakunin, an anarchist who favored a looser federation of workers' groups. After the First International disbanded in 1871, Bakunin's followers retained control of worker's organizations in Spain, Italy, and a few other Latin countries. When they were able to achieve some measure of power, as in local elections. These people showed themselves to be, in general, terroristic, anti-religious, and oppressive.

In Europe, some of the anarchist workers' groups retained a measure of power until they were decisively crushed by so-called Fascist governments in the years immediately preceding World War II.

Bakunin's followers emphasized the use of violent acts, such as assassinations, for the ostensible purpose of revealing the vulnerability of capitalist nations. Among the prominent leaders killed by anarchists was President William McKinley of the US in 1901. Other victims of the anarchists were President Sadi Carnot of France in 1894, Empress Elizabeth of Austria (1898), and King Umberto I of Italy in 1900. There were undoubtedly other victims who, because they were not prominent enough to be mentioned in the history books, perished without a trace.

In spite of the anarchists' evil record, their advocates did not become discouraged. One authority tells us, "Owing to their repudiation of political action and to their vision of a just and harmonious society of individuals linked only by voluntary associations, many anarchist thinkers" such as Peter Kropotkin, "tended to take a high moral tone."

Anarchism as a world-wide social movement declined in numbers but did not wither away after World War II. Cells of anarchist activists and talkers are still quite numerous and in recent years there has been a tendency to expand the membership of the many small cells through use of the Internet. More about this e-anarchist community can be found elsewhere in this chapter.

Non-viability of Anarchistic Societies

No true anarchistic society ever existed — the adjective and the noun are incompatible. Anarchism by its very nature presumes the non-existence of a society. It is predicated upon an assemblage of persons who reject unified direction, and this makes an anarchist community an easy target for any predator who commands an organized force.

All history shows that disorganized groups rapidly become dominated by the most powerful or determined persons in the group. Leaderless groups, such as are advocated by the anarchists, are also easy victims of outside individuals or groups having better weapons, greater organizational skills, or a lifestyle more conducive to innovation. Anarchy is like the dream of a willful infant, whose needs are expected to be met at whatever cost by means he knows not of.

The Bolsheviks found anarchistic politics very helpful in their campaign to destroy the Czarist government and the somewhat simplistically democratic activists whose government immediately followed the fall of the Czar, but which lasted for only a brief time and had little real power at any time.

The Bolsheviks loved the anarchists because:

1. The anarchists proposed to destroy all existing authority, so they could not allow any of the old administrators and officials to remain in power without being inconsistent. Also, they had not prepared any system to put in place once the old regime was abolished and, in fact, would have left an organizational vacuum if they were true to their principles. Perhaps some of the leaders had secret plans to implement a dictatorship once the old guard was destroyed, but, if so, they either delayed too long or were not able to establish the necessary power center.

2. By removing the old officials and not replacing them with representatives of their own group, the anarchists caused a collapse of the executive branch of government, and the Communists were quite willing to fill the void.

3. During the interregnum, when a very confused situation existed (a result of the anarchists' dislike of organizations, among other reasons) the Communists were able to put into effect a program to seize power by a method which seemed on the surface to be democratic.

4. Once in power, the Communists were able to forestall any anarchistic interference with their government by killing, imprisoning, or exiling the anarchists and nihilists.

Since the nihilists were principally concerned with destroying things, they had no opportunity to organize or to assemble the materials which could have served as the basis of power. Their "army" was basically a group of independent assassins. They were easy marks for any determined and ruthless group of whatever persuasion. It is unfortunate that the Czar or some democratic group did not immediately destroy the nihilist/anarchist nucleus — a step which would have been very simple at one point in time.

The preceding analysis is a simplified view of the events in question. There is certainly no intention of implying that the only two groups or parties which were struggling for power in the interregnum were the anarchists and the Communists. It is clear this was not the case, at least in the first few months after the Czar's supporters were convincingly neutralized. But, in my opinion, the anarchists and (to a lesser extent) the nihilists played a key role in establishing the power vacuum which the Communists were able to fill. Philosophy had nothing to do with it — organization, strategy, determination, outside financing, and ruthlessness had everything to do with it. And in the end, it was the most pitiless of all those vicious gangsters who had held some fraction of the power from the early stages who emerged triumphant with all the power.

That is History. What we have at present are new generations of restless, rebellious, dissatisfied, bored, hedonistic, and narcissistic young men and women who are looking for a spiritual home — a philosophy that will allow them to express the destructive, nihilistic, sadistic urges they feel, while they are saying (and perhaps even believing) that their supreme selfishness is justified by their adherence to an advanced philosophy. For some of them, anarchism will meet these needs. What religion could suit them better than one that says it is good to remove all restraints, to do what feels good, to smash those that seek to "oppress" you by making you conform to rules? In other words: anarchism.

Anarchism Today

Anarchists are spiritual twins of Reds. Our category of "red" includes the subcategory of anarchists. Some persons have called them the Black Reds since they fly a black flag.

No matter how much anarchists may claim to be interested in abolishing the government, all government, it becomes clear as soon as they get a little power that freedom for everyone else (or *anyone* else) is not on their agenda. Reaction of the budding red to the anarchists' teaching is a matter of personality, or, if you prefer, of their hormonal and neuronal constitution, i.e., their genetic makeup as modified by the environment.

Today's apprentice anarchist spends his time applying graffiti to other people's buildings, breaking windows, dropping objects out of tall buildings, shoplifting, fighting randomly selected foes, and rioting whenever it is safe to do so. From these activities he graduates to mass demonstrations, large scale arson, and the like. Graduation to hero status may require assassination of a policeman or mass murder.

History of English Anarchism

Throughout history there have been many groups and individuals who might be regarded as having had some influence on the development of anarchism. I think, however, that the idea of doing away with the boss so as to take over his goods, land, and women is nearly as old as the human race, and we can be sure the most aggressive of the plotters always, or nearly always, promised his co-conspirators that, when the old man was killed, his goods would be equally divided and no person would have power over any other. Of course, it never turned out that way, and it never will.

During Wat Tyler's insurrection of about 1381, John Ball made a speech at Blackheath in which he spoke the famous phrase [converted here into more nearly modern English]:

"When Adam delved and Eve span, who was then the gentleman?"

The 1381 uprising called Wat Tyler's Rebellion (Oman 1968) very nearly succeeded in overthrowing Richard II of England. The chief resentment of the rioters who turned into rebels as they gained power was the instituting of a poll tax, but they spoke of many other grievances as well. Through a series of miscalculations by the king's partisans, a large number of the rebels gained control of most of London. Although they had previously retained a fair measure of discipline, they soon began breaking into mansions and warehouses. They drank heavily from the stores of wine and ale, and then began looting on a large scale. In other words, they behaved much as we would expect anarchists to do. This uprising seemed to have very little permanent effect on English government or on anything else. It failed utterly, and Tyler was killed. Thus, we have the story of anarchism in a nutshell.

It is not unreasonable to call Wat Tyler's Rebellion am example of anarchism. Although the expressed goals of the participants, insofar as they expressed any goals, did not seem to include the complete over-throwing of the government, the action of the rebels certainly showed a tendency toward seeking the chaotic endpoint that true anarchy seems to aim for.

About 1647, in the time of Charles I of England and of the Commonwealth which followed his execution, a group of nihilists or anarchists called the Levellers appeared. Most of this party's adherents had some connection to the army of the English Long Parliament. As its name indicates, the primary goal of this movement was to "level" all ranks so as to establish a more democratic government, particularly by making all men eligible for public office. The Levellers were suppressed in 1649 (Pease 1965). This group certainly exhibited anarchistic tenden-cies, and its final collapse due to inadequate leadership might be regarded as typical of anarchistic outbreaks.

In Irish history, there was another group or movement called "Levellers." This was the name given to certain 18th century agrarian agitators. They began by destroying the hedges that had been put around areas supposedly dedicated to common use. Their program soon escalated into a demand for the general redress of a wide range of agrarian grievances. On the basis of their actions, it is easy to impute anarchical or even nihilistic tendencies to the leaders, although solid evidence of a conscious program in this direction does not seem to exist.

The Diggers were Levellers who took over the commons and began to till them, and in this respect they approached more closely to anar-chists than did the parent group. They called themselves, "The True Levellers," and their spokesmen (or some of them) "may also have reflec-ted agrarian communist ideas which had long circulated in England, reinforced by Anabaptist theories which the Thirty-nine Articles of the Church of England fiercely denounced ... both Spenser and Shakes-peare had clearly heard communistic propaganda" (Hill 1972).

Some anarchist writers (and communists) include Levellers and

Diggers in their line of predecessors, but it is difficult if not impossible to see a clear connection through the centuries. In the first place, these early reformers never had a stable, coordinated program of any type; their agenda was almost entirely negative. It also appears that most of the Levellers were not in favor of eliminating all government.

Ranters were members of a certain pantheistic and Antinomian sect which has been called the extreme left wing of English 17th century religious individualism. They, too, have sometimes been included in the genealogy of anarchists though the practices they wished to change were almost entirely of a religious nature.

Success Brings Imitation

The American Revolution and the French Revolution of the late 18th century, being successful, each in its own way, gave new hope to the unruly elements of society. It was believed by many that these rebellions showed it was possible for the common people to overthrow kings and emperors, and to gain wealth and power in the process. This hope gave encouragement to violence prone individuals in the population, and outbreaks of meaningless destruction and murder, as well as individual assassinations, supported by anarchistic slogans and the like became more or less de rigueur for the dedicated anarchists of the time.

Later Anarchists

Two major heroes of the early anarchistic movements were Emma Goldman and Pierre-Joseph Proudhon. In point of fact, their actual contributions to the development of social movements were almost insignificant. Their only claim to fame was gained by writing down and publishing their anarchistic escapades. Their minor and temporary achievements did, however, influence and encourage their contemporary, Karl Marx, whose effect on history was anything but minor.

Emma Goldman — This not-so-nice Jewish girl was born in Lithuania (then a part of Czarist Russia) in 1869. She was the daughter of a government official who managed a theatre, and Emma lived mostly in Königsberg, Prussia (later Kaliningrad, Russia) until she emigrated to the US at age 16. She worked for a time in a clothing factory in Rochester NY where she became involved with German socialists. Then she spent some time in New Haven CT where she became acquainted with a group of Russian anarchists, and joined their movement. By age 20, she had moved to NYC and at about that time became a protege of the Russian anarchist Alexander Berkman.

Berkman attempted to assassinate the industrialist Henry Flick during the Homestead steel strike in Pittsburgh PA. He was convicted and sentenced to 22 years in prison but served only about 12 years. When he got out, he re-connected with Goldman, who had in the interim served a short prison term for inciting a riot in NYC. This pair of jailbirds continued their disruptive activities, including the publication of *Mother Earth*, an anarchist magazine. In 1917, they were convicted of obstructing the military draft and served two years, after which they were deported to Russia (1919).

The socialist paradise wasn't quite what Emma expected. She managed to last two years before leaving to go to England, and later to Canada. She also went to Spain during the civil war in that country. If there was anywhere she could create trouble, Goldman managed to get there. Somehow the means were provided.

She wrote a book, *My Disillusionment in Russia* (published 1923) and eight years later, her autobiography, *Living My Life*. Other publications included pamphlets and magazine articles on anarchism, feminism, and birth control. She always managed to find a publisher for her tripe. Emma Goldman died May 14, 1940 in Toronto.

Pierre-Joseph Proudhon — This inveterate troublemaker was born in 1809, son of an unsuccessful barkeeper and barrelmaker in Besançon France. He became an apprentice to a printer at a fairly young age, and in that trade naturally met many socialists. About this time, Proudhon began to write some prose works. At the age of 29, he was awarded a scholarship which supported him while he studied and wrote in Paris. In due time, he published a book (English title, *What is Property?*), in which he wrote, among much other garbage, the statements, "I am an anarchist," and "Property is theft."

His type of anarchism would allow the small farmer to possess the land he worked and the craftsman to possess his shop and tools. And, he critized Communism because it destroyed freedom by taking control of the means of production from the individual.

In about 1842, he published what has been called an inflammatory sequel to his earlier work, the new one being *Warning to Proprietors*. For this he was put on trial, but escaped conviction because, it is said, the jurors could not understand what he was talking about.

After this, he went to Lyon and worked for a time as a clerk with a commercial firm. There, he became associated with a weavers' secret society, called *The Mutualists*, who believed they could transform society by operating factories managed by associations of workers. This, they thought would reform the culture by economic action rather than violent overthrow. *Mutualism* was the name Proudhon adopted for his own system of anarchism, although it might be more appropriate to have called it a form of *Syndicalism*.

In Lyon and during visits to Paris he met many of the leaders of revolutionary politics, including Karl Marx, Mikhail Bakunin, and Alexander Herzen. Proudhon and Marx became bitter enemies, due to their different philosophies and their individual desires to be pre-eminent in their circles. Marx wrote a book, *The Poverty of Philosophy*, which attempted to deconstruct Proudhon's theories. Bakunin seems to have accepted much of Proudhon's thesis, and this led eventually to a bifurcation of the Socialist movement into anarchists and Marxists.

In 1848 Proudhon settled in Paris, where he edited several newspapers and took a small part in the revolution of that year, though he disclaimed any dedication to the theoretical basis of the fighting. He was elected to the Constituent Assembly of the Second Republic. However, Louis-Napoleon became president of the republic and threw Proudhon in jail because of his writings and other activities. It must have been a modern-style prison, for he managed to get married and beget a child while he was in stir. He was released in 1852, and subsequently wrote a number of other books. In one of these, he advocated a federal world society with no national boundaries, and with authority decentralized among communes or local associations. Contracts of some kind were to replace laws. That is not anarchism.

Proudhon was in almost continual trouble with the police in his later years, and finally fled to Belgium where he continued to write. However, in 1862 he returned to Paris. A considerable number of craftsmen in this city adopted his views, at least in part, when they founded the First International in 1865. His last work set forth the concept that liberation of the workers must some about through their own efforts, as a result of economic action.

Proudhon has been given a great deal of attention by academics and agitators, who regard him as one of the foremost theoreticians of anarchism. As shown by the preceding discussion, Proudhon was not the first to advocate anarchism, and the type of society he favored was not a typical anarchy by any means.

Analysis and comparison of Proudhon and Goldman — The recognition craved by Proudhon and Goldman could not be obtained by productive means so they chose the destructive route. The gratification of sadistic desires, by killing and maiming more or less at random, was perhaps a major goal of their agitation, as it is in all anarchists' theorizing and publicizing activities. However, Proudhon cloaked his desires in a less transparent cloth. The insight of Goldman was much less than that of Proudhon, she was in fact hardly more than a tool in the hands of more determined and knowledgeable partisans. Neither person considered the damaging consequences of their activities to be a factor worthy of their attention.

Failure to Comprehend Technology

Because of its inherent limitations and as a result of the nature of its advocates, anarchism totally fails to take into account the role that advances in technology play in improving the lot of humanity.

The whole trend in anarchist thinking, from the earliest times to the present, is toward a more primitive type of society. The modern anarchist, as he types out his threats on a computer freely available at the library or on one purchased by his parents, or on one he has stolen, does not understand and does not want to understand, that the components which make up the computer and Internet are products of free enterprise and capitalism, and could never in a million years have been developed by a society that resembled an anarchy in any significant way.

The anarchist also does not realize, and must not realize if he wants to retain any illusion of self worth, that he is a totally useless relic of a primitive past, a pathetic ne'erdowell dependent for his livelihood on the largesse of the very society he professes to despise.

Even worse, some of these dodos advocate the use of criminal acts to support themselves and to give themselves a sense of power they are unable to achieve by any legal method. They advocate criminality quite openly in their printed literature and on the Internet.

Anarchism in the New Millenium

Self-proclaimed anarchists of the present day are often found in the front lines of demonstrations (1) against globalism, (2) for animal rights, (3) against Christian works and symbols, and (4) for abortion "rights" and the like. Any riot is a good riot seems to be the maxim guiding their activities. This is in perfect accord with the anarchists' basic beliefs, of course.

Typical of many such is the action described in the news report (Anon. 1999A) entitled *Anarchist group is blamed for vandalism in Seattle.* "Much of the vandalism that provoked police action here [Seattle] is being blamed on a band of self-dubbed anarchists from Eugene OR. The group of young men and women ... wore dark clothes and black masks as they prowled downtown streets Tuesday, smashing windows at McDonald's, Starbucks, and other multinational chains. They left their calling card, a spray-painted 'A' — for anarchy — on walls and windows.

"The disturbance enraged many of the Seattle activists who had hoped to express their opinions nonviolently. 'This was a handful of idiot anarchists who have no relation at all to the labor and environmental activists' said Arlie Schardt, president of Environmental Media Services, a Washington DC group helping to coordinate environmentalist activity here." Arlie, an ex-flac for Al Gore, is quite a big bug in the business of organizing and inciting demonstrations of any sufficiently left-wing type.

"Known by such names as the Black Army Faction and Black-Clad Messengers, the Eugene OR youths are said to have led the rampage during the mostly peaceful demonstrations."

A report filed a few days later by Schwartz (1999), amplifies the preceding comments. "The world has watched in bafflement as Seattle, home of computer geeks, stock options, espresso boutiques and other expressions of yuppie modernity, has descended into anarchy. But the virulent protests against the World Trade Organization are very much in keeping with the city's history . . . But Seattle's progressive mentality — like the very concept of American progressivism — was always Janus-faced. One generation was anarchist; the next believed in big government. The children of the Wobblies became 'Scoop' Jackson Democrats, who prized their union cards and jobs at Boeing, while the offspring of that wave turned against the hawkish Sen. Jackson for his quite logical dislike for the Soviet Union.

Schwartz continued, " . . . the same ecological extremism and fear of change led many locals to feel more than a touch of sympathy for Unabomber Theodore Kaczynski, whose 'manifesto' read like a transcription of conversations in Pike street bookstores and coffeehouses . . . And leftists were once defenders, not enemies, of free trade. Karl Marx himself was an eloquent advocate of the beneficial effects of international commerce, and Friederich Engels even argued that the arrival of a single world market would mean the de facto achievement of a united global society — the ostensible aim of socialism. But all such details are forgotten in the fog of demagogy that has descended upon Seattle. The shrinking ranks of professional protestors hailing from the 60s, now very long in the tooth and exemplified by Tom Hayden, began by hailing street crime as a form of rebellion, then promoted the Stalinist dictators of Hanoi. These racketeers of rhetoric have gravitated from fake cause to phony crusade for so long they know no other means of existence."

Further comment on the Seattle free-for-all was provided by Mitra (1999). "The range of free-trade opponents who assembled here was truly amazing. It spanned the political spectrum — organized labor, militant greens, animal rights activists, self-proclaimed consumer advocates, anti-immigration bigots, anarcho-nihilists and sundry professional protesters . . . There were other absurd examples of the protester's ignorance and hypocrisy. There was the young man wearing Nike sneakers kicking in a Nike sign . . . Then there was the young lady who looted a downtown shop while talking on her cellular phone . . . Quite a few of the protesters wore gas masks long before the police actually fired tear gas, giving the impression that they wanted to stir up trouble. Many chanted their slogans simply to raise the level of hysteria but were not willing to discuss the issues . . . The attempt to demonize biotechnology and genetically modified organisms was perhaps the best indicator of the true agenda of many of the activists: a desire to impose their own Luddite vision on the rest of the human race. Choice is anathema to these activists." Just good business for Arlie Schardt, however.

There can be little doubt that many of the demonstrators are indigent and are receiving unemployment benefits, disability payments, student grants, free medical treatment, social security money, and free transportation, and that funding for these expense comes out of the public purse. It is possible that some of the persons are on temporary release plans from jails and mental institutions, to which they return after their campaigns. It may indeed be possible that some of these people are using computers in their prison cells to conduct their businesses and spread their inflammatory propaganda.

The public has a right to know the names, addresses, and affiliations of these blatant outlaws, but such information can seldom be obtained, even if the person has been arrested (unless the crime is a major one). Some of the demonstrators no doubt use their young age as a defense against criminal prosecution — it is absolutely essential for the public peace that their parents or alternative custodial persons be held responsible for their actions and, in addition, the caretakers should be prosecuted for child endangerment if they have fail to exercise due diligence in keeping their charges safe and under control.

Organizations and Activities of Present-day Anarchists

The desire for notoriety of any kind seems to overcome caution when anarchists, particularly young anarchists, establish web sites or enter chat rooms. They tend to expose their souls in all their loathsome details. For the researcher, there is an embarras du choix.

Burn! is described as "A great anarchist site sponsored by what calls itself [sic] a collective of students at the U CA — San Diego, with plenty of art. They have a wonderful collection of poster art from the Spanish Civil War." And, they do all of this on college premises and they probably use the school's facilities without charge. They may even be receiving various government subsidies for their "research project."

Their website *burn.ucsd.edu / ~acf / news / index* describes a number of sparkling events that benefitted from anarchists' assistance. Several of these took place in England. For example:

•There are monthly meetings in London to protest the impending execution of America's best known cop killer, Mumia Abu-Jamal.

•A "three-headed demonstration" against Porton Down Research Centre.

•National Speakout week in London, an event which gives homeless persons a voice and a platform directly into decison makers.

•Demonstration in support of Paul Robinson outside the Swedish embassy in London.

•A Fiesta for Life Against Death, protesting something called the DSEi Arms Fair, also in London.

•"Beginning of the trial of Euromin boss on charges of corporate manslaughter for the death of Simon Jones." Jones was a young man who, according to the anarchist version of his tragedy, was minding his own business in the hold of a ship under construction, when a device attached to a crane nearly decapitated him. Somehow, this accidental death was attributed to negligence by an official who had never been near the ship. The anarchists, or some of them, are trying to turn this into a cause célèbre, or perhaps they are trying on a little extortion.

One of the complaints listed at www.simonjones.org.uk, is that "harassement [sic] Simon got from the dole made him take any job on offer for fear of having his benefit stopped." Translated, this means that Simon had been on welfare so long that, even in the peculiarly lax British system, the folks administering his case decided he had to do some kind of work. The anarchist view is that most people, particularly anarchists, should get paid essentially from birth to death, whether or not they do *any* kind of work.

Internet Sites

"Heatwave CAF," self-described as a communist-anarchist federation site, can be reached at the net address: *flag.blackened.net*, hosted on the Proudhon Memorial Computer (yes, really). They seem to base their curious philosophy on the writings of Piotr Krotopkin, "as briefly described in his essay *Anarchism*."

They preface their web paper with a quotation from Noam Chomsky, who seems to have no difficulty positioning himself anywhere on the political spectrum — as long as there is money or notoriety in view. This time we are fortunate to receive a really deep insight from this noted academic: "Organization has its effects. It means that you discover that you're not alone. Others have the same thoughts that you do. You can reinforce your thoughts and learn more about what you think and believe. These are very informal movements, not like a membership organization, just a mood that involves interactions among people. It has a very noticeable effect." The effect that will be noticed by most people reading this is a sense of utter boredom.

The spokesperson for Heatwave CAF says, "We are not Communists because Communism has given state power to butchers like Josef Stalin and Mao Zedong; it has created totalitarian police states and manipulated the efforts of such revolutionaries as Nestor Mahkno and Buenaventura Durruti. Instead, we are Anarchists — if the state is a tool of the ruling class, if it protects their interests and upholds their authority, then the state must be abolished. However . . . we consider ourselves communist-anarchist."

Further, the spokesperson says, "One of the advantages of communist-anarchism is that it mixes easily with lots of issues — labor, ecology, anti-racism, feminism, and likewise the society we are aiming for is flexible in putting these issues in practice." In other words, we get a kinder, more sensitive genocidal organization such as we would expect from a blending of historical anarchist and historical communist strategies.

The website *unseelie.org/anarchy/links* is composed mostly of a list of hundreds of anarchist websites. Some of them appear to be very strange and very dangerous indeed.

Modern Anarchists Glorify Criminality

From the very beginning, anarchism was associated with criminality. Its exponents permitted and encouraged violent acts including murder, arson, and expropriation of real estate as well as old fashioned sneak thievery and vandalism. Modern anarchists are no different from their historical counterparts. Although they have toned down somewhat their public endorsement of homicide as a tactic, they seem to have no compunction about publishing recommendations for committing lesser crimes, including detailed descriptions of methods for accomplishing them. What is particularly disturbing is that much of this material is devoted to encouraging wanton destruction which cannot possibly be of any benefit to the criminal or anyone else. Breaking the law to obtain their little necessities like drugs, disks, and petroleum jelly is just a joke to many of these people, as is all conventional morality.

Much of this poisonous anarchistic literature can be found on the Internet, thus being readily available to every person who has access to a computer, which is to say virtually everyone in the country, including prisoners and lunatics. None of the 20 or more libraries I have personally canvassed bars childrens' access to such material.

Examples of Internet Anarchism

In a particularly obnoxious and illiterate piece entitled, *How to turn the work life of a local 7-Eleven employee into a living hell*: (www.phonelosers.org/issue/pla008), the author (RedBoxChiliPepper) begins by telling us, "Most of the more destructive ideas have been tried by me and friends while working the graveyard shift at the Han-Dee-Mart as it gets extremely boring there at night. Keep in mind that a conveinence [sic] store gets pretty busy sometimes and the cashier can't watch every section of the store all at once so don't worry about him/her seeing you do most of this stuff. Even if you're caught, the worst that happens is you get kickedout [sic] for the day." The author tells how to steal, commit vandalism, harass employees, etc. All good fun — for an anarchistic imbecile.

At a site *www.theft.demon.co.uk*, you can get advice from overseas about shoplifting — not how to prevent it but how to do it. Its author states: "Shoplifting is less immoral than big business: It doesn't exploit workers, kill animals, destroy rain forests or give cancer to children.

"Shoplifting is the perfect crime — easy, quick, effective, and satisfying. See what you want, work out the best way to get your hands on it, then just take it. Shoplifting improves your lifestyle and pokes a finger in the eyes of big business at the same time. In fact, its [sic] such a normal part of everyday life for so many people that its difficult to think of it as being a crime at all."

"To be honest [sic], it seems that its [sic] actually easier to justify shoplifting than to justify paying for the things we need. Shoplifting can have a personal impact, too. As well as making life easier, it can help change the way you see shops and the things they sell."

The shoplifting expert gives us his/her "Top Ten Tips." Among these are: "•Take a knife to cut plastic security tags off clothing . . . Changing rooms are usually the best place for this.

"•Work out ways to throw detectives off the trail . . .

"•Always remove price tags and brand labels as soon as you can — go to a public toilet (watch out for plain clothes police) or examine your goodies at leisure over a cup of coffee."

And, much more.

At a site address *www.nothingforbidden.com/anarchy_info.*, we find "1500+ Anarchy Guides," which includes, among other things:
- How to pass a lie detector test
- How to beat any drug test
- 22 ways to kill someone with your bare hands

Among other means of thievery discussed in their list:
- Free entry and drinks in bars and clubs
- Getting into theme parks for free
- Bootlegging concert tapes
- Electronic and computer scams of ATMs

They also tell you how to kill people:
- Letter bombs
- Manufacturing explosives
- Building a delay detonator

For a fee of $15.00, cash in advance, you can get unlimited access to the above, and much more. And you can trust them to treat you right.

chapter three

SOCIALISM AND COMMUNISM

> The world will become a heavenly commune to which men
> will bring the inmost treasures of their hearts, in which they
> will reserve for themselves not even a hope, not even the
> shadow of a joy, but will give up all for mankind. With one
> faith, with one desire, they will labour together in the sacred
> cause — the extinction of disease, the extinction of sin, the
> perfection of genius, the perfection of love, the invention of
> immortality, the exploration of the infinite, and the conquest
> of creation.
>
> *The Martyrdom of Man*, Winwood Reade

History and Definition

Gerrard Winstanley, an English writer active in the mid-1600s, advocated a political or cultural condition that closely resembled either anarchy (but subservient to God's will) or communism/communalism. Communalism has been defined as a system in which communes or other small political units have large powers, as compared with both the individual and the central government; it has many similarities to communism. The end result envisioned by Winstanley was a rational acceptance of a self-imposed labor discipline within a cooperative community.

The term, "red," signifying an anarchist or revolutionary, predates the Communist Third International. It is found in the literature at least as far back as the French Revolution, and is almost always associated with incidents of uncontrolled rioting, wholesale murders, mindless destruction, and pillage.

The dictionary definition of socialism is:

"A political and economic theory of social organization based on collective or governmental ownership and democratic management of the essential means of the production and distribution of goods; also a policy or practice based on this theory. Socialism aims to replace competition by cooperation and profit seeking by social service, and to distribute income and social opportunity more equitably than they are now believed to be distributed. These aims have given rise to many distinct schools: *Christian Socialism* promulgated in England by Thomas Hughes . . . and others; *Owenism* and *Fabianism* in the same country; *collectivism, Saint Simoniansm,* and *Fourierism* in France; the *communism* of Brook Farm and the *nationalism* of the followers of Edward Bellamy in America; the *socialism of the chair,* the *state socialism,* and the *social democracy* of Germany; the *syndicalism* of France; and the *Bolshevism* of Russia. Usually, *socialism* denotes the doctrines developed by Ferdinand Lassalle and Karl Marx, especially the *scientific socialism* of the latter and his followers. From the point of view of economic determinism the scientific socialists predict developing antagonism between capitalists and workers as capitalistic control becomes more concentrated and the misery of the working classes increases, the consequent decline of the middle classes, and the final triumph of the proletariat. An antiutilitarian and aesthetic type of socialism was developed by Ruskin and William Morris and found a few followers in America. On questions of policy, moderate or democratic socialists believe in a slow evolutionary transformation of capitalist into socialist society, while radical or revolutionary socialists believe in class war and the overthrow of capitalism by political uprising or a general strike."

An excellent treatment of the history, development, and justification of socialist/communalist/communist theory and practice is *The Socialist Phenomenon,* by Igor Shafarevich, first published (in the Russian language) in 1975. Much of the following discussion of variant species of the type of social organization (or disorganization) called "Communism" is based on the English translation of that book (Shafarevich 1980).

Shafarevich reached the conclusion that socialism existed as a unified historical phenomenon, having four basic principles (or distinguishing features). They are:

• Abolition of private property

- Abolition of the family
- Abolition of religion
- Equality, especially the abolition of hierarchies in society.

It should be pointed out that one or more of these points may have been either ignored or treated in a brief or desultory manner by each of the "thinkers" when they spoke or wrote on the subject. In addition, many theoreticians tended to vacillate over a period of time in their emphasis in, and interpretation of, these points. And, when it became possible for some of the promoters to actually implement a communist type of government, no point of theory was regarded as of the slightest importance when it seemed to conflict with strategic necessities or with the leaders' desires.

Differentiating the Leftist Philosophies

If we chart the philosophies we have been discussing according to the degree of organizational complexity they envision as endpoints, the graph would look something like the following:

<--Increasing danger from individuals

NIHILISM->ANARCHISM->SYNDICALISM->SOCIALISM- >COMMUNISM

Increasing danger from organizations-->

The author intends to show by this simple graph that:

1. As personal freedom increases due to the relaxation of governmental controls, the likelihood of individuals being harmed by actions of their fellow citizens increases.

2. As the power of government increases, the chance that individuals will be harmed from government actions increases while the chance of being harmed by individuals (or non-government groups) decreases.

Libertarianism can't be fitted into this simple graph because there is no present-day definition of this philosophy which can be agreed to by a majority of the faithful. The life-style libertarians, whose principal aim appears to be to gain the freedom to use any kind of drug for recreational purposes and to practice almost any kind of sexual perversion without penalty, would fall in the nihilistic category, but they would probably be more comfortable somewhere to the right of communism in most other respects. Political libertarians would probably fall somewhere between syndicalists and socialists. Ayn Rand types, whether they want to call themselves libertarians, objectivists, or something else, would certainly be placed to the right of communism.

Capitalism, democracy, monarchy, feudalism, and the like fall into a different sphere of the societal universe, and cannot be fitted into the preceding description, which is based on a linear graph, but a brief discussion of democracy is apropos at this point.

The virtue of democracy is that, in the best cases, it enables a constant trade-off of power between the general populace and elected officials. Of course, this is more or less an idealized concept, usually much damaged in the realization, but even flawed attempts to approach democracy yield results that are superior in terms of human values as compared to the other types of government. People are imperfect — neither banding them together in large units or isolating them in smaller units will make them perfect. Distributing power dilutes the effects of would-be tyrants. "Power tends to corrupt; absolute power corrupts absolutely," wrote Lord Acton and, if he could get the picture, anyone can.

Personalities in the Red Order

The following tables give an overview of the principal organizations active on the far left region of the political spectrum at the end of the 1960s. This is about the time when the gradual decline (later to become precipitous) started in the influence exerted by Soviet agents on American groups. It led to the formation of pressure groups based more on environmental topics which the reds believed would enable them to obtain financing and mission support from a more diverse set of sources. It is this fragmentation (and its results) which is a subject discussed in considerable detail later in the present book.

Table 3.1

ORGANIZATIONS OF THE FAR LEFT IN THE 1960s [1]

1. Students for a Democratic Society (SDS)
    1.1. The Weatherman or Revolutionary Youth Movement (RYM-I)
    1.2. Progressive Labor Party — Worker-Student Alliance (PLP)
    1.3. Revolutionary Youth Movement II (RYM-II)
    1.4. Trotskyite groups.
        1.4.1. Young Socialist Alliance (YSA)
        1.4.2. Youth Against War and Fascism
        1.4.3. Johnson-Forrest Group
        1.4.4. Sparticist League
    1.5. Communist Party — USA (CP-USA) and its youth group, the DuBois Clubs of America
    1.6. Independents (radicals who opposed the Vietnam war and the establishment but did not endorse revolution)
2. Black Panther Party (BPP)
3. Student National Coordinating Committee (SNCC)
4. Black Student Unions (BSU)
5. Revolutionary Action Movement (RAM)
6. Republic of New Africa (RNA)
7. Youth International Party (Yippies)
8. Freelancers: David Dellinger, Dr. Benjamin Spock, Rev. William Sloane Coffin of National Committee to End the War in Vietnam (aka, New Mobe), Student Mobilization Committee to End the War in Vietnam (Student Mobe), Staughton Lynd of the Union of Organizers, Herbert Marcuse of U of CA at San Diego, RESIST, Liberation News Service, Underground Press Syndicate, Newsreal, Ramparts Magazine, "an estimated 100 militant black groups such as the Nation of Islam and US (United Slaves)."

[1] Based in part on: Anon. 1970A. Communism and the New Left. Books by US News & World Report, Washington DE

Table 3.2
LEADERSHIP CADRES OF FAR LEFT ORGANIZATIONS IN THE 1960s [1]

Communist Party — USA
Gus Hall, General Secretary
Henry W. Winston
Claude Lightfoot
Michael Zagarell
Daniel Rubin
Herbert Aptheker

Students for a Democratic Society
Mark Rudd
Milton Rosen
Jeffrey Gordon
Michael Klonsky
Carl Davidson
Rennie Davis
Alan Haber
Tom Hayden
Bernardine Dohrn
Carl Oglesby

Young Socialist Alliance (Trotskyites)
Larry Seigle
Carol Lipman
Nelson Blackstock

Progressive Labor Party (Mao-ists)
Milton Rosen
Jeffrey Gordon
John Pennington
Jared Israel
William Epton
Allen Krebs

Youth International Party (Yippies)
Jerry Rubin
Paul Krassner
Ed Sanders
Abbie Hoffman
Keith Lampe

[1] Based in part on: Anon. 1970A. Communism and the New Left. Books by US News & World Report, Washington DC

New Guises for Old Geeks

The disinformation specialists' litany is, "Don't worry about the Communists. Communism is dead. You can forget about Communism. It is no longer a threat." This is far from being the case. Reds are still out there, and they are willing to work at their old trade if they have an opportunity to do so. The label is a bit different, but the product is the same — though perhaps a bit spoiled.

A great many of the orphaned Reds find a secure base in academia, those protected enclaves which harbor every kind of vice, corruption, and treason. As recommended in *The Virtual Campus* (Foulke-ffeinberg 1998) and *Twilight of the University* (Foulke-ffeinberg 1995), a beginning to the solution of the red disease could be made by abolishing all public support, direct and indirect, of all institutions of higher education, and by the instituting of **true** freedom in higher education through the great increase of internet instruction facilities. The asymptote of this curve would be the complete elimination of all campus-based colleges and universities.

One of the characteristics of the Bolshevik-lovers who became deeply embedded in the structure of American society during the glory years of Russian espionage is their penchant for giving rewards to aging veterans of the "class struggle" — the red murderers and traitors who have got a bit long in the tooth and who tend to drool when drinking their borscht. They give them professorships, grants, awards, book contracts, speaking assignments, and as many other money-making opportunities as are in their power to deliver.

We have the example of Antonio Negri. He is the co-author of *Empire*, a book published in 2001 by Harvard University Press. Pryce-Jones (2001) describes it as "a political manifesto with the aim of laying out a new guise for Communism, in other words modernizing the Last Big Idea Which Did Not Come Off."

In academia, primarily, but also in all other branches of the intellectual and activist communities, we find even at this late stage in the dissolution of the heaven of Bolshevism, i.e., Soviet Russia, there are indefatigable prospectors trying to find some nuggets in the garbage dump. Many of these characters can be found in environmentalist circles, and they are willing to instruct all who listen of the advantages of applying the teachings of Karl Marx to environmental problems.

The Role of Reds in Environmental Activism

The reader is no doubt aware that there have been for decades, if not centuries, organizations which promoted environmental issues, kindness to animals, equal rights for women, etc. But they were generally under the control of middle-of-the-road activists who lacked the destructive or anarchistic spirit which is so prominent in the environmental groups controlled by Reds.

This new spirit came into the movement when the "sensitive, compassionate" activists formed connections with groups resulting from the dispersion and re-aggregation of members of the hard left and with previously unaffiliated radicals taking advantage of the lessons learned from the hard left during the Vietnam-era protests. The core from which members and contributors arose to populate New Left causes is the garbage bin of restless, idle, dissolute, amoral, and ignorant students and professors populating the institutions of higher education.

"The leading role in the development of socialism passes to a new type of individual. The hermetic thinker and philosopher is replaced by the fervent and tireless publicist and organizer, an expert in the theory and practice of destruction. This strange and contradictory figure will reappear in subsequent historical epochs. He is a man of seemingly inexhaustible energy when successful, but a pitiful and terrified nonentity when luck turns against him" (Shafarevich 1975).

Stalin Lives!

Of course, Communism in the traditional sense is not entirely dead. China gives lip service to the old maxims while vigorously promoting their version of capitalism (and doing rather well at it, too). The head reds issue fearsome threats while carefully avoiding any open confrontation that might result in a military disaster. Cuba and other tattered remnants of the glory days remain more or less faithful to the dear old red flag. It is even possible that some of their leaders are optimistic enough to believe that the successes of the Bolsheviks can be repeated if the proper conditions develop. However, they are doomed to failure — that egg can't be unscrambled.

Is China the exception that proves the rule? Mao was a true red, one of the "kill 'em all, some of them are bound to be guilty," crew. His organizational and administrative failures were legend, but his willingness to commit any enormity to sustain the atmosphere of terror within his country, and the protection from outside incursions he received from world leaders of the communist persuasion, enabled him to continue in power until he died — presumably a natural death. He was the Stalin of Russia — one of a long line of historical despots who have died in their beds.

But the present rulers of China are pragmatists, not for them the Charge of the Light Brigade, especially if it requires the leader to be on the front horse. They are willing to blow the trumpets loudly and then retire to their tents.

They have avoided attempts at conquest because they understand the difficulties and riskiness of absorbing additional subjects when they are having a hard time controlling the ones they already have. Besides, their fleshpots are full, what material need do they have that cannot be filled without additional risk? The idea that they will take personal risks for the sake of dear old Marx is hardly realistic. Booze and bhang, broads and boys are readily available, as is cable TV in all its variations. Such a life is even better than immolating a few hundred clumsy peasants or chopping off the heads of dozens of overly cautious soldiers — it is almost better than torturing to death a few of the usual suspects, though that, too, can be arranged, if custom palls.

Kibbutzim

The kibbutzim of Israel are enclaves of socialist and religious extremists that wanted to isolate themselves from the surrounding, imperfectly Judaic, society that constitutes the majority of the country. Meld a monastery and a convent, junk the crosses, sell the jewelry, and jazz up the sex activities, and you have a kibbutz. Kibbutzim have also been described as prisons with work release programs, spousal visitation rights, and glatt kosher cuisines. One would think that, if communism (communalism?) was ever going to work, it would work here.

Few opportunities for envy? — Schoeck (1966) believes that the kibbutzim in Israel are true examples of places where there are very few opportunities for envy to develop. Perhaps he relies too much on published reports. From eyewitness reports, admittedly second hand, and in some cases, third hand, gathered by your author, it would seem that aggression, envy, and hate are ever present in these isolated settlements. Just as these emotions were constantly present in convents and monasteries, where there was also great uniformity in living conditions and possessions, especially at the lowest levels. Of course, the hierarchy imposed by the church certainly gave opportunity for ostentation and luxurious living at the highest levels.

"A number of social scientists have rightly described the kibbutz as one of the most important laboratories for the study of human beings under special conditions. For these represent the first 'utopian' communal foundation, literally and deliberately based upon socialist ideas and emotions, and one which, instead of disintegrating after a year or two, has continued to function for half a century" (Schoeck 1966).

"The aim of the kibbutz is to make communal life feasible in the pure and full sense of Ferdinand Tönnies' famous and influential work of 1887, *Community and Society*."

According to the present author's information, recruits to the kibbutzim turn over all their possessions to the kibbutz, and if they manage to leave the kibbutz alive, after their disillusionment, none of their property is returned. In other words, the escapee starts at the very bottom of the social scale, no money and only the clothes on his back as property. This keeps defections at a low level.

"Today, in many cases, the kibbutzim make use of modern technological methods; processes are modernized, agricultural machinery is imported. Yet there can be no doubt at all that such methods could never have been invented or developed by a people which had never emerged from the form of community represented by the kibbutzim. In other words, the purely socialist community, and more especially the kibbutzim in the singularly difficult environment that is peculiar to them, can exist and function only by making use of the products, the technology and the achievements of individualistic societies" (Schoeck 1966).

Another bubble bursts — A brief report published in 2000 by the Staff of *The Jerusalem Report*, says, "The [Israeli] government has written off about $1 billion owed by kibbutzim under an early-1990s debt arrangement. Banks wrote off another $1.8 billion and other creditors another $200 million. The remaining $2 billion will be paid off under a long-term payment schedule or has already been returned in asset sales and land transfers." Here we have another failure of socialism, this time in the form of restricted communities of presumably well educated and relatively competent people (I'm sure they would tell us so) who voluntarily accepted the rigid format of the kibbutzim in order to practice the sacred rites of communism and Judaism. They couldn't make it work — no one can make it work, whether participation is voluntary or mandatory, whether it is in Israel or Russia or China, whether it is subsidized or supposedly self-sufficient.

chapter four

BOLSHEVISM AND TERRORISM

The Bolsheviki were the members or adherents of the radical wing of the Social Democratic party which favored immediate full introduction of the Marxian Socialist program, using for this purpose a dictatorship of the proletariat. They formed the Third International. In 1918, this group adopted the name, "Communist party." In the present discussion, "Bolshevik" will refer to adherents of Lenin and later Stalin during the early part of the group's takeover of the Russian government.

For most practical purposes, Bolshevism can be considered synonymous with Stalinism, and very close in definition to Communist absolutism as developed in the actions (not necessarily in the speeches and writings) of Lenin and, to a lesser extent, of Trotsky. In reality, most of the programs initiated by Stalin and his henchmen were either in place or under consideration before Lenin became incapacitated by syphilis. Among these are the one-party state, the official cult of the infallible leader, a pervasive policing and investigative system, a widespread web of citizen informers, and a network of gulags to intimidate and isolate the leader's enemies.

Terrorism

A number of different definitions of "terrorism" will be found in the literature. The tactic itself is certainly an ancient concept — the Old Testament describes many examples of terrorism, as when Moses and his masters sought to demoralize first the Pharaoh, then the Israelites, and, finally, the native peoples of Palestine.

In the first century AD, the Jewish sects of Zealots and Sicarii assassinated fellow Jews, mostly in Judea, in order to punish their co-religionists who had collaborated with Roman rulers.

The Assassins, a Muslim sect, were active from about the 11th through the 13th century AD. They relied on daggers wielded by assassins to murder leaders of their own religion who were believed to have corrupted Islam. The killers often operated in ways that ensured their own death — suicide stabbers, in effect.

During the Middle Ages, individual murders for political purposes were common, probably a great deal more common than history would have us believe. Although some of these were undoubtedly committed in ways intended to inspire terror in some group identified with the victim, we do not have space to examine them in this book.

In modern times, terrorism was recognized as a major tool in the destruction of first the monarchists and then the enemies of Robespierre during the French Revolution. In fact, the phrase *Reign of Terror* has been used by historians to describe this period. It has been defined as, "A period of anarchy, bloodshed, and confiscation in the French Revolution, during which the country was under the sway of an actual terror inspired by the ferocious measures of its temporary rulers. It began in the spring of 1793 and practically ended with the fall of Robespierre, July 27, 1794."

This bloody, chaotic period was evidently initiated and controlled (for a time, before it went out of control) by the Jacobins, a society or club of radical democrats in France that became prominent during the revolution of 1789. The society (originally a loose organization known as the "Club Breton," which met at Versailles) was called by its members the "Society of Friends of the Constitution." Its opponents called the members *Jacobins*, from their meeting place, an old Jacobin convent in the Rue St. Honoré, Paris. The society came to be controlled by violent agitators, and, under the leadership of Robespierre, conducted the Reign of Terror. With his fall, their power was broken, although the society was not finally dissolved until 1799.

An important ingredient was added to this devils' brew when the concept of Internationalism became an official tenet of the Soviet government. No other religion (and it *was*, to all intents and purposes, a religion) in the world's history exhibited a more ambitious plan or a more rigid gospel, or inspired proselyters with greater dedication.

"What do terrorists want. They want The Revolution, a total transformation of all existing conditions, a new form of human existence, an entirely new relationship of people to each other, and also of people to nature. They want the total and radical breach with all that is, and with all historical continuity. Without a doubt they are utopians ... They pretend to serve 'the people,' but the people exist only in their imagination. And they are interested in Marxist or Leninist theory only to the extent that they hope to find in it some effective methods of revolutionary action"(Rohrmoser 1992).

A Chilling Example

According to Kellen (1990), "On 19 January 1976, when [Gudrun] Ensslin was co-leader of the Red Army Faction, she stated: "The canard that we have moved away from Marxism is nonsense. We have applied the Marxist analysis and method to the contemporary scene — not transformed it but actually applied it. Only an idiot can seriously believe that the Marxist analysis of capitalism and the Marxist concepts are obsolete. They will only become obsolete when the capitalist system has been abolished." But Ensslin also said, shortly thereafter, "As for the state of the future, the time after victory, that is not our concern . . . We build the revolution, not the socialist model."

The communist may discard the outward garb of the violent radical as age begins to cool down his drive toward overt destruction (with all the dangers to the perpetrator those operations involve), but the Red cloak is still waiting in the closet of his mind. Kellen (1990) further states, "One interesting study, conducted by A.J. Nassi in the United States, examined 15 years after the event, a large group of activists of the Free Speech Movement who were arrested at the Sproul Hall sit-in at Berkeley in 1964. The study compared them with student government members and with subjects from the general Berkeley student population. The activists appeared not to have abandoned their radical political philosophy, but they were less politically active and they accepted the fact that changes can happen within the political system. They endorsed leftist politics, and they held social service or creative [sic] jobs."

Ferracuti ends his essay with a paragraph that is perhaps more revealing than he realized: "In citing these findings I do not mean to imply that exiting a life of terrorism can be accomplished simply by, say, entering an ecology group or getting a job at the Environmental Protection Agency. Terrorists are more extreme than the kinds of political activists who sat in at Berkeley, and their return to legitimate, nonviolent roles in a democratic society is inevitably wrenching and difficult."

Communism itself is but a new mask on an old monster. History provides us with many examples of attempts to implement the concept which forms the centerpiece of Communist ideology — and they all failed. The special status of Bolshevism in modern history is due primarily to the fact that its adherents, which the author chooses to lump together under the term "Reds," were tremendously effective during the twentieth century in utilizing terror to gain control of a large part, perhaps a major part, of the world's population.

Beginning of Modern Terrorism

The Bolshevik-orchestrated plague that began to infect the world in 1918, and which is still operative, is a mutation of a cultural fungus, or disease, that had its origin in ancient deviltry and which has existed continuously throughout history, assuming different forms in different ages, and not infrequently being represented by different phenotypes in the same place at the same time.

Bittman (1985) says, "The Soviet love affair with terrorism is deeply rooted in Russian history . . . [but] It was only after WWII that Western governments began to think seriously about Soviet terrorism."

Terror has been defined by the FBI as the unlawful use of force and violence against people or property to intimidate or coerce a government, the civilian population, or other segments to further [i.e., advance] political or social objectives.

This definition represents the necessarily limited viewpoint of a law enforcement agency which has to have some sort of legal infraction on the record before it is justified in taking official cognizance of a person or group. The definition seems to be somewhat inadequate, however, because (1) the use of propaganda, or even of so-called nonviolent protests, are integral parts of the terrorist program, and failure to take action against them exposes the populace to future dangers of severe types, and (2) "force and violence" hardly seems to encompass bioterrorism which does not necessarily involve either of these elements, as they are commonly defined.

Furthermore, not all terrorism can be said to have the objective of advancing a definable politicial or social objective, in some cases it might be merely terror for the sake of terror, for the gratification of the sadistic impulses of a person or group who have at best only a superficial or incoherent commitment to the changing of political or social conditions. In the Red terror in Russia, the government terrorism against the people had only the most tenuous connection to policy, being motivated principally by the destructive and murderous impulses inherent in the leaders, Lenin, Stalin, and Trotsky.

Terror is a tool available to all political parties, and even to individuals — whether they are on the left or right, whether religious or atheist, whether rich or poor — but Communists and groups allied to them have been among the most diligent users of this tactic. Reds of various hues were much more successful than any preceding cohort in using terrorism to achieve their goals — at least in modern times.

Why Terrorize?

As has been stated or implied a number of times in the preceding discussions, one of the most common characteristics of Red activists is their tacit or implicit support of violent and disruptive acts. This attitude results (at least in part) from the appeal that subversion and violence have for individuals who are attracted to Bolshevik-sponsored movements.

The choice of methodology and the timing of red terroristic episodes and their relationship to underlying causes or principles to which the individual practitioner supposedly adheres are seldom, if ever, the result of a logical decision-making process, but often are the consequences of a concatenation of chance events, expediency, and the influence of a charismatic leader.

According to Reich (1990), "The era of modern terrorism is usually said to have begun in the nineteenth century with the rise in Russia of the Peoples' Will party (Narodnaya Volya). In 1879, that party's program spoke of 'destructive and terroristic activity.' Its methods involved assassination of Tsarist officials in the hope of provoking Russian society into revolution. They were opposed by later Russian revolutionaries, particularly the Bolsheviks [!] who believed that revolution could be attained successfully not by individual terror carried out by a small clique of intellectuals but by class struggle carried out by the masses. Such individual terror came to be called 'propaganda by the deed' — that is, the method of using extreme acts, by which the masses would be stirred not only to understand the depth of their subjugation but also the vulnerability of the authorities."

"For many anarchists, terror itself was an end; indeed, one anarchist group in Russia during the revolution of 1905-7 advocated unmotivated terror. For anarchists, the invention of dynamite introduced an era of exciting destructive possibilities in which individuals could be, in their actions, as powerful as governments. Some anarchists advocated violence aimed not just at authorities but also at the general public, particularly those parts of it, such as the bourgeoisie, who could be identified as supporting the existing order merely because they profited from it. 'There are no innocents,' Emile Henry, the young French anarchist said at his trial for throwing a bomb into the Cafe Terminus."

The Bolsheviks are sometimes equated with Leninists and, indeed, their name was coined to refer to the "minority" party led by Lenin. His group was more militant, more devoted to force and violence, and more accepting of terrorism. It is certainly true that Lenin is on record as objecting to "terrorism," but he was speaking about the use of undisciplined terror, as when some individual or small group, operating independently of party control, kills an enemy they have selected. He never showed any disapproval of murder and destruction when they were conducted at the party's behest. And, of course, the many outrages committed by communists of the Bolshevik-Stalinist era clearly showed they regarded terrorism as a highly effective tactic for maintaining control of the masses.

Lenin's philosophy deviated from pure Marxism (however that is defined) in many respects. He had no faith in the ability of the proletariat to overthrow the capitalist hegemony. In *What is to be done?* he wrote, "The history of all countries shows that the working class will of itself develop only trade union consciousness." That is, it will opt for higher wages rather than control of the system. Lenin had a solution, of course (he always did): the workers would be guided by professional revolutionaries who would be a combination of the sages and generals of the proletariat. And, these sages and generals would be guided by the bourgeois intelligentsia, as typified by Vladimir Lenin. He believed, or said he believed, that socialism was the product of profound scientific knowledge born in the heads of individual members of the bourgeois intelligentsia, and that the persons able to understand this "science" could not be found among the proletariat. Lenin was an elitist of the most blatant type, consumed by envy of the aristocracy and contemptuous of the common people.

Lenin's faction believed their version of truth must be delivered to the whole world, and persons who refused to believe it and conform to its dictates must be neutralized so that they would not interfere with the historical imperative of a worker-peasant state. To propagate this doctrine, it was necessary to destabilize existing governments and to incite the underclasses, the proletariat, to revolution. An essential tactic in this destructive program was terrorism, applied as a means of inciting fear and passivity in the affected populations, so that the taking of control by the dedicated cadres of Communism would not be opposed.

Theoretical Justifications of Terrorism

Terrorism is certainly not something invented by the Bolsheviks, We can find mentions of it in some of the earliest historical texts. From the first, terrorism was described by Lenin and other Communists as a necessity in establishing the heaven on earth that was their promise. For example, Lenin said terror was legitimated by dangers to the Revolution. Later, Stalin attempted to justify the retention of the terror apparatus by pointing to the enemies which still existed in Russia. "These questions not only betray an underestimation of the capitalist encirclement, but also an underestimation of the role and significance of the bourgeois states and their organs, which send spies, assassins and wreckers into our country and are waiting for a favorable opportunity to attack it by armed force. They likewise betray an underestimation of the role and significance of our socialist state and of its military, punitive, and intelligence organs, which are essential for the defense of our socialist country from outside attack" (quoted in part from Fainsod 1953).

Thus, there were recognized advantages in using terrorism as an educational and governing tool. When Lenin issued statements that he opposed individual terror, he apparently meant assassination of public figures by persons working on their own initiative, but he undoubtedly accepted and advocated terroristic acts by agencies of his government. Even more, there is no evidence that he ever punished *any* murder by his agents even when an individual was the target and pure terror was the object. Some quotations from his works may be helpful in understanding this apparent contradiction.

In *A contribution to the history of the question of dictatorship*, he said, "the scientific concept, dictatorship, means neither more nor less than unlimited power resting directly on force, not limited by anything, not restrained by any laws or any absolute rules. Nothing else but that." He explained "The point of the revolution is the seizure of power; afterwards we will see what we can do with it."

Paul Johnson (in *Modern Times*) said of him, "No man other than Lenin personifies better the replacement of the religious impulse by the will to power. In an earlier age he would surely have been a religious leader. With his extraordinary passion for force, he might have figured in Mohammed's legions. He was even closer to Jean Calvin, with his belief in organizational structure, his ability to create one and then dominate it utterly, his puritanism, his self-righteousness, and above all his intolerance." He would have made a good Mafia godfather, too.

In the period from about 1917 to 1934, the most intensive application of terror was reserved for the kulaks of Russia, the small landowners who resisted the expropriation of their property by the Bolsheviks. Lenin and his successors were dedicated to the mission of liquidating this class, which, in effect, meant killing as many of them as possible — some quickly, others more slowly in the gulags. Also subject to the Terror during this period were former White Guards, the bourgeoisie, miscellaneous political enemies of the rulers, individual traders, and members of the intelligentsia

General Applications of Terror

Terrorism can be considered both as an inevitable accompaniment of Bolshevism and as a tactic of any other philosophy dedicated to enslaving, despoiling, and murdering members of the human race. To persons for whom this type of action seems desirable, the act is the reward, the philosophy is the excuse, and the result is a bonus. Therefore, the name, tenets, and history of the cause are largely irrelevant to the final result. Nonetheless, an examination of these factors is necessary to understand the reasons the Bolshevists were able to seize power and hold it for so long a time.

Terrorist acts in many parts of the world starting about 1971 had been presaged by the violent student protests which began occurring about 1968 in the US and some other democratic countries. These episodes led to the coalescing and focusing of US groups such as The Weatherman and the Symbionese Liberation Army, whose members committed many horrendous terroristic acts. In France, the main group was Action Directe, in England the Angry Brigade, in West Germany the Baader-Meinhof gang, and in Japan the Red Army Group. There can be little doubt that the basic philosophy behind these organizations was Bolshevism, and the hidden commanders controlling all these organizations were in Soviet Russia, even though that country had begun to drift into chaos.

Seeking Oppression

A central strategy used by communist organizations to justify their terroristic and destructive activities is to claim that their group, or a subset of its members, or even an identifiable fraction of humanity not directly connected to the party, is being oppressed by some especially privileged fraction of the population. "Rich Texas oil men" are always popular as oppressors; so are racist heterosexual rednecks and Christian fundamentalists. When speaking of such despicable tyrants, one need not specify exactly what the "oppression" consists of, you just know it's there — if you're a liberal.

The existence of "oppression," or of a potential oppressor, is claimed to legitimate the expropriation of goods and land as well as the indiscriminate murder or imprisonment of large numbers of innocent persons who could not by any reasonable process of logic be considered to be members of the hated class. Vide the Russian Revolution, the French Revolution, the Khmer Rouge, Bela Khun, etc.

The claim of oppression as a justification is intended to lull into inactivity and neutrality those persons of limited comprehension, who are able to convince themselves that they will not be affected by the changes advocated by their leaders because they have not themselves engaged in the "oppressive activity." Such dupes ignore the fact that all around them people who could have had no part in any kind of oppressive activities are not only being deprived of their natural rights, but are even being tortured, maimed, murdered, or sent to the gulags.

The other side of the "oppression" coin is that chronic malcontents and misfits of all descriptions recognize the claim as an invitation to murder, rape, pillage, and engage in all sorts of deviant behavior, knowing (or believing) that there will be no retribution forthcoming because the victims have been dehumanized.

A Need for New Flags

When the Soviet Union collapsed, most if not all of the red groups and persons outside of Russia who had been getting money and direction from Russian intelligence agencies lost their source of funds and their supervisory contacts. Perhaps more importantly, effective coordination of the programs of various Soviet espionage groups broke down. Of course, these external agents and groups did not simply disappear, they remained in place — many of them in very high places — but they had to re-orient their mission statements and consider how to reposition certain elements of their public images.

Finding a replacement job giving them equivalent satisfaction was often rather difficult, since many of these doctrinal orphans had strong emotional ties to Communism, indeed had often based their whole careers on subverting their own countries, denying truth, defrauding their employers, and corrupting their students and friends (and even their own offspring) in the name of Communism/Bolshevism. In most cases, however, these disappointed individuals found their philosophy was either disposable or could be put into cold storage until the Red corpse was revivified. Their local organizations often underwent manipulation in their internal operations and camouflage in their outward aspects to meet the demands of the changed environment.

A Utopia, with Some Reservations

The enthusiasm of American traitors for the "worker-peasant state," as they often described Soviet Russia, was not due to any improvement made by that government in the lot of workers or peasants, which would have been shown by the availability of better food, housing, medical treatment, or other creature comforts, but to the destruction of not only the upper classes but also the hated middle class.

These American enthusiasts were not (and are not) deterred in the slightest by clear proofs of Lenin's and Stalin's sadistic and genocidal practices. Though they may have professed a disbelief in reports of repressions and massacres, they secretly hoped the reports were true, because that is the way they would have handled the situation. They were exhilarated by thoughts of killing and torturing thousands of human beings, and wished they could have participated directly in these practices, or at least could have been spectators so they could have enjoyed the victims' sufferings directly.

In addition, most of these traitors appear to have had a innate love of conspiracy, to have reveled in the belief that they were "putting something over" on their bosses, spouses, neighbors, co-workers, the government, or the human race. There appears to have been something in their genetically determined, "hard-wired," thought patterns that delighted in a conspiracy, took satisfaction in the belief that they were members of a limited group, even though the group might have only two members (one of whom might have been imaginary), a group that had a special knowledge not obtainable by anyone who was not a member of it or who did not have a unique status for some other reason. This condition of belonging made the group member a "special" person, a status that he believed (usually correctly) he could never have attained in the wider society by any open and constructive efforts he was capable of making.

Those traitors to their fellow men who considered themselves communists were and are, in fact, morally no better than the common criminal who imagines that he has a special (and, of course, privileged) status in society because of his membership in a gang, even though that membership (however informal) confers many more disadvantages than advantages, when examined through the eyes of objective observers.

The special status of the illuminates confers (as all true believers "know") absolution for behavior that is not considered acceptable in the general community, thereby removing feelings of guilt and replacing them with feelings of superiority for aberrant practices such as drug addictions, sexual perversions, sadistic tendencies, and generally boorish behavior. Thus, we find a much higher percentage of sexual perverts, thieves, sadists, dopers, and drunks among the traitorous class than in the ethnic and social groups from which they sprang.

Cynics and Dupes

It would be wrong to give the impression that all persons working Red scams are dedicated anti-civilization freaks. There are some persons seeking financial benefits (profits, grants, etc.) from red organizations who have no commitment to any coherent philosophy or ethical system. Money is their god. They may even regard their associates with contempt.

Such opportunists are totally cynical and are willing to advocate patriotism, good schools, better law enforcement, and any other element on the right wing's agenda if they think they can profit by this kind of activism. They are capable of being agnostics rather than atheists, capitalists rather than communists, patriots rather than traitors, homebodies rather than seekers of casual sex if that is where the money is. However, their dedication to these ideals is no deeper than the first bill in their wallet, the last digit in their bank balance. They are not to be excused because of their lack of dedication, however. They can do as much harm to innocent citizens as any doctrinaire communist.

Another group in the red universe consists of those persons who have never joined an organization they knew to be controlled by Soviet agents, and who have never even considered joining such an organization, but who have become affiliated with one or more red causes inadvertently. Such persons do not comprehend the hidden agendas and the covert manipulations controlling some of the organizations having attractive names and sporting mission statements that can probably best be described as "compassionate."

And, many of the spiritually orphaned Communists might not have wanted to join any of these groups after they learned of the demise of Mother Russia, concluding (perhaps wisely) that these cheap substitutes did not fulfill all of their desires, either because the organizations' missions were inappropriate, the modes of implementation were ineffectual, or their comrades daffy.

The author seeks to provide evidence that the Red/red causes and groups which are described in this book offer congenial ambiances to persons having psychological traits that would have led them to become active and faithful members of Red-dominated movements of the old type, and that many "new" groups were initiated for the specific purpose of providing rallying points for persons having the Bolshevik type of behavior and thought patterns.

The new organizations may support many of the same goals as groups which more-or-less openly proclaim the Bolshevist anti-human views.

Lenin on Terrorism

Lenin's " . . . entire life was spent among the members of his own sub-class, the bourgeois intelligentsia, which he saw as a uniquely privileged priesthood, endowed with a special gnosis and chosen by history for a decisive role. Socialism, he wrote (quoting Karl Kautsky), was the product of 'profound scientific knowledge. The vehicle of this science is not the proletariat but the bourgeois intelligentsia: contemporary socialism was born in the heads of individual members of this class.' "

Lenin's speech at the Congress of the Swiss Social-Democratic Party on November 4, 1916 sheds some light on the apparent ambiguity in his attitudes toward terrorism. " . . . we do not know whether the assassination of Stuergkh by Comrade Fritz Adler was the application of terrorism as tactics, that is, systematic organization of political assassinations unconnected with the mass revolutionary struggle; or whether it was a single act in the transition from the opportunistic socialist defense of the fatherland tactics of the official Austrian Social-Democrats to the tactics of revolutionary mass struggle. The latter assumption appears to fit in more with the circumstances. The message of greeting to Fritz Adler proposed by the Central Committee of the Italian party and published in *Avanti!* of October 29, therefor deserves our fullest sympathy. At all events we are convinced that the experience of revolution and counter-revolution in Russia has proved the correctness of our Party's more than 20-yr struggle against terrorism *as tactics* [emphasis added]. We must not forget, however, that this struggle was closely connected with a ruthless struggle against opportunism, which was inclined to repudiate the use of all violence by the oppressed classes against their oppressors."

"We have always stood for the use of violence in the mass struggle and in connection with it. [emphasis supplied].

"We have regarded the armed uprising not only as the best means by which the proletariat can retaliate against government policy, but also as the inevitable result of the development of the class struggle for socialism and democracy.

"Thirdly, we have not confined ourselves to accepting violence in principle and to propaganda for armed uprising. For example, four years before the revolution, we supported the use of violence by the masses against their oppressors, particularly in street demonstrations. We sought to bring to the whole country the lesson taught by every such demonstration. We began to devote more and more attention to organizing sustained and systematic mass resistance against the police and the army, to winning over, through this resistance, as large as possible a part of the army to the side of the proletariat in its struggle againsat the government, to inducing the peasantry and the army to take a conscious part in this struggle."

It is clear enough that Lenin supported violence and directed assassinations. The kind of terror he objected to was violence, assassinations, and destruction that had not been previously approved by him.

Trotsky on Terrorism
In his essay, *The Defense of Terrorism*, Trotsky said

[paraphrased]: In the composition of the working class, there occur various elements, heterogeneous modes, different levels of development. Yet the dictatorship pre-supposes unity of will, unity of direction, and unity of action. What other path can it use to succeed? The revolutionary supremacy of the proletariat presupposes within the proletariat itself the political supremacy of a party, with a clear program of action and a faultless internal discipline.

Stalin on Terrorism

Stalin's attitude toward terrorism was clear: if any activity involved killing people and destroying property he liked it a lot. If it furthered an objective he approved of, that was an added bonus, if it didn't, it was still good entertainment. Stalin had been a terrorist and thief from an early age. He utilized violence and murder as standard operating procedures at all levels of his adult career.

There were very, very few people who seemed to be relatively safe from his savage hatred, so easy to incite and so impossible to assuage. His first wife, Ekaterian Svanidze, was apparently of middle-class parentage and not particularly involved in any political movement. She died of tuberculosis in 1909 after having borne a son, Yakov. He officially married his second wife, Nadezhda Alliluyeva, in 1918 after first raping her. She bore Stalin a son, Vasily, and a daughter, Svetlana, who actually managed to survive to adulthood and leave Russia.

Nadezhda was a neurotic who argued and fought with Stalin as she sought to pursue a career of her own (Vasilieva 1992). She died of a bullet wound to the head while alone with Stalin in their apartment. The story that finally became the official record of the incident stated that she had killed herself, but it is highly likely that she was shot by Stalin who had finally become fed up with her neurotic behavior and insolence.

Stalin showed very little sympathy with his children, but they remained alive until adulthood. Very few of his other "friends" and comrades were as fortunate.

Although persecution and murder had become a part of the Russian internal security mechanism in the earliest actions of the Lenin regime, this period came to be regarded as relatively mild after Stalin assumed power. Genrich Yagoda was removed as head of the NKVD in 1936, because Stalin regarded him as insufficiently opposed to Trotskyism. His replacement, Nikolai Yezhov presided at the largest scale peacetime persecution and blood-letting in European history (Andrew and Mitrokhin 1999).

section two
THE ENEMIES WITHIN

Although the Bolshevik subverters of civilization who were active primarily in the period from the 1920s to the 1980s were determined to co-opt or destroy every institution that offered any resistance to their takeover of the world, they realized they could achieve the greatest influence with the least expenditure of their scarce resources by targeting in each country those institutions which were the most effective indoctrinators of youth. With this goal in mind, Reds applied much effort to controlling US (1) colleges and universities, (2) religious organizations (including especially, the Christian churches — the Jews having been co-opted previously), and (3) the media (all print and broadcast organs).

The Reds were eminently successful in diverting almost completely the thrust of academia and the media to their own destructive programs. Religious organizations proved somewhat more difficult to subvert, but great successes were achieved in many cases. When the Soviet Union collapsed, the indoctrinated cadres it had inserted into US (and world) institutions remained in place without significant diminution either in number or influence. However, their rate of growth was hampered somewhat by the changed climate.

In the US today, the arts and entertainment community, institutions of higher education, organizations engaged in international finance, and many branches of the government (including particularly the judiciary) are filled with persons who obtained their initial positions and subsequent advancements (and, in many cases, great wealth) through networking with other Marxists, or in blunter terms, either by slavish obedience to their superiors in the KGB and other Russian intelligence agencies, or by following without direct contact those agencies' ultimate goal of destroying Western Civilization. None of these people will permit their co-conspirators to be dislodged from their unmerited positions without engaging in concerted and vicious attacks on their opponents.

The chapters in this section will describe the campaigns of Reds to infiltrate schools, churches, and media, and use their facilities to promote their own programs.

chapter five

ACADEMIA

Marxism survives [as rooted policy] in only two places on the planet: on Castro's island empire and on the American university campus. With the Soviet Union gone, the most socialistic, the most Godless, enterprise on earth is America's educational system. Draper (1994)

Dr. Draper summed it up very well, though he may have been too optimistic about the limited extent of the traditional form of Communism. We don't doubt that he would agree that North Korea is an unabashed outpost of Bolshevism in its original beastly form, while the rulers of mainland China are more or less committed to the Stalin type of Communism but in a more pragmatic form— China is to Bolshevism what the United Methodist Church is to Christianity.

In this chapter, we will concentrate on Red influences in campus-based universities.

The Root Cause

It is the desire for money, power, prestige, and privilege — a set of intertwined goals each of which may be given different emphasis in different situations — that drives the deviant behavior of college administrators and faculty members. These people spend most of their lives in enclaves insulated to a considerable degree from the investigative and corrective activities of police and other law enforcement agents. This protection enables faculty members to remain free from any effective oversight or control by the public's elected and appointed representatives. They also receive special treatment from the news media.

These unique privileges make academia very attractive to persons having many kinds of personality defects. The congenital red sees Shangri La (or Sodom) when he views the campus.

Understanding these simple facts helps us to understand the seemingly self-destructive actions of many college administrators. Such goals as improving the intellectual level of the university, assisting the students to be better qualified in real life activities, or advancing the welfare of the country as a whole have absolutely no weight in the educationists' decisions.

To the positive reinforcements previously mentioned as affecting their behavior, we should add the negative motivation, fear — fear of losing their positions, fear of ridicule, fear of ostracism, and fear of premature death.

Reds are Congruent in Three Dimensions with Academia

Today, Marxism (in one guise or another) thrives on university campuses all over the world. Of course, its adherents may not call themselves "Communists." Less confrontational names are usually adopted — but, then, that has always been the practice of the Bolshevists. The brilliance and saturation may be different, but the hue is always red.

The infiltration of campuses by Red professors is not a movement that started when the Soviet Union collapsed. It was occurring even before the Soviet Union was established. Communism, anarchism, nihilism, and other disruptive and violence-oriented philosophies always had attractions for the bored, dissolute, dissatisfied, and fundamentally incompetent faculty members in public schools of all sorts, but especially in institutions of higher education..

There was a major influx of Communist professors from Europe into American colleges and universities during the years immediately preceding World War II. These immigrating academics foresaw a bleak future for themselves in the areas of Europe not yet under Soviet domination and sought greener pastures elsewhere. Their spiritual and ethnic comrades — who had been infiltrating all levels of the teaching profession for decades — provided support and cover for the new arrivals. Conservatives or other staff members without red "rabbis" found themselves shut out of favored positions and deprived of grant money by persons who could barely speak English and who, in many cases, had very dubious academic credentials.

This migration continued throughout World War II, but abated somewhat after the Allies were victorious and Soviet hegemony was established over most of Eastern Europe. There, Red governments provided some openings for party members, but most of these positions were very inferior in amenities and salaries to those available on US campuses. Also, the competition was greater for the European openings. The possibility of winding up in a gulag was not considered a plus, either.

When the Soviet domination of Europe collapsed, there was another increase in the movement of Red professors to the US. These people came not only from the newly freed nations surrounding the Russian kernel, but from the mother country itself. Many of these immigrants understood the advantages of dissociating themselves from the catastrophic failure of the despotic Soviet Union, and so they downplayed their philosophical preference for Communism in their new homes. But they had been indoctrinated during their entire lifetime with the dogmas of Marx, Lenin, and Stalin, and that — plus an ingrained cynicism — made them incapable of accepting the traditions and democratic ideals of the US. They had been Reds, they were and always would be reds. Whatever their academic achievements, they were exceedingly inappropriate choices as teachers of impressionable and inexperienced youths.

Historical Patterns

Beginning no later than the latter part of the nineteenth century, the personal welfare and career status of certain "scholars" have been facilitated by a network of Marxists. The influence of crypto-communists and their sympathizers grew slowly until about 1920, when direct control from Moscow, accomplished by more sophisticated recruiting, stronger control, more unified direction, and the financial awards distributed by their agents, provided the impetus for the Reds' complete take-over of the US university system. Killing a few of the malcontents and obstructionists was another useful and relatively inexpensive corrective measure.

Gimme That Old Time Religion

We often hear that Marxism has been thoroughly repudiated and that virtually all political students now realize (after 80+ years of studying it) that Communism was a failure from the start, and that its principles are now and always have been invalid. These conclusions are widely accepted, at least in free societies and by unbiased scholars, but what is so often ignored is the clear evidence that doctrines originating from the Marxist icons — Marx, Lenin, Trotsky, Stalin, Mao, Castro, Pol Pot, etc. — have exerted an overwhelming influence on the educational establishments of the free nations of the world, and that adherents to these doctrines have had tremendous (actually unprecedented) success insofar as the implementation of their program of infiltrating and subverting all democratic institutions is concerned.

According to a very penetrating and discerning article by Bennett (1994B), "Marxism may be dead to most of the world, but it's alive and well here in the US — at least on college campuses. Many American Marxists say that, far from making Marxism obsolete, recent events in the East have rekindled their enthusiasm. At the annual meeting of the American Economics Association, earlier this year, a session entitled 'What it still means to be a Marxist in Economics' drew a standing room only crowd . . . making it one of the best attended gatherings. And, in 1992, an academic conference titled, 'Marxism in the New World Order' drew 1,500 people, many of them economists."

Bennett continued, "So how do many of today's American Marxists cope with the widespread fall of Eastern economies? Easy. They say they were never truly Marxist — or even socialist — economies, but were failed experiments . . . Mainstream economists scoff, 'Some Americans went from believing in the Soviet Union and becoming disillusioned, to believing in Castro's Cuba and becoming disillusioned, to Mao's China and becoming disillusioned,' says Paul Samuelson . . . 'If you're a serious student of history, you have to ask yourself if it's the system that can't work.' "

Red Fortresses Protect Psychopaths

Through both the deliberate orienting of their institution's recruiting efforts toward persons of their own political stripe and the subsequent weeding-out of those persons who do not fit the radical left's requirements, the faculties and administrators at institutions of higher education have become a cohesive group of activists who not only harbor a strong antipathy to all American traditions and history, but are convinced haters of scientific truth and the objective evaluation of phenomena. This group is leavened by a significant number of persons who are clearly enemies of humankind as a species.

Other writers have pointed out that a source, or the source, of our present educational problems is the Balkanizing of the universities. For example, Anderson wrote (1992): "America's academic intellectuals are largely insulated from the discipline of free markets, each university or college a tiny oasis of quasi-socialism . . . [They] pretend to teach, they pretend to do original important work. They do neither . . . And from these impostors most of the educational ills in America flow . . . The death of integrity in the heart of higher education is the root cause of the educational troubles which afflict us today." He described fraud, sexual harassment, plagiarism, and the pitiable condition of graduate students. Congressman Armey (1992) agreed, "As a former academic, I'm very familiar with the sad reality of life on a college campus, as Mr. Anderson relates it."

Radical activist professors collect about themselves a coterie of worshipful devotees and use these students and staff members to apply peer pressure to potential antagonists, thus either converting their opponents into true believers or intimidating them into silence and impotency. They may arrange safe houses for violent agitators and other criminals, thereby adding to the build-up of terrorist operations on campuses. And, they are in the forefront of activities intended to hamper the peaceful practice of beliefs that are not red enough to meet their standards.

Jean-Francis Revel (1991), whose powerful book, *The Flight from*

Truth, dissected many of the myths and mores of leftist educators, says the primary reason for the recourse of radicals to terrorism remains the fundamental hatred for civilizations based on freedom. "If not . . . why should we have witnessed the holding of a symposium devoted to the theme of 'Talking Terrorism' which was held . . . at Stanford University's prestigious School of Education. The list of invited speakers had been drawn up in such a way as to guarantee that the speakers would end up exalting international terrorism and reviving the standard old thesis that it is the democracies that are intrinsically terrorist."

An Endangered Species

As a result of these concerted and long-continued Red programs, true conservatives have become exceedingly rare in academia, and patriots are virtually non-existent. Occasionally, the academics will trot out a token conservative, exhibiting him to visitors with the rather self-conscious pride a sculptor might display when unveiling an obscene work of art. The rara avis will have qualified as a conservative (if not a reactionary) in the view of his colleagues and the administration, because at some time he expressed his view that perhaps Ronald Reagan was not really a demon from hell. In social and economic matters he will be found to hold views about a half-step to the right of Josef Stalin. As a result of these cultural deficiencies, and in spite of his tokenism value, he is certain to be precluded from further advancement, ostracized from staff social functions (this likely to be considered a benefit by normal persons), and never included on the list of persons eligible to attend meetings in Las Vegas, Aspen, or San Francisco (much less Paris, Venice, or Rio de Janeiro) at the expense of the university or the nonprofit foundations associated with it.

Examples of academia's hostility to traditional American culture are plentiful, and more are being reported every day. Roberts (2001) described many examples of interventions undertaken by The Foundation for Individual Rights in Education (www.thefire.org). This organization aims to expose administrators who "intentionally stifled patriotic expression and retaliated against those who voiced support for our country." Some of the examples of abusive actions by educationists were:

• At Central Michigan U, students were ordered by university administrators to remove patriotic posters and the American flag from their dormitory. They were told these items were offensive.

• Duke U in NC shut down a professor's web page because he posted an article that called for a strong military response to the terrorist attack of September 11, 2001.

• At Lehigh U, the vice provost ordered the American flag to be removed from the school bus.

• At the U of MA (one of the leading academic zoos), students were granted a permit to protest the war against terrorism, but students who wanted to rally in support of US policy were denied a permit.

• At FL State Gulf Coast U, the dean of library services ordered some of his employees to remove stickers reading, "Proud to be an American," because such expressions were offensive to foreign students.

• At the U of MO, the director of the university's TV station told employees not to wear red-white-blue ribbons in memory of the victims of the September 11 attacks.

After several more examples similar to the ones reproduced above Roberts ends his very informative essay with, "We must . . . end taxpayer and donor subsidies to politically correct universities, which are fifth columns within our country." Similar advice was given by Foulke-ffeinberg in "Twilight of the Universities" (1995) and "The Virtual Campus" (1998), who envisioned the eventual shut down of all taxpayer-subsidized campus-based institutions of higher education.

We cannot expect help from the few academics who have managed to retain their positions in spite of not being reds and of having a more or less conventional life style. The survival strategy of these misfits consists largely of trying to stay out of the way of leftist activists, hoping no one will notice them. They have dug their hole and are hibernating in it, hoping to survive until the ice melts. Their hopes are likely to be futile, this ice age will be longer than their lifetime; they are occupying room that can be put to better use by the predators, and as soon as their space is needed, they will be forced out. But, in the meantime, they cannot be counted upon to assist in introducing or supporting any significant changes — they are afraid that doing so will make them targets. The fact is, they are already targets.

Dr. Mark Draper (1994), an astute observer of the campus scene, said "Today, academic freedom means that if your ideas are not politically correct, you are free to seek employment elsewhere. Today, the university no longer trains leaders but indoctrinates followers. Harvard hates America. They hate the middle class precisely because of its common sense and its unshakeable virtue . . . Karl Marx conceived of two ways to destroy the bourgeoisie he so despised; one was violent revolution, the imposition of a new world order by force, the other, a gradual takeover by slowly increasing state power, spreading social services and regulation, raising taxes to support ever growing programs of public assistance, simultaneously encouraging dependency and discouraging enterprise until individualism is replaced by collectivism and American freedom is smothered by a vast bureaucratic blob."

Behind the Red Curtain

The motivation of many Marxist educators, often unrecognized even by themselves, is not a commitment to socialist theory, which they may understand only vaguely if at all, but a deep-seated, uneradicatable hatred of American culture. This hatred may be based on a feeling that the commonality does not value the educator's abilities sufficiently, or more realistically, on a recognition by the reds that they are misfits in and parasites on, a culture that is superior to them in so many ways. In addition, there is an understandable desire to advance themselves by conforming to the pattern of the people they correctly recognize as being the true movers and shakers in the intellectual milieu. Alexander Zinoviev, a Russian emigré writer, described these Marxist ideologists as sworn enemies of democracy, who have colonized our universities and churches, Hollywood and television (Beichman 1988).

A deeper truth is, most persons who are capable of developing a fervent commitment to Marxist doctrines are constitutionally incapable of being content with any government under which they function. If their government were Marxist, they would be fighting Marxism, becoming dedicated perhaps to anarchy or even (temporarily) to democracy.

Academic Marxists, like all Marxists, loved Lenin and Stalin not in spite of their heinous crimes but because of their crimes. They were fascinated and exhilarated by the massacres and contrived famines, they were proud to be part of a system that was responsible for the show trials and for the executions resulting from them. They experienced a warm feeling when they thought about the gulags. Their own failures and inadequacies, their own perversions and debauches, were washed away by the flood of massively greater crimes committed by their heroes — they were 'redeemed' by a baptism of innocent blood.

Although they felt no shame for their actions, public relations considerations suggested the need for a pretext they could use to justify the campus violence they were planning as a way to consolidate and extend their power. They needed a socially acceptable goal or higher principle which would establish their moral superiority over their opponents and give them an excuse for completing the destruction of the few remaining conservative elements in the university systems.

In the 1960s, this putative reason or point d'appui for the violent and destructive forces that are inherent in the political left was the Vietnam War. The demonstrations, assaults, murders, vanadalism, arson, and other crimes related to Vietnam protests can be found at their bottom to have been planned by academics and carried out by their lackeys, the radicalized students. A typical professor said, (as reported by Collier and Horowitz 1988), "We hated the [Vietnam] war, but we loved it, too. Vietnam made us special, a generation with a mission. The war justified every excess, every violent thought and deed. Trying to set fire to a university library, we said to ourselves, 'This is for the Vietnamese.' The war also gave us an addictive sense of moral superiority." It also gave them a new source of recruits: the men who were afraid of being drafted into the armed forces.

Hazard Adams (1988), a retired dean, gave his opinion that, "The student movement — associated with war protest and drugs — turned quickly into a historically familiar mode of negative romanticism and then decadence."

The Net Effect

In the US, as in many other countries, Marxism was very success-ful in some respects — it created a conspiracy, or a network if you prefer, of persons who recommended each other, hired each other, pro-moted each other, gave their comrades awards, grants, and degrees, all on the basis of their devotion to the great cause and regardless of their gross deficiencies of scholarship. Today, these conspirators are present at every level of virtually every academic institution in the country. They are also found at all levels of government and in many commanding posi-tions in commerce, as has been documented in great detail in other publications.

In most cases, these red educationists achieved their positions (and many of them reached very high positions) not as a result of their teaching or research ability, but because their competitors for a particular post were not members of the favored sect or were less subservient to the conspiracy. Now, in less felicitous times, they find it is necessary to protect their positions by assuming a camouflage super-ficially compatible with the changed political environment. But, you will find no patriots among the redeemed.

When reviewing the newsmedia files for evidence of the domi-nance of leftists in university faculties, one is confronted by an embarrassment of riches. So many examples, so little space. Therefore, the reader should understand that the following examples do not exhaust the supply.

We learn (Anon. 1988C) that, "The faculty senate [of Stanford] voted . . . to abolish existing 'Western Culture' courses . . . in favor of a program in 'Cultures, Ideas and Values' . . . At a gathering in New

York City ... a professor [women's studies specialist Paula Rothenberg of William Paterson College] challenged her colleagues to harp on race, gender and class issues in *all* of their courses ... Most Stanford professors would describe themselves as liberal Democrats, but the faculty senate has just voted to introduce the far left's educational progrsm into the one course required of all students."

The Chronicle of Higher Education, in reporting on the 10th Annual Socialist Scholars Conference in New York: "Judging by the heavy turnout, socialist values are far from dead in the academy." The Chronicle's editors knew something significant was happening even if they didn't quite know what it meant. Frances Fox Piven thinks the left will now organize around gender and race, plus class. "Does identity politics supersede class politics? In a way it does." The writer states, "Just as we expected, Marxism is therapy for an identity crisis."

Not Dead Enough

Today, the leftists are well-organized, and they make no particular effort to conceal their less violent actions and goals. The following is from a report on the third international convention of the Young Communist League in July of 1988, held at U MA Amherst (Anon. 1988A). "About 200 devotees of Marx, Lenin, and Stalin from countries including the Soviet Union, Cuba, El Salvador, and the United States gathered to attend a variety of workshops and seminars. Typical seminar topics included how to oppose CIA recruitment on campus; how to pressure universities to divest their holdings in corporations which do business in South Africa, and how to take over student governments throughout the country ... According to the conservatives, the traditional left wing groups on the UMass campus have been supplanted by the Young Communist League over the past two semesters."

According to a Campus Report article (Anon. 1988B), "Boston University's mega-Marxist Howard Zinn is leaving his comfy perch in BU's political science department ... Zinn, who relives the '60s heyday of civil rights demos and antiwar violence in class, was rated the most popular prof at BU, according to the April issue of Newsweek on Campus. More than 300 students per semester reportedly register for Zinn's class to hear him rant about how Columbus raped the New World, and the rights and privileges of people like Norman Mayer, who tried to blow up the Washington Monument. In Zinn's world, social progress is achieved not by passing laws but from mass protests, a view he backed up by testifying last year in behalf of Abbi Hoffman and Amy Carter [in their trial for violently protesting CIA recruitment at U MA Amherst]. Then, too, he allegedly tried to skitter around the rules by allowing students to forge his signature on their class signup sheets to save time.

Bennett (1990) quotes Richard D. Wolff, A Marxist professor of economics at U MA Amherst: "Freed from the association with the Soviet Union, Marxian economics has regained the liveliness, the debates. It's fun." Bennett concludes, "Many Marxist professors, who started out as 60s radicals, see Marxism not as the basis for a new society but as a tool for critiquing [i.e., destroying] existing ones. 'The status of Marxism as a school of thought is going to stand or fall according to whether it is an insightful view of how capitalism works,' says Samuel Bowles, another Marxist economist at U MA Amherst."

Strangers in a Strange Land

Persons who have been successful in the normal world sometimes are gripped by a self-destructive urge to reform academia from the inside. Those who survive the experience have some curious tales to tell.

David Bromwich (1992), a professor of English at Yale, says that academics justify their indoctrination tactics and other political activities in and around the classroom by reasoning such as: "Since nothing we teach can be altogether isolated from the moral and political views we hold, let us, as efficiently as possible, adopt our own morality and politics as the self-conscious message of everything we teach."

A former CEO retired in 1968 and became an emeritus professor of the School of Social Work at Southern Illinois U at Carbondale. He said, "In academe, there is as much ruthless competition, personal and political malevolence, sneaky backbiting, toadyism and 'old-boy' favoring, racial and gender prejudice, as there is in the business world. Perhaps more" (Auerbach 1992).

Charles Steinberg, who left his job as vice president of CBS-TV to become a professor at Hunter college, said: "Academe . . . can be a jungle more terrifying than a real jungle . . . Academic people on the make have an instinct for the jugular that is driven by a malevolent, sadistic, pleasure . . . Academe is ruled by a rigid hierarchy of presidents, chancellors, provosts, deans, chairmen, tenured faculty committees that would make a military force look like a children's playgroup. You play ball with the power structure or you're deprived of any goodies and frozen out of the club. If you don't have tenure, you aren't reappointed — in other words, you're fired. In academe, there's no effective way to evaluate results, as there is in industry. Any new finding is usually made by someone working like a private entrepreneur" (Auerbach 1992).

The Rewards of Activism

Among the privileges deemed by many professors to be among the implicit entitlements of their their positions, is the "right" to join demonstrations in any part of the country (indeed, in any part of the world) as a means of showing the professor's unity with socialists, freedom fighters, and other murderous thugs. Of course, the ostensible motivation is the professor's love for humanity, though we can't help but believe that the ready access to sex, drugs, and rock and roll — the activists' lode stars — has something to do with it. Whatever the motivation, activist professors feel it is their absolute right, or rather, their duty, to abandon all their campus obligations in order to attend these functions. Somehow, their finely tuned sense of righteousness never extends to the repaying of the employer's added costs for instructors needed to teach their classes in their absence and for students' lost instruction hours.

Speaking out for Marx and money — A sure way to obtain lucrative bookings for speeches on campuses is to be a vociferous communist propagandist, and it helps if you have a background of violence in supporting your cause. Such lectures, which more correctly could be called radicalist ranting, are paid for out of the mandatory student activity fees collected at each semester's registration.

As a practical matter, individual students have no voice in deciding how their fees will be used. Although some students have sued their universities for refunds when the money has been used for unconscionable purposes, this is not a redress available to the average student. The occasional legal defeats suffered by university administrators in these court actions have not to any degree destroyed their appetite for radical speakers. Of course, the individual administrator will never lose a cent of his money as a result of any legal action, and any inconvenience resulting from a court appearance will be offset by some sort of compensatory time off.

Fees to a "star" lecturer can exceed $10,000. Such a star is Karen Wald, a freelance journalist who lived in Cuba for over five years. She " . . . denounced native Cubans who criticize the Castro government's human rights abuses, and described Cuba as a 'democracy.,' and not a 'dictatorship.' Wald's views were challenged by Reginaldo Lopez-Lima, a recently released political prisoner held for 23 years in Cuban prisons. After the presentation, he said Mrs. Wald's personal attacks on Bofill [a Marxist former university professor who has been jailed by the Cuban regime] resembles the line taken by the Castro regime. 'She is getting her stuff from the Cuban government.' Wald recently covered the UN human rights conference in Geneva, and just returned to Cuba after completing a series of lectures at Brandeis, Smith, Trinity, and other universities. She was invited to Johns Hopkins by Dr. Wayne Smith, a professor of Latin American Studies, and chief of the US interests section in Cuba during the Carter administration."

If You Liked Bonnie and Clyde, You'll Love Bernardine and Bill

The gross indecency of the appointment of Angela Davis to the faculty of U Cal has been equaled, if not exceeded, by the appointment of Bernardine Rae Dohrn and Bill Ayers to the faculty of Northwestern University Law School. Dohrn and Ayers were among the founding members of The Weatherman (sometimes given as "The Weathermen") in 1969. They planned or conducted bombings of public places, among other crimes. She went into hiding after a bomb explosion killed some of the members of her group. After she resurfaced, Dohrn was sentenced on a couple of relatively minor charges, including a short jail term for refusing to testify about a 1981 robbery in Nyack NY. The latter event involved the killing of two officers and a security guard who were gunned down by members of the Weatherman who had turned to robbery as a short step up from their former calling.

Ayers is the son of former Commonwealth Edison Chairman Thomas Ayers (Swanson 2001). No doubt he has had access to the family funds over the years. This may have something to do with his success in obscuring a past that would seriously hamper a less well-endowed individual. It would also answer the question as to why his companion is still having legal troubles and he is not.

As an example of Dohrn's general moral tone, we quote from a contemporary account of her comments at a convention of Students for a Democratic Society (Bugliosi and Gentry 1974). She was giving her views on a particularly gruesome mass murder committed by followers of the cult leader cum assassin Charles Manson. "Offing those rich pigs with their own forks and knives, and then eating a meal in the same room, far out! The Weathermen dig Charles Manson."

According to the Wall Street Journal (Anon. 2001J), Northwestern has shown "contempt for the law ... by [placing] on its faculty someone who could not pass a character and fitness test and who could not be admitted to the bar. The university's representatives point out that membership in the bar isn't a requirement for the law faculty. Dean David Van Zant issued a statement on academic freedom, saying that the law school's ability to understand and relate to controversial views was one of its strengths and that Ms. Dohrn, *director of a family law center*, channeled 'her energy and her passion into making a difference in our legal system.' " Yes, killing policemen does make a change in our legal system.

As the WSJ pointed out, Ms. Dohrn is an unrepentant lawbreaker who never took responsibility for her own crimes. One of her paramours, later her husband, managed to get his memoirs published, which, considering the character of the US publishing industry, is no surprise at all. At the party this lovely couple gave to celebrate Ayers' official entry into the intelligentsia, they gave out stick-on tattoos of the Weatherman symbol. Some of the guests thought this was quite humorous — would they have thought it humorous if she had passed out swastika stickers? If not, why not? What is the difference?

When Ayers was asked if he had regrets about the several bombings in which he had some complicity, he said "no." He also said he did not want to discount the possibility that he might commit more bombings, and, one is entitled to extrapolate, more murders.

Ayers and Dohrn, a modern day version of Bonnie and Clyde, but without the latter's panache, should have been convicted of their crimes and executed years ago. However, they now find a good living as celebrities, one as director of a law school service and the other as a writer, plus whatever sidelines they may have to subsidize their style of living, which is apparently quite comfortable. Perhaps they have grants from tax-advantaged foundations and income from various welfare plans. And they have their pick of dinner invitations from the degenerate rich and famous who are in the throes of nostalgie de boue.

Above all, we see in the Ayers-Dohrn story an example of the sheer unbridled arrogance of the educational establishment, members of which not only make but defend as noncontroversial or run of the mill, the most outrageous and disgusting appointments. And, they do this with no oversight or fear of retaliation. It is clear to this writer that the cause of the problem is the saturating of institutions of higher education with administrators and faculty who despise and even hate, normal, ethical, and responsible human behavior. They are, indeed, "reds," enemies of the human species.

The Facade Is All There Is

Marxists/socialists are very compatible with the intellectual community as it exists today. There may be a few intellectuals who do not care to claim philosophical kinship with the communists, but it is rare to find a communist who does not imagine himself to be an intellectual. Though very similar in their goals and methods of operation, the two groups can be distinguished by, among other things, their approach to public relations problems. There is a difference in coloration, the intellectual being better camouflaged than the out-of-the-closet Marxist.

Brian Timmons, at one time a law student at Harvard, has a most trenchant and often amusing style of writing. He commented (Timmons 1990) on some of the more absurd pretensions of intellectuals, particularly university faculty members. He mentioned the proposal of one of Harvard's most notorious left-wing professors, Duncan Kennedy, that all Harvard law professors regularly change places with the school's janitors. "I sprang Mr. Kennedy's proposal on my grandfather, an elementary school janitor. He was offended by two assumptions behind the job-switching plan: that there was something wrong about being a janitor and that there was something good about being a Harvard Law School professor ... I never told my grandfather about the Jaguar that Duncan Kennedy drives to school" (Timmons 1990).

What They Really Want

The true agenda of most of the academic establishment, and particularly of the deconstructionists who have evolved from the radical leftist groupies of the '60s (and their disciples) is cogently summarized by Seltzer (1991): " ... those who cloak themselves in intellectual systems and arcane jargon have a negative view of society in which they feel insufficiently empowered much the same as many insecure people attempt to present themselves larger than they are ... every deconstructionist has a private agenda for which his philosophy is merely a means. It is no different with anyone else – the deconstructionists are simply more ambitious than most."

A large percentage of persons who are and have been involved in the continuous degradation of higher education have participated in so many immoral and illegal acts in the past, that any reduction in authority or status which might allow their misdeeds to come to light is resisted with desperate intensity. Many of the professors and administrators currently occupying prominent positions in academia have received their jobs, their promotions, and their protection from retribution only because they are slavishly devoted to extreme left-wing politics, including in many cases active cooperation with communist governments abroad.

Those in the inner circles have slandered, disgraced, physically injured, intimidated, and possibly even killed, or caused to be killed, persons who stood in the way of their advancement or who proposed to expose their illegal actions. Their dupes, lackeys, and lovers, as well as the students, media representatives, and politicians that form the infantry platoons of academia, have cooperated in those policies with the emotional fervor of true believers.

John Silber, at the time president of Boston U, speaking at the opening reception for the university's Center for Defense Journalism, said, "No university worthy of the name can pretend to be value-neutral in the assessment of the US and the Soviet Union. A university that promotes the doctrine of moral equivalence between these two nations, presenting them as two equally valid systems of government, or as two equally guilty parties in the political realities of our time, repudiates the conditions for its very existence. The pernicious assertion of the moral equivalence of the US and the Soviet Union is nothing more than the expression of an ideology that seeks to eliminate the very freedom on which universities depend" (Silber 1988).

The Faint at Heart

Occasionally, persons having a far-left orientation, formerly proud to bear the communist/socialist label, will come to realize that this category is a trifle passé, even in academia, and they try to adopt a more obscure coloration, using neologisms to describe their philosophy or, perhaps, using incantatory words and phrases which have significance only to the illuminated.

LaBarbera (1994B), quoted Dr. Paul Rahe, a Tulsa history professor, who expressed some opinions on " . . . the latest revisionist theory, known as 'New Historicism.' Rahe said this teaching approach is grounded on the presumption that 'all human thinking is historically determined,' i.e., a mere by-product of social forces. Such a philosophy, he said, rejects reason and holds that 'all thought is incoherent,' hence unverifiable. Rahe called the New Historicism a species of sophistry, that devalues human reasoning [and] that in the eyes of its adherents . . . 'All thought and speech is merely a secretion.' He said most New Historicists are former Marxists, and named Frank Lentricchia, director of undergraduate studies of Duke U's literature department, and Berkeley English professor Stephen Greenblatt as among the leading academic proponents of the theory.

Rahe said the goal of New Historicism is to domesticate history; "They debunk the past so it makes no claim on you." The downfall of the New Historians, according to Rahe, is that " . . . they fail to apply their deconstructionist model to their own thoughts and [to] obscure the authors they lionize in their teachings . . . Those who attack reason often do so . . . [in order] that they can defend something without reason." He urged students to ask their New Historian professors why they never apply their debunking theories to maxims favored by The New Historians.

Relative to the drive by tenured socialist/communist radicals to take over the American education establishment, Somkin (1990) has this to say: "Sweet reasonableness will get us nowhere in this matter because it is not an academic, an intellectual or even a moral question that confronts us but purely and simply a struggle for power — or jobs, money, control of budgets, and ultimately the real estate and endowments of institutions."

Other Attacks on Western Values

"The demand, 'Western culture must go' has been made of late by significant groups of students at Stanford and elsewhere, with increasing support from professors, politicians and others" (Lewis 1988). "It is not always clear whether what must go is Western culture itself, or merely its teaching in the universities, but given the central role that Western culture assigns to universities in our life, the two may in the long run come to the same thing."

A useful book documenting the causes and effects of enforced political correctness is J. Leo's (1994) *Two Steps Ahead of the Thought Police*. A representative extract will give the general flavor: "Stanford, which is now turning out more and more racially alienated graduates . . . [and] whites are leaving Stanford less sympathetic to minority causes than when they arrived . . . the damage speech control inside academia has caused. The nation's colleges are places where authorities monitor dormitory posters, wisecracks, comments on physical appearance and such forbidden classroom opinion as, 'I think men are better than women in this field.' "

The Clash between Incongruent Philosophies

Since most of the parasites who have intrigued their way into permanent status on today's campuses know very well they are unable to meet any objective standards which would be set for determining their capabilities, they are always looking for protective camouflage. Some of them believe they have found it in logical positivism, urbane gallic theories, or other abstractions.

The network of overt and covert Marxists remains so powerful today, that they can introduce — and have accepted by a large fraction of the educationist establishment — certain deviant and irrational philosophies that provide safe havens and a source of employment for their co-conspirators. Consequently, we find them solemnly discussing "post-modernism," "subjectivism," and "constructivism." These are doctrines that have been hashed, rehashed, and abandoned over many decades by droves of clerical and secular philosophers. Nonetheless, they will again be resurrected, renamed, and used as the subject of countless class synopses, seminar topics, journal articles, and books. And they will, during the process, justify the jobs of hundreds of professors who have no capacity for doing useful work.

Logical positivism — This philosophy or school of thought has, as its basic premise, the dogma that the only route to valid knowledge is based on sense impressions. Anything not observable with the unaided senses is metaphysics. Thus, to the logical positivist most modern science and all disciplines depending on the quantitation of natural phenomena are false and irrelevant in everyday life. See Goode (1995).

There seems to be little or no difference between logical positivism and subjectivism. The latter is a philosophy that has become essentially dormant over the last few hundred years, except in certain religious communities.

Modern intellectuals benefit greatly from such a set of beliefs, since it leaves intact the web of conspiracy by which they have achieved their positions, awards, and other benefits, while demolishing the value structure of scientists, engineers, technologists, and the like, who might displace them if any objective scale of abilities was used to measure suitability for a position on the faculty or in the administrative ranks of higher education.

The eminent physicist, Edward Teller has been a staunch suppor-ter of reason and justice in higher education for several decades. Recently, he wrote, "According to professors at the best universities, science is a network of myths fabricated by a white male ruling class bent on keeping minorities subjugated. Now any oppressed minority has a right to be heard, but the fact that a group has been oppressed does not guarantee it is right" (Teller 1994).

The subjectivists who say that feelings are the true standards by which our lives should be conducted, and that physical evidence should be ignored if it is not compatible with their system, may be correct according to their own belief system. It is completely futile for the objectivist to point out that virtually every material thing and energy source the subjectivist is using every minute of his or her daily life is a product of objectivist reasoning, or that stepping in front of a speeding automobile is not a good idea even if one feels perfectly confident about the insubstantiality of the vehicle just before the impact.

Urbane Gallic theorists — The criminal goofiness that permeates nearly all departments of nearly all institutions of higher education today has many roots and many fruits, but the bedrock seems to be an implacable hatred of humanity as a whole and, more specifically, of normal humans as they follow the dictates of nature and their religion in founding and nurturing families.

For perhaps a hundred years the aberrancies were centered on, and ostensibly derived from, Marxism in all of its many ramifications, but after the Soviet Union collapsed, and the spiritual and financial backing and the direction that formerly came from Russia was no longer available, the intellectual crowd had to seek another lodestone.

MacDonald (1978) wrote, "Starting in the 1970s, a fatal encounter began that has profoundly disfigured the American university; that between the French literary intellectuals and the American humanities professors. Bored with explicating such mundane writers as Shakespeare and Kant, scholars in America's most prestigious universities seized on something far sexier — urbane Gallic theorists who claim, in prose of unbelievable opacity, that language is meaningless and truth an illusion." She goes on to quote examples from the writings of Jacques Lacan, psychoanalyst and literary theorist, which it would be useless to reproduce here, since they resemble typing exercises submitted by a mildly retarded chimpanzee.

The basic argument of "postmodernists,"appears to be that language obscures, or is inadequate to represent, reality. What we consider the real world is just another text. I assume that these high-minded philosophers continue to ask for their pay to be real money, their food to be real food, etc. Although many of them have undoubtedly benefitted from the achievements of modern science, they claim that science is really just a narrative that can be deconstructed into the triumvirate of race, gender, and class. Aren't race, gender, and class merely "another text?"

Sokal and Bricmont (1998) wrote a book-length discussion revealing the asininity of these and other propositions. Mr. Sokal had previously authored a parody mocking postmodern thought, in which he claimed that "physical reality" is only a "linguistic construct" and called for a new "postmodern and liberatory science." The editor of *Social Text*, said to be one of the leading journals of postmodern theory, accepted this satire and had it printed as a legitimate scholarly study.

MacDonald (1978) said that the book by Sokal and Bricmont, " . . . exposes the breakdown of intellectual inquiry in much of the academy. It can now be said confidently that the thousands of professors who have parroted the scientific contortions of Mr. Lacan and Ms. Kristeva, who have sneered at scientific positivism along with Mr. Baudrillard and Mr. Latour, understood not a word of what they were mimicking — because there was nothing to understand."

Gay rights, radical feminism, abortion rights, anti-white racism disguised as tolerance, animal rights, eco warfare, earth or nature worship, and all the other "compassion" related movements are but pigments in a dreary gothic landscape painted by the haters of humanity.

Creationism — What has not been generally recognized is that the battle between objectivists and subjectivists is analogous to the dispute between creationists (typically, those who advocate "literal" acceptance of the Old Testament) and evolutionists (typically, Darwinists).

We cannot fit the beliefs of creationists into the framework of evolutionists, because the dimensions are totally different. Similarly, we cannot package the beliefs of the subjectivists in any form compatible with the evidential structure of the objectivists — it's the wrong box. To put it a different way, the evidentiary frameworks are totally incongruent, they do not overlap at any point. When the orthodox Jew says the world was created 5762 years ago, there is no point in a scientist trying to rebut his statement by pointing out that thousands of bits of physical evidence prove (to him) that the universe is over 3 billion years old or that a flourishing civilization existed in Egypt, and probably elsewhere, more than 6000 years ago. The physical evidence is irrelevant to one kind of believer and the spiritual evidence is irrelevant to the other, because there is no congruency between the two frames of reference.

Similarly, the belief that all men are brothers in the sense that every one is completely equal in all meaningful characteristics in spite of the overwhelming physical evidence to the contrary is no doubt a wonderful exhibition of the believer's sensitivity, but such a person should (for his own psychological comfort) be prepared to admit that his belief pattern cannot be shared by others who use a more objective standard of appraisal.

The subjectivists and the objectivists make the same error as the creationists and evolutionists. Each group wants to verify its claims by tearing down the other group's basic assumptions, and, when this proves to be unacceptable to their opponents, they want to convert the unbeliever by arguments inappropriate to the unbeliever's system of proof. Thus it is useless to present objective proofs of racial differences to the racial flatlander, who will consider such proofs to be false because they are outside his universe of acceptable data.

The problem for the average citizen, who is almost always a practicing objectivist, is whether the taxpayer should subsidize the teaching of creationism or subjectivism. If it is the religious belief of a professor that "feelings," i.e., individual emotional responses to stimuli (or, perhaps, emotional responses supposedly independent of external stimuli), are the guiding principles of the universe, should that professor be subsidized in the teaching of his beliefs to persons who are going to be designing bridges and balancing accounts — or for that matter, someone who

is going to spend his life digging up potsherds in Mesopotamia and interpreting their significance to world history? Going a step further, if it is
agreed that it is suitable to pay teachers of subjectivist theory, why is it
not proper to subsidize (with public funds) the teaching of creationism?

Can There Any Good Thing Come Out of Academia?

It is characteristic of the leftists that, having achieved a position
in academia that facilitates their peculiar beliefs and inflammatory declarations, they will hold on for dear life, resisting all efforts to dislodge
them, all the while complaining bitterly about oppression, although they
are probably the most oppressive group to be found on any campus.

Finding a method for uprooting the weeds from the academic
garden is a problem that has concerned many commentators. A book by
Bernstein (1994), *Dictatorship of Virtue*, is an important contribution. As
reviewed by McGowan (1994), the book "describes how extensively ideologies of the cultural left have built up a multicultural bureaucracy
within the major institutions of American life, from newsrooms and
museum offices to government agencies, elementary schools and, of
course, university campuses."

There have been many calls for reform, but any change extensive
enough to remedy all, or even most, of the problems of institutions of
higher education will leave a structure that cannot function. In the current situation, removal of all objectionable personnel would leave too few
people to conduct business in a normal manner. On the other hand, eliminating a few figureheads will accomplish nothing of value; the radical
activists who remain at lower levels will continue to exercise the power
of their network, converting new personnel to their views and assisting
their co-conspirators to achieve positions of power and influence. As
Irvine (1994) states, "The leftist seizure of American academia is now an
established fact." Nothing worthwhile remains to be saved.

Any attempts to improve the efficiency and raise the level of
instruction at institutions of higher education will always be opposed by
those who know only too well that they are incapable of handling even

their current duties. Such persons will be willing to tear down the whole structure rather than submit to changes that will adversely affect their own comfort or prestige. They are the Luddites of the education industry. This group is comprised of liberals, intellectuals, anarchists (within which category we can include some factions of the amorphous group that prefers to be called "Libertarians"), radicals of other types, and socialists (this last term includes a wide range of variously denominated activists acknowledging Marx and Engels as their role models).

The real solution would be to simply defund all campus-based institutions of higher education and replace them with distant teaching methods responsive to the needs of individual students and completely separated from colleges and universities as they exist today. Details of this approach can be found in "Twilight of the Universities" and "The Virtual Campus," by Foulke-ffeinberg (1995, 1998).

Partners in Crime

Many people believe that universities and the professors infesting them depend mostly on tax money and tuition income to pay their expenses. Certainly, these are sources of enormous amounts of money, and would be enough to pay for the services rendered to students, if institutions of higher education were run by conventional business principles. That is not the intention of the modern educationists, however. They must have more money, much more money, to fund their hare-brained research projects and the "scientists" and "scholars" who cannot and will not perform any useful work. This money comes partly from bequests and gifts from wealthy alumni, grants from various foundations, and various forms of payments from the government.

One hand washes the other — Working hand in hand with the universities are the nonprofit ("charitable") foundations which are the source of much of the money that pours into the outstretched hands of left-wing educators.

Horowitz (1997) points out, "An irony missed by our left-wing critics was that the 'ruling class' foundations, such as Carnegie, Ford, and Rockefeller were solidly behind the programs and ideas favored by Edward Said and his allies — multiculturalism, affirmative action, radical feminism, black separatist studies and the political redefinition of the university mission. Tens of millions of dollars had been invested by America's biggest capitalist fortunes in these antidemocratic and anticapitalist agendas... One left-wing foundation, MacArthur, which was only half the size of Ford... MacArthur was a funder of *Harper's*, Lapham's left-wing journal, and the pro-Sandinista Christic Institute, a conspiracy-minded think tank whose wild-eyed theories had been thoroughly discredited in the courts. MacArthur's signature program was its prestigious 'genius' awards, which took the form of fellowships to individuals identified as creative thinkers. In addition to funding... reasonable recipients, the five-year grants (roughly $250,000 each) provided an endowment program for the socialist left. Five editors of the tiny ideological journal *Dissent* had already received the grants (*Dissent's*... Irving Howe, was an adviser to the program ... "

Looting endowment funds — The endowment funds of IHEs are targets for looting by reds. Directors' positions are often sought, and obtained, by radicals of the deepest red. It is then a simple matter to lose applications from centrists and right-wingers, or disqualify them on technicalities, while approving applications from reds, regardless of their suitability. The board members, honorary appointees in most cases, usually accept the director's recommendations with few or no questions.

The grant and bequest seekers employ skilled solicitors to massage potential donors. Their requests are framed to match the suckers' enthusiasms. Middle-aged, financially successful men, who are important targets for such solicitors, are often very interested in sports, especially if there is a team they can relate to, either because of the team's success in contests with other schools or as a result of the presence of charismatic individuals (coaches or players). Therefore, free trips to games, good seats, and free mementos are given to the potential donors. Elderly widows gently slipping into senility are often easy targets for smooth-talking professionals who are willing to listen to their babble and treat them to an occasional outing.

Hartle (1999) points out that 90% of the nation's post-secondary institutions have endowments under $50 million, and the vast majority have endowments well under $10 million. The question might be asked, why should any going concern, such as a university, be allowed to have a large slush fund? Why should a government funded school have *any* endowment fund? Why should alumni, or anyone else, be solicited for the privilege of having attended the school? Do the alumni who are shaken down for funds they could use for better purposes know about the wasteful expenditures of the money the college has already collected?

Spending apparently averages about 3% of the endowment per year. Mabry (1999) said, "Colleges have become a new kind of investment business. They don't think of the endowment as something that was created to pay for the costs of education; they think of it as something that guarantees their survival: They're bankers."

The Results

Levy (1999) made many of the same points presented by F X Foulke-ffeinberg in his earlier books, "Twilight of the Universities" (1995) and "The Virtual Campus" (1998). Levy feels the culture has not been improved by decades of increased spending for higher education. He wrote, " . . . although there may [now] be more wine-sipping museum-goers, the bulk of the population is ill-informed . . . An inescapable conclusion must be that the educational establishment is at fault. There have been many complaints about the defects in education, and many suggestions on how to remedy them. But few if any point to the root of the problem, which is the basic principle on which it currently rests. It is that everybody is equally educatable. It is this false and entirely novel doctrine that colors everything. It is rigidly held, despite thousands of years of experience that people are not equally able to absorb knowledge."

Simple Corrective Actions

Removing the red influences from institutions of higher education would be an insurmountable task. The cleaning of the Augean stables was child's play in comparison. There are no obvious methods by which all of the red faculty and administrators could be removed. A drastic revision of the whole concept of higher education is necessary. As your present author has stated elsewhere, the following program is necessary:

1. Discontinue all money from government sources now being transferred to campus-based institutions of higher education (IHE). This action will include the discontinuance of all municipal, state, and federal subsidies to staff (administrators and faculty), to students, and to all other persons connected either temporarily or permanently with the institutions. Foundations, centers, institutes, and all other appendages of the college will be included in this prohibition. If the institution can continue to function on the income willingly spent by consumers of the services it provides, so be it.

2. Discontinue all tax forgiveness measures now benefitting campus-based colleges and universities. This includes, among many other items to be discontinued:

(a) Eliminate the charitable donation deduction obtained by individual and corporate tax payers for sums transferred as "gifts" to institutions of higher education.

(b) Discontinue all tax advantaged savings plans that contemplate the transfer of money (on which income taxes would otherwise have been levied) to college students as some form of aid or fee-cancellation.

3. With a small part of the added income tax collected and the saving of government funds that would have otherwise been spent, subsidize the development of a gigantic distant-teaching organization, which will give any student in the country an opportunity to study the subjects he is interested in, and only those he is interested in. The new institution would allow the students free choice of instructors as well as classes, and relocation of students to campuses would be no part of the scheme.

chapter six

RELIGIONS

The principles and practices of Bolshevism would seem to be clear and direct indications of that philosophy's unshakable enmity to the Christian church. After all, Marx wrote, "Religion . . . is the opium of the people." He also wrote, in 1843, "I have just been visited by the chief of the Jewish community here, who has asked me for a petition for the Jews to the Provincial Assembly, and I am willing to do it. However much I dislike the Jewish faith, Bauer's view seems to me to be too abstract. *The thing is to make as many breaches as possible to the Christian state and smuggle in as much as we can of what is rational.*" It would appear that what he considered rational would have to have a Jewish element. This is, in fact, perfectly in accord with all of his actions, as opposed to some of his pronouncements. He promoted the welfare of the Jews at the expense of the Christians, members of other religions, and even atheists.

It is true that Marx occasionally used outrageous insults to describe his ethnic mates: he described Ferdinand Lassalle as Izzy, the Yid, and the Jewish nigger, and speculated that he might be descended from the negroes who accompanied Moses' flight from Egypt. These were merely the fireworks he sent up to distract the goyim's attention from the landmines he was planting around their feet.

In the book, *Karl Marx* (Wheen 1999), the author declares the tract, "On the Jewish Question," though often regarded as evidence that Marx was antisemitic, does not provide such proof. "In spite of the clumsy phraseology and crude stereotyping, the essay was actually written as a defence of the Jew." Wheen, it should be mentioned, is actually a fan of Marx, and certainly no lover of the Christian religion. In fact, Wheen's first chapter begins with a lengthy discussion of an episode related to "The Holocaust," the latter being a sequence of events presumed to have occurred about a hundred years after Karl Marx flourished, and which has no discernible connection to the rest of his book.

It does not matter that Communism is completely antithetical to religion, their agents were willing to assume any role to secure the effects they wanted. Lenin wrote, "Every religious idea, every idea of God, every flirting with the idea of God, is unutterable vileness of the most dangerous kind."

Unfortunately, there are many Christians who are not able to understand that, while Marx and nearly all other Reds push for the abolition of all religions, they don't include Jewishness in that category. Jewry is a racial matter to them, not a religion. The great number of dupes who have been unable to understand this interpretation provided valuable assistance to Red recruiters, and have caused immense harm to traditional religious organizations and to sincere believers in Christ.

Judaists have been closely enmeshed with communism and its modern variants Leninism, Trotskyism, Stalinism, and Bolshevism since those movements came into being. Rich Jews from all corners of the world provided financial assistance to revolutions in many countries, and were crucial supporters of the violence and disruptions that ultimately led to Lenin's acension to power. This is a matter of record which no knowledgeable person disputes, except for propaganda purposes.

The relationship of other religions (e.g. Mohammedism and Buddhism) to Bolshevism has been somewhat less direct and often considerably less positive than the Jewish connection.

In summary, it can be said with great confidence that Karl Marx, and all those associated with him in the communist movement, hated Christianity and made this hatred a commandment in their new religion, which was, to all intents and purposes, a branch of Judaism. This commitment did not prevent the Bolsheviks from assuming the guise of Christians if that pretense helped expand their brand of atheism. Among them was Liberation Theology, a brilliantly designed invention, which proved to be very effective in neutralizing the negative effects of the Roman Catholic Church on the growth of Communism.

The Russian Orthodox Church

The earliest and most successful attacks on religion by Soviet agents were directed toward taking over the Russian Orthodox churches and its priests. This operation began shortly after Lenin seized power. Each successful encroachment was followed by further attacks. According to Andrew and Mitrokhin (1999), "The Council for the Affairs of the Russian Orthodox Church (later the Council for Religious Affairs) worked in close cooperation with the NKVD and its successors to ensure the subservience of Church to State."

After the Soviets had installed their agents, Patriarch Aleksi I and Metropolitan Nikolai of Krutitsky and Kolomna, as first and second authorities in the Orthodox hierarchy, these prelates began to infiltrate international organizations. They joined the World Peace Council (the Soviet front organization founded in 1949) and were highly regarded by the KGB as agents of influence. Aleksi declared in 1955: "The Russian Orthodox Church supports the totally peaceful foreign policy of our government, not because the Church allegedly lacks freedom, but because Soviet policy is just and corresponds to the Christian ideals which the Church preaches."

On the occasion of the beatification of 28 bishops, priests, monks, and nuns by Pope John Paul II at Lviv in the Ukraine, Karatnycky (2000) provided the following report. "These Ukrainian martyrs (and a Russian one) were not the victims of medieval torture. Most suffered and died in the 1940s as part of Soviet Communism's suppression of Ukraine's Greek Catholic faith." The Red campaign was part of a program to ban the church, which was thought to be supporting Ukrainian nationalism. Stories of terrible atrocities, including boiling priests in cauldrons, crucifying others, are told. At Bykivnia in Kiev, 120,000 Ukrainians (mostly Orthodox Christians) were shot by Stalin's stooges. News reports of many of these occurrences must have been suppressed by the media, but word of mouth relay of some of the details must have reached religionists of this denomination residing in free countries.

Andrew and Mitrokhin also say that, "In 1961, with the KGB's blessing, the Orthodox Church joined the World Council of Churches. At that very moment, Kruschev was in the midst of a ferocious anti-religious campaign which closed down many of the reopened monasteries and seminaries and disbanded half the Orthodox parishes ... The head of the Second Chief Directorate, General Oleg Mikhailovich Gribanov, reported in 1962 that over the previous two years, the KGB had infiltrated reliable agents into the leading positions of the Moscow Patriarchate, the Catholic dioceses, the Armenian Gregorian Church, and other religious groups."

And, "The most important of the agents at the WCC central committee meeting in Canterbury [1961] was the leader of the Russian Orthodox delegation, Metropolitan Nikodim, whose meteoric rise through the Church hierarchy was in itself unmistakable evidence of KGB approval. In 1960, at the age of only thirty-one, Nikodim had become the youngest bishop in Christendom." Well, not quite — some of the bishops in the Church of Jesus Christ of Latter Day Saints have been younger than this.

US Fifth Columnists

The World Council of Churches [WCC] and Union Theological Seminary [UTS] of New York came to be completely dominated by Soviet sympathizers and agents. Thus, the alleged Christians in these organizations — with very few exceptions — provided cover for the government that had caused "... the four million Uniate Christians to become the world's largest illegal church [1946] almost overnight. All but two of its ten bishops, along with many thousands of priests and believers, died for their faith in the Siberian gulag" (Andrew and Mitrokhin 1999).

In the US, the WCC and the UTS were lauded by the non-Christian-controlled media moguls and promoted by their servile hacks as the most sensitive and dependable Christian authorities of Russia. Their influence was effective in many countries, and the Soviet worldview came to be dominant, especially in Central and South America. The religious interfered with legally elected governments in all manner of ways.

As the movement's leaders became bolder, they felt free to encourage allegedly religious leaders of poor people to use terroristic methods to kill, steal from, and destroy the property of, more fortunate members of their society without regard to the effects of these crimes on the poor people of the country and on persons who relied on the church for guidance. Thus, we arrived at Liberation via Theology.

Liberation Theology

The term, "Liberation theology" was supposedly coined by Gustavo Gutierrez, a Peruvian Roman Catholic priest (Gutierrez 1983). It implies, we are told, that "the Gospel of Christ demands the church concentrate its efforts on liberating the people of the world from poverty and oppression." In practice, however, this movement or philosophy has nothing to do with liberation and very little do do with theology.

"Liberation Theology" was described by one critic as "Communism in a cassock" and by another as a "Roman Catholic movement dedicated to correcting the social abuses originally caused by the Roman Catholic Church." Neither of these definitions seems satisfactory, because the rogue clergy of the Roman Catholic Church are by no means the only religious pretenders using the communist-style destabilizing techniques which are the distinguishing features of Liberation Theology, and the philosophy was never adopted by a large percentage of the influential members of the RC Church.

In practice, as compared to theory, Liberation Theology has come to mean the use by allegedly religious leaders (often passing as Jesuits) of terroristic methods to kill, steal from, and destroy the property of more fortunate members of society without regard to the effects of such tactics on the rebels or their families.

The development of Liberation Theology — For about a decade after the term was first introduced, the methodology and message of Liberation Theology underwent a gradual development, including a re-orienting of some of its goals. As it became more radical, the usual kind of malcontents began to be attracted to the movement. A new impetus was provided by what seems to have been a crucial conference in 1968 — perhaps the founding event of the Latin American Liberation Theology movement. This conference was a meeting of South and Central American Bishops of the Roman Catholic church in Medellin, Colombia. Three persons who became very active in the movement at that time were Dom Helder Camara from Brazil, Jose Comblin, said to one of the earliest theologians of liberation, and Gustavo Gutierrez (a Peruvian priest).

Juan Luis Segundo of Uruguay was another early Liberation Theologist. Two members of Nicaragua's Sandanista leadership were RC priests — one a Maryknoll and the other a Jesuit. Leonardo Boff was regarded as one of the most radical exponents of the philosophy.

A predisposition to terrorism — The type of clerical meddling and indiscriminate terrorism which Liberation Theology encourages and attempts to justify is very attractive to certain types of persons, especially those who have lived for long periods in the restrictive confines of the religious establishment. These bored, egotistical, frustrated, and cynical individuals look for a new outlet for their "talents," and many of them find it in liberation activism.

Their participation (though sometimes vicarious) in the murdering, pillaging, and sexual exploitation of innocent victims by their client thugs satisfies the same sadistic proclivities that led to witch hunts. Inside every liberation theologist is a Savonarola struggling to get out. These debased appetites make their possessors easy prey for the Communist manipulators who are the real controllers of Liberation Theology and who benefit most from its depredations.

In 1999, Daniel Levine, professor of Political Science at U MI, said Peru was " . . . one of the originating points of liberation theology and there in the late 60s liberation theology comes together with an immense popular movement of grass roots organizations and trade unions and teachers' organizations and neighbourhood groups. There was a great effervescence at the time and I think that they drew force from the fact that a lot of normal politics and a lot of normal channels for activists had been closed down by the power of authoritarian and military region [sic] across the regime — *there were no normal channels for politics so a lot of activists, I think migrated into the Church* " [emphasis added]. This supports the claim of the present author that activists are a special breed whose personality causes them to seek out causes that will provide them with certain kinds of satisfaction having little or no connection with the publicly expressed motives of the movement.

Pre-empting the Religious Establishments

Although the doctrines on which Christian religions are based might seem to be totally incompatible with the justifications for Red rebellion, the Reds were not going to allow a little thing like that bother them. We know from records in the Soviet archives, and from other historical documents, that Lenin began to take over the Russian Orthodox church almost as soon as he achieved the power to do so. Corrupting those churches headquartered outside the USSR took a little longer.

The Roman Catholic church was one of the designated victims of this campaign because of its worldwide presence, its vast treasures, and its pervasive influence on members' lives. Much effort was exerted over several decades on attempts to subvert the RC hierarchy so as to bend this giant organization to the uses of Communism. One of the chief agents in this program was Saul Alinsky. We'll analyze his tactics in some detail.

A Soviet operation in the US — An important and authoritative book, *The Thirty Years War*, by Tom Pauken (1995), gives some significant insights into the planning that went into the corrupting of Catholicism in the US. The process started with introducing nuns and seminary students to poverty theory, continued with converting them to liberation theology, and eventually conducted them into a life of radical activism. Much of the text under this sub-head was adapted from Pauken's book.

"The late Saul Alinsky wrote the leftist organizing bible, *Rules for Radicals*. In the forward to the book, Alinsky offered: 'an over-the-shoulder acknowledgement to the very first radical . . . who rebelled against the establishment and did it so effectively that he at least won his own kingdom — Lucifer.' " Alinsky's brazen flaunting of his indebtedness to the devil is typical Jewish chutzpah.

Pauken wrote, "Over the years, many young nuns and priests had fallen under the spell of Saul Alinsky, who based his community organizing operation in Chicago. Alinsky had decided early on in his career that he had to change the attitudes of the Catholic church in the US, which traditionally had been viewed as a conservative, anti-Communist institution. His objective was to use his young 'recruits' from the religious ranks as a wedge inside the institution of the church in order to change it. As the Alinsky-trained recruits grew older and gained more power within the Church infrastructure, the Catholic Church in America began to show the effects . . . His decades of hard work paid off as the religious who shared Alinsky's radical brand of politics moved into key positions of influence within the bureaucracy of various religious orders, Catholic dioceses, and even the US Catholic Conference itself (the national organization of the American bishops)."

The foregoing account, and other evidence, leaves little doubt that the corrupting of the Catholic church was deliberately planned and partially executed by Saul Alinsky, a Jewish agent of the Comintern.

Considering the known methods of operation of Soviet intelligence agencies, there is a very high level of probability that operations similar to that of Alinsky were conducted in other parts of the U.S. and throughout the rest of the world, wherever there were institutions for educating the religious.

The role of Pope John Paul II — Although Pope John Paul II of the Roman Catholic Church has not been as diligent in reproving the excesses of liberation theologians as some would like, he is far from being a supporter of the Soviet brand of rebellion and banditry which appears to be the scenario from which these activists take their cues. It is a reasonable assumption that the Pope does not regard the disruptive actions of renegade priests as compatible with his own view of the Church's mission.

In 1984, the Vatican Congregation for the Doctrine of Faith issued "An instruction on certain aspects of the theology of liberation." Basically, it said that liberation theology is based on the Marxist philosophy of the class struggle and generally makes the plight of the poor worse. Few non-Communists would argue with this analysis.

One of the official statements of the Catholic Church's attitude toward Liberation Theology is: "Let us recall the fact that atheism and the denial of the human person, his liberty and rights, are at the core of the Marxist theory. This theory, then, contains errors which directly threaten the truths of the faith regarding the eternal destiny of individual persons. Moreover, to attempt to integrate into theology an analysis whose criterion of interpretation depends on this atheistic conception is to involve itself in terrible contradictions. What is more, this misunderstanding of the spiritual nature of the person leads to a total subordination of the person to the collectivity, and thus to the denial of the principles of a social and political life which is in keeping with human dignity." (VII, 9) We should also recall the words of Pius XI in 1930 that "No one can be at the same time a sincere Catholic and a true Socialist."

The former Jesuit priest Leonardo Boff, whose writings and oral statements have been dealt with in considerable detail elsewhere in this chapter, was silenced by the Vatican and subsequently left the priesthood. Cardinal Ratzinger said, "He [Boff] has chosen his own way, he has taken a path that goes away from the doctrine of the Church."

Of course, the Pope's opinion is of absolutely no consequence to the average Liberation theologist, whose allegiance to the Catholic church, and even to Christianity itself, is a formality at best. Their god is the triple-headed monster Marx-Lenin-Stalin.

Standard operating procedures — There is every reason to believe that the Russian hierarchy considered Pope John Paul II a major enemy, a man who was especially dangerous because of his opposition to the Russians' program for keeping Poland inside the Bolshevik empire. It surely is not a coincidence that on May 13, 1981, the Pope was shot (and nearly killed) by a Turkish assassin. The Italian police could not find a connection between the assassin and any outside agency. If they *had* found a connection, do you think they would have publicized it?

Since (1) the Russians would have gained the most from the Pope's removal, (2) assassination was (and is) a very common tactic in the Bolshevik repertoire, and (3) there seems to have been no other group with a strong reason to kill the Pope, we are justified in concluding there is a very high probability the would-be assassin was operating under Soviet control.

In 1999, solid evidence was unearthed that threw a new light on the plan to assassinate the Pope. Carroll (1999) published extracts from Czechoslovakian secret service documents obtained by the Italians in 1990. Among the information bearing on the Soviet attitude toward the Pope and on Catholicism in general, Carroll commented:

"Appalled at the prospect of an anti-communist Pole leading the Roman Catholic church, KGB bosses allegedly gave orders to destroy John Paul II hours after his election in 1979.

"Operations — code-named Pagoda and Infection — allegedly instructed intelligence agencies in the Warsaw Pact countries to 'discredit the church and the pope with disinformation and provocations that do not *exclude* his physical elimination.'

"The archive vindicated claims that the Soviet Union was behind the March 1981 assassination attempt on the pope in St. Peter's Square (Rome), according to excerpts published in Thursday's *Il Giorno* newspaper.

"It has never been proved that the gunman, Mehmet Ali Agca, a Turkish member of the Grey Wolves terrorist group was working for Moscow.

"KGB agents plotted to plant a bug in a statue of the Madonna kept on a table in the private study of the late Vatican secretary of state, Cardinal Agostino Casaroli, according to the files. A plan to put another bug in a picture frame was also alleged. The KGB wanted to be able to anticipate and combat the Vatican's stoking of anti-communist sentiment in eastern Europe.

"Markus Wolf, who headed East Germany's Stasi secret service, has claimed that a Benedictine monk who worked inside the Vatican was a mole.

"The Italian secret service is believed to possess another 600 pages of Czechoslovak documents. They were handed over after Vaclav Havel became president. Enzo Fragalo, a member of the right-wing Alleanza Nazionale, said it was clear that the Soviet Union wanted to destroy one of the gravest threats to its empire. 'The Soviets succeeded in organizing a frontal attack on the Vatican and the Pope,' he said."

Who goes there? — Our contention is that communist agents developed the theories and controlled the strategy of liberation theologians. They intended to destroy the religious commitments of Christian institutions and then to redirect their funds and manpower toward Soviet goals. As part of their plan, they schemed to place communist sympathizers in the colleges and seminaries that trained the future leaders of the religious communities. They chose to advance the weak, the gullible, the perverse, and the corruptible.

In spite of ample evidence disclosing the evil intentions of its practitioners, many prominent halfwits and venal agnostics in the community of American church leaders supported Liberation Theology, just as they had given their approval and assistance to other Red front movements without hesitation.

Right-wing Death Squads

In the propaganda lexicon of Liberation Theologists, the term "right-wing death squads" occupies a prominent place. It is a phrase reds apply to military and police units who are operating under a legally constituted government to rescue the populace from the tyranny of communist oppressors who have tried to set up their personal kingdoms in the countryside, or in sections of cities. The news media establishment slavishly follows this terminology without question.

Have you ever seen the term "left-wing death squads" in the news media, or in academic writings, or anywhere except here? Were the millions of persons who perished under Lenin, Stalin, Pol Pot, Mao, Bela Kuhn, or Ho Chih Minh the victims of "left-wing death squads?" Or, were they merely collateral damage, the unavoidable result of corrective actions taken by Communist freedom fighters? Perhaps the victims should have been grateful that they were able to contribute their lives to the great and noble schemes of Stalin.

Why It Doesn't Work

Such authorities as Leonardo Boff and Clodovis Boff (2001) of Brazil, who are responsible for the book, *Introducing Liberation Theology*, still claim to believe that the pathetic state of some of the Inhabitants of the less industrialized nations can be improved by a redistribution of existing material assets. The truth is, the wealth that remains in these backward countries is insufficient to bring the populace to a modern level of comfort and safety even if *all* existing wealth were to be divided equally among every man, woman, and child in the nation.

Industrial development accompanied by technological advances and a vigorous commercial system is the only way any kind of lasting prosperity can come to the inhabitants of any country. This has been proved time and time again. Democracy of the US type is helpful but not essential to such achievements. Such concepts are dismissed out of hand by the likes of the Boffs. Typically, they will say something like, "The middle and upper classes benefitted, but the farmers and laborers were no better off." History proves otherwise.

The problem of Jesuits — The history of the Liberation Theology movement provides us with classic examples of communistic infiltration and takeover of an opposing pressure group. There is very little doubt that the Jesuit seminaries are at present largely under the control of persons who at one time took orders from Soviet intelligence agents and who are and always will be devoted to the vicious philosophies of Marx, Lenin, and Stalin. The goal of this controlling group is to subvert and eventually destroy not only the Society of Jesus but all of the institutions of the Roman Catholic Church.

It seems that Pope John Paul II became aware of this program, at least in its broad outline, and did his best to blunt the effect of the renegade Jesuits. Unfortunately, he was unable to completely reverse the results of the program because of its deep roots, but he was somewhat effective in slowing the spread of the disease.

A more forceful prelate, or one with more reliable lieutenants, would have first reduced the whole Jesuit order to a core that consisted of a few priests who were known to have fought the communist takeover. He would have closed and dismantled the Jesuit seminaries (devoting their properties to other uses), and would have excommunicated (or at least segregated and isolated) all members of the order (at whatever level) who refused to submit to these moves or who were found to have had contacts with Soviet agents from any country. Then, if he wished, he could have slowly rebuilt the order, and opened a new seminary under close control of the Vatican.

None of these things were done, and Papal opposition had little effect on the infiltration of reds into the Jesuit order, or on their destructive effects on the mission of that group. We are now faced with a widespread and continuing propaganda program and an accompanying attack on freedom and social advancement by their agents. Unfortunately, there are no obvious ways to reduce the deleterious effects on humanity.

The Art and Practice of Liberation Theology?

Movements such as Young Christian Students, Young Christian Workers, Young Christian Agriculturalists, and the Movement for Basic Education established the first "base ecclesial communities" and set up educational radio programs. Agents planted by the Soviets in all parts of academia, and in the seminaries in particular, had gained a high degree of control over the instruction and indoctrination of students, and their converts began to exercise a direct and malign influence on religious practices in many nations.

A "base ecclesial community" is a sort of commune or collective dominated by, e.g., a Jesuit activist and devoted to Christian living and redeeming the poor. That's how the prospectus reads — in reality they become, or start out as, safe houses for drug peddlers and terrorists.

Continuing with our analysis of the justification of Liberation Theology by the Boffs, we find the following passage: "The work of these — generally middle-class — Christians was sustained theologically by the European theology of earthly realities, the integral humanism of Jacques Maritain, the social personalism of Mounier, the progressive evolutionism of Teilhard de Chardin, Henri de Lubac's reflections on the social dimensions of dogma, Yves Congar's theology of the laity, and the work of M.-D. Chenu. The Second Vatican Congress then gave the best possible theoretical justification to activities developed under the signs of a theology of progress, of authentic secularization and human advancement."

The actual philosophical forefathers of Liberation Theology are none other than our old friends Karl Marx and his disciples Lenin and Stalin. Teilhard de Chardin and the other dead fish who appear on the label have nothing to do with the actual contents of this package. It is an old trick of the reds — they appeal to the spirit of Aristotle, the humility of Saint Francis of Assisi, the non-violence of Gandhi, and the like to characterize their philosophy, to give it a more nearly human face, when they should be referring to Bela Kuhn, Ho Chi Minh, and Pol Pot. Truth-in-packaging is badly needed here.

Wealth will always be distributed unequally — surely not even the Boffs believe each of the world's inhabitants should have exactly 0.7 automobiles and 2.5 children — but the vast differences in availability of consumer goods which so trouble the tenderhearted reds are due to restrictive laws and customs which prevent the flowering of innovation and entrepreneurism and the free flow of commerce. And, the disruptive and destructive effects of Soviet-style activists are major contributing factors.

In a closely reasoned metaphysical (!) study of Liberation Theology, Fr. Bill Leaming (2001) manages to clarify some interesting points for the few non-metaphysicists among his readers. For instance, he writes " . . . as a class, they [the victims of oppression] are sometimes defined dialectically, and not just economically. They represent any group on the downside of oppression: exploited females, or laity in a clerically dominated church, or immigrants in a hostile country. Indeed, suffering is considered almost exclusively as a result of oppression. There is no consideration of disease, pain, depression, bereavement, mortality, or any impoverishment except what has been inflicted by others." He quotes Leonardo Boff, "The first to benefit . . . are the victims of injustice, oppression, and violence. The powerful, the rich, the proud will be toppled from their places. Thus they will be able to stop being inhuman. Freed from the schemes that made them oppressors, they too will have a chance to share in God's new order . . . It is this condition [poverty] that makes them the preferred people of God." Leaming points out, "this favors the poor for no other reason than that they are poor . . . I find it impossible to square with Christian revelation any doctrine that Jesus shows preferential love toward any single class of people."

Why not liberation technology? — Technology, not theology, is the answer. The first problem with Liberation Theology is that its leaders haven't a clue as to the real sources of community plenty and individual advancement. The two prongs of economic advancement are technology and capitalism — goods must be produced efficiently and distributed by a freely operating market system before the masses can benefit. This implies that articles must be produced and services must be provided by persons who are rewarded for their achievements. Artisans and entrepreneurs must have a scope for their activities which provides rewards for innovation and production targeted to the needs of others, not guided by a blueprint drawn up by some ecclesiastic or academic (or, even worse, panels of them) in a seminary or university.

Liberty is meaningless without opportunities for those to advance materially who wish to do so and who can provide benefits to others that justify their own economic success. The advocates of Liberation Theology believe (or purport to believe) that something must be taken away from those who have it before those who do not have it can achieve their desires. The real answer is that, even if the top 10% of the population were simply exterminated, and their goods were distributed to the poorest segments of the population, the conditions of everyone, including the poorest, would within a matter of weeks or months be worse than ever. And, there would be no one else to steal from, so everyone's plight would be hopeless.

In practice, the application of free enterprise to the enrichment of the general population is not simple. The idea that everyone has the freedom — and the responsibility — for taking charge of his own life is very daunting to some people, especially if they have been taught by clerics or communists that God, or nature, or civilization, or the government owes them a living. Many persons growing up in the kinds of cultures that predominate in parts of Africa, Asia, and South America are very uncomfortable with the idea of open-ended achievement for everyone, and are simply unable to visualize the benefits that would accrue to them from implementation on a broad scale of improved methods.

Therefore, it may be necessary to teach the poorest some basic skills, to expose them to the elements of personal economics, to show them (by example) the advantage of self-control in their individual careers, and to wean them away from dependence on counseling by spiritual leaders, most of whom have never earned an honest peso in their entire lives and who wouldn't even know how to go about earning one by doing constructive work.

Once the basics have been grasped, there is an opportunity for the development of a relatively prosperous class of laborers, farmers, and artisans. This can be expected to lead to a continued upward trend in health, freedom, and the availability of comfortable living conditions. In this type of social climate, technological advances will occur, will be commercially applied, and will enrich the entire society.

Proof of the pudding — Wherever Liberation Theology advocates have had free rein to practice their ruinous teachings, in South and Central America and elsewhere, they have terrorized and enslaved the underclasses, and have eliminated whatever chances there may have been for improving the common people's health and welfare. Neither Liberation Theology nor any other kind of theology will ever allow poor people to rise above their present level of living unless they understand the necessity for ecouraging the application of technology to the satisfying of wants and needs of individuals.

Of course, it is also necessary to inculcate the idea that each individual must take the responsibility for performing a useful function in society. And this requirement does not include forming another mariachi band, painting crude political cartoons on buildings, singing folk songs in a mezcalera, harvesting coca leaves, or joining some coked up activist in a peace demonstration.

Liberation Theology failed to improve the lot of the poor because (1) it was based on the abdication of personal accountability and (2) it failed to acknowledge nature's rule that material rewards follow material achievements. Furthermore, even the untutored masses eventually realized the folly of entrusting the responsibility for their lives and fortunes to the tender mercies of the paranoid and sadistic invaders who, so often, used religion as a cloak for their own foul practices.

It is important to understand that the improvement of people's living standards and the enhancement of their personal freedom was never a part of the real agenda of the Liberation Theologists. Probably, the subalterns in this conspiracy had very little faith in the correctness of the Red tenets, either. Instead, the secret intent of these activists was to carve out little empires for themselves — or big empires if conditions permitted — and to satisfy their own peculiar sexual appetites using the unfortunate persons who came under their control.

Probably, few of the "theologians" really believed any part of the religious doctrines they so forcefully proclaimed — they would have espoused any cause, flown any flag, that allowed them to gain the power they hungered for.

Same old, same old — The preceding examples of the current activities of red groups in Central and South America, who are cut off from the sacred ground of Bolshevism, but who still function as convinced and determined terrorists, killing, raping, and committing every other type of atrocity in pursuance of their inherent sadistic orientation. One is tempted to conclude that some other international operation of a violent and ruthless minority, not connected with the Roman Catholic Church or any other conservative religious organization, but well-financed and tightly controlled, has taken charge of these field groups.

It may not be entirely correct to lay all of the blame on Castro, because he no longer has the money, and he probably can not furnish the manpower, to keep these South American campaigns going. The drug trade could be part of the answer, but I am inclined to think it is only a peripheral segment of the total picture. One might look for members of a more cohesive and less constrained brotherhood, more ancient than the church and more ruthless by far.

What's next? — In the year 2002, we find that Liberation Theology, as it was originally promoted by reds in the Roman Catholic priesthood (and by other, nominally Christian, activists), has been thoroughly discredited by its opponents, and by history. Even its major proponents, after being responsible for killing and torturing hundreds if not thousands of innocent people, and destroying untold amounts of property, and delaying for decades the entry of whole countries into the modern world of advanced technology and prosperity, are admitting their basic precepts were wrong. But, of course, they have suggestions for fixing their plans so that they will be workable. And, they have supporters in the media and in politics. One despairs of the human race — let us hope God has an improved model in the works.

Red Protestant Denominations

The preceding discussion is heavily oriented toward descriptions of the problems encountered by the Roman Catholic Church in trying to deal with infiltration and subversion by Red agents. Protestant churches have had their difficulties, too, but the gravity of their situation does not seem to be as great, perhaps because they do not present such a concentrated target. The Reds can find more attractive victims elsewhere.

All of the Protestant churches have had some difficulties with Reds, and the trend in thinking and preaching in the middle and top management levels has definitely turned to the left during the past few decades. A fairly typical example is the United Methodist Church, which is today unmistakably red. The Quakers have for many years pursued goals which are little different, in most cases, from those of the Communist Party — of course the church's rhetoric is slightly less strident.

Individual preachers pursue many different angles, but their thinking is always strongly magnetized by contributions and the potential bequests. Reinhold Niebuhr, a Protestant theologian who was proud to be a Socialist, received good press coverage for many years, because he supported programs which were highly favored by the leftist establishment. For example, he was strongly in favor of a the US entering the war in Europe in 1940, before most other Socialists had got their options straightened out following the break in the German-Soviet entente. Once his clients had succeeded, he again became a vociferous pacifist.

An example of misplaced compassion — "The Fifth Avenue Presbyterian Church has been encouraging up 45 derelicts to sleep on the sidewalk outside its walls, in multiple violations of city law. This is a classic piece of Manhattan 'compassion;' maximally visible with no sacrifice to the self. The homeless can't actually come inside the church, and they have to leave early in the morning so church employees don't have to step over them" (MacDonald 2001).

"Recently, the police have tried to move the vagrants into shelters, where they could receive treatment for mental illness, addictions, and infections, and where they would not endanger the public. Three times in the past two years, deranged vagrants have pushed two people in front of subway cars, killing one woman, severing a man's legs, and, just this November, fracturing a mother's skull.

"That's apparently OK by the church, however, which has screamed 'rights violation!' against the city's efforts to enforce the law, and which just won a preliminary court ruling to keep its homeless on the streets."

SUMMARY AND CONCLUSIONS

The Christian religion has faced many internal and external threats over its two millenia of existence. Many of the internal dissonances have been silenced by fragmentation and pre-emption strategies, but the basic message of all the major branches has remained essentially the same. The most serious threat it has ever faced was communism, and in particular the Soviet brand of this philosophy, which itself had many of the characteristics of a religion.

The communist proselyters recognized from the first that established religions in general, and Christianity in particular, were major hindrances to the spread and acceptance of their philosophy. Therefore, they established as major goals the invading and subverting of Christian sects. They had varying degrees of success in these maneuvers.

It is certainly true that many other religious organizations suffer from the same disease. Methodists, Presbyterians, Quakers, Episcopalians, certain branches of Methodism, and several kinds of Baptist churches are under the influence of left-wing organizers and executives who are determinedly anti-Christian.

So far as Judaism is concerned, it is a question of who would preempt whom. Jews were among the first promoters and advocates of Communism of the Marxian type, and they remain a powerful influence in all branches of that movement today. At best there is an "understanding" which is of mutual benefit to Judaism/Zionism and international communism. At worst, we could consider that liberation theology and similar movements are just additional tools to make the whole world eretz Israel. It is unquestionably true that vicious propaganda campaigns by both Jews and Reds have been very effective in distorting the Christian message so as to gain political advantages for non-Christians.

Islam seems to be in somewhat the same position as Christianity with regard to Communist influences, i.e, there are segments of the membership in which substantial penetration has been made, but the administration of this religion is so fragmented that an overall conclusion can not be made by this writer. Terrorist acts have certainly been committed by Muslims, but it seems doubtful that there was a direct Communist line to any of the events. Future revelations may help us decide.

Established religion is, of necessity, almost by definition, a foe of revolutionary movements. But, in every religious organization, there will be disruptive and destructive persons. As long as they remain isolated, or consist of small groups arguing among themselves as to the best course to take in opposing the establishment, little harm will come to the establishment.

But, when opponents begin to coalesce around one or two major centers, they constitute a potential danger to the entrenched power system. This threat may or may not be recognized by the often somnolent executives in time for them to take effective protective measures.

The establishment may attempt to pre-empt some of the goals of these disruptive elements, or may relinquish some of its powers in attempts to placate the rebels. These tactics may succeed in holding the animals at bay for a time, but the religion's actions will always be weakened by its baggage of sinecure-holders (who will do nothing to help) and malcontents, who are foolishly gladdened by signs of impending destruction of their own institution. Many of these freeloaders and losers accumulate through decades of easy times.

Furthermore, the initial appeal of the established religion will often have been diluted and even deformed by a sequence of additions to and subtractions from the simple message of its founders, so that it no longer be understood by the masses, and often not by anyone else.

chapter seven

MEDIA AND THE ARTS

In the sense in which the word is used here, "media" signifies the corporations, persons, physical plants, and products involved in the businesses of distributing to the public news and other supposedly factual information, entertainment, and propaganda (such as advertisements). A few examples of the many products in this field are: (1) ephemeral print media such as newspapers and magazines, (2) books, (3) broadcast media such as radio and television, and (4) recorded media such as visual and sound events that have been filmed, taped, or preserved by other methods. Producers of live performances which are not put in recorded form for sale to the general public are generally not thought of as being in "the media."

"Arts" overlap, to some extent "the media," or perhaps it would be preferable to say the dividing line between the two is diffuse. In the arts we can recognize subdivisions such as drama, musical performances, ballet and other dance exhibitions, opera, and many others. Painting, photography, sculpture, non-technical books, and static representations form other important classes of idea transfer. And, of course, video and radio performances of all appropriate kinds are compatible with our specifications. Professional sports could no doubt be considered a type of "art," but they will not be considered further in this section.

This list is not only incomplete but somewhat redundant, since the reader will undoubtedly have a very good grasp of the concept without further elaboration.

The Arts

Anything and everything that can be described as "art" is considered by its practitioners to be beyond the ken of ordinary people, that is, Philistines such as you and I. Well, you anyway. Non-artists are not supposed to have the ability to evaluate "art." The outsider who, upon viewing (or hearing) an artistic production, comments, "I don't understand it," is likely to provoke a snicker or at least a despairing shake of the head from those who operate within the sacred confines of art.

This makes "art" an easy vehicle for the disinformation expert: the product doesn't have to pass any of those silly tests of verifiabilty that are required in science, technology, or even (sometimes) the news. This viewpoint converts art into a kind of religion based on faith alone.

The infiltrating of decadent art into the community is a tactic that is useful for promoting the red goal of destroying the spirit and will of free societies. It also provides an avenue for transferring funds from nonprofit foundations to useful members of the wrecking crew.

In the year 2002, the prestigious Turner Prize, which is awarded annually to a British artist, was given to Martin Creed, who entitled his work, *The Lights Going On and Off*. This consisted of an empty room in which the lights went on and off at five second intervals. Nonsense art of this sort, or Dadaism as it was called in the years just before 1920, is a simple way to attract publicity and to transfer funds (in this case 20,000 pounds) to a red, a lover, a relative, or some other worthy person, who perhaps will give a bit of it back to the donors.

According to BBC news, the runner-up work to Creed's master-piece consisted of "a dusty room filled with an array of disparate objects, including a plastic cactus, mirrors, doors and old tabloid newspapers." The prize was presented by that perpetual celebrity Madonna, another piece of nonsense art that was created, named, and used by anti-Christian zealots.

Things may actually be getting better, though. In 1995, the Turner prize was given to an "artist" who exhibited a cow and a calf cut in half and preserved in formaldehyde.

Disinformation and Censorship

Red doctrine demands the perversion of truth to advance the cause of the greater good of Communism. Lenin's message was that truth was whatever helps the cause, that lies which advance Bolshevism are good, a truth which retards its advance is bad. Arthur Koestler said (in *The God that Failed*) that he gave a talk in the late 1930s to a group of German exiles which was about half Reds, and he included in his speech the statement that a harmful truth was better than a useful lie. His Communist friends later told him they knew then that he had renounced his allegiance to the Party.

Mossad influence on media — For many years, Victor Ostrovsky was an agent of the Mossad, the principal spying, disinformation, and dirty tricks arm of the Israeli government. It has had an intimate and long-standing relationship with the Red subversion and disinformation bureaus. He later defected and wrote a book, *By Way of Deception* (Ostrovsky and Hoy 1990). This led to a series of personal difficulties including situations which he regarded as life-threatening. He described some of these experiences in *The Other Side of Deception* (1994), from which has been taken the following discussion of the working methods and general philosophy of Israeli disinformation agents.

The Israelis were determined to establish as much control as possible over the media, and, as part of this plan, would planted false information in US newspapers, magazines, books, movies, etc., whenever they thought it was necessary or desirable. Some of the tactics used to prevent publication and distribution of Ostrovsky's book are described in the following paragraphs.

Mossad operators gave reporters documents revealing some of the Mossad's secrets. Ostrovksky said, "I believe this was in Canada. Then the reporters were told that they had to return the press release because Israel had taken legal steps to block the book's [TOSOD] publication. "To my surprise, the reporters returned the papers without a murmur."

"Then Mossad made its move in the US and managed to temporarily block further distribution of the book there. This was an unprecedented move, and the reaction in the States was much more vocal and furious than the Canadian reaction."

"Then several Israeli newspeople showed up, acting both as reporters for their own papers and as commentators for other media. One by the name of Ran Dagony, reporting for a daily newspaper in Israel called *Maariv*, published an extremely devastating interview with me that he claimed to have conducted in Toronto. The interview covered almost two full newspaper pages. The man only neglected to mention that we'd never met and that I'd never spoken to him . . . "

The case of Kosinski — "Another widely used disinformation technique is rumor, employed particularly against political exiles, refugees, and defectors from Communist countries (Bittman 1985). Jerry Kosinski, a refugee from Poland and a prominent writer in the US, has for years been a target of Communist slander. The campaign seemed to reach its zenith on June 22, 1982, when *The Village Voice* of NY published a lengthy article accusing Kosinski of two unforgivable sins: plagiarism and cooperation with the CIA. The paper stated not only that Kosinki's novel, *The Painted Bird*, was written in Polish and translated into English without crediting the translator, but it also said that the author had fabricated facts about his biography... And the paper charged that the CIA 'apparently played a clandestine role' in the publication of his first two books. The article opened an argument with strong political overtones in several prominent publications, including the *New York Times, Newsweek*, the *Boston Globe*, and others" (Bittman 1985).

Kosinski, who had become a highly successful writer of English novels was considered an important target for destruction not only because he served as an example and an inspiration for many young Poles but also because he made strong political statements against the Polish government, which was dominated by the Soviets at that time. The source of most anti-Kosinski disinformation has been Wieslaw Gornicki, a correspondent for the Polish Press Agency at the UN in the sixties and a high official in General Jaruszelski's military regime in the early 1980s (Bittman 1985).

A disastrous dereliction of duty — The following discussion is included at this pointbecause it describes what would be called by any reasonable person a clear-cut failure by the news media to reveal the true nature of a totally evil organization — the People's Temple of "Reverend" Jim Jones. This failure resulted in the deaths of hundreds of people and the loss of millions of dollars in funds extorted by Jones from Temple members and outside supporters of the organization.

The People's Temple tragedy shows clearly that the news media will attempt to disguise or minimize serious threats to masses of people, if the threat is in the form of a "progressive," "activist," or "liberal" organization or person. The following discussion of this point is largely based on an article by Richard Jencks, *The Press and Jim Jones* (1978).

"In retrospect, it is apparent that Jim Jones succeeded for the better part of five years in manipulating the San Francisco media in order to obtain a consistently favorable image . . . Jones seems to have found safety in playing on liberal and progressive sentiments — nonviolence, concern for the poor, racial justice — that made him a sacred cow to some journalists . . . There appears to have been little that a determined reporter could not have learned about Jim Jones before the Guyana tragedy that wasn't learned after it was too late."

For example, the general public and law enforcement officials in California could have learned about the first suicide rehearsal in 1973. Members of the press certainly knew about it, and, if they had publicized it, they might have prevented the sect from acquiring members who were later killed. And, they might have gained public support for defectors from the group and for family members who were trying to rescue their minor children from the Temple.

Mark Kilduff of the San Francisco Chronicle got his investigative report on the Temple rejected by his employer in early 1977. It was also initially rejected by New West magazine, but then was accepted by that periodical after a management shakeup changed its editorial policies. The Northern California chapter of the American Civil Liberties Union attempted to kill the story by claiming that "People's Temple has made a solid contribution to social justice in our community." Acceptance by the ACLU, that foul conglomeration of subversives and oppressors, is a reliable token of approval by the establishment.

Jones had a simple and direct approach to co-opting the media — he used flattery and bribery. "In 1973 the Temple awarded 'free speech' prizes totaling $4,400 to 12 newspapers and magazines, including the New York Times, The Christian Science Monitor, and three San Francisco newspapers." These media powerhouses, when accepting their crumbs, could have mentioned that the peerless leader did not extend his idea of freedom to converts, who were not allowed to leave the organization for any reason — in fact, members of the Temple were slaves, for all practical purposes.

"[Jim Jones] . . . used all the liberal buzzwords. He was an 'activist.' He was a 'peacemaker.' He was dedicated to 'nonviolence.' He denounced 'racism.' Favorite reporters got special interviews with Jones." Reporters described his teachings as "Radical Christianity."

"[The People's Temple]...was a cloak for Jone's avowed if twisted Marxism...his People's Forum house magazine was full of his hatred for American institutions."

"Mark Lane asserted at a press conference that his client was being persecuted because he was a Marxist..."

How to get a manuscript accepted — It is easy enough to get rapid production of a manuscript which fills a specific propaganda need. The assassination of President John F. Kennedy at first appeared to be the work of a "lone assassin," Lee Harvey Oswald. There were, however, some details which strongly suggested the participation of Soviet agents in the planning of the murder. For example, Oswald had spent time in the Soviet Union, and had remained an ardent Communist supporter after he returned to the US. There were other links of Red agents with the JFK assassination which space limitations do not permit us to explore. For further information, see *The JFK Assassination*, by Christian Hartwright (1999).

The important problem facing the Red apologists was the need to keep control of both the temporary and the permanent records being developed so that attention would be diverted from the red assassin story to a version that can be summarized as "red defector assisted by right wing fanatics." Many obvious defects in this theme began to appear, and the communists apparently decided to settle for a version that we might call, "the lone assassin who had by a strange coincidence been in Russia for a while." The disinformation activity was greatly facilitated when Oswald's own version of his motivations was abruptly obliterated by a bullet from a gun wielded by a homosexual Jewish thug.

The lone assassin story which the reds intended to have accepted by historians and, hopefully, by all the official investigators, was never questioned by any of the establishment's journalists. The news media in America were almost 100% committed to this disinformation effort, and slavishly parroted the Red-invented scenario. Although the news outlets were not a problem, the conspirators evidently thought it would also be desirable to have a book or two available for historical researchers to consult when they wrote about the assassination.

As a result of the Red's speedy reaction to this perceived need, the first volume on the Kennedy assassination to gain wide circulation in the US was *Oswald: Assassin or Fall Guy?*, by the German writer Joachim Joesten. The author had a Communist background and the book was published by Carl Aldo Marzani, owner of the Liberty Book Club. Marzani was an American Communist, born in Italy, who received both funding and direction from Soviet agents.

Joesten wholeheartedly supported the Soviet's original disinformation theme that the assassination was a conspiracy by right-wing racists, among them the familiar punching bag for Reds, "oil-magnate H. L. Hunt," who was, at the time, probably the "usual suspect" most popular with the left-wing disinformation experts when public attention had to be diverted from some new red atrocity (Andrew and Mitrokhin 1999). Occasionally, they seemed to confuse HLH with E. Howard Hunt, a totally different person.

Oswald was, according to Joesten's hypothesis, an FBI stooge supported or encouraged in some manner by the CIA. In these few words, we can see the nucleus of the original program of the Soviets as they attempted to deflect attention from their own participation in the Kennedy assassination, *a program beginning before the actual deed*. Even today, their dupes and accomplices continue efforts to promote this scenario.

One piece of "evidence" used by left-wing assassination theorists to connect E. Howard Hunt, a Watergate "conspirator," to the murder in Dallas, is a letter supposedly written by Oswald to Hunt shortly before November 22, 1963. According to evidence revealed by Mitrokhin (Andrew and Mitrokhin 1999), this letter was a complete fabrication, having been drawn up under the direction of the KGB. They had the handwriting "authenticated" by three "experts" as well as by the ever flexible and cooperative Marina Oswald. The KGB was disgusted to find that some people were identifying the addressee as H. L. Hunt.

The forged letter used words and phrases taken from material written by Oswald during the time he lived and worked in Russia. These were assembled and put into final form by KGB forgers. Documents seen by Mitrokhin showed the final document was checked two times for suitability by the Third Department of the KGB's Office of Technical Operations.

In 1975, photographs of the letter were sent to "three of the most active conspiracy buffs, together with a covering letter from an anonymous well-wisher who claimed he had given the original to the Director of the FBI, Clarence Kelly . . . " No one acted on the provocation for about two years. Then, Penn Jones, retired owner of a small Texas newspaper and self-published author of four books on the assassination, began writing articles about the letter. The fable soon acquired a life of its own, and the forged letter from Oswald to Hunt is now a widely accepted piece of evidence among the establishment's assassination theorists.

Movies

Soon after Hollywood CA became the center of film production, communists began to infiltrate the movie industry. By about the time of WWII, they had achieved almost complete control of the "creative" side of film making, and few movies were produced that did not have some sort of left-wing propaganda embedded in them. Perhaps musicals were less affected than most other films because the crude Bolshevik message was rather difficult to adapt to a melodic line. Also, musicians of that era seemed to be, for some reason, less interested in the politics of rage than the less ethereal dramatists — a difference that no longer exists.

Bits and pieces of propaganda could be found in most film productions, and even more importantly, rabid communists received very large sums of money from the movies they made, and some of these funds went into the support of extreme left-wing organizations, causes, artists, activists, and spies.

There is a seamless connection between television programming and movies. Obviously, there are no significant barriers to presenting in one of these outlets what is available to consumers in the other — and the Reds control both. In the last decade or so, the Internet has become a third important outlet for red propaganda but it is still not subject to the complete control by Soviet sympathizers that is so evident in other recorded media.

Print Media

The indefatigable Communists used print media from the start as important methods of propagandizing and proselytizing. All of the early anarchists, communists, Bolshevists, and even nihilists depended heavily on pamphlets, posters, circulars, booklets, and the like to get their messages into the hands and heads of potential recruits. These paper products were, in fact, one of the most effective tools in attracting converts to the cause — the other being the numerous small "clubs" that were organized by left-wing enthusiasts. Now, we have the Internet, which enormously increases the potential audience of every budding Bakunin.

Books — Books can be considered an important part of the print media complex available for use in disseminating Red propaganda, along with newspapers and magazines. For many decades, both fictional and "scholarly" books have been powerful tools in the hands of red propagandists. The principal book publishing firms, or at least the employees of those firms who are responsible for choosing which books to publish and the amount of money and pressure to be used in promoting them, are composed almost entirely of persons with a strong liberal/anti-American orientation, that is: "reds." It is also of considerable interest that most of them are Jews and a high percentage of them are headquartered in or near New York City.

The red establishment's keen perception of the need to keep intact the relatively permanent archives of their version of history is evident in the de facto censorship and blacklisting of all manuscripts that present a truthful view of certain critical events. The initial filtering step is the layer of agents which has been interposed between the publishers and authors. It is this author's opinion that persons operating this screening process are approximately 90% red and roughly 95% Jewish. A Christian patriot hoping to get his manuscript published by a top NYC firm has approximately the same chance as the proverbial snowball in hell.

Direct Actions of Soviet Agents

Bittman (1985) described Russian methods for placing agents of influence in positions of power in US media companies: "According to Soviet intelligence doctrine, an influence agent is an individual who occupies an important position in the governmental, economic, journalistic, scientific, or social hierarchy of the target country and in one way or another, is capable of influencing the decision-making process or public opinion. Candidates for this demanding role *are not necessarily in total agreement with Soviet political perceptions.* For example, foreign students attending East European universities are potential agents of influence recruited during their stay in Moscow or East Berlin on the basis of their anticipated careers upon returning home. This long-term approach pays handsome dividends in Third World countries where a university education is an extraordinary asset." College graduates can be expected to advance relatively rapidly in the government, and in educational circles, perhaps even in business and technology, greatly increasing their value to their spymasters.

They Call It "News"

The tendency of some well-known writers in the print news business to fake all or part of their stories in order to attract more readers, or perhaps to give their stories a strong leftward bias, is too well known to require proof at this point. The only thing that continues to amaze some readers is the sheer effrontery of these lying cheats, as shown by the crudity of their lies and their willingness to present them to persons who are certain to know they cannot be true.

Although dishonest reporters predated even Josef Stalin, not to mention Karl Marx, their personalities have always been red all the way through. They have always been spiritual brothers to Bakunin, Lenin, Stalin, Trotsky, and the like. Even after the Communist Manifesto appeared, left-wing reporters who might never have had any interest in joining a socialist group or bombing the local police station, hated the US and most other countries except Russia, and they despised ordinary citizens. In fact, they hated most people, and considered them to be dullards and unsophisticated clods — not at all like journalists.

A few examples of the apparent inability of newspaper writers to understand the moral value of truth will be given in the following text.

The New York Times is usually held up by the liberal newsmedia as a highly reputable, very truthful paper. It is neither. It biases its reports and selects the news it prints on the basis of how closely the text fits its far left bias. Evans (2000) described an error-filled report the Times printed on May 24, 2000. The story said that Oscar Shaftel, a professor at Queens College in the 1950s, lost his job because he refused to answer some questions posed by the investigations subcommittee of the Internal Security Committee headed by Senator Joseph McCarthy. Evans points out that McCarthy had nothing to do with the recently expired professor, with the committee that questioned him, or with "his ensuing hardships." Although the Times said Shaftel was relieved of his position without good cause, he had in fact been identified under oath as a Communist operative. Evans and some friends tried to get the Times to publish a retraction, but only a partial and very inadequate correction appeared, and that not until three months after the erroneous story had been published.

Facts too obscene to publish — In the heat of the 2000 presidential primaries, Marvin Olasky wrote a column for the Austin American-Statesman which, by viewing the Bush candidacy with mild approval, caused turbulence in the mainstream media's copious flow of pro-McCain propaganda. What was even more stirring, was his criticism of three so-called journalists who are Jews, i.e., William Kristol, David Brooks, and Frank Rich. As a justification for even sterner corrective measures, his tormenters discovered that Olasky is himself a "former" Jew who converted to Christianity from Judaism (by way of Marxism!). This was, of course, considered an exacerbation of his heinous crime.

The coordinated attack on Olasky included, for examples, bitter comments in *The Washington Post*, *The New York Post*, and *The Jerusalem Post* ostensibly based on his allusion to Judaism as the religion of Zeus. According to the excerpt of the article provided by him (Olasky 2000), this interpretation is a far stretch. As a side comment, it seems to the present writer that modern Jews do themselves too great an honor if they imagine their religion is that of Zeus. But the mere accusation, based on a suspicion arising out of a misinterpretation, provided enough of an excuse for the Judaists and their shabbes goyim to join the attack on Olasky.

The rapidity with which the establishment media put their coordinated smear attack into effect is absolutely astonishing, even to this cynical writer, and suggests the many participants were taking their cues from a playscript provided by some central director via e-mail. Olasky asked Eli Lake of *Forward*, " . . . why this became a story in the first place but [he] told me his editor had assigned him the task and he had to do it."

Our Crowd

The people who rose to the top in the various branches of the news and entertainment media varied greatly in some respects, but the group as a whole exhibited several characteristics which were present in percentages much higher than in the general population. A composite example would be a male with far-left sympathies, who was active in "compassionate" causes and was an atheist or Jew. He would probbly be a sexual pervert (homosexual or bisexual), a first or second generation American, and a psychopath.

Networking — Persons in the red networks helped each other in getting their art and media products financed and promoted. In an online commentary by film director Michael Moore, we find the following. "I will never forget the day when, over lunch, I asked one of the Warner Bros. executives why they wanted to distribute my film. This person leaned over and said, *I was one of the early students in the S.D.S.* [he was referring to Students for a Democratic Society, one of the leading student radical/anti-war groups of the 1960s]. My jaw must have dropped. I didn't know what to say, it seemed so surreal at the moment. But over time I've had similar things like this happen. Here and there in the media world there are those who haven't checked their consciences at the studio gate, baby boomers from the '60s who may have cut their hair and put on a suit but didn't sell their soul to the devil. They do their little subversive actions because they never lost their values or forgot what we all went through."

We also find some interesting facts about the general disposition, including sexual traits, of one of the better known Hollywood figures in a review by Teachout (2000) of a book allegedy authored by A. Laurents (1999). Laurents was, or is, a Hollywood writer who participated in productions such as *West Side Story* and *Gypsy*. The reviewer says Laurents is bisexual, but mostly prefers men, and is very promiscuous. "Virtually everybody he meets is rated in terms of his or her imagined sexual potential." His politics were "hot pink." And, "if you disagree with him about anything, you're a bigot . . . Like so many liberals of his generation, he finds it inconceivable that anyone of intelligence or common decency would voluntarily vote Republican, dismissing such Hollywood 'right-wingers' as Ronald Reagan, Barbara Stanwyck, and John Wayne as 'stars born on the wrong side of the tracks who thought playing footsie with conservatives would allow them to cross over.' "

Laurents once told Teachout, "I believed it wasn't un-American to be a member of the Communist Party, it was un-American to be on the House Un-American Committee." Of course, Laurents was a strong supporter of the Hollywood Ten, that clique of movie industry communists who were exposed by a Congressional committee and other investigators.

The Hollywood Ten — The individuals who came to be known as "The Hollywood Ten," were men who had risen to important positions in the movie making industry. They worked mostly on the so-called creative side and had been identified as CP-USA members or communist sympathizers by government investigators.

These men were subpoenaed by a Congressional committee and questioned about their alleged traitorous activities. Several refused to answer any questions, and after a series of court cases, some of them served jail time. Two or three persons cooperated to a certain extent with the Congressional committee, and as a result they were stigmatized and essentially blacklisted by their comrades in the industry, with the result that they could not find jobs, or at least no work at the level they had occupied when they were "good" communists.

The refuseniks generally prospered. If they could not get work in the movie industry, they wrote books, articles, etc., describing their wonderful courage and their liberal attitude in refusing to rat on their fellow criminals. One or two of them changed their names and continued to work on movies. The Hollywood in-group would have undoubtedly put them all back to work immediately on the best possible assignments, if they had dared to do so, but they were apparently afraid this would have an adverse effect on the consuming public, to the extent that potential customers might boycott movies on which the Reds had worked. Also, the Red disease was so prevalent, that many of the comrades who hadn't been forced out of the closet were probably afraid to call attention to themselves by giving work to any of the Ten.

The heroization, almost deification, that was given by the media to those communists who refused to cooperate with government investigators was proof enough that the accused men were indeed members of the inner circle of Bolshevik infiltrators of the movie industry and were thought to be entitled not only to protection but to rewards by all types of media managers.

The extreme left never made much of a pretense that the Ten were not Communists. Here is what Larry Ceplar said (from Ryskind 2002): "Ceplar admits the Hollywood Communists tried to politicize the films, conceded the 'absolute control Moscow maintained' over Communist parties both here and abroad, agrees that Hollywood Reds became allied with *Nazi* Germany [while the German-Soviet pact was in effect] and confirms that, *under Stalin's instructions*, American Communists turned against the US with a vengeance after the war." [emphasis added]

At times, an egomaniac in the upper levels of movie and television production will lose control and announce their true feelings about their host country to the news media. But, the damage control squads will immediately go into action, plugging their message, "Never mind folks, it is just a humorous example of artistic temperament" . . . or an overdose of cocaine. Pressure is put on the news media to discontinue all coverage of the incident.

The far left film director Robert Altman, has been quoted as saying, "When I see the American flag flying, it is a joke." He is thinking of moving out of the country, because (among other reasons), "There is nothing here he would miss at all." And, "This present government in America I find just disgusting" (from Colvin 2002). Altman had already threatened to move to France if G.W. Bush was elected president, but he still seems to be receiving mail at a US address. Maybe he is waiting for final election results from Florida. We're disappointed.

Messages from Hollywood

The propaganda delivered in the form of movies produced by Reds involved not only direct glorification of Russia and Communism and admitted Bolshevists, but of fellow travelers as well. That was the positive thrust. The negative messages included those ridiculing and even demonizing straight society, most businessmen, patriotism, family values, and the like. Violence was condoned, and swindles, gambling, and other kinds of theft were often given a humorous twist, but blackmail and snitching on the mob were always regarded as being on the outer limits of evil behavior.

Square society, especially the Christian religion and aspects of conventional married life, was often satirized or even harshly ridiculed, while the decadent lifestyles of singers, musicians, actors, and gangsters were romanticized. Homosexuality, though not often shown in direct terms, was presented as a humorous, harmless eccentricity. Young girls were more or less indirectly suggested as sex objects. Excessive alcohol consumption was harmless, even funny — several character actors made a good living by portraying advanced alcoholism in a humorous light.

Patriotism was, of course, an emotion to be destroyed at all costs, except when it served the specialized needs of the machers. The armed forces were glamorized when it was considered necessary to increase their numbers and generate enthusiasm for an all-out assault on enemies of the Soviet Empire, as in World War II. But, heroism and faithful duty were presented in an extremely negative light during other conflicts such as the Vietnam and Korean wars. In fact, peace at any price seems to have been their motto, so far as the US was concerned. The executives who make crucial decisions at the studios, however, seem to lose their devotion to pacifism when conflicts between Zionists and Palestinian Arabs are being discussed.

Webb (2002) " . . . mainstream America is too often the whipping post in modern films, constituting the 'evil' in the traditional Hollywood formula, against which the struggles of 'good' — all manner of politically correct agendas — are measured."

Testing the limits — Of course, the financial aspects of films are always kept in mind, so the Hollywood moguls make efforts to avoid direct confrontation of the movie-going masses, a large percentage of whom would be offended by insults directed at their way of life, provided they understood what was being done. Segmentation of the market is one of the ways to maintain share while pressing the boundaries of perversity.

The limits of customer acceptance, in terms of the extremes of sexuality and violence which the targeted audience will tolerate, are constantly being tested. In recent years, maniacal killers have been presented in a favorable light in movies intended for general audiences. Various types of internet and mall games allow the user to participate vicariously in homicide for sport. And, sexual displays have become remarkable for their crudity, flagrancy, and perversity.

Encouraging Crime and Violence

Persons who have a liking for violent confrontations and other antisocial activities certainly will find their desires fulfilled in products of the US entertainment industry. Sadistic, antisocial violence and perverted sexual practices are very much à la mode in the movie industry and theatrical circles.

Foreign terrorists are said to cater to Western journalists because they know they will be glorified and treated as though they were heroes. This insight was provided by Kellen (1990), who wrote "In that sense the United States is the terrorists' greatest booster, not only because it gives them so much media attention, but even more so because US leaders make thunderous declarations to the effect that they will destroy the terrorist root and branch, thereby paying them high tribute."

As might be expected, spending a lot of time viewing or listening to glorifications of violence leads susceptible customers to attempt to put some of these concepts into practice. It is to be expected that persons who repeatedly view scenes of death and destruction on their television sets or in movie theatres may begin to imagine that such activities are normal and to be expected, well within the range of acceptable behavior, and a lot of fun to boot. Personality changes of this type have been scientifically confirmed as shown in studies discussed below.

A team of psychiatrists and other medical doctors investigated the effect of television viewing on the aggressive behavior of adolescents and adults (Johnson et al. 2002). The 707 subjects were evaluated over a 17-year period. Investigators found there was a significant association between the amount of time spent watching television during adolescence and early adulthood and the likelihood of subsequent aggressive acts. The connection remained statistically significant even after the factors of previous aggressive behavior, childhood neglect, family income, neighborhood violence, parental education, and psychiatric disorders were taken into account.

Anderson and Bushman (2002) pointed out, in their comments on the Johnson et al. study, that by 1972 sufficient empirical evidence had accumulated for the US Surgeon General to comment, " . . . televised violence, indeed, does have an adverse effect on certain members of our society." The popular press, however, seems intent upon downplaying this connection. "We recently demonstrated that even as the scientific evidence linking media violence to aggression has accumulated, news reports about the effects of media violence have shifted to weaker statements, implying that there is little evidence for such effects. This inaccurate reporting in the popular press may account for continuing controversy long after the debate should have been over, much as the cigarette smoking/cancer controversy persisted long after the scientific community knew that smoking causes cancer."

As further evidence of the connection, Anderson and Bushman describe the following study. "Results of a meta-analysis of *all available studies* investigating the hypothesis that exposure to media violence increases aggression . . . [indicates a] positive link between media violence and aggression regardless of research method is clearly shown ... " Furthermore, "Experimental studies demonstrate a causal link." The authors point out that the effect is long-lasting and damages adults as well as children.

Rock and Rap Music

The messages dinned into the ears of adolescents and youths by rock bands and musicians of certain other types surely must affect adversely the values and emotions of listeners. Lyrics of these "songs," insofar as they are understandable, tend to encourage violence, sexual abuse of women, destruction for its own sake, and a generally nihilistic attitude toward police, the military, and government in general. It would be a reasonable assumption that the entire rap and rock segments of the entertainment industry are intertwined in some manner not only with Reds of the deepest dye, but also with criminals who distribute narcotics.

Bozell (1999) wrote, "Rage [Against the Machine] hit the scene in 1992, and since then, has sold more than 5 million records in the US alone. It has always carried a left-wing political message, and today remains far, far left of center, as its new release, 'The Battle of Los Angeles' — which debuted in the top spot on the Billboard chart — indicates." Bozell gives several examples of the Rage's excesses which are too extensive to reproduce here.

"Elsewhere, a nasty anti-police rant surfaces in 'Mic Check' (Who got the power/Tha pig who's free to murder one Shucklack (sic)/Or survivors who make a movie and murder one back?" They praise the convicted and condemned Philadelphia cop-killer Mia Abu-Jamal as well as Leonard Peltier, killer of an FBI agent.

Bozell continues, " ... it seems that Rage would be even more militant if they thought it would be effective." It seems the band members freely use the Marxist cant of governmental and quasi-governmental elites and cabal in conversation. " ... In fact, Rage's real heavy-duty politicking comes when the music's over. Included in the 'Battle' album package are the names and web addresses of more than a dozen organizations, most of them on the leftist fringe. Fairness and Accuracy in Reporting (FAIR) for example, is so radical that it sees a rightwing bias in the news media, and Refuse and Resist! was founded in 1987 to combat the issue agenda of Ronald Reagan, which, it declared, 'had a distinctly fascist aura and raised the specter of a police state. Refuse and Resist! is "proudly pro-abortion'... [it has a goal of changing] the climate from one where abortion providers are vilified and attacked to one where they are honored and upheld as the heroes they are.' " This demonstrates beyond a reasonable doubt that whoever controls the Rage has a deeply embedded hatred of the human race.

Criticisms Are Not Welcome

W. A. Rusher (1988), who was publisher of *National Review* at the time, wrote a book, "The Coming Battle for the Media: Crushing the Power of the Media Elite," in which he suggested (among many other improvements) a greater degree of legal liability for publishers and writers who issue defamatory and false reports.

Rusher's book was reviewed by Tim W. Ferguson, editorial features editor of the Wall Street Journal, who evidently poses as a Libertarian. Ferguson (1988) damned Rusher's book with faint praise, but he did make a significant comment on press bias: "No serious, disinterested observer ought to dispute that most in the media today hold political views best described as reformist-liberal. Libertarians suffer from this bias as much as anyone, but they do not answer with briefs for state remedies."

In the first place, the very fact that Ferguson has the gall to describe the media slant as reformist-liberal, rather than leftist-Bolshevist, is enough to cast doubt on the rest of his observations. He appeals to freedom of the press, and in his lexicon, "press" evidently includes all news media, but he seems to be unable to explain how there can be meaningful freedom of the press or even freedom of speech when the distribution of news is under the rigid control of a clique of extreme left wing managers/censors.

The news media has become, in a sense, a government in itself, a monopolistic controller which is inimical to the intent of the signers of the Declaration of Independence, and indeed to the best interests of the US. It seeks to restrict access of the people to facts respecting their government and the Constitution (which, contrary to some opinions) contains more than the Bill of Rights. Mr. Ferguson thinks that the reason that more "individualist thinkers" have not been hired by media moguls is their lack of "technical competence!"

Ferguson also says, "In this country, the most outrageous cases of one-sided news judgment and arrogance occur in broadcasting, especially at the Big Three networks." He blames, principally, "soulless corporate advertisers." Most corporate advertisers, soulless or not, have no interest in promoting Red and Zionist agendas, which are the dominating influence in print, broadcast, and virtually every other kind of media, except (perhaps) the Internet.

Other examples — In the book, *Moscow's Words, Western Voices*, Campbell (1994) discussed the careers of four Communist apologists who were active in English language print media for many years, and who managed to make a living, meet famous people, travel, get awards, and achieve a certain type of fame in spite of their constant, unwavering support of the Soviet Union on every detail, and despite [because of?] the vituperation they directed against the US on every possible occasion. These four men were:

Isidor Feinstein, later known as I.F. Stone. 12-24-1907 to 1989.

Wilfred Burchett, born in Australia. 9-16-1911 to 1983.

Walter Duranty, born in England. 1884-1957.

Alexander Cockburn, born in Scotland, grew up in Ireland.

It is important to note that each of the above "journalist-authors" was able to get his extremely anti-American articles published in the US and elsewhere over a period of many years. In some cases, these agents of influence won prestigious awards (e.g, the Pulitzer Prize), in spite of the unabashed Communist propaganda they produced. The point is not that some crazy, dishonest, or hate-filled journalists are willing to work for the Reds, it is that they can always find an outlet for their propaganda when better writers have difficulty in finding a market for their more objective reports. To this author, such evidence is simply another proof that American media is, at its base, anti-American in orientation. We can also conclude that it is anti-Christian.

Reasons for bias — Why are the "machers" in Hollywood so devoted to a left-wing agenda? Webb (2002) thinks he has part of the answer. "First and foremost, for all its international reach, Hollywood's management is largely inbred, and the very notion of voluntary military service is an anomaly to its members. For every person who is hired at a studio or major agency or production office there are probably ten with the talent and desire to work there. In a business that is intensely relationship driven, the tendency is to hire those with whom one is most comfortable,   both   philosophically   and   in   terms   of   background . . . Rather than externalizing the conflict, the struggle between good and evil in more recent war films has taken place *within* the American military, usually on issues of corruption or morality. This is   especially   true   with   respect   to   films   about   the   Vietnam War . . . Hollywood was the most virulent antiwar culture in our society during that war, and has been reluctant to show American soldiers fighting, and usually defeating, a determined enemy."

The antiwar stance is present in all types of media. Pauken (1995) describes the television career of John F. Kerry — onetime soldier, later an antiwar propagandist, now a Senator, always a red.   Kerry " . . . who would make regular appearances on the 'Tonight' show, all decked out in his military fatigues, where he would proceed to denounce the American effort to defeat Communism in South Vietnam. He also made   numerous   appearances   in   Washington,   becoming   a regular . . . on the Georgetown cocktail party circuit . . . Kerry was purely and simply an opportunist, parlaying his involvement in the antiwar movement into a budding political career." Kerry later married the widow of Senator John Heinz, a lady from Mozambique who had inherited a very large estate when Heinz was killed in an "accident."

No heroes in the media — Despite all their posing as "fearless," "unbiased," etc., US media managers are extremely weak in resisting demands that certain politically incorrect views be eliminated from the airwaves. A recent example was the campaign by the Gay and Lesbian Alliance Against Defamation (GLAD) to get Dr. Laura Schlesinger's radio show downgraded so far as its time slot, frequency, etc., were concerned. GLAD's first approach was to demand that Schlesinger's show be dropped altogether. The fruit fanciers objected because the doctor had announced her opinion that homosexuality was bad (Ryan 2000). The ACLU, which is also against prayer in schools, joined the lynch mob without delay, as was easily predictable.

Books exposing cultural and political bias — Over the past two or three decades, many articles and several books dealing with media bias have appeared in the US. Most of the books have been issued by small or boutique publishing houses. In spite of the limited number of reviews in the popular press which such publishers can obtain, a few of the books have sold at a fairly good rate. Evidently there is an usatisfied market for the truth. A few of these publications (articles and books) will be briefly excerpted here.

"A Roper-Freedom Forum study of 136 Washington reporters and bureau chiefs ... found that their 1992 votes went 89% for Bill Clinton and 7% for George Bush. Other studies have shown that the elite journalists are especially 'liberal' on lifestyle issues such as abortion, sex and drugs. The reason for this is simple and powerful: self-selection. These are the people who want to go into journalism, as opposed to business, engineering, medicine or whatever" (Bartley 2000).

The Media Elite, by Lichter, et al. (1986) is an establishment-oriented study of media bias and other pressures which influence published news and analysis. Although a bit out of date in terms of the exact figures, the study is still useful as evidence of the long-standing tendencies toward leftist sympathies. A few of Lichter's data are shown below.

•54% of the panelists are left-of-center, 17% claim to be rightists, 29% centrists.

•56% say their colleagues are mostly leftists, only 8% are rightists.

•In the 1972 election, 80% voted for McGovern (whose popular vote was less than 40%)

•Over a 16-year period, less than 20% of the media supported *any* Republican presidential candidate.

•"Are environmental problems exaggerated?" 1% strongly agree, 54% strongly disagree.

Edith Efron (1972) analyzed media coverage of the 1968 presidential election for possible distortions, bias, and conflicts of interest. The results were quite conclusive, and not surprising to those of us who have recognized for decades the far-left orientation of the executives who hire the staffs for TV and radio networks. Commentators, producers, and top executives hardly bothered to conceal their indifference to truth and objectivity. Walter Cronkite, regarded then as now an elder statesman of the news reporting racket, ends a paragraph or two of turgid self examination with the conclusion, "Objectivity is when one tries to be objective." As Ms. Efron comments, "It is rather circular as definitions go." Fred Friendly, at one time President of CBS news, opines "I think fairness is something you know in your gut you're doing." Bill Moyers, sometime publisher and a commentator during the campaign period, said, "Of all the myths of journalism, objectivity is the greatest." David Brinkley, another liberal icon from the news media, was content to say, "Objectivity is impossible to a normal human being."

Efron's book is filled with documentation showing that, whether or not objectivity is possible, it was never exercised at the major networks during coverage of the 1968 campaign.

A recent book, *Bias*, by Bernard Goldberg (2001), was described by a reviewer (Smith 2001) as "an exposé of the hypocrisy, elitism, and tendentiousness that define the major television networks, as well as the institutions such as the New York Times and Washington Post." One of the quotes in Smith's review perhaps sums it all up. "Andrew Heyward, the president of CBS News . . . said . . . 'Look, Bernie, of course there's a liberal bias in the news. All the networks tilt left . . . if you repeat any of this, I'll deny it.' "

Goldberg describes a clear trend in nomenclature. "On the network news, Robert Bork is the 'conservative ' judge: Laurence Tribe, merely a Harvard professor. Mr. Goldberg notes that the major networks, in a fit of political correctness, reported during the 1980s that AIDS was a menace to everyone — even heterosexuals who engaged in no-risk sex — despite facts that proved otherwise."

section three
GREEN TERRORISM

Although it is generally admitted that Marx had nothing specific to say about the beneficial effects of Communism on topics that currently concern environmentalists, left-wingers continue to assault credulous readers with declamations about the opportunities we missed by not following Karl's advice on how to make a greener world. These unreconstructed Marxists resemble nothing so much as the eager terrier described by P. G. Wodehouse, which repeatedly laid a dead rat at his master's feet, in spite of every indication by word and deed that such a gift was not appreciated. So is the decaying carcass of Marxism flung into our living rooms and classrooms in current sociopolitical discussions.

The Reds became discouraged: People were such fools — they just didn't want to listen to the socialist message. A new product seemed to be necessary, or at least a new disguise for the old product. Bring in the marketing group — will a new logo be sufficient, or do we have to redesign the entire package?

What could they advocate that would attract donors and activists? How about protecting animals? Even better, how about taking up the cudgels for the earth — Gaea? Surely, one is a better person if he is the pal of something as big as that. And, it isn't going to vanish suddenly, as did Marxism, leaving you standing alone with a foolish grin on your face and a "Death to Capitalism" placard in your hand. So it was: persons who had been effulgent Reds became reds with a greenish tint.

Of course, eco-centric causes pre-dated Marx. One doesn't have to have a socialist outlook to be an environmentalist wacko. In fact, an unmistakable capitalistic motif appears when some of these movements are closely examined. Activists opposing nuclear energy seem to have received considerable encouragement, financial and otherwise, from oil-producing interests, while the anti-globalism rioters receive support from both unions and capitalist sources who have an interest in decreasing imports. Such ethical conflicts are of small consequence — it is the outward appearance and the expressed goals of the cause that attract the congenital trouble-makers who are indispensable ingredients in every successful demonstration and destructive outbreak.

chapter eight

OVER ALL IS THE LAND

Though every prospect pleases,
and only man is vile . . .
> R. Heber (1783-1826) *Missionary Hymn*

In this Second American Revolution, we are
fighting for the rights of the land itself.
> Paul Brooks

After one reaches the conclusion that man is vile and the enemy of, and a parasite upon, all other organisms, only a small step is needed to reach the ultimate "truth" — that man is inferior not only to every member ot the animal kingdom, but to all inanimate things as well. This is the basic but sometimes unacknowledged tenet from which springs the wilderness worshippers' personification and deification of "The Land," a globe that existed before any living thing developed or was created, where the only sounds were the trickling brooks, the distant thunder, and the whispering winds, where the only visual disturbances were the auroras, the lightning, and the rainbow.

Or, perhaps the true finality, the goal which remains unrevealed, is the Chaos that existed before Gaea. Granted, this is an endpoint in mystical thinking which even the most ardent nihilist or naturist might find difficult to acknowledge or accept, even in their secret ponderings. But, many of them are warily circling the edges of this thought, like jackals around a jungle encampment.

Earth-worshipping Cults

The deification of the earth (or of nature as a whole) is an old religion; it may be the oldest. Some historians have called it the first form of monotheism. In Greek mythology, the earth (Gaea or Gaia) was a goddess. Hesiod, the Greek philosopher who lived about the eighth century BC, said that she was the eldest offspring of Chaos, and the mother of Uranus and the Titans. Gaea became the focus of many cults. The famous Delphic oracles claimed to get the straight dope from Gaea, allegedly by breathing fumes emitted from a deep crevasse in a cave that was located under the Delphic temple.

Some reds find worship of "the land" provides a comfortable spiritual home because it is compatible with the deep and abiding hatred of all mankind which is at the core of their destructive and nihilistic mindset. They firmly believe that, if *Homo sapiens* could be eliminated, all would be well with with the nation, the earth, and the universe. This is the end point toward which the tree huggers and the bug saviors instinctively move. To make the discussion more convenient for the reader, the author will apply the name of "landgod" to the "object of their affection."

Although their beliefs are ill-formed and mushy at best, it appears that some of the tenets of those who worship "the land" differ only quantitatively and not in their essential tenets, from most of the principles expressed by animal righters, greenies, biodiversity fanatics, global warming hysterics, and econuts in general. The characterizing difference is that landgod worshippers endorse the extreme position that the ideal world is an earth in which no men and no works of man appear. They may not acknowledge in so many words that such an endpoint is their goal, and they may control their own lives (and finances) in manners quite contrary to their expressed beliefs, but their public statements clearly point to that goal.

It is this fundamental difference in their philosophies that dictates the author's treatment of land worshippers in a separate chapter instead of combining it with the chapter on ecological fanatics.

The Source of All the Trouble

Obviously, to get the purest kind of wilderness, we have to eliminate the presence of people. And, of course, the whole earth should be (ideally) a wilderness, because that is the highest state of nature. Where does that leave you and me? Nowhere — in the literal sense.

This is not a rational goal, you might say. Our subsequent discussion will show, however, that some of the landgod worshippers — the true believers — are not completely irrational. In their literature they often limit their goals to some hypothetical end point that is at least conceivable, even if it isn't practical under any normal set of conditions. Many of them, however, haven't a clue, no real conception, no visualization, of how the climax of their scenario would affect them personally.

Their dislike of animals in general and of people in particular is the reason that land worshippers seek out the wide open spaces; why the wastelands of the subarctic or the deserts of the tropics are so attractive to them; why seascapes stretching to the empty horizon so often appear in their books and articles as things to admire. That is why, in their tracts, TV spots, PBS specials, and other promotional efforts, you will often see photos of their camps, with tents perched on the edge of nowhere, with no person in view, and for that matter, very few animals in sight. This is how the whole earth should be, they think — and in unguarded moments they sometimes say it.

Big Bucks in the Wilderness

Saving the earth is big business. The customers — it would be more accurate to say "suckers" because they get nothing for their money — who are ultimately stuck with the bill for all of the public demonstrations, literature, traveling expenses, and salaries, are the taxpayers. Also damaged are the putative heirs of senile magnates who find, when the old fool finally dies, that their expected windfall has vanished into the coffers of The Sierra Club or one of its numerous imitators.

A fairly large number of nature lovers seem to make a very good living from the earth — Paul Brooks and Rachel Carson are prime examples of this phenomenon. Such persons may get a position on the faculty of some university or college and stick to it as though Superglued until they die (just like most other academics) or they start a non-profit organization having the avowed goal of preserving the universe, or some part of it. Still others, like Mr. Brooks, will find that publishing is a facet of capitalism with which they can manage to coexist. In instances of really bad luck for the taxpayers, people of this ilk may get themselves elected to important political positions. But, in whatever way they make their money, they manage to prove that hypertrophy of sensitivity is not necessarily accompanied by atrophy of acquisitiveness.

The most successful earth-saving foundations have honed their marketing skills to a fine point. They collect money from naive folks who believe that the outdoorsman wearing neatly pressed and cleaned garments and unscuffed shoes from the most exclusive outfitter, who is shown in their literature in a picture taken just after he completed a two-week tour to the Amazonian jungles (with his spouse, if any, nowhere around) is *so* cute, *so* compassionate, *so* intelligent. Or, perhaps we will be granted a view of the sensitive person in his university office, in front of his computer, stroking his little doggy — *so* kind to animals and *so* scientific.

Anyone who believes such persons will apply more than a token percentage of the money they collect to "saving" the environment/earth/planet/universe needs to cast a more critical eye on the available evidence. Any donor who believes these dilettantes will spend the funds he gives them wisely and carefully by alleviating the sad condition of a lost butterfly, a starving hummingbird, or a lonely walrus, or even of a grizzly bear suffering from a shortage of tasty hikers, is rather more gullible than the average taxpayer. If everything goes well, perhaps as much as 10% of the credulous donors' money will be spent on the needs of the intended beneficiaries, and you can be sure it will be spent in a manner calculated to gain as much favorable publicity as possible for the person or organization doing the spending.

Not all of the funds collected by wilderness societies come from disoriented do-gooders. Careful research will often show that some foundations, far from being established and led by fanatics, obtain most of their financing and nearly all of their mission statements from entrepreneurs (or their surrogates) who plan to make a great deal of money from selling solar panels, wind-powered generators, fluoride dispensers, smoke scrubbing technologies, newly patented insecticides or artificial sweeteners, auto air bags and seat belts, proprietary vaccines, etc. And, in some cases, we find organizations supported by people who have *very* practical reasons for wanting to keep the supply of oil (and of energy in general) in short supply, so they vigorously fight all attempts to drill new oil wells, huild new pipelines, construct new dams with hydroelectric generators, or establish nuclear power plants. And the opening of new residential tracts in the wilderness (or anywhere else) will be vigorously fought by big city politicians who want to keep the population densities in their bailiwicks at high levels, and who are willing to do this by making commuting more difficult and expensive. They think they can accomplish this goal by vetoing the construction of outlying airports and suburban living areas and by keeping gasoline prices high, and they are probably correct.

Listening to the Babbling Brooks

One of the most prominent gurus of the save-the-planet wackos was Paul Brooks, who graduated from Harvard in 1931, then spent most of the subsequent 44 years attached to Houghton-Mifflin (the Boston book publishers) in one post or another. He was a director of The Sierra Club for seven years starting in 1966, and he was appointed a vice president of this organization in 1968.

Boston being a noted area of unspoiled natural beauty, Brooks was able to absorb the aesthetic principles of naturism during his educational and professional tenures while residing in one of its suburbs. He was extremely active in the landgod business most of his life, and was regarded as an authority on the subject by many people. We will be devoting a great deal of space to the analysis of Brooks' views, because they can be regarded as representative of those of a large part of the wilderness-preservation movement. He died in December of 1998.

Although Brooks was responsible for getting Rachel Carson's books published, and even wrote a book describing Carson's work, he apparently did not share that lady's fervent love of fish and other wildlife. In this respect, as well as in other ways, he is a much better representative of the landgod view than Carson was.

In addition to other print publications, he was able to get at least four books published. These are:

Roadless Area, 1964

The Pursuit of Wilderness, 1971

The House of Life, 1972. Re-issued as *Rachel Carson: The Writer at Work*,

The View from Lincoln Hill, 1976

Other positions and awards which Paul Brooks acquired included:

Member, Board of directors, Public Lands Institute

Chief of book section, ETO, Office of War Information, 1945

Director of the Massachusetts Aububon Society, 1943-1947

Vice President of the Sierra Club in 1968; director 1966-73

Edited two Rachel Carson books: *The Edge of the Sea* and *Silent Spring*.

In the Rachel Carson Council News, Spring 1999, No. 91. we find the following: "To those who had the privilege of meeting Paul Brooks, he was as unforgettable an individual as is the bird that to many symbolizes the place he loved and about which he wrote, 'The purest voice of the north country, the wild unearthly cry of the loon ... pulsating through the darkness like northern lights through a night sky.' " To many other people, as well, Mr. Brooks seemed very like a loon.

Brooks' basic philosophical bent may be expressed by the following statement taken from page xii of *The Pursuit of Wilderness*. "Central to the modern conservation movement is the principle that a citizen has a legitimate interest in the environment as a whole, not merely in the piece of real estate to which he happens to hold title. This is indeed a revolutionary doctrine, if one interprets the so-called 'free enterprise system' to mean freedom to exploit one's property at whatever cost to others. But actually it represents a return to an earlier ideal; an ideal underscored by the significant change in the original wording of the Declaration of Independence, from 'Life, Liberty, and Property' to 'Life, Liberty, and the Pursuit of Happiness.' [He relies upon the Declaration of Independence rather than the Constitution, and he does not understand that the change was intended to incorporate "property"in the wider definition of "pursuit of happiness"] Young Americans in particular reject the assumption that the gross national product is the measure of the good life — as if exploitation of nature were synonymous with success. Everywhere there is springing up a new 'land ethic,' a respect for the land itself, independent of any monetary use to which it may be put. This attitude finds its purest expression in the value we attach to our remaining unspoiled wilderness."

If Brooks is trying to say that property rights are not protected under the US Constitution, he will not be able to quote any respected legal authority to support his view. If he is using Karl Marx as his authority, then — we would not be surprised.

On page 3, Brooks names some of the books that have influenced his thinking: "It may be a book like *Deserts on the March* by Paul Sears, *Sand County Almanac* by Aldo Leopold, *Road to Survival* by William Vogt, or *Silent Spring* by Rachel Carson, where eloquent words, backed by irrefutable scientific fact, have been used to shock us into realization of what we are doing to our environment." The problem with this statement is there are no irrefutable scientific arguments in these books. They are polemical works, perhaps of some literary value, but, where any data appears (rather than tedious and repetitious paeans to the landgod), it is usually from a questionable source, not representative, not available to other researchers, or capable of various interpretations. Brooks was not a scientist, and I do not believe he understood, or wanted to understand, science as a process for solving problems. My opinion is, he thought science was irrelevant to his views, which are more spiritual than technical in nature.

On page 4, we find the following revealing passage. "It [the conservation movement] suffers . . . from a severe handicap: scarcely one of its key words has been defined with precision. Some of them have mutually exclusive connotations, depending on the background of the person being addressed. In short, there is no accepted vocabulary to express a set of values which need to be presented precisely and persuasively." Contrast this admission with Brooks' claim on page 3, quoted above. So, we are being presented with a philosophy, or creed, which has no firm foundation of definitions for the specialized words its believers use to support and defend their theories. This means that the claims of the conservationist movement are impossible to either prove or refute, because no one knows for certain what its missionaries are talking about. Many of us have suspected this from the start.

He goes into a bit more detail about the lack of precision in defining the words central to the wilderness program, and on page 5, after discussing the historical development of the meaning of "wilderness," he writes, "Presumably, a 'wilderness conference' in those days would have been a sort of witches' sabbath." And not just in those days, Paul. That is one of the traditions which is still preserved.

The Trappings of Civilization are Evil

The thought processes of Brooks are often obscure. He wrote, "A man in an automobile consumes space many times faster than a man on foot" (page 9). Well, no. He doesn't consume space at all, he traverses it. The space remains intact after he has moved over it. Look at it this way. A person on a bicycle can traverse a ten mile trail in perhaps half an hour, while a hiker would take perhaps four hours. The hiker is using the trail (i.e., contaminating the wilderness with his disgusting human presence) for eight times as long as the cyclist; that is, he occupies space that could be better used by (e.g.) wolves for eight times as long as the wheeled trespasser.

On page 13, we come to an important declaration: "We shall never understand the natural environment until we see it not as just so much air, water, or real estate, but as a living organism." A separate being, the landgod, now comes into view — there is no other way of interpreting Brooks' statement. He says the earth as a whole, "the natural environment," is a "living organism." The stones, the water, the snow, the vegetation, etc., constitute one living thing.

Also on page 13, we find that ownership of all land should be vested in *everyone* — which means, of course, that *no one* owns it. "Our present attitudes and laws governing the ownership and use of land represent an abuse of the concept of private property. Land is treated like a commodity when it is in fact a trust." He compares land ownership to slavery. This is pure communism. He nowhere offers a justification in law for this view, but, of course that is not necessary (in his view) because all land is part of the landgod, and you must surely know a god cannot be owned by anyone. How simple! Who needs definitions and logic to win an argument when you have a god on your side.

Of course, if the land is a living thing, as we have learned from the preceding discussion, people are doing terrible things to it every day. Murder is one of these things. Brooks says, " . . . in America today you can murder land for private profit, as is being done, for example, on a vast scale in the southern Appalachians." Now, he is referring to land developers as murderers.

On page 14, he goes into greater detail about these heinous crimes. "You can kill land by skinning it alive or by slowly poisoning it, and it is murder all the same. In the modern world, no one should have life and death power over his land any more than he does over another human being."

We are told on page 18, et seq., how the activists mean to go about stopping all this murdering and maiming of the landgod. We are told, "The birdwatchers, the photographers, the campers and the climbers are making themselves heard above the chain saws and the bull-dozers . . . They have become organized, sophisticated, articulate. The intangible values they stand for have caught the attention of the giant foundations which are concerned with the future pattern of the good society . . . Congressmen who want to be re-elected are forced to listen. Indeed, Congress itself officially recognized the existence of wilderness, when it passed the Wilderness Act in 1964, and . . . President Johnson went down the line for 'natural beauty.' "

LBJ is a poor example of environmentalist fervor. He was a noted deer slaughterer, preferring the simple and safe method of shooting baited animals from a tower after he had blinded them with a spotlight. In addition, he actually was a conspirator in a number of murders of his opponents, so he is a rather unsatisfactory reference for those interested in sensivity.

On a two-week camping trip, previously mentioned, Brooks went by horse and pack mule into the North Cascades (p. 25). "To the wilderness lover it was also jarring. Here was the beginning of a cross-mountain road, the first to be cut through this hitherto roadless area. There is something almost obscene in the power of modern technology to subdue the landscape ... Not till we had turned off the main trail, with its ominous surveyors' ribbons, and climbed up to a high mountain tarn did we sense that lifting of spirit that comes on entering the true wilderness." Where no sign of man can be found, that is where the landgod is most evident.

He becomes almost poetic as he describes how wonderful it is that there are some places where the works of man cannot be seen. For example, on page 29, he tells us: "The forest below showed a curious pattern of dark and light green vertical stripes; through the binoculars one could see that these were not the result of lumbering — for this is still virgin land — but of old snow and rockslides, the bright green being a carpet of new growth where the big trees had been sheared away." It's OK for the trees to be sheared away by rock slides, but not by lumbering crews who would turn them into useful timber. The hatred of mankind that is typical of the landgod worshipper has seldom been more clearly expressed.

Continuing with our review of *The Pursuit of Wilderness*, we find on page 30, " ... we passed a sign: North Cascade Primitive Area, Mechanized Equipment Prohibited. This was off bounds for scooters or 'tote goats,' those new destroyers of wilderness peace." Real goats would be much better, of course, though still not as good as wolves.

He dislikes the stance of the Forest Service in the Cascades development program (page 33), because this agency " ... spoke too often with the voice of the lumber industry. Only such areas were recommended for preservation as were good for nothing else; wilderness, in other words, was synonymous with wasteland." But isn't this exactly what he wants? No. "Those who used this argument ignored the fact that the trees in the high country are worth more as scenery [to whom?] than they are as lumber." How does one evaluate the trees' value as scenery? We have experts who can value them as lumber.

Brooks becomes sarcastic when writing about "multiple use." He writes, "There is no virtue in multiplicity unless the 'uses' are mutually compatible . . . Logging and scenery do not go together." Who is to say what is scenery and what is not. Logging is a way to get something that is worthwhile from a human perspective out of a wilderness, and the amount of its value can be measured. If necessary, controls can be instituted so that only as much timber is removed as will grow back before the next visit of the lumberer. Yes, this may mean that tourists will have to change their itineraries a bit to see "unspoiled" views. So what? They've come several hundred miles to see some mountains, what is ten miles more?

On page 35, we find, "Dams . . . may provide some types of recreation and may also destroy a wilderness. Wildlife (as contrasted with mere numbers of deer to be hunted) achieves its maximum variety and interest in those biotic associations which have been least altered by man." The book is full of these blanket statements, completely without foundation in data or references, which seem, in fact, to be irrational.

"Management for 'multiple use' tends to be management for maximum dollar return, which is to say, for salable timber — this in a nation that no longer has a shortage of timber [no thanks to him and his supporters], but will soon be facing a shortage of wilderness."

"Logging or mining an area like this is like ripping the corner off a classic Chinese painting" (page 36). No it isn't: productive use is not the same as unproductive damage. The artwork presumably couldn't be reproduced, the trees will replace themselves. The artwork is unique (in a way), the scenery is undoubtedly reproduced a hundred times with slight variations, all through the Cascades. Who says anyone has a Gaea-given right to see a specific site at any time he or she wishes, while a productive enterprise at that site is delayed indefinitely, perhaps forever? And, if a forest fire takes place, millions of dollars worth of useful timber will have been lost because we should, it is said, save every view, every landscape, everywhere for potential viewing by the casual tourist.

Another off-the-top-of-head claim is found on page 37. "And in the nation as a whole, everyone knows that we are going to need more wilderness, not less." What percentage of people in the US give a damn about the existence of National Parks? How many would spend their vacations in The Wilderness, if they were given a choice between roughing it there for a month, or, e.g., staying a week at Disney Park, or Las Vegas, or even Branson, or attending a few ball games?

He calls the mayor of a small town in Washington "xenophobic," because the man said (p. 41), "We resent that people from the outside who have never fully explored our North Cascades area should tell us what to do with it [Brooks spent a total of about two weeks there]. It would take more than a lifetime for any person to see all this rugged beauty, and we could lose every member of the Sierra Club in only a part of the proposed large National park area." And what a very good thing for the country *that* would be.

On page 43, we find the following: "And the very heart of the park is now threatened by the dam-building proposals of the public utility, Seattle City Light — one of which would raise an existing dam in the 'recreational area' by 125 feet, inundate the access to the greatest wild area, and destroy one of the finest parts of the park." Is the energy deficiency on the West Coast due, at least in part to the maneuverings of these east coast liberals and communists who have fought *every* sensible energy expansion project for forty years.

"So we are faced with the inevitable question: To what extent does a great corporation have an obligation to serve the public interest, as well as its own executives and stockholders?"(page 44). For one thing, the market for the corporation's products is determined by how well it fulfills the needs of its customers, while a non-producer such as the Sierra Club doesn't have to satisfy anyone except the gaggle of freaks who contribute to it, mostly rich persons to whom the damage done by the Club is of no consequence, and their much more important donors who have a strong financial interest in seeing that all attempts to increase energy supply and vacation spots are bushwhacked.

He views with alarm (again) the possibility that (page 48) "a view described as the scenic climax of the entire North Cascades," which few people know exist, might become "exploited." Does it bother him, did it even occur to him, that maybe most people really don't want to take the trouble to go to this God-forsaken spot just to look at another mountain? Flying over it in a plane would give the viewer a much greater experience.

"Unhappily, we cannot automatically expect such self-denial, least of all on the part of great corporations" (page 49). Where in this 200+ page screed does Brooks make a suggestion that the lookers-at-mountains, the landgod worshippers, should make some concessions? Nowhere, that's where. The total self-absorption, the utter contempt for others' wishes (or even their welfare), is very typical of a sociopath.

A mining company proposed a scheme to mine millions of tons of copper ore from a very small percentage of the Cascades (page 53). It is obvious that gainful employment would have been provided for thousands of people over a period of many years, and that the project would have yielded a product essential to industry and to the enjoyment of life by millions of people. But this is of no interest to Brooks.

From p. 59, he discusses the history of Project Chariot, a plan to either blast out a harbor in Alaska or dam a river, possibly by using atomic explosions. Alaska . . . "contains . . . the greatest remaining areas of wilderness in North America." How may people go there to look at the wilderness? "One would have to travel as far as the Florida Everglades to find so fragile an environment under such deadly attack." Fragile? Deadly? Again and again the use of superlatives without justification. The landscape in this area has probably existed without major changes for thousands of years, perhaps since the end of the last Ice Age. What makes this particular conformation of land, rocks, ice, swamp, etc., of any particular importance? Is it attractive? To whom? To Brooks, it is important simply because it is (it can be called?) "a Wilderness."

He fears an Eskimo community of about 300 people would be disturbed by the work (page 61). Much of their livelihood depends on killing caribou, the rest upon killing fish. It would be a fairly safe gamble to bet that everyone of these 300 Inuits would take $20,000 to clear out and think that it was not only better than winning the sweepstakes but one more proof that all white man are crazy. All over the country, all over the world, many larger communities are being displaced because of public developments and commercial improvements. In the US, environmental decisions by government agencies are the cause of displacing several times more people every year than are present in the Eskimo community. Mr. Brooks should have shown some interest in them.

"Another danger from the Chariot explosion was of concern to conservationists everywhere as well as to the local Eskimos (p. 70). The sea cliffs north of Cape Thompson constitute one of the principal nesting areas of several species of seabirds ... " P. 71. " ... the available breeding habitat of these highly specialized birds would be greatly reduced." So what? Has the bird population remained constant for millennia? Where is his evidence? Have the birds nested anywhere else? Can't they nest somewhere else? If they can't, who cares?

On page 77 and elsewhere, we find a discussion of "The Plot to Drown Alaska," i.e., the US Army Corps of Engineers' scheme to dam the Yukon River at The Ramparts in east-central Alaska. "To conservationists, the most valuable part of the river is the area known as Yukon flats ... this vast network of sloughs and marshes and potholes provides ... one of the finest wildfowl breeding grounds in North America." We come again to the necessity for preserving swamps, not a goal many of us would care about.

It appears the dam would have provided new and reliable sources of electric power, greatly expanding the industrial potential of Alaska and adding much wealth to the country as a whole (page 79). Again, these considerations are of no concern to the conservationists.

Brooks opposed this dam project, which would have benefited all of Alaska and much of Canada and brought power and other benefits to much of the rest of the US, because it would spoil "wild country, and its values are wilderness values" (p. 83 et seq.). He became an expert on this part of Alaska by making a trip down the river in flat-bottomed boats with outboard motors. This took only a few days, but he was a fast learner. He also hired a plane for a one-day excursion. This taught him all he needed to know about Alaska.

On subsequent pages, he shares his concerns about the effects of man's activities on birds: their nesting places, etc. He worries that 10,000 little brown cranes (and some other birds he lists) would be without "nesting habitat." How does he know these birds would not simply relocate to another area? He is very concerned about the possible effects of the proposed development on the breeding habits of salmon, etc. Is the development of land for the benefit of the human population as a whole to be prevented because of such considerations?

In speaking of the power that would be generated by the hydro-electric facility to be built in Alaska, he complains that it would be in excess of present needs. He seems to think demand would never increase, which may be perfectly logical for a person who doesn't want modernization, but not so logical for people who wish to provide both for the needs of an increasing population and for the factories which will enable these people to be productive and comfortable citizens. Since Brooks wrote his book, the power shortage on the West Coast has become critical.

From page 101, he discusses, "Super Jetport or Everglades Park?" This refers to an ingenious and colossal project to convert part of the Everglades, that very thinly populated swamp that spoils a large part of the south end of the Florida peninsula, to an immense airport and city. Since the project would convert waste land to practical and profitable use, benefitting millions of people every year, it was strongly opposed by worshippers of the landgod, i.e., wilderness conservationists.

The tract under consideration was just north of Everglades National Park, the latter being a vast acreage of what is essentially swamp land regardless of whatever specialized name the conservationists try to apply to it to conceal the fact that its most noticeable inhabitants are mosquitos, ticks, buzzards, and alligators. In terms of visitor-days, the park is not at all a popular destination for vacationists, those who come there doing so mostly out of blaze of curiosity which is quickly extinguished by a cloud of mosquitoes.

Part of the plan of the developers of the airport and improvements which would have accompanied it, including such amenities as highways, cities, etc., was to control the flow of the nearly stagnant water which constitutes such a tremendous health hazard to all of south Florida. The flow of the so-called river is seasonal, and, on this intermittent sluggish movement, according to Brooks (p. 106), "... the entire character and life of the park depends." That's too bad. Someone should try to remedy it, shouldn't they?

"No," according to Brooks. He is indignant that farmers got water for irrigating their crops, while some of the swamp land was allowed to dry up. He seems to imply, that we should allow the farmers to go bankrupt, and vast supplies of fresh food for humans to be lost, so that the scum-dwelling biota in the swamp can get their needed supply of mud.

Brooks does not believe parts of the swamp can be drained without "affecting the quantity and quality of water flowing through the Everglades (p. 108). Pollution is inevitable." Polluting a swamp? "For example, on takeoff a jet plane discharges about a gallon of unburned fuel." He doesn't want this to fall on the swamp. He doesn't care, presumably, that the planes (which will certainly be taking off from somewhere nearby, if the market demands it) deposit their fuel on inhabited areas, because the latter are not "wilderness." Again, we have an example which suggests to us that Brooks' basic motivation was a hatred of people, of humanity as a class.

Brooks frequently uses pejorative terms and broad, sweeping claims for which he has provided absolutely no justification, no data, no references. For example, "The entire environment 'downstream' — which is to say all of central Florida — would be subject to creeping death. This is not just horrid fantasy; serious effects have already been observed. *Replacement of one type of algae by another is already taking place* [!], and pesticide levels found in the tissue of fish taken from the park are already alarmingly high"[emphasis supplied].

Brooks calls it "effrontery" when developers call attention to the fact that the swampland partly surrounding the proposed Everglades super airport, would serve as a sound barrier absorbing the noise of plane take-offs (p. 109). Why? Is it because wasteland and wild animals are more important than residential areas and people? Yes. Furthermore, he apparently has no objection to the propeller driven "airboats" which ply the waterways and mudflats of Okefenokee, and which must certainly furnish louder noise (though localized) at waterlevel than the jet planes would. He and his wife explored the swamp in a low-flying airplane (p.112). How totally inconsistent and arrogant was this man.

He is bitter that (p. 119) "The Port Authority's objective was, and still is, the economic development of southern Florida." Seems to most of us to be a worthwhile objective. But it would benefit millions of people, not wild animals, so Brooks is indignant. He describes (p. 120-124) an onslaught of "conservationist" organizations and some state and federal employees on the Everglades airport plan, starting in about 1969.

Brooks is indignant that (p. 125) "The present priorities of the Corps [of Engineers] and of the state are clear; people first, agriculture second, Everglades National Park third ... " Incredibly, he thinks the Park, as a piece of land, should come first in the series of priorities.

"The Secretary of State of Florida says that it must [continue development] (p. 140). 'Both intelligence, and, for those of you who wish, the Bible, dictate that man is to have dominion over all the resources of the earth. Since most of us either believe in our own intelligence and/or in the Bible, let us be about the task of exerting our dominion over these resources.' " Seems fair enough to me, but Brooks becomes indignant again, he says, "An admirably clear statement of the philosophy that is bringing our world to the brink of ruin." It hasn't been this kind of philosophy that has brought ruin and chaos, it is the anarchical and Ludditical approach of the reds both here and abroad that have brought death and destruction and starvation to millions.

He describes (p. 143) a machine which is being used to clear away trees and other heavy vegetation in the swamp, as "an *obscene* symbol of man's war with the wilderness. We left the scene of *carnage* with relief." The "carnage" was some cleared ground, with trees as the corpses.

Environmentalists recruited foot soldiers to stop progress on the project (p. 150). Brooks gives great credit to "Florida Defenders of the Environment." It would be interesting to know how many staff members and students from institutions of higher education were on this project, and where the funds came from to get them to the hot spots. "As of this writing, construction has virtually ceased. Eureka Dam remains high and dry, the tree-crushing monster lies rusting on the shore; and the river beloved by William Bartram and Sidney Lanier, though sorely injured [!], is still alive [personification again]. Future generations may yet enjoy, as Coleridge wrote in his notebook, 'some wilderness-plot, green and fountaineous and unviolated by Man.' " That opium sipping esthete is a poor example of a nature lover — his view of beauty was mostly obtained in a drug-induced delirium, and he knew as much about nature as others of the same type. Perhaps he was typical of a landgod worshipper after all.

From page 151, Brooks describes his experiences on "The Golden Plains of Tanzania." Some new aspects of his peculiar philosophy come to light in this travelogue. "It is a land of vast wealth, but of a kind that cannot be possessed. Indeed, its unique asset, wildlife, exists by virtue of not being possessed . . . For in an age of triumphant technology, whatever we don't understand we sooner or later destroy." Perhaps his message is in code. It doesn't seem to make a lot of sense as written. His paradoxes are too paradoxical: "exists by . . . not being possessed." He describes an asset which cannot be converted into useful materials.

The following statements can be found on pages 157 through 171 of Brooks's book.

"Can the needs of wildlife and native tribes be reconciled?"

" . . . the Masai — with due regard for nature's cycle — layout their dead on the open plain to be eaten by the hyenas." Perhaps part of their evening's entertainment is taking the kids out to see the hyenas chewing on grandma.

He describes the milking procedure of the Masais. "Modern sanitary dairy farmers might question this procedure — including the rinsing of the kibuyus [gourds into which the cows were milked] with cow urine — but to the visitor from a prepackaged pasteurized world it was singularly refreshing."

"By fighting off the agricultural tribes, they have preserved the habitat of the wild animals among whom they live in mutual tolerance . . . But by overgrazing the range with their cattle — and worse with their sheep and goats — they have turned some areas of Masailand into near desert."

" . . . in recognition of the Masai's claim to grazing rights — which of course cannot be allowed in a national park."

"So those of us who recognize man's kinship with wild nature are diminished whenever, through man's agency, another form of life becomes extinct"(p. 176). I presume, if it becomes extinct because of predation by some other species, that's all right. This brings up the principle of preserving biodiversity, which will be discussed in detail elsewhere in this book. Suffice it to say that there are millions of species, and some of them become extinct every year. The great majority of these lost species were not known to man, and never will be known because they leave no traces.

Brooks tells us about "The Conservation Revolution" (p. 199 et seq.). In this, he clearly points out that drastic changes have to be made before his vision of a universe acceptable to the landgod can come into being. He quotes with apparent approval George Perkins Marsh (1864), an early landgod worshipper: "Of all organic beings, man alone is to be regarded as a destructive power . . . He wields energies to resist which nature is wholly impotent . . . [Brooks' ellipsis] Though living in physical nature, he is not of her." This is pure paranoia, all living beings are programmed to survive and reproduce as much as possible even though they may drive to extinction one or more competing species.

Brooks is in favor of revolution, but he doesn't think we should stop our piecemeal reform actions while waiting for the right time to burn everything down. He writes, "I cannot wholly agree with those who inveigh against 'piecemeal' actions as almost worse than nothing, who say that what we want is not reform but revolution, that it is futile to clean up rivers and purify exhaust from automobiles when we should be banning all automobiles and challenging the ethics of our society. This is the either/or fallacy. *We need* both reform *and* revolution [his emphasis]. Of course the aims of conservationists are revolutionary — they are radical in the literal sense of that term, since they go to the root of our system of values . . . If you believe, as some do, that increasing populations will cause us to starve in twenty years, how can you even work on thermal pollution?" How indeed — and why indeed. Brooks wrote that more than 30 years ago, and most of us haven't starved yet — in fact, overweight is a much more serious problem than starvation.

He refers once again to Carson's *Silent Spring*, and says that the book, in only eight years, " . . . has had an effect comparable to that of the bomb or the population explosion." Yes, it sold millions of copies and made Carson and Brooks rich, and it didn't do any harm to Houghton-Mifflin either. Of course, a lot of trees had to be "killed" to furnish the paper for *Silent Spring* and the other books manufactured by H-M. But, hey, it was for a good cause. If Carson's book had never been published, the conservation movement would have found, or would have created, a different bible — to provide a little red book for greenies.

Brooks believed a shortage of food is not the only disaster that will occur. "We had better brace ourselves for an attempt to condition us to accept the unbearable boom of the supersonic transport" (p. 207).

Brooks' Luddite attitude toward technology becomes very clear at some points. He says (p. 210 et seq.), "One doesn't need a Ph.D. in physics or chemistry to understand that crops can be successfully grown without indiscriminate use of persistent poisons, that technical means exist for controlling smog and for keeping industrial wastes and raw sewage out of our rivers, that the lumber industry can exist and flourish without raiding our remaining virgin forest, that strip mining is not the best way of obtaining coal — in terms of land use — but only the quickest and the cheapest [also the safest, but he doesn't care about that]. In other words, the public knows that we can save the environment if we will ... To say that 'we can't afford the cost of saving the environment' is absurd. It is not an economic, but a political decision."

The landgod worshippers know they have to denigrate the work of scientists and technologists, because their own efforts to frighten the populace into ill-considered actions are based on unsound assumptions and junk science that can be refuted quite easily by any good scientist, regardless of whether or not he is familiar with the specific problem under discussion. In fact, many of the radical conservationists know that the mere application of common sense to some of their proposals will show the average citizen how ridiculous they are. So, the average citizen can't be given time to consider the effects, he must be pressured to act solely on impulse, and be motivated primarily by fear.

"Wilderness is as essential to our way of life as our laboratories, museums, libraries. For our need to understand the world of nature signifies something in us deeper than mere curiosity. Here, we feel, is some statement of the truth, if we only have the wisdom to read it" (p. 212). Brooks presents us with the sealed book, which can be read only by the illuminated. What could be clearer proof of the religious status of wilderness worship than this obeisance to the landgod?

Gaea is Good to Them

Gaining money and notoriety are the main goals of the professional wilderness activist. The Sierra Club is a very wealthy organization, with oil wells and other good investments in its portfolio. There are some members who believe, more or less, in the stated goals of the Club — they pay the bills. Then there are the executives and consultants and grantees — they get the money.

Some of the money going into the wilderness activist organizations is obtained by means little short of extortion.

Anti-development activists will claim, and some of them may even believe, that by preventing the conversion of empty tracts of land to capitalistic purposes, they are depriving investors of gains, which seems to be a highly desirable accomplishment to them. But consider the net effect of their operations. The closing of large tracts of lands to development greatly increases the value of land already converted to profitable uses, whether it is in the form of residential, commercial, recreational, drilling, or mining use. Thus, current owners of residential developments, operating oil fields or mines, or recreational facilities (e.g., Las Vegas) will greatly benefit from the conservationists' efforts to remove potential competition from the market.

Who contaminates land the most? — Hikers, campers, and nature worshippers in general contaminate the land much more than people who work on the land. The nature buffs defecate and urinate on the land and leave behind food scraps and other debris. Occasionally, they cause forest fires. Their untreated garbage and sewage serves as foci of disease-causing organisms which can spread far from the specific location of the deposit. Living organisms of all other kinds (e.g. wild animals such as wolves) are even worse — the residue of their living processes, and their bodies after their death, contaminate the forests for miles around. If the wild animals are carnivorous, the scraps of their kills rot; if the animals are vegetarian, they may destroy large areas for a relatively small amount of food, they are not delicate eaters. And no, they do not have an innate, God-given respect for their environment.

Don't give me any static — One of the more curious fantasies prevalent in the landgod congregation is the concept that the wilderness is "unchanging," that the land has been there "forever," that the landscape and its constituents are eternal. Not so. The land is ever changing, on any time scale the observer may select. Life and land is never static. Any unprejudiced observer knows this very well.

Anyone with intelligence and experience greater than the average kindergartner, and with perhaps more insight and honesty than the average college professor or foundation representative [this part can't be difficult], can easily comprehend this fact. Under our feet, though it may be separated by many layers of concrete and steel, lie hundreds if not thousands, of layers of sand, gravel, consolidated sediment, lava, and mixed organic materials, deposited by glaciers, streams, wind, gravity, and the workings of microscopic and macroscopic organisms, including people. But, whatever the source, whenever it was deposited, it represented a change in the earth, a potential change in the landscape, and thus a failure of the landgod to perpetuate his "unchanging" image.

Characterizing the Econuts

From examples readily available to us, some of which have been presented earlier in this chapter, we see that worshippers of the landgod are, by and large, selfish, arrogant, elitist, unscientific, and infantile. If *Homo sapiens* had followed their principles from the start, we would still be living in the Stone Age, if, indeed, any specimens of the race would still be extant. We would be dying at an average age of about 15, living in constant peril from the ravages of "nature," suffering our whole lives from diseases transmitted by uncontrolled biotic vectors, and without heat and light except from the sun. We would be the favorite prey of countless species who would have laughed, if they had been capable of that form of vocalization, at the idea they were created to be brothers to mankind.

But, looking on the bright side, there would be wilderness everywhere — and there wouldn't be any books by Paul Brooks.

Getting in Touch with the Land God

David Abram, who is, evidently, the guiding spirit of an organization called "Wild Earth," and by his own account an ecologist, philosopher, and magician, published an article of interest to us in the Nov.-Dec. 2001 issue of the UTNE Reader. This magazine deserves a few pages of critical commentary of its own since it is an pre-eminent source of touchie-feelie junk. Unfortunately, the space is not available here to deal with their problems.

In Abram's article we find the following comments: "If . . . we view matter as animate (or self-organizing) from the get go, then hierarchies [of sentience] vanish, and we are left with a diversely differentiated field of animate beings, each of which has its gifts relative to the others. And we find ourselves not above this living web, but in the very midst of it, our own sentience part and parcel of the sensuous landscape."

And, "If we really wish to awaken our senses, and so to renew the solidarity between ourselves and the rest of the earth, then we must acknowledge that the myriad things around us have their own active influence upon our lives and our thoughts (and also, of course, upon one another). We must begin to **speak** of our sensuous surroundings in the way that our breathing bodies really experience them — **as active, as animate, as alive**" [emphasis added].

Nothing could be clearer: Abram believes every material thing is active, animate, and alive. We have here another unequivocal acknowledgement of the all-encompassing landgod, presented by Abram as the thinking, feeling, pulsating web which includes human beings as well as every lump of filth in existence.

As we consider Abram drawing in deep breaths of the Wilderness air in order to get in touch with the greater realities and the most obscure truths, our thoughts are inevitably drawn to the Pythia at Delphi, who breathed the effluvium (toxic fumes?) of the earth in order to reach a mental condition where the future was revealed. Of course, Pythia did it for pay, just as Abram does.

What passes for logic/science in the environmental community consists largely of reiterations of doubtful evidence that can not be related in any scientific way to the actions demanded by environmentalists, and which, when dispassionately analyzed, can often be shown to provide a justification for proceeding in a direction diametrically opposite to the program of the activists.

The Great Divide

The present author believes the environmentalist community can be shown to be divided into four parts — like most other activist groups:

1. The professional managers, lawyers, fund managers, etc., who do not care a whit for the rightness or wrongness of a program, so far as its ultimate effects on humanity are concerned, but are interested in promoting their own careers and enlarging their own lifestyles by garnering fees and establishing connections.

2. The front line soldiers, who are looking for some cause to fight for, as a means of bringing meaning and consequence to their otherwise pointless lives.

3. The thrill seekers, those bootless, rootless trouble-makers who seek action, adventure, and novelty regardless of the cause, and who would be as comfortable supporting free trade as they are supporting restrictions on international commerce. In general, however, it can be said that these foot soldiers of the environmental battalions demand entertainment in the form of sex, drugs, and the opportunity to destroy things. A good organizer sees that his recruits are promised these goodies, even though he may have no intention of providing them.

4. And, at the bottom, or perhaps it should be regarded as the top, we have the real motivators, the long-term planners, the furnishers of seed money, who never appear in the press releases, or in the table of organization. These are the persons who anticipate large gains from the social disruptions caused by the activists. They fit each riot and destructive rampage into their own master plan which, when completed (and, if successful) will show results which are completely different from those anticipated by any of the other participants in the program.

chapter nine

PRESERVING HABITATS

Deification of "The Environment," is generally accompanied by the anthropomorphizing of Nature, a process which will include, in the minds of some fanatics, geographical features as well as the biota — and perhaps may include some aspects of nature which are completely imaginary. Among the ideas generated by the econuts is the concept that animals should not be crowded out of their present homes by human residences, or as a result of the by-products of human activities. Their "natural" homes should be maintained without any substantial changes (intentional or otherwise) caused by humans. This is the "habitat preservation" doctrine that has resulted in so much grief and monetary loss to humans who may have inadvertently caused some inconvenience to animals (not necessarily a separate genus or species) that are currently residing on valuable land.

It is important to understand that, in many of these situations, we are discussing nuisance animals who are moving into areas of human habitation (including fully built-up and fully improved suburbs) because pressures of excessive numbers of animals in the original home areas have driven out some of the less competitive individuals. In other words, animals are not "repossessing" former habitats but are attempting to create new living space out of human residential areas.

Also discussed in this chapter is the concept that geographical areas which have some special identifying feature attractive to environmentalists should be maintained forever without change, usually because a supposedly unique biota of mixed but perhaps common animals and plants are thought to be characteristic of the area. It is very difficult to understand the rationale, if we can call it that, behind some of these crusades, if for no other reason than the specifications of such "threatened areas" often change overnight, as does the site itself.

"Habitat preservation" differs from "Biodiversity protection" (which will be discussed in another chapter) in that the former is concerned with species whose numbers and distribution may be considerable (or even excessive, by any reasonable evaluation), and which are in no danger of extinction on a global scale — it is only a geographically delimited mixture of animals and plants which is alleged to be in trouble. Biodiversity protection deals with animals of species (or varieties, races, types) which seem to be so limited in their distribution, or their total population in the world seems to be so small, that once the targeted individuals die out, members of the species will no longer exist anywhere.

Principles of Habitat Conservation

The basic though unannounced principle of habitat conservation, is that the comfort and well-being of animals — any animal — deserve to take precedence over any project which enhances the comfort, safety, or material welfare of humans. This basic guideline is disguised in various ways, as will be seen elsewhere in this book, but it becomes obvious when the maneuverings of econuts are examined closely and without prejudice.

Protecting natural ecosystems — At the website library.thinkquest.org we find the following. "Endangered species are not the only organisms that desperately need to be saved. In order to save organic diversity, we must not only defend populations and species but protect natural ecosystems as well. This is done by minimizing destruction of habitat . . . " It probably could be shown that every cubic foot of earth contains a "unique" mixture of numbers and types of plants and animals (including microorganisms) so we seem to have arrived at a point where the endangered species zealots are trying to establish their hegemony over every bit of the planet.

"To protect natural diversity, we must focus on protecting entire ecosystems. It is impossible to maintain entire biospheres in zoos, laboratories, and botanic gardens. Wherever possible, attempts should be made to rehabilitate the natural environment. It is a good idea to plant native vegetation and provide homes for associated animals . . .

the rainforests, especially, are a natural wealth of animal and plant diversity, and should be preserved at all costs. In order to help save them, ruined croplands and other free land could be planted over with forests, to make less the need of clearing forest for timber."

Habitats should be preserved forever — A nonprofit called *American Wildlands*, says there should be sufficient wilderness areas to allow "viable populations of native species to exist in perpetuity." And, "From a conservation standpoint, the sensible strategy is to ensure that we err on the side of preservation; no further degradation of wildlife habitat is allowed to proceed until it is scientifically determined how much habitat is adequate and where critical habitat is located." In other words, persons who oppose American Wildlands restrictions are required to prove a negative.

The Natural Resources Defense Council tells us, "Aiding wildlife by protecting wild places grows ever more difficult in the face of sprawling development and relentless pressure from the logging, mining and other industries. NRDC fights to save the homes [sic] of diverse animals including polar bear and caribou populations in the Arctic, British Columbia's rare Spirit Bear, the Pacific gray whale and south Florida's Cape Sable seaside sparrow by pressing the government to set aside protected wilderness and other areas and by developing practical plans to avoid new development by making already developed areas more livable. We also take legal action under the Endangered Species Act and other laws and mobilize citizens to use their consumer and political power on behalf of preserving habitat."

Use of Habitat Preservation to Block Projects

Many useful and indeed necessary public and private projects involving the development of substantial land areas have been delayed or prevented indefinitely by claims that the project will threaten an endangered species. If federal funding is required for any phase of a project's construction, an environmental impact statement is required, and approval may be refused (or indefinitely delayed) for a number of ecological reasons. Proof of the econuts' allegations is seldom required. Following are some recent examples of their work.

The Tocks island dam, a major hydroelectric project, was held back for years by the claim that a small fish, the brown snail-darter would have its habitat destroyed. There never was any proof that this was the only population of the animal.

Spotted owls in the forests of the Pacific Northwest were said to be endangered by lumbering activities, so a major part of the local economy was essentially destroyed by a refusal to grant the necessary approvals. Endangerment of a species, if it was a distinct species, was never proved.

It is certain that many parties who wish to prevent a development for financial reasons may oppose approval for a project on the pretext that a unique habitat will be damaged. Some of the reasons for this are to prevent new supplies of a raw material coming to market (as when petroleum companies wish to prevent oil fields not under their control from being developed), or to prevent competition in the form of housing construction that would compete with existing developments.

An interesting example of conflicting interests being activated by a habitat preservation problem arose recently in the Washington DC area. The project involved was the construction of the Woodrow Wilson Bridge which was intended to speed up traffic around the Washington Beltway. The bridge and associated roadways would have made commuting much easier for the bureaucrats who lived in the suburbs and worked in the city. According to the Wall Street Journal, " . . . even though construction would imperil several endangered species, including the bald eagle, bureaucrats at federal agencies — from Fish and Wildlife to the National Marine Fisheries Service . . . had quickly waved through the project. The hypocrisy is so blatant that the National Wilderness Institute, a group usually critical of the Endangered Species Act, has felt compelled to sue to halt the project . . . the Washington politicians and commuters are shocked . . . that an ESA lawsuit is being used so blatantly to halt human activity . . . The Endangered Species Act was passed nearly 30 years ago in a show of bipartisan good intentions, to help animals on the brink of extinction. But since that time, environmental groups have hijacked the act, turning it into a bludgeon by which they can enforce their vision of a development-free America" (Anon. 2002B).

"It's rural parts of the country, where small landowners lack deep pockets and political clout, that bear the brunt. The ESA's capricious and uneven enforcement only underscores the utter bankruptcy of the law. According to a 1999 report from the House Resources Committee, while 543 species were listed in the five Far West states, only 39 were listed in the Northeast. Critical habitats were designated for 96 species in the West, for just nine in the East. Fish and Wildlife spends more than half its ESA budget in just five Western states alone" (Anon. 2002B).

Germany Leads the Way

According to a news brief in Science (Vogel et al. 2002), "Favored fauna animals in Germany, which already enjoy some of the strictest legal safeguards in Europe, are about to be labeled a protected resource ... the Bundestag voted overwhelmingly to include animals in a phrase pledging the state to protect 'natural resources' for 'future generations ... [ignoring] objections from the country's leading research organizations ... [T]he upper house, the Bundesrat, is expected to go along ... many scientists worry that it will give activists new grounds on which to attack the use of animals in research.' "

In an earlier but related report, we learn The European Commission threatened to block development of a $72 million business park near Aachen (Germany) because it is a habitat of the black-bellied European hamster. The developers pointed out that no one had seen a hamster on the plot for several years. But, by using satellite data, an environmentalist located two sets of hamster burrows about six feet underground. A legal authority said the hamsters are protected under European Union law, and the developers can either stop their project or relocate the hamsters, which would cost millions of marks (Anon. 2001F).

The Mud Police

The fanatics who believe they can turn back the clock and recreate aboriginal landscapes and prehistoric faunal populations on developed sites, are wrong. The goal itself seems bizarre because of its necessary lack of specificity — any given plot of land must have had hundreds of different animal and vegetable (and, for that matter, mineral) profiles during its existence. An example would be, recreating the prairie as it was before *Homo sapiens* arrived on the scene, as though man could make greater changes than volcanoes, glaciers, earthquakes, erosion, and thousands of other natural occurrences had already made. And, we must also consider the effects of natural selection, or evolution, which has undoubtedly changed details of the flora and fauna countless times before any kind of "man" existed.

Government policy for the past several years has been that an artificial wetland can replace a natural one. Kaiser (2001) tells us, "Recreated wetlands are no match for the original," whatever "original" means. But, " . . . in unusually blunt language, a new report by the National Research Council says that the current approach, designed to ensure no net loss of wetlands, is a failure and that handmade eco-systems are often a poor substitute for the real thing." Does this mean that the NRC now recognizes that all nature is transient, and a swamp with mosquitoes and snakes is not spiritually superior to a supermarket and parking lot? No, it doesn't.

The disputed policy gives developers an opportunity to build on top of a "water-logged" spot if it is necessary and if the builders restore the conditions or create a marsh nearby. The sheer lunacy of this concept should not need to be pointed out.

The government, or the part of it devoted to protecting mud, claimed they were really concerned about maintaining wildlife habitats (why?) and controlling floods by maintaining reservoirs for excess rainwater (how can a saturated soil absorb more moisture?). In fact, they were concerned with protecting their jobs and increasing their salaries. They knew that opposing the big foundations would result in the application of economic and political clout by the activists which the federal employees did not have the resources to combat. So, they did not oppose them.

Don't Damage the Mud

In 1980, the Environmental Protection Agency began using the amended 1972 Clean Water Act as a basis for stipulating that landowners who get a permit from a state agency or the US Army Corps of Engineers to build on a marsh may be required to make up for the "damage."

"The NRC expert committee, formed at the request of EPA, found that although various factors, including less destruction of wetlands for agriculture, have stemmed their overall loss, mitigation wasn't working. According to the corps, 17,000 hectares of wetlands have been created for 9,500 lost between 1993 and 2000. Yet despite almost double the area of loss [created vs. lost], 'the goal of no net loss is not being met,' said . . . an ecologist from the U WI at Madison" (Kaiser 2001).

One of this panel's complaints was that many of the recreated wetlands don't function in the same way as the original ones, which often (allegedly) depend on intermittent water flows to support a specific mix of plant and animal species. Evidently, the panel wanted someone to turn the water [rain?] off and on at specific times — how they would have determined the correct times and quantities, no one knows.

Swamps are called "the rainforests of the North," and "kidneys of the earth" because they allegedly filter slow moving water courses and collect sediment. "Rainforest" is an incantatory word for econuts, with its mystical power often increased by adding the prefix, "Amazon."

So, this highly scientific panel recommended that wetlands which can't be replicated with certainty, should be left in their primitive state, until nature decides to step in and change them. Wetlands that must be harmed should first be studied so that permit holders know what they're trying to reproduce. Before issuing permits, regulators must look at the entire watershed to see if creating a different, more distant wetland would ultimately be better than building an identical one nearby.

To achieve these lofty goals, the panel recommended a new database to track permits, a research program to find out what works (!), stricter enforcement, and long-term monitoring. In other words, lifetime careers for another army of mud protectors. The first step, says a spokesman, is increasing the corps' $125 million budget for wetland mitigation. How is it that this recommendation does not come as a surprise to the author? Or, he hopes, to the readers?

Other examples

"Anthony Palazzolo . . . wanted to build on . . . coastal property he had owned for 40 years" . . . but "At some point in his tenure, the land had been designated protected wetlands" (Anon. 2001L). So, his requests for a building permit were all rejected. He sued for compensation, and the state courts said there was no case. However, the Supreme Court, in a 2001 decision, said the state court should decide whether he had received adequate compensation for the "regulatory taking" of the wetlands designation.

Palazzolo was one of thousands of property owners whose land use has been arbitrarily restricted, and the value of the land thereby reduced, by regulatory actions. Our Constitution prohibits any government (municipal, state, or federal) from taking a citizen's land for public use without paying for it. Government officials and activist groups have attempted to get around this restriction by claiming that regulations which restrict the use of land, or in some other way depreciate its value, are not "taking" and so they pay nothing for them. This policy has resulted in numerous outrages supposedly justified by so-called environmental considerations. A few examples follow:

• A retired contractor in Virginia was unable to build a house on a lot he owns in the middle of a development, because the construction noise might distress a bald eagle which has settled nearby.

• Owners of 37 acres of commercially harvestable forest land in Oregon were forced to dedicate it to the welfare of the northern spotted owl.

• In California, grape growers and farmers have been put out of business because their activities might discomfit the tiger salamander, which is on the emergency list.

• Owners of land in the stomping ground of the silver rice rat, were barred from commercial use of the land.

Organizations formed to protect the property rights of persons affected by such government regulations estimate that land owners have suffered billions of dollars in lost value because of government actions based on the endangered species legislation.

First attempts at restitution — Some states, such as Florida and Oregon, have passed laws allowing owners just compensation for loss in land value resulting from new restrictions applied to the land. Various organizations dedicated to "the environment" have attempted to overturn these laws and have encouraged state officials to ignore them. Politicians in Oregon have explained that the government could never afford to compensate landowners for all the property it takes ($5.4 billion a year, according to state authorities). The option of seizing less property was evidently not considered as an option.

Farmers in the Tulare Lake Basin of California sued the state when they lost their water supply in 1992 and 1994 because of restrictions imposed to protect certain species of fish. In 2001, the US Court of Federal Claims held that the loss of water constituted a clear government taking of property, and that the farmers must be compensated. The court said the Fifth Amendment is intended to bar government from forcing some people to bear public burdens which in all fairness and justice should be borne by the public as a whole.

In mid-2001, "Oregon Senator Gordon Smith offered an amendment that would have released water to 1,500 farmers in the Oregon/California Klamath Basin (Anon. 2001K). Those farmers have been left high and dry for months because of a junk science opinion from the Fish and Wildlife Service saying nearby endangered sucker fish needed more water to survive.

"Evidently, humans don't merit such concern. In the end, 52

members voted to kill the amendment. Every Democrat save two — North Dakota's Kent Conrad and Oregon's Ron Wyden — happily paid fealty to the super-enviro crowd. California's Barbara Boxer, in voting to condemn thousands of her own constituents to misery, nobly noted that someone had to be the voice of wildlife. Certain Republicans also felt fish ranked higher than humans, including Pennsylvania's Arlen Specter, Rhode Island's Lincoln Chafee and Illinois's Peter Fitzgerald.

"Of interesting note was Democrat Max Baucus. Mr. Baucus appeared in front of a Senate environmental committee as recently as May to talk about reforming the Endangered Species Act. 'The ESA was never, never supposed to trump good and necessary projects that can and should move forward.' He was speaking of the highway projects the ESA had obstructed in his home state of Montana. Now if only 'good and necessary projects' could be defined to include humans." And, to include projects outside of Montana.

Pity the poor Monarch

According to Lovel (2001), "Tom Turpin of Purdue is right to remark that Bt corn's effects on monarch butterflies obscures wider issues. Once we release genetically modified organisms, we may never be able to recall them. As Turpin notes, we don't know the long-term effects of Bt toxin on soil organisms. There has been only the barest investigation of the effects of Bt corn in animal feeds, let alone in the human food chain. The monarch question, while worth consideration, pales in comparison with these issues."

But, Taylor (2001) wrote, "As a lepidopterist for over 40 years, I found the discussion about Bt corn and monarch populations ludicrous. If monarch-overwintering habitat in Mexico disappears, as seems all too likely, the only US population [of these butterflies] will be west of the Rocky Mountains, well away from the corn belt and further exposure to Bt corn pollen. If only a portion of the effort and money spent to prove the safety of Bt corn in monarchs were expended helping Mexico to save Monarch's winter habitat, we'd be dealing with a really important issue."

This appears to be an issue over which there is disagreement among the econut community. We can expect to see more of this in the future as the irrationality of the various programs leaves much room for confusion and controversy.

The Beavers Vote "Yes!"

"Nearly a year after Washington state voters banned most forms of trapping, land owners, wildlife officials and trappers say they are dealing with the consequences. Dam-building beavers flood timber land. Coyotes snatch more lambs. River otters treat salmon hatcheries as all-you-can-eat buffets.

"Initiative 713 bans the use of body-gripping traps to capture any animal for recreation or commerce in fur. It also outlaws two specific poisons . . . Initiative sponsors, primarily the Humane Society of the United States, argued that such methods are cruel and inhumane . . . The measure was approved in November with nearly 55% of the vote.

"The result is that fewer beavers are being caught — leaving more of them chopping down trees and building dams.

"For landowners, especially owners of timber, that means more young trees in reforested areas dying in beavers' jaws and more mature timber drowning in beaver ponds.

"Initiative sponsors say that is OK.

" 'People are now supposed to be focusing on non-lethal ways to deal with their wildlife problems,' said Lisa Wathne of the Humane Society of the United States.

"Before Initiative 713, sheep rancher Fred Blauert used foothold traps to catch the coyotes that burrowed under the fence that protects his 300-ewe flock near Washington.

"Since the measure's passage, Blauert said his losses to predators have jumped from 5% to 15%, a tough hit in an industry already hurt by cheap imports of wool and meat from Australia.

"Body-gripping traps also were standard in Washington for the wildlife managers who tend the public's lands and private operators who make their living removing nuisance wildlife.

"Those operators are suffering under the initiative's restrictions . . . It was much broader than just affecting commerce and recreation in fur," said Lt. Steve Dauma, who oversees enforcement of the measure for the Department of Fish and Wildlife.

"Among the initiatives's consequences is an increased demand for the help of an obscure federal agency known as Wildlife Services, which specializes in protecting livestock, crops, people and property from wildlife . . . Blauert said his neighbors recently called in the agency's aerial gunners to thin out the coyotes attacking their stock, effectively using wholesale coyote killing to replace their piecemeal efforts.

"Bill Clay, the agency's deputy administrator, concedes such methods are controversial, but notes that by outlawing foothold traps and a poison used against coyotes, the initiative cut down on his options.

"John Consolini of Northwest Nuisance Wildlife Control also says he's hamstrung by the initiative's rules as he tries to get otters out of koi ponds, raccoons out of rhododendrons and moles out of lawns.

" ' We're getting more and more damage to properties because of this,' Consolini said. 'The customer's paying another 30 to 40 percent for our services than if we could use the proper equipment' " Queary (2001).

It's the Taxpayers Who Suffer

Investigators and reporters have publicized numerous examples of absurd attempts to apply legal sanctions against human disturbers of plant and animal life. Many of these programs involved heavy costs to taxpayers, even if the salaries and expense accounts of the biodiversity police are not considered. Even worse, small businesses, including farmers, have been ruined by police enforcement actions conducted in the name of biodiversity. Many times, the convicted party had no idea he was doing anything that was against the law.

Saving the kangaroo rat and other diversions — We learn from news reports (Anon. 1994) of another outrageous example of official oppression. "In Kern County, California, Vietnam refugee Taung Ming-Lin, made a living growing alfalfa, bamboo, and bok choy on his 720-acre farm, unaware that his land is home to the endangered Tipton kangaroo rat. Earlier this year *two dozen* state and federal agents invaded his farm *by land and air* in search of rodent body parts. They found five carcasses." As a result, Lin faces up to a year in prison and $300,000 in fines for violating the Endangered Species Act. The court documents filed by the government state that Lin 'did knowingly take and abet the taking of an endangered species of wildlife, to wit, Tipton kangaroo rats.'

"As if that was not enough, the Endangered Species Act 'authorizes the confiscation of instruments of crime,' so the government seized Lin's machinery as the murder weapons . . . Lin told the Pacific Legal Foundation, 'I wanted to make bamboo and bok choy part of the American diet. But the government showed me this dead rat and then they took my ($50,000) tractor. Now my land is worthless.' " We suggest that some restless, bitter, nonproductive informer, no doubt affiliated with an institution of higher learning, spent much time and grant money searching out this industrious farmer as the subject of persecution in order to further his own career or to enhance his self-image.

The pigeons weren't interviewed — John R. Undeland (2002) was saddened and surprised when the Wall Street Journal published an editorial saying, or implying, that the Woodrow Wilson Bridge project threatened bald eagles and other species (see page 174 for more details). He responded: "With a pair of bald eagles having established a nest nearby . . . the project undertook an exhaustive biological assessment to catalog the raptors' habits and habitat — where they hunt, roost and otherwise exist. In response, the US Fish and Wildlife Service mandated a series of rigorous conditions, including broad seasonal limitations on work near the eagles, 'no-go' zones of protection, extensive tree preservation and the creation of a 10-acre eagle conservation preserve.

"While complying fully with the strict requirements, the project has gone still further to protect bald eagles. Fully 32 acres of forested property were acquired — three times what was required — as well as an additional 51 acres of submerged property to create permanent eagle sanctuary. These efforts are apparently paying off: three eaglets hatched last spring [83 acres of land in this area must have cost the taxpayers tens of millions of dollars, multimillions per eaglet].

"Similar levels of effort, consuming enormous resources and time, have been devoted to protecting other endangered species. These are hardly the actions of a project looking the other way with regard to species protection."

The amount of money spent on protecting these birds could have been better spent on improving the welfare of humans in the city, or better yet, returned to the taxpayers, the vast majority of which do not care whether the eagles live or die. And, the pigeon fanciers would much prefer that they die.

Cases similar to the above have proliferated in recent years. Only a few of the most outrageous examples can be reported in the space available in this book.

There goes the neighborhood — An article by Sterba (2002) discusses the problems arising from wild life invasions into residential areas in Massachusetts. It seems that the do-gooders made hunting and trapping virtually impossible in or near the wooded suburbs of the state. As a result, there is now an out-of-control white deer population, beaver dams, garbage hunting bears, and other wildlife problems. Sterba explains, "By keeping out hunters as unsafe and trappers as inhumane, suburbanites unknowingly favor some species, such as deer, over others, such as songbirds." In addition to 3,000 black bears, 70,000 beavers, there are many deer, and other wild animals in or near suburban areas.

"In 1996, an animal-welfare coalition called ProPAW (Protects Pets and Wildlife) led by the Humane Society of the US ... and the Massachusetts Society for the Prevention of Cruelty to Animals

(MSPCA), organized and funded a Bay State ballot initiative around the theme: *Ban Cruel Traps*. They spent heavily on media ads. One showed a dog with one leg missing, another, a cat writhing in a leg-hold trap." The zoophilists managed to get passed a "Wildlife Protection Act" which banned leg-hold and body-gripping traps.

The National Audubon Society, which was not in favor of the act, reported, "The cruel Conibear traps, which cost $18 each, weighed two pounds and killed instantly, have been replaced by 'humane' 25-lb traps that cost $250 each and hold the terrified animals for hours until they can be bashed on the head and thrown away." As a result of the Wildlife Protection Act, the number of beavers caught by trappers in Massachusetts dropped to about 5% of its former level, and home-owners began to find beavers building dams across the streams running across their back yards, then their back yards became ponds. All the result of a few thousand feel-good voters.

What does the head of the MSPCA say about the results of her organization's successful initiative? "People have much to learn about living around wild animals" (as reported by Sterba 2002). The editor of Wildlife Control Technology, said, "A big part of the job [of wildlife control] is assuaging the fear and/or guilt of the people who call to solve the problem. Many are in denial."

Caribou capers — Before drilling for oil began in Prudhoe Bay, Alaska, over 20 years ago, there was a hysterical outbreak from the eco-nuts, who were certain the activity would disturb the caribou and lead to a catastrophic drop in the numbers of these animals. There were about 3,000 Arctic caribou in the herd then. There are now about 27,500. Since the Bush administration began pushing for rights to drill in the Arctic National Wildlife Reserve, the same old complaints are being made by the environmentalists (Feder 2001). And, they again speak of a "pristine wilderness," but the region that would be affected is among the bleakest, most inhospitable land in North America. In the nine winter months, the temperature drops to as low as 70 degrees below zero.

The environmentalists never learn from their mistakes, because they are "saving the earth," and that requires penalizing human beings for the sake of animals, whatever the ultimate cost. Their religion is dependent upon revelation, and facts do not matter to them any more than they do to a true believer in any other religion.

A Spark of Sanity

Ayers (2001) summed it up very succinctly in a letter referring to an article indicating that "Fish stocking may transmit toad disease." He wrote, "In the past 15 years or so since we became aware of significant declines in amphibian populations, I have seen at least five reasons given for this. They are: (1) global warming, (2) chemical pollution, (3) the ozone hole, (4) parasites, and (5) habitat loss. With limited data and unlimited faith in their assertions, the articles often were more evangelistic than scientific. At last, someone takes some suggestive data and draws reasonable but tentative conclusions. As yet, I have read nothing of scientists trying to get a realistic assessment of the normal population cycles for these animals. Without the background estimate, you don't really know if you're looking at anything at all. Too much faith and evangelism is passing for science these days."

The World Needs More Turtles

The following extract was taken from Dixie Lee Rays' excellent book, *Environmental Overkill*, which contains more wisdom than you would find in the entire Harvard faculty . . . much more.

"The desert tortoise is listed as 'endangered' even though it is common in the land surrounding Las Vegas. The city agreed to place 400,000 acres of surrounding Clark County in a Desert Tortoise Management Zone. In the zone there will be no grazing, no mining, no off-road vehicle events, no hunting, and no hiking. In exchange for being allowed to build downtown, Las Vegas surrendered a total of 1.4 million acres of Clark County and nearby Lincoln County to the Desert Tortoise Management Zone. But in a document announcing the new program, the

Fish and Wildlife Service threatened further confiscations: 'There are 50 other threatened or endangered species for which provisions also must be made.' All this because the government did not have courage to fight the Humane Society. If only the government were as solicitous of the rights of ranchers, miners, recreationalists, and the city of Las Vegas.

"Is there really a dearth of Desert Tortoises? Is there a likelihood that the species might not survive? No, they are abundant in Nevada, as well as the desert areas of California, where highway signs, 'Warning: Tortoise Crossing,' abound.

"If we're not to lose our communities, our civil liberties, and our traditions of individual freedom and common sense, we're all going to have to band together to beat back the depredations of cynical environmentalists and bureaucrats who value their own power more than the Constitution."

Cougars and Humans: Who is attacking whom?

Wolves and coyotes are not the only killers found to be worthy clients by the habitat preservation crowd. Mountain lions — cougars — also find favor in their eyes.

The heading for this segment is taken from an article in *San Diego Earth Times*, dated March 1996. Interested researchers can find the website at www.sdearthtimes.com.

Kelly Cowan, the author, intends to imply that cougars are getting a bum rap because they have killed a few people. It is the old story: humans kill cougars, so why isn't it fair that cougars kill humans, especially if the humans are inconsiderate enough to violate the cougars' space? Cowan says that opponents of cougars claim there were 322 serious incidents in 1995, but only 100 were actually confirmed. Somehow, this argument is not very convincing — 100 attacks on humans by cougars seems to be at least 99 too many to this writer.

Cowan likes to compare numbers — people are complaining about their pets being killed by cougars, so she points out that *coyotes* take hundreds of outdoor pets every year. Again we must ask, what does this prove — one thing it proves is that we ought to exterminate the coyotes as well as the cougars. Cowan also quibbles: it is known that mountain lions kill livestock, but "most livestock taken [i.e., killed] is due to domestic and wild canines." Why should the threshhold of acceptability be adjusted upward because of other threats?

Cowan's article was motivated by a desire to activate voters to cast their ballot against a proposition to allow hunters to kill mountain lions. Here is an opportunity to eliminate a hazard at no cost to the public, and the voters are encouraged to reject it. Strange.

The Conservation Business

A brief glimpse of the particulars of one of the mid-tier green organizations may help the reader understand the big business aspects of nonprofits exploiting this segment of the conservation racket. The National Fish and Wildlife Foundation has its headquarters in Washington DC (of course), but it has a total of ten offices around the country (Maher 2002). It began operations in 1984, and since then has made more than 5,000 grants dealing with conservation of fish, plants, wildlife, and habitats. There are about 2,000 projects currently being funded with a total outlay of around $40 million annually. The chief operating officer earns between $100,000 and $120,000 plus fringe benefits, but he doesn't have much time to spend among the fishies and birdies. Multiply this operation by 100 or more to encompass all the variations possible on the green theme, and you have a fairly substantial chunk of the national economy going into what are essentially non-productive endeavors, and that does not even take into account the real giants, such as the Sierra Club, whose total income is many times that of a run-of-the-mill foundation such as the NFWF.

chapter ten

GLOBAL WARMING

> *Global warming is an outright invention. It is*
> *absolutely unproven, and in my view it is a*
> *lie ... that will cost billions of dollars*
> *annually ... There is no danger to the ozone*
> *layer from the CFCs, nor is there any kind of*
> *danger from carbon dioxide, no greenhouse effect,*
> *nor any risk of any kind of global warming. It is, to*
> *me, a pure falsehood.*
>
> Haroun Tazieff (as quoted by Ray 1993)

The connection of global warming with terrorism and Reds may not be immediately obvious to the reader, but the author believes that further consideration will justify his regarding of global warming as a crusade which is very attractive to people who were comfortable under the Red banner in its glory days, a cause which allows activists to fight and kill for the whole earth, while other, wiser, persons benefit enormously from their actions.

Is Global Warming Bad, Good, or Neutral?

Is the earth getting colder? Is it getting warmer? Will all of us soon be charred like a buffalo wing at a Texas barbecue? Would it be a tremendous disaster if the climate at International Falls MN, in a thousand years or so became similar to that presently affecting Miami Beach? Would a 2°F rise in temperature drive all the senior citizens out of Ft. Lauderdale — and back to Brooklyn? Though most of them seldom leave their air conditioned rooms even now. Do we find the Eskimos/Inuits in the forefront of complainers about global warming? Would all the tanning salons be put out of business — and if so, who cares?

Is it *immediately* necessary to make drastic changes costing in the trillion dollar range (just to begin with) — changes which would affect the lifestyles of everyone in the world — to offset climatic fluctuations that may not be occurring and, if they did occur, might have effects that are, on balance, beneficial? Should we work to make the earth's surface one uniform temperature everywhere, everday? Does anyone really believe this could be accomplished?

By the way, is our goal to be global cooling, or are we expected to keep the temperature finely tuned to just exactly the temperatures that existed in, say, 1900? That is, if a fractional degree of cooling is observed in a future year, do we reverse the changes we have made up to that point so that the "ideal" climate — which existed everywhere just before the internal combustion engine was invented — can be maintained? How do we do this? Do we start the engines in a million autos in each state and run them day and night until a warming trend is observed?

The Kyoto Accord

This agreement-in-waiting, or pending accord, or botched treaty, has served as a rallying point for the more radical global warming activists, including such scientific luminaries as Christie Todd Whitman, as of this writing head of the Environmental Protection Agency.

According to published summaries of this document, as analyzed by supposedly objective scientists, if all proposed signatories to the treaty abided by its provisions, the climate would be less than 1°F cooler a hundred years from the treaty's implementation than it would be if current practices remained in effect. President Bush has, said, "The Kyoto treaty would severely damage the US economy, and I don't accept that" (Anon. 2002B). Or, the game wouldn't be worth the candle, and there's a high degree of probability we don't know the rules of the game.

The publicity machines of the left wing radical groups brought out their deep thinkers to add validity to the global warming claim. For example, "Such intellectual luminaries as Bianca Jagger and Robert Redford have weighed in recently with their thoughts that President Bush is playing 'Russian roulette' with the planet (Bianca) because he 'has not understood that we live in a global village' (Redford). On Tuesday a professor even suggested that if Mr. Bush refuses to ratify Kyoto, environment 'victim' nations like, say, Bangladesh, could sue the US for billions of dollars" (Anon. 2001H).

The Postulated Causes of the Postulated Warming

Several factions have offered different views of the causes of global warming, but the politically correct reason is "man and all his works." In order to give the cause and effect scenario a bit more stringency, most of the most prominent "experts" have gone a step further, and proclaimed the establishment's official "usual suspect." The choice was, "Greenhouse gases."

It has been characteristic of those "scientists" and "activists" clamoring for action to solve global warming, that they fix their attention on some small factor that might or might not participate to some extent in the modification of climate in some part of the world and select data, or, even worse, design computer models, that ignore an entire universe of other factors. Some of the ideas that have had, or do have, boosters who have been sure they knew the answers include: the ozone layer over Antarctica and greenhouse gases.

Greenhouse gases — Gases such as water vapor, methane, carbon dioxide, and ozone are normal atmospheric components that have been classified as "greenhouse gases." Some marketing genius originated this term to create uneasiness and fear in the minds of gullible observers. It is a catch phrase of indeterminate meaning. Its main application, at least in the popular media and in certain purportedly scientific publications, has been to carbon dioxide.

We are told that carbon dioxide is making the earth warmer because it tends to entrap solar radiation which would otherwise be reflected back into space. Consequently, we should stop burning fossil fuels, stop fermentation operations (no more beer, wine, or other alcoholic beverages, and no bakery fermentations), and stop other operations which yield carbon dioxide — exhaling is very bad, we must stop it at once, but don't worry, it's OK to inhale.

The strong emphasis in press releases and in many so-called scientific studies has been on carbon dioxide *from industrial and vehicular sources* as the cause of global warming. In point of fact, there are other gases which could have a much more potent effect on climate than carbon dioxide. Water is one of them, methane is another.

Only four percent of all carbon dioxide emissions, the (or one of the) major causes of global warming according to some experts, are man-made, the other 96% being more or less uncontrollable. Solar activity (as manifested by sunspots) has closely tracked global temperatures for more than 200 years. Temperature readings by instruments mounted on satellites and weather balloons have shown almost no increase in global temperatures over the past 20 years, contrary to the predictions of computer models (Lee 2001, and others).

How it all came about — During the International Geophysical Year (1957-1958), a carbon dioxide monitoring station was put in place at the top of Mauna Loa in Hawaii. The original justification for the location, and in fact for the whole project, is not entirely clear to this writer, but the providing of employment for additional bureaucrats may have been a factor.

Data that was accumulated over the following decades confirmed that the level of carbon dioxide in the atmosphere was rising at a "significant" rate. This finding was said to negate the previously held notion that oceans would buffer atmospheric carbon dioxide. The new findings led to the conclusion, or assumption, that large bodies of water could release more carbon dioxide than they absorbed, evidently as a result of the life processes of the plants and animals living in the seas. Gas issuing from vents of the volcanic type on the ocean floor might also be a factor.

The highly publicized discovery of fluctuations in the dimensions of the ozone "hole" over the Antarctic a few years later provided another talking point for persons who wanted to intensify the populace's concern about changes to the Earth's atmosphere that were being caused by human activity. No plausible cause and effect relationship of ozone hole dimensions and climatic changes has ever been shown. There may or may not be concurrent changes in atmospheric carbon dioxide concentrations and climate (and other data), but this does not confirm a close link between these two sets of data.

By 1988, the UN was ready to profit further from the scare, so the World Meteorological Society established the Intergovernmental Panel on Climate Change and charged it with assessing the current state of knowledge regarding global warming. This panel gave employment, grants, and cachet to dozens, if not hundreds, of bureaucrats and academics — which is certainly one of the deleterious effects of climate change.

The IPCC's report came out in 1990, and it stated that human activity was leading to an increase in greenhouse gases in the atmosphere and was, consequently, causing the earth to warm. The report further stated that unless industrial and commercial emissions were limited and/or reduced, the planet would suffer the consequences. In 1995, the IPCC's second report confirmed their original conclusion.

Oceans and carbon dioxide — According to Fenchel (2001) and Kolber et al. (2001), "Oceans are thought to act as carbon sinks: Atmospheric carbon dioxide is assimilated during photosynthesis by plankton in the ocean and is converted to organic carbon, which then enters the food chain. Twenty-five years ago the flow of carbon through organisms in the open ocean appeared simple: Algae 'fix' carbon dioxide during photosynthesis and are eaten by zooplankton, which in turn serve as food for fish. Since then, however, the simple diagrams of plankton food chains in ecology textbooks have had to be redrawn many times as new findings have added extra layers of complexity. For example, ubiquitous unicellular cyanobacteria are important producers of organic carbon. Carbon and other organic compounds dissolved in the ocean are metabolized by heterotrophic bacteria, and these bacteria are eaten by protozoa. To complicate matters further, viruses regulate bacterial populations, and photosynthesizing protozoa can also be predators.

Bureaucrats Agree

A report, produced "with unusual swiftness" by the Academy of Sciences (NAS) in Washington DC claims a strong scientific consensus regarding climate trends. The panel headed by "atmospheric scientist Ralph Cicerone of the U of CA Irvine" agreed that an accumulation of carbon dioxide and other greenhouse gases could heat the planet between 1.4° and 5.8°C in this century. The zealots say such a shift "could well have serious adverse societal and ecological impacts." Of course, more money would pour into studies conducted at all of the think tanks, including any affiliated with Cicerone, if these conclusions were accepted by the government. Not exactly an unbiased report, some neutral observers might say.

The NAS report came to much the same conclusions as a longer scientific report the UN compiled in January to guide nations considering the Kyoto accord. A comparison would doubtless show the wording and "data" (if any) in the quickly produced latest report were very similar to those in the earlier paper.

The US and UN reports also concluded that human activity "very likely" has caused the increase in global temperatures since 1900 (that increase is estimated now at 0.6°C). Both of the reports acknowledge that uncertainties remain concerning the role of human-generated gas emissions because of lack of knowledge about natural climate variations.

President Bush said data were insufficient to justify sweeping revisions in the way we live and vast expenditures on questionable technology. "Environmentalists saw little substance in the President's proposal. 'Where is the actual cut in pollution,' asks Kalee Kreider, global warming campaign director of the National Environmental Trust." Kalee is not about to give contributors to the NET a chance to cool down.

Other "Greenhouse" Factors

As explained in the preceding text, carbon dioxide has been assigned the role of "usual suspect" because it fits in with the Greenies' desire to cut back on travel, production of goods, etc. There are, however, other possible "villains."

Water — Theoretically, water vapor should be far more potent than carbon dioxide in causing the retention of heat from solar radiation. This is generally accepted. But, the global warming scaremongers have no interest in emphasizing the connection of water vapor and climate changes because they can see no way of profiting from that relationship. Instead, they have developed the concept of "climate forcing" by water vapor, which seems to mean that water in the atmosphere can act as a magnifier of the effect of carbon dioxide, but does not itself have an effect on warming, or at least not an effect that can be modified by any manipulation by humans.

Incidentally, hypothesized changes in atmospheric water vapor, caused by various unknown factors and not supported by *any* data, are often blamed for failures of computer modeling to explain past climate changes which do not seem to be related to any known differences in carbon dioxide concentrations.

Del Genio (2002) discussed some of the problems involved in calculating the effect of atmospheric water vapor on global temperature changes. He says, "The direct warming caused by greenhouse gas emissions is modest, but positive feedbacks in the climate system *may* [emphasis supplied] amplify the effect . . . Water vapor should almost double the sensitivity of climate to greenhouse gas increases. However, doubts about the sign [he doesn't know whether it is positive or negative!] and magnitude of the effect persist because of coarse model resolution and limited understanding of cloud processes that supply and deplete water vapor . . . Water vapor responds differently to global and regional climate changes, making it difficult to separate water vapor feedback from other effects . . . The same model may thus show either decreases or increases in subtropical water vapor when subjected to different types of climate warming . . . After a major volcanic eruption, global climate may cool for several years until the aerosols settle out of the atmosphere."

Methane — Methane, a ubiquitous gas of simple structure (CH_4), is the smallest molecule in the series which includes the straight chain hydrocarbons ethane, propane, butane, etc. It is said to be 21 times more "potent" a greenhouse gas than carbon dioxide. It is found in natural gas and has been emitted from the earth's surface in large quantities since the world assumed its present form, thus being "natural" in every sense of the word. It is also emitted from the intestinal tracts of ruminants, and probably of other animals. Methane has assumed an importance in the demonology of conservationists that is only slightly lower than that of carbon dioxide.

Part of this emphasis has resulted from the recognition that a considerable part of atmospheric methane is emitted from the digestive system of ruminant animals such as cows. The gas is generated by methanogenic bacteria (organisms ordinarily present in the animals' rumen) which act on partially digested plant materials. Since these organisms are present in all healthy adult ruminants, it would appear their functions are integrated into the animals' metabolism, otherwise evolutionary pressures would have driven them out of existence. Getting rid of ruminant-derived methane thus would seem to require getting rid of ruminants, not a happy thought for the meat-eaters and milk drinkers on the planet — and probably not in accord with the thinking of zoophilists in general.

Other Possible Causes of Climate Changes

Extreme climate changes, as seen during the ice ages and in past millenia-long warming trends, must have been due to factors which could not possibly be related to the activities of humans. This has always created a problem for computer modeling promoters, a problem which they have treated, usually, by simply ignoring it. Some braver, or more audacious, modelers stick a few more variables in their formulas and come up with equations which give answers of a reliability similar to that which could be obtained from a Ouija board.

The inorganic materials forming the core of the earth are at high temperatures, and the materials (perhaps a mixture of metals) near the center are thought to be molten. It is an easily demonstrable fact that, in deep bore holes and mines the temperature at the bottom is higher than at the surface immediately above the hole. It is also known that magma, molten rock, is emitted from deep natural holes (clefts in the sea bottom and volcanoes). Hot springs of water are well known features in many parts of the world. If there were but a small fraction of an increase in amount of hot material coming to the surface (or to the bottom of the sea) from deep layers of the earth, we could expect an effect on the surface temperature that would exceed anything predictable from the carbon dioxide effect. Generally, the variations in such factors, however they occur, have not been considered in climate predictions, and, indeed, it would seem that geoscience is not capable of taking them into account in a quantitative manner.

Dziak and Johnson (2002), wrote, "A swarm of micoearthquakes on the East Pacific Rise [a sea-floor structure] increased fluid temperature by 7°C at a hydrothermal vent located directly above the swarm — but only after a delay of 4 days. Vertical cracks propagated into a previously isolated high temperature region of lower crust, and it took days to transfer this heat upward to the seafloor."

Volcanic eruptions can have a significant cooling effect over rather long periods. This phenomenon, which is due to the sun screening effect of the microscopic dust emitted from the crater, is well known. It is unpredictable, and has been largely ignored (at least as a quantitative factor) by computer modelers.

Combatting the Scare Tactics

"Alaska's coastal permafrost is eroding," says the headline on an article in Science News of June 16, 2001, but we learn that, in fact, "recent losses fall within the normal variation seen along this coastline in the past. More analysis would be needed before anyone culd pin the apparent surge in erosion on factors associated with global warming."

Hoffheiser (2001) points out that "Famous entertainers, major national media sources and Pulitzer Prize winning columnists tell us that human activity is causing a dangerous global climate change. They say that computer models can accurately predict the climate 50-100 years from now. On June 5, Tropical Storm Allison suddenly began dropping heavy rain in the Houston area. Sophisticated computer models failed to give even an eight-hour warning.

"How can these world-wide 50-100 year models be more accurate than those used to make short-term weather predictions in a small area of the Gulf of Mexico? Thirty years ago, other 'experts' theorized that continued combustion of fossil fuels would cause global cooling due to a buildup of greenhouse gases in the atmosphere. They claimed that, within 20-30 years we would expect a cooler climate that led to shorter growing seasons, resulting in world-wide famine. But a funny thing happened on the way to world-wide disaster. Their computer models weren't accurate, and we have yet to have a world-wide famine caused by global cooling.

"The National Research Council and the rest of the 'global warming crowd' are promoting a treaty that is nothing more than a recipe for global socialism."

Role of the Sun in Global Warming — The editor for an article by Rind (2002) asks, "Is the sun the controller of climate changes, or only the instigator of changes that are mostly forced by the system feedbacks, or simply a convenient scapegoat for climate variations lacking any other obvious cause?"

It is quite amazing that so few of the publications that dwell at great length on the possibility (many say, "certainty") of global warming give any attention at all to fluctuations in the sun's radiation as a source of the supposed rise in temperature. The sun is certainly the source of nearly all the energy that is supposed to cause alterations in surface temperatures. It is also known, without question, that variations in the sun's radiation do occur, the result, in part, of fluctuations in sunspot number and size. Unfortunately, the sun's radiation has been measured accurately by satellite for only about 20 years.

Rind (2002) pointed out some other long term trends affecting earth surface temperatures: orbital variations, icesheet instabilities, and lithosphere deformation.

Confounding Factors

In the following text, the author gives a summary of some of the confounding factors discussed elsewhere:

• Volcanic emissions — all of them, not just those resulting from violent eruptions.

• Forest fires — obviously, these inject massive amounts of carbon dioxide and particulates into the atmosphere. No one knows how much, or what effect these particulates have on global temperatures.

• Shifts in air currents, affecting the moisture content of the atmosphere, which is much more effective than carbon dioxide in affecting net solar input to ground level.

• Ocean currents — such as El Niño.

• Variation in energy emitted from the sun — the sun-spot factor and other, perhaps as yet unknown, forces modifying radiant energy.

• Questions about reliability of data, especially comparability of all data at one given time with all data at another given time, considering the nature of the sensing stations and the quality and motivations of persons operating the stations.

• Lack of justification, or validity, of computer modeling programs, and failure to disclose all factors used when designing the programs.

In an article in Environmental Science and Technology (p. 190a, issue of May 1, 2001), workers at the Massachusetts Institute of Technology and NASA-Goddard Space Flight Center suggest that high-level cirrus clouds over the tropical Pacific Ocean decrease when sea-surface temperatures increase. This natural vent provides a heat release mechanism so strong that it could significantly diminish global warming. These workers compared detailed daily observations of cloud cover from Japan's GMS-5 Geostationary Meteorological Satellite with sea-surface temperature data from the US National Weather Service's National Centers for Environmental Prediction from January 1998 to August 1999. The data revealed fewer cirrus clouds were produced over warmer ocean regions. The authors proposed that higher sea-surface temperatures directly cause the decline in cirrus clouds by changing the dynamics of cloud formation and rainfall.

It's Necessary to Do Something Now!

It is characteristic of global-warming alarmists that they insist it is necessary to do something *immediately*. Often, the "something" involves spending billions of dollars more for research. It may also involve major changes in the lifestyles of Americans and the stalling of industrialization in the less developed nations. The tone is often shrill, the statements dogmatic, and the standards obscure.

For example, we refer to an article by Alverson and eight co-authors (Alverson et al. 2001), in which we find "A major obstacle to producing reliable predictions of climate change and its impacts is a lack of data on time scales longer than the short instrumental record.

Recently initiated climate observation programs will need to be continuously operated for at least 50 years before they begin to provide information that is relevant to this problem. In contrast, natural archives of past climate variability can provide relevant information now. Unfortunately, some of the most valuable paleoclimate archives are being rapidly destroyed, largely as a result of human influences. *We cannot afford such an irreversible loss* [emphasis supplied]. The Past Global Changes (PAGES) program of the International Geosphere-Biosphere Programme therefore calls for scientists, funding agencies, and institutional partners to *establish immediately* [emphasis added] a coordinated international Global Paleoclimate Observing System (GPOS) to complement the Global Climate, Terrestrial, and Ocean Observing Systems . . . that focus on contemporary observations.

"An example of the loss of paleoarchives is the rapid retreat of alpine glaciers in the tropics and temperate latitudes. Ice cores from such glaciers have been used to reconstruct temperature, precipitation, and atmospheric dust levels, and to provide records of changes in the strength of the Asian monsoon and El Niño-Southern Oscillation . . . the total area of the summit glacier on Mt. Kilimanjaro decreased by 82% between 1912 and 2000. Soon, the only information left from the Kilimanjaro ice will be what is contained in the cores extracted last year and stored in freezers at Ohio State University. The situation on Kilimanjaro is not unique. Tropical warming is causing the rapid retreat of ice caps and glaciers at high elevations in the tropics and subtropics around the world.

"A second example of paleoarchives that are being lost is the widespread damage to tropical corals. Measurements in corals have been successfully used to reconstruct sea surface temperature, salinity, and the surface circulation of the tropical oceans for the past several hundred years, and for isolated windows in the more distant past [however, what has not been reconstructed, and cannot be reconstructed, are the possible changes in the corals' metabolic processes which may have influenced their residues in ways that served to adapt the living cells to different climatic conditions].

"Another biological source of paleoclimate records are tree rings, which have the potential to yield information on many aspects of tropical climate, from the Asian monsoon and El Niño to the factors controlling the storage of carbon in tropical forests.

Unintended Consequences

From another grant-funded think tank, *Resources for the Future* (Toman 2001), we receive the opinion, "It is true that the magnitude of benefits from reducing CO_2 and other greenhouse gases over time is uncertain. But recent reports by the National Academy of Sciences and the Intergovernmental Panel on Climate Change indicate, notwithstanding political spin, that this is indeed a problem requiring attention. Uncertainty about how much to control carbon dioxide can be handled by initially setting a modest emission reduction goal, and then tightening or loosening the targets over time. Since the controls would be flexible, the possibility of error is no reason to proceed." Except that a wrong decision can result in the waste of trillions of dollars *and the possibility of actually exacerbating the problem or creating problems which have not even been thought of by the constructors or the plan.*

Some obvious problems are: (1) the negative effects of a poorly based and poorly motivated set of regulations cannot be predicted with a satisfactory degree of certainty, (2) once in place, controls of this sort are almost never removed and never ameliorated, but often intensified, (3) any moves of this sort are always accompanied by the formation of government departments, committees, panels, and non-profits, and other sets of parasites, that are themselves a drag on the economy and which are virtually impossible to inactivate, and (4) the "temporary and mild" levels of control become the "non-negotiable" base for further tightening.

Computer Modeling

If a skeptic casts doubt on the reality of global warming, the latter being defined somewhat variously, but surely indicating a continuous increase in annual mean temperatures throughout the world for the last hundred years or so (and preferably much longer), the advocates of immediate action leap to the attack, with qualitative and suppositive data. They appeal especially to "computer modeling," the latter being a "proof" that has been somewhat discredited in recent years. For example, see the comments of Trenberth (2001), who says, "Unfortunately, in the NRC Report [which had cautioned about placing unfounded faith on fluctuating and uncertain data] two aspects of natural climate variability are conflated. First, there is natural variability that is tied to external forcings, such as variations in the Sun, volcanoes, and the orbital variations of Earth around the Sun. The latter is the driving force for the major ice ages and interglacial periods. Second, there is the natural variability that is internal to the climate system, arising, for instance, from interactions between the atmosphere and ocean, such as El Niño. This internal variability occurs even in an unchanging climate.

"In the NRC report and in its summary, natural variability is said to be 'quite large,' but both kinds of variability are treated as if they are internal. Glacial to interglacial swings are discussed without mention of the known causes. Several lines of evidence, from the instrumental and paleoclimate records and from climate models, strongly suggest that the recent increase in global mean temperature is *beyond that possible from internal processes and thus must be caused by an increase in heating.* [emphasis supplied] This reasoning also puts limits on how large aerosol cooling could be. Further, known causes such as changes in the sun and volcanic activity in the past 50 years *have, if anything, led to cooling in this interval,* leaving only the human-caused increase in greenhouse gases as the culprit. This reasoning has also been quantitatively confirmed *with climate models.*

"A consequence of mistreatment of natural climate variability in the NRC report is that the caveats are overstated" [based on what evidence?]. Natural climate variability is dealt with much more thoroughly in the recent Intergovernmental Panel on Climate Change (IPPC) assessment, which was developed over about 3 years (versus one month for the NRC report) [the longer it takes, the more reliable it is, unless it is contrary to the party line]. The summary from the IPCC is that '[t]here is new and stronger evidence that most of the warming observed over the last 50 years is attributable to human activities.' " But only a small number of alternative causes have been considered.

More on volcano emissions — Volcanic eruptions have a significant effect on the temperature and rainfall in the months (or even years) following the occurrence. This is due mainly to the large amount of aerosols ejected high into the atmosphere. The explosion of Krakatoa in 1883 affected weather all over the world for many months, leading to the so-called "year without a summer." It is not at all clear that the data used by researchers in this field are corrected for such events. If not, the overall climate for the 1880-1890 decade would tend to show a much cooler earth at that time, and much more global warming in subsequent decades than resulted from any steady trend in the upward direction.

More on this subject can be found in the Soden et al. (2002) article on the effects of the eruption of Mount Pinatubo in 1991 on global *cooling*. As stated by these scientists, "Water vapor plays a key role in regulating Earth's climate. It is the dominant greenhouse gas and provides the largest known feedback mechanism for amplifying climate change. Because the equilibrium vapor pressure of water increases rapidly with temperature, it is generally believed that the concentration of water vapor will rise as the atmosphere warms. If so, the added radiative absorption from water vapor will act to further amplify the initial warming. Current climate models suggest that this provides an important positive feedback, roughly doubling the sensitivity of the surface temperature to an increase in anthropogenic greenhouse gases. *If the actual feedback by water vapor is substantially weaker than predicted by current models, both the magnitude of warming and range of uncertainty resulting from a doubling of carbon dioxide would be substantially diminished.*"

These writers claim the difficulty in verifying [computer generated] climate models stems partly from the lack of observed climate variations that can provide quantitative tests of the feedbacks in question.

Other failures of computer modeling — A recent report prepared by the National Research Council (Windham 2001) supported findings by outside agencies that the computer models used by the EPA to estimate the effectiveness of vehicle emissions inspection and maintenance programs were inaccurate. Declines in overall pollution due to these programs were said to be less than half what the models projected. Ralph Cicerone, chancellor at the U of CA-Irvine, conducted the survey over a period of two years, using a team of 12 people, most of them college educators. Despite the many deficiencies of the system, Wyndham suggested it shouldn't be drastically changed or dropped. We can understand this — after all, it is a government program, so it will never be dropped if other bureaucrats have a say in the matter.

Establishing the Basis for a Decision

The first questions we should answer before we even consider making *any* changes in our way of life in attempts to ameliorate global warming are:

1. Is there any solid evidence that the earth, *as a whole*, is becoming warmer on a year to year basis? Obtain answers to the following questions.

1.1. Are there *objective*, quantitative data showing there has been a year-to-year warming trend over the whole earth's surface during, say, the past 100 years? And, if so:

1.2. Is there any logical theory, or hypothesis, justifying the extrapolation of the verified warming trend into the future?

1.3. How far into the future are we justified in extrapolating trends according to the hypothesis or theory?

2. What are the natural long term balancing or counteracting effects (causes of cooling) that may come into operation during the next 50 or so years? There have been ice ages in the past — when does the next one begin?

3. If there is a high degree of certainty the earth will become warmer, according to the extrapolation suggested in point 1.3 as offset by the answer to 2., would that be a bad thing, a good thing, or neutral insofar as the human species *as a whole* is concerned?

4. If the earth is becoming warmer, and it is decided this is bad for the human species, *as a whole*, is it within our power to change the trend? Use the following steps.

4.1. What are the scientifically sound methods for halting a warming trend? Arrange these trends in order of their likelihood of success.

    4.2. Estimate the cost, per degree, per year, of decelerating the warming trend using each of the methods.

    5. Are we willing to pay the price required by *any* of these agendas?

    It is most important to have the proofs and conclusions reached by following the above protocol examined thoroughly by persons with enough scientific ability to judge the validity and pertinency of the evidence (both published and unpublished) on hand. These judges should be totally separated from any possible rewards accruing from the emplacement of programs that could yield direct or indirect benefits to them: benefits either of money in terms of grants, salaries, profits, or capital gains, or of position (i.e., academic or electoral offices). Furthermore, they should be persons having no direct connection with any previous investigations of the problem. Retired physical scientists and statistical experts might be suitable referees. Members of foundations, societies, and the educational establishment should be precluded from having any part in the investigations.

    And, operating separately from, and independently of, all of the other investigators engaged in this project there should be a panel of theoretical and practical statisticians who will evaluate the data in terms of its statistical significance so this type of guidance will be available to the persons who will have to make the final decisions and write the report. Such a filter is needed because, as the present writer has observed, many reports and conclusions being published and relied upon today are based on (1) data which are incomplete, fragmentary, and poorly documented, and (2) computer modeling projections which depend upon programs that have been insufficiently described and validated, and will therefore yield numbers which no amount of mathematical massaging can make into reliable data.

Ways to Decrease Global Warming

    The reds always wish to blame the world's troubles on human beings, and if they can't find a deleterious change that fits their needs, they are willing to make one up. Then, they sound the alarm, and suggest ways to alleviate the problem, all of which involve some restrictions on human activities, and usually on the numbers of humans. The net effect is to make is to make a reduction in the number of people seem a highly desirable goal. Global warming is such a cause.

Renewable fuels — The "Renewable Fuels" pressure groups seek to have petroleum, natural gas, and coal phased out in favor of fuel made from plant products such as corn. This is, in the author's opinion, a scheme based entirely on a desire to increase the prices of certain plant crops, and it is without any technical or economic merit at all. One of the basic reasons is that the energy consumed in preparing land for planting, cultivating the crops, harvesting the crops, making a usable fuel from the crops, and disposing of the worthless residue (which will be enormous) from the harvesting and processing operations will totally swamp the energy which can be obtained from the finished products.

A second reason is, there is not sufficient land of suitable quality available to grow enough plants for a quantity of fuel that can replace any significant amount of petroleum. Virtually all the best land for growing food plants is presently being used for that purpose, and expanding the arable land base (by clearing forests, introducing irrigation, etc.) would result in enormous costs and drastically reduce "wilderness." Still further, the water available for the irrigation which would be required, is not available — we are very short on reliable water sources even without the water that would be used in growing the plants needed to yield the amount of starch or sugar which would be used as the raw materials for the sustainable fuels.

It is certain (the author believes) that the advocates of sustainable fuels (or, at least, the people who are paying the activists for their propagandizing efforts) know all about these limitations. This does not deter them. They want to sell the factories (thereby making money from land, land preparation, plant design and construction, etc.), operate the plants and sell subsidized fuels, until the public rebels; then they will walk away with their profits, to run another scam. This is simply a scheme to expand the ethanol-for-fuel racket many fold.

Problems with ethanol as a fuel — Many people not directly involved with either the ethanol producing industry or the petroleum industry are becoming aware of the problems created by the laws which require the addition of ethanol to gasoline which is intended to be used as a fuel for automobiles. A few critics have started to publicly denounce this practice. Some recent adverse comments are reproduced below.

Mordecai Shelef, who has a Ph.D. in fuel science, wrote, "The impeccable analysis of Prof. Pimentel was preceded by several similar studies over the past 20 years, demonstrating the negative energy balance [i.e., more energy is used in making the ethanol than can be obtained from it] of making ethanol by using mainly fossil fuels. Moreover, the largely abandoned 1980s experiment in Brazil where (a) there is much more sunshine than in the Midwest [so that theoretical yields of ethanol raw material from sugar cane should be much greater per acre], (b) the crop, sugar cane, is a better converter of solar energy to biomass than corn, and (c) the agricultural labor is much cheaper, should have served as a lesson" (Shelef 2002).

Harry S. Crowder (2002) wrote, [There is] " . . . a basic problem with corn: It is highly subject to crop failure due to drought, cold, or too much rain. It is unstable as a source for fuel. It's just a cheap political boondoggle."

A somewhat satirical viewpoint [some would say, "realistic"] is expressed by C. Fountain (2002). He writes, "Well sure, it may cost 131,000 BTUs to produce 77,000 BTUs of ethanol, but what's that when it comes to garnering Iowa primary votes? The most enjoyable aspect of this political boondoggle (for cynics) is that the stuff is completely worthless for cleaning up our air. Some extra oxygen is needed in gasoline to reduce the production of carbon monoxide. Ethanol served as just such an 'oxygenator' back when cars had carburetors, but that was long ago, before fuel injection systems, which automatically provide the necessary oxygen, became standard equipment. Eric Stork, head of the EPA's Mobile Source Air Pollution Control Program from 1970 to 1978, once said that, 'the idea of oxygenating gas to reduce carbon monoxide was brilliant 30 years ago. But in cars built in 1983 and later, oxygenates are obsolete and pointless.' "

Reduction in methane production by ruminants — Reese (2001) reported on experiments conducted in Australia. "By early June [of 2001], Australian farmers had signed up more than 635,000 sheep and 410,000 cattle to take part in a methane vaccine program proposed by CSIRO Livestock Industries, a division of Australia's national science agency, the Commonwealth Scientific and Industrial Research Organization. The idea is to reduce the animals' emissions of methane, a greenhouse gas, and thus slow global warming. Rob Kelly of CSIRO Livestock Industries says, 'Our goal is to have 1 million cattle and 2 million sheep available for vaccination every year from around 2005 to 2012.' The methane vaccine 'discourages' methanogenic ... organisms in the animals' rumen that produce methane by breaking down feed. As a greenhouse gas, methane is around 21 times more potent than carbon dioxide. Sheep and cattle produce about 14% of Australia's total greenhouse emissions, measured in CO_2 equivalents. Current experimental results [in sheep] suggest that the commercial vaccine will reduce methane emissions by about 20% in those animals, the greenhouse equivalent of about 300,000 metric tons of carbon dioxide annually. Reduction of methane from feed leaves more nutrients for the animal, so the vaccine also is expected to yield modest gains in animals' liveweight and, in sheep, wool production. Summing up, CSIRO anticipates that the methane vaccine program will offer the following benefits:

• Vaccine at minimal cost or free for some or all participants in the program.

• Productivity gains.

• Greenhouse gas abatement.

• Possibility of labeling/marketing/trading sheep and cattle as environmentally friendly and sustainable enterprises."

Have experiments been conducted to determine the long term effect on animal survival and on efficiency of feed utilization by animals which have been treated with these vaccines? If so, the results do not seem to have been published.

The proponents of this program claim that reducing or eliminating the bacteria will leave more of the feed for the animals' use, that is, more nutrients will be absorbed from the gut by the animals if the bacteria's demands are not met. No experimental results showing this benefit were cited in the references consulted by this author. If the material normally used up by the bacteria passes through the animal's gut and is deposited in the soil, to be further processed by soil organisms, then carbon dioxide (or even methane) may be generated from it. In such a case, would the vaccine result in a net reduction in greenhouse emissions?

We can be sure that the enthusiasts who are promoting this curious experiment have been benefited in some way by the manufacturers of the vaccine and/or by the owners of patents on the process of making or using the vaccine. Perhaps the benefit was not as straightforward as a *cash* payment (although that must be considered as a possibility), but the *publicity* gained by the bureaucrats' advocacy of a point dear to the econuts, i.e., reduction of global warming.

Oxygenates in Gasoline

One of the truly hare-brained schemes evolved by bureaucrats and their buddies in academia was the addition of various substances to gasoline so the fuel would "burn more cleanly." The 1990 Clear Air Act requires 2% oxygen by weight in gasoline in regions where pollution exceeds certain limits. As a matter of fact, there are only two substances that are produced in sufficient quantities to meet the requirements. These are methyl-*tert*-butyl ether ("MTBE"), which is produced from petroleum and ethanol (ethyl alcohol). After these materials were approved — to the great financial benefit of the producers of MTBE — it was found that MTBE had leaked out of underground gas storage tanks and was polluting the water, giving the ground water a bad taste and very possibly causing serious health problems.

There is now a demand for phasing out MTBE and requiring ethanol (only) in gas at the 2% level. This alternative is highly pleasing to the National Corn Growers Association and to the producers of industrial grade alcohol, who see demand for their product increasing enormously and, since it is a monopoly situation, generating vast profits to the producers. Ethanol is, even now, more expensive than MTBE. In addition, gasohol (a highly unpopular fuel containing 10% ethanol) receives a 5.3 cent per gallon exemption from the 18.4% excise tax on gasoline for cars. This exemption *isn't available to gasolines containing synthetic ethanol made by non-fermentation means.* And, it amounts to a 53 cent per gallon of ethanol, pure gravy to the producers of ethyl alcohol from grain. As a result, it is reported that dozens of proposed new fermentation alcohol plants will be constructed. Archer-Daniels-Midland, or ADM, accounts for about 50% of US production, and it expects to produce 900 million gpy in 2001.

The plain fact is that addition of MTBE or ethanol to gasoline has never been proven to significantly reduce air pollution or to alleviate other environmental problems.

Furthermore, federal investigators suspect the manufacturers of fuel ethanol may have been inadvertently generating pollutants which can have, or are having, serious effects on the environment. Fialka (2002) reported, " Federal regulators are investigating emissions produced by the nation's ethanol industry, concerned that the work of turning corn and other agricultural materials into fuel may be violating the Clean Air Act. The EPA inquiry, disclosed in a letter sent to ethanol producers last month, comes as lawmakers from farm states are pushing a 'renewable fuels' mandate in an energy bill, passed by the Senate, that would triple the size of the rapidly growing industry . . . EPA's regional administrator . . . said an agency test showed that an ethanol plant in the St. Paul MN area was producing volatile organic compounds, which can cause urban smog and carbon monoxide. These, in turn, can lead to heart disease in very high concentrations. He called them 'additional emissions that weren't anticipated' in prior tests . . . Mr. Shaw said the industry was surprised by the EPA test, which was different from those used to measure emissions from ethanol plants . . . [the test] showed that the emissions from the ethanol plant were coming from a drying process that turns the mash, or residue of corn and other materials that have been used to produce the ethanol, into cattle and chicken feed."

The other anti-smog additive for gasoline, methyl tertiary butyl ether (MTBE), is regarded by some gasoline refiners as a problem they want nothing to do with. It is possible they see environmental damage occurring from its use and they do not want to take the chance of being held liable. The refiner, BP PLC, announced in 2002 that it intends to switch (in 2003) to ethanol, and Chevron Texaco says it will switch to ethanol as soon as possible. Transportation problems have arisen, however, since there is only one commercial pipeline for carrying gasoline to California and the operator says it cannot switch to the ethanol-added product by year's end (Herrick 2002).

Collateral deaths — A major auto producer released a study asserting that federal regulations mandating greater fuel efficiency for automobiles would lead to more highway deaths (Ball 2001). The basic contention, that making vehicles lighter makes them more dangerous, is not a new idea. But the new report showed that even with new safety devices such as driver-side air bags, the lighter cars might lead to an additional 400 deaths per year — also 1,000 to 2,000 more injuries. Of course, the advocates of smaller cars say that weight doesn't make much difference, one of them making the perfectly asinine statement that putting a 100-lb bag of sand in a car wouldn't make it safer.

The Plot Begins to Unravel

As more and more solid data accumulates negating the theory that there is a worldwide warming trend, and we begin to explore the possibility that warming would have many beneficial effects, establishment publicists start to bring in data, theories, and interpretations that are even more weakly related to the basic hypothesis than those previously exhibited. Evidence hastily assembled from sources of questionable dependability, often consisting merely of a rehash of previously discredited studies, is slapped down before the naive audience, with a "see, I told you so" attitude that is supposed to quell those weak-willed viewers who may have been wavering in their commitment to the revealed truth.

Beautifully colored graphs, photos of expiring dolphins and cadaverous wolves, and attestations by Chomsky, Madonna, and similar celebrities, are publicized without question by the servile press. International eco-conferences are held in permissive environments for those who are pining for fun and games at the taxpayers' expense. White-blue-green-buff papers and petitions are signed by academics roused from their post-semestrial stupor, and the usual suspects in the political racket are called upon to kiss it one more time.

Sadly, one cannot say with certainty that truth will prevail.

Advantages of Global Warming

It is unfortunate that global warming is not a reality. Gradual increases in the average temperatures on the earth's surface would provide more and better places for people to live and grow food crops. There are billions of acres of land which are totally unsuited for growing any kind of plant crop because of low temperatures, but there is no place on earth which is too hot for all kinds of plant crops (assuming an adequate supply of moisture is available during the growing season).

A rising global temperature would open vast tracts for growing crops, and there is no place on earth where surface temperatures would become too high for all food crops under any scenario the doomsday predictors have dared to advance. In North America alone, every few degrees of average temperature increase would enable the planting of more grain crops, sugar beets, and the like, and much of the released acreage would be in regions where there are large supplies of surface and sub-surface water. The practice of double-cropping — two plantings a year — would become possible in much larger areas.

A whole continent (Antarctica) is at present closed to any kind of plant cultivation because of low temperatures. A sufficient increase in global temperatures could allow the populating and cultivating of the continent. This alternative is undoubtedly far in the future, even if we accept the worst-case scenarios of the doomsday prophets. But, we can readily imagine the opening of millions of acres in Siberia, Scandinavia, Mongolia, Alaska, Canada, etc., if the summers became warmer and longer, and the winters somewhat less harsh. Of course, these beneficial effects are not likely to come about in our lifetimes, but we certainly want to take the long view, as all of the scaremongers tell us.

Mountains and high plains in the temperate zones would also become more adaptable to various kinds of agricultural pursuits, and the types of products that could be grown in regions that now have a temperate clime would increase. Crop failures due to untimely freezes would be less likely.

If temperatures of ocean water increase, we would expect to see a more rapid proliferation of plankton, and this should be followed by increases in every kind of sea animal used as food by man.

In short, the best thing that could happen to the earth would be to have a gradual warming trend lasting over a couple of centuries.

section four
TERRORISTIC ZOOPHILISM

The place that people find for non-human animals within their individual image of the universe is extremely varied. The impression one gets from reading a screed by a convinced zoophilist is that mankind is an interloper on the planet and can be welcomed (or, perhaps, barely tolerated) here only as long as its representatives acknowledge their inferiority to every other species and take every possible measure to avoid offending or even discommoding all other living creatures.

The author suggests that four broad categories (admittedly, with diffuse boundaries) include all, or almost all, of the possible attitudes humans have with regard to animal welfare. These are:

(1) The category the author calls *sauve qui peut*, which can be translated as "Save himself who can" or "Everyone must look out for himself." It is intended to mean that persons in this group believe animals are entitled to the protection and advantages they can provide for themselves, and nothing more.

(2) The animal welfare segment of the population, very likely including the majority of US citizens. This consists of persons who believe that treatment of animals with random cruelty is ethically undesirable. The ASPCA would be regarded, rightly or wrongly, by most people in this group as the arbiter of correctness in regard to animal treatment.

(3) The animal liberation groups, members of which believe, or pretend to believe, that every living creature (or, perhaps, every animal capable of feeling pain) should have rights equal in all significant respects to those expected by every human.

(4) The zoophilists, who would elevate some, or most — perhaps all — living things other than *Homo sapiens* to a special category *above* human beings. Voting rights for oysters but not for humans, etc. It would appear that only a few percent, perhaps even less than a full percentage point of the population, falls into this category. But, the group seems to be growing and it has always been very obtrusive.

In terms of increasing "compassion," this spectrum could be represented by the following simple graph:

sauve qui peut—>animal welfare—>animal liberation—>zoophilism

chapter eleven

ANIMAL LIBERATION

The ultimate expression of self-hatred and hatred of the human race which is at the base of the red activists' portfolio of "Rights" is Animal Liberation. Advocates of the most extreme form of this doctrine, a subset of humanity which includes a significant number of academics and other ne'er do wells, purport to believe that members of the species *Homo sapiens* should not only be placed on a level playing field with all other living things — i.e., all animals including, presumably, cockroaches, leeches, and cobras — but should in fact abstain from all activities which *might* cause some non-human organism discomfort or inconvenience, or which would interfere with reproductive *rights* of such species.

Most people would tend to describe persons holding such beliefs as extremely weird. But, of course, many of the originators and exponents of this ethical system do not believe any part of it — they have found a way to prosper by peddling such views, and they give no more ethical or moral weight to the effects on the human race of their activities than the gourmet gives to the feelings of the live lobster he cooks in boiling water.

It is certainly possible that the ranks of the animal liberationists may include some people who actually believe all species of animals (including humans) should have the same rights, or approximately the same rights, but the majority of the persons marching under this banner are motivated by the expectation of obtaining the kinds of rewards which motivate all reds.

Among the benefits they may expect to receive are: (1) Opportunities to express their hatred of all humanity, (2) participation in terroristic acts which exhilarate and gratify the sadistic impulses of the perpetrators, (3) receipt of economic rewards in the form of money from foundations, charitable organizations, and the public, (4) media attention, which not only provides immediate gratification but can also lay the groundwork for personal advancement, and (5) social satisfaction (increased access to music, dope, and sex).

When all is said and done, however, money is the medium.

Aspects of Speciesism

"Speciesism" is the awkward word that has been coined by certain Animal Rights promoters to describe the holding of beliefs tending to elevate the human species to a unique status in the animal kingdom. Taking actions based on such beliefs is just as wrong, in the minds of animal liberationists, as enslaving someone or practicing cannibalism. For example, if you shoot a dog that is trying to mangle your baby, or if you swat a mosquito to avoid getting malaria, you are a "speciesist." Such words allow the promoters of animal liberation to fit their program into a very profitable group of "isms" that have previously entered the marketplace: racism, sexism, lookism, anti-semitism, etc.

It is our duty to love our dumb chums — Ms. Briggs, President of the National Humane Education Society, proclaimed, "I believe we have a responsibility to these creatures to give them a decent life: food, water, a home, and respect for their lives. That's not a lot, but for millions of animals in the United States it means the difference between life and death." Presumably joining her in this all-encompassing love for our dumb chums are such non-profit groups as the American Humane Association, Defenders of Wildlife, The Humane Society of the United States, the Wildlife Management Institute, the World Society for the Protection of Animals, and the Massachusetts Society for the Prevention of Cruelty to Animals. There are undoubtedly many more organizations of this type that could be identified with a few minutes search of the Internet, but the author believes his point has been made.

Briggs had still more to say about the sad plight of our speciesist-threatened neighbors: "From dogs and cats to mice, birds, and elephants, animals are seen in all the ways they 'serve' humans: as objects of affection, education, research, and testing; as sources of food and clothing; and as contestants in sporting activities" (Briggs and Clark 1994). We need, it is said, " . . . to alter our behavior to better meet their needs and their rights . . . By pooling our resources, humane groups not only can produce more persuasive arguments for their causes, they also stand to persuade more people to the fact that animals deserve our love, our respect, and our thoughtful stewardship."

Our kindly lecturer says she learned from the Talmud, that "He who saves a life saves a world." Palestinians and other goyim were never intended to be covered by this, of course. By drawing a line from this beatitude, through the "Holocaust " to pets who "get no respect," she arrives at a need for 10 million people to adopt a dog or cat from the local animal shelter.

Projects for the future — After reading Ms. Briggs' heart-rending appeal, and learning that large amounts of money are being contributed to animal rights activists for the alleged purpose of benefiting the life styles of certain animals, an acquaintance explained to the author that fruit flies (*Drosophila melanogaster*) are the most widely used laboratory animals because of the peculiar advantages they have for genetics research, e.g., they can be kept in glass jars and fed fermenting fruit juices. In the course of the experimentation, these creatures are killed by the millions virtually every week, if not every day. Furthermore, they get very little respect.

My ingenious entrepreneur friend had developed the idea that a foundation should be established for the purpose of expressing our concern and respect for these unfortunate victims of scientific cruelty. It is highly probable this nonprofit charitable organization would garner large amounts of contributions from the rich and clueless. Not only would the usual gaggle of animal rights freaks pitch in to protest the daily holocausts, but our friendly innovator expected to elicit the interest of gay rights groups who might be attracted by the "fruit fly" cognomen.

And, on being told that the species name, *melanogaster*, meant "black belly," he saw prospects of help arriving from the NAACP and the Rainbow Coalition. That is not all, however. The flies are often fed on fermenting fruit juices, suggesting a possible appeal to Alcoholics Anonymous; and, the demeaning and disgusting practice of transferring large numbers of adult male flies into an unprotected population of virgin females, the latter with their intellects possibly clouded by unwise consumption of the fermented fruit juices, will certainly attract the attention of all feminists, not to mention the family planning enthusiasts.

Don't blame the poor little doggie — Claudia Rosett (2001) discussed the case of Diane Whipple, a San Francisco woman who had been bitten to death by a pair of dogs belonging to a neighbor. "One of the dogs, Bane, the lead aggressor, has been euthanized. But the other dog, Hera, has had an *animal rights lawyer* arguing its case and generating such headlines as this, from the San Francisco Chronicle: *Lawyer says dog in fatal mauling didn't get fair hearing.*

"Due process isn't the only constitutional right people are asserting on behalf of animals. Last month, after a shark bit off eight-year-old Jessie Arbogast's arm, a New York Times editorial sided with the shark ... The attack should be seen, opined the Times, as a chance to understand sharks and remember 'how much we have to learn about them and their waters.' *Their waters?* [Rosett's italics] The Times is not known as a defender of property rights for people. What will the paper advocate next, the right to arm bears?" Hey, Claudia, don't give those loonies any more ideas!

A Rainbow Coalition for Cats and Dogs?

Let us consider the Community Led Animal Welfare (CLAW) project operating under the direction of the International Fund for Animal Welfare, a nonprofit foundation based in Maine. "CLAW" is "dedicated to bringing basic veterinary care to the poorest of South Africa's poor, the dogs and cats of the country's townships." We learn from Block (2001) about some of the exploits of Cora Bailey, founder of CLAW, who is doing the publicity interviews in South Africa, while the executive director counts the donations in Bangor.

For about ten years, Bailey and an assistant "have been navigating the dirt roads of western Johannesburg in cars and trucks loaded with pet food, flea dip, syringes, serums and pills to stop worms, rabies and distemper. People wait for them by the hundreds in empty fields or on street corners carrying their best friends in blankets, cardboard boxes, in canvas bags and on pushcarts. Mrs. Bailey and Mr. Katywa, neither of them formally trained as veterinarians, see more than 700 animals a week . . . In the slums and shantytowns where she works, even dogs have venereal diseases. 'It's poverty and too many sexual partners,' Mrs. Bailey explains as she examines the raw underside of a small mongrel brought to her by a toothless, drunk young man. 'It's the same with their owners,' she whispers, pulling out a huge syringe and vial of doggy medicine. She knows this from personal experience. Two years ago, people living around the dump started approaching her and dropping their pants to reveal their own sexually transmitted diseases. 'It was incredible,' she recalls, 'They would take De Villiers and me around the side of the truck and say, Look, I have the same as Fluffy. Will your medicine make me better, too?' "

Bailey has never seen any signs of government attention to sexually transmitted disease since she has been working in South Africa. And, she never will.

This lady sees some of the incongruities of her role. "I know it seems crazy to care about animals in the midst of so much misery. But we have to try to create a gentler society." She believes her activities will serve as an example to the children, teaching them to show respect to people. Maybe. But more likely it will convince the kids their parents were right when they told them that all white people were crazy.

Singer's Animal Liberation

Peter Singer is an Australian-born Jew, whose book *Animal Liberation: A New Ethics for Our Treatment of Animals,* has attracted worldwide attention. In the last few years he has received much favorable publicity, several awards, and a plum job at Princeton U.

Singer unquestionably is positioned at the extreme left end of the Animal Liberation movement. For example, he indicates that some babies deserve less consideration than animals. He does not believe animals should be used in medical research, as pets (which he regards as being equivalent to human slavery), as work animals (no more sheep herding, bomb sniffing, or guiding the blind), or as exhibits in zoos and the like. They should not be used as sources of milk, wool, etc. They should not be confined (fenced, tethered, etc.), and they should have family rights (the ability to live with mates and create offspring).

He informs the reader that animals have emotions just like humans: they feel pain, fear, and other unpleasant sensations just like humans. This makes them equal to normal humans, and superior to those human beings who, for example, cannot feel pain. It is not clear to this reader whether or not he is speaking of temporary or permanent anesthesia as being a justification for euthanasia.

The following selection of direct quotations from his book is included to verify the preceding statements.

p. 19-20. He decides to put aside the religious view that humans have immortal souls while other species do not, because "Logically, however, these religious views are unsatisfactory . . . [and] comes under suspicion as a form of speciesism." Besides, he says, " . . . these doctrines are no longer as widely accepted as they once were." Unfortunately for humanity, he is correct.

But, since Singer does not accept the doctrine that humans possess souls, any appeal he makes to the reader's kindness, mercy, justice, etc., is ridiculous, and any objection to killing animals (including humans) for any reason, including amusement or the whim of a moment, cannot be based on moral or ethical grounds since these precepts are always founded on the concept that humans have special status and special responsibilities — i.e., souls and/or a mission defined by a supernatural force or being. We can see clearly from this point alone (though confirmed by many other statements) that Singer's basic goal is not an ennobling (or empowerment) of animals, but a debasement of humanity — one of the major goals of the cultural extreme left.

Singer's equating of human rights with animal rights is based, at least in part, on the concept that all animals feel pain just like (some?) humans. This is a difficult sell, but Singer is willing to plug away at the concept for many pages.

p. 18. "How bad a pain is depends on how intense it is and how long it lasts, but pains of the same intensity and duration are equally bad, whether felt by humans and animals." Prof. Singer increases our humanity, because he gives many of us a pain that is very intense and of long duration. But, how does he know or how would he measure the intensity and duration of a sensation on a non-speciesist scale in order to compare human and animal pains? Is there a difference in perceptions between tapeworms and infants?

p. 232. "But pain is pain [good thinking here!], and the importance of preventing unnecessary pain and suffering does not diminish because the being that suffers is not a member of our species." Most of us would say that we do prefer to have our pain relieved even if the method caused discomfort to one or more animals. The rat in the trap may not feel comfortable, but few of us would be willing to spend any time trying to quantitate his pain.

p. 234. "It is often said . . . that people in the animal welfare movement care more about animals than they do about humans. No doubt there are some people of which this is true." Peter Singer, for example?

p. 236. "Animals feel a need to exercise, stretch their limbs or wings, groom themselves, and turn around, whether or not they have ever lived in conditions that permit this. Herd or flock animals are disturbed when they are isolated from others of their species, though they may never have known other conditions, and too large a herd or flock can have the same effect through inability of the individual animal to recognize other individuals. These stresses reveal themselves in 'vices' like cannibalism." The quotation marks around "vices," as the word applies to cannibalism is a nice touch.

p. 236. " . . . to part a human mother from her child is tragic for both; but neither the farmer nor the breeder of pets and research animals gives any thought to the feelings of nonhuman mothers and children [children?] when he routinely separates them as part of his business." As, for example when the cattleman separates the cow and her weaned calf without consulting them, not even getting written approval from the bull. There are times when Singer seems to approach sheer lunacy, but the explanation for his outrageous statements is even simpler than that — this man has made a very lucrative career out of his program, and show business people (to which Singer is akin in approach and style) flourish by causing shock and outrage. He was wise enough to recognize there was a market for this kind of silliness, and he is milking it [excuse me, Bossy] for all it's worth.

Some inconsistencies — Singer does admit that the existence of carnivorous animals poses a bit of a spiritual problem for the animal liberation zealots. On page 238, et seq., he writes:

"It must be admitted that the existence of carnivorous animals does pose one problem for the ethics of Animal Liberation, and that is whether we should do anything about it. Asssuming that humans could eliminate carnivorous species from the earth, and that the total amount of suffering among animals in the world were thereby reduced, should we do it?"

" . . . any attempt to change ecological systems on a large scale is going to do far more harm than good." In other words, let animals kill each other, except of course for one species of animal . . . *Homo sapiens*, who doesn't have a "license to kill."

"My point is not that animals are capable of acting morally, but that the moral principle of equal consideration of interests applies to them as it applies to humans." Do animals apply the doctrine of "equal consideration of interests" to humans?

He concludes, " . . . once we give up our claim to 'domination' over the other species, we have no right to interfere with them at all. We should leave them alone as much as we possibly can. Having given up the role of tyrant, we should not try to play Big Brother either." In other words, let the cats eat the mice, the dogs eat the cats, etc. However, under Singer's plan, Chinese gourmets definitely cannot eat the dogs. But, we must never interfere with those man-eating tigers — that would be "dietism."

Although Singer has expressed his dislike of the idea of making animals into pets for human enjoyment, he seems to waver in his commitment to the remedial program this suggests, i.e., the "liberation" of all pets. But, the least one can do is to ensure that cats and dogs, for example, are fed vegetarian diets. Singer even gives a source for leaflets describing how to make vegetarian food for pets. He does not seem to consider that this may not be the type of food preferred by, e.g., cats, and that, in fact, foods derived from plants can cause serious disorders of the digestive tract in animals who are genetically carnivorous. How does does forcing an animal to eat an inappropriate selection of foods contribute to its "liberation"?

The approval, however limited, that Singer gives to the "enslavement" of animals, i.e., making pets of them, is completely at variance with his general thesis. The probable explanation for this inconsistency is that Singer ran into a firestorm of objections from fanatical pet lovers when they learned he advocated releasing all pets into the wild. This was a constituency (perhaps better described as an audience), which he could not afford to lose, so he modified his product to fit their requirements. Good marketing skills!

Singer seems to think the kid who buys a hamburger at McDonald's is just as delinquent as the hunter or fisher who kills a duck or trout for food. "Why, for instance, is the hunter who shoots wild ducks for his supper subject to more criticism than the person who buys chicken at the supermarket? Over-all, it is probably the intensively reared bird who has suffered more," At least, Mr. Tyson has protected his birds from chicken hawks, foxes, and other predators, and fed them to their hearts' content, and used disease prevention techniques to modify their discomfort. It could probably be shown that a farm-reared chicken has a longer life (on average) than a bird hatched in the wild, lives under better conditions, and dies a less painful death.

"I do not believe that consistency [in applying Animal Liberation Standards] is the same as, or implies, a rigid insistence on standards of absolute purity in all that one consumes or wears" (p. 245). So, Singer would allow the wearing of shoes and other clothing made of leather, provided the user had purchased the material before he or she decided to join the Singer Crusade. The moral justification for this escapes me, but the obvious practical justification is that Singer doesn't want to scare off potential converts who refuse to throw away those $300 leather shoes or that $30,000 mink coat.

What about farmers and ranchers who suffer large losses from the depredations of animals — such as the killing of sheep by wolves or the destruction of growing crops by rabbits and the like? Singer has an answer: Put out as food for the animals and birds baits containing chemicals that will cause sterility. The asinity of such a suggestion is probably too obvious to require discussion, but, as one point out of many: the existing population of pests (which will not be reduced by the baits) can cause the loss of an entire harvest. Also, a few fertile animals can quickly expand to reach a number limited only by the available food. His suggestion is so poorly supported by facts and logic as to seem almost irrational. Furthermore, it is inconsistent with his other principles: using Singer's own moral standards, it is unethical to prevent animals from having a normal family with offspring by sterilizing them with poisoned baits.

We read, on page 252, "... if human beings have a right to relief from acute physical pain, it is not a specifically human right, in Wasserstrom's sense. Animals would have it too." Would this lead to aspirin dispensers in the wilderness for alleviating pain of wildlife?

"They [other philosophers] resort to high-sounding phrases like 'the intrinsic dignity of the human individual.' They talk of 'the intrinsic worth of all men' as if men had some worth that other beings do not have or they say that human beings, and only human beings, are 'ends in themselves' ... " Princeton is doing its part to give dignity to animals

— it awards professorships to jackasses.

"The truth is that the appeal to the intrinsic dignity of human beings appears to solve the egalitarian philosopher's problems only as long as it goes unchallenged. Once we ask *why* it should be that all humans — including infants, mental defectives, criminal psychopaths, Hitler, Stalin, and the rest — have some kind of dignity or worth that no elephant, pig, or chimpanzee [or oyster, or tick, or buzzard?] can ever achieve, we see that this question is as difficult to answer as our original request for some relevant fact that justifies the inequality of humans and other animals." Well, we could put forward the religious justification for man's superiority, and there is the evolutionary justification that each person is one of Nature's implements for improving his or her own species and/or creating new species. It is not clear why Singer believes he can disregard these points, or the source to which he appeals for justification of his own views. Everything he advocates seems to be based on eternal truth as revealed to (or by) Singer.

Infanticide may be acceptable — Singer seems to see no particular problem with euthanasia, abortion, infanticide, and, in fact, the killing of all persons "who quite clearly are below the level of awareness, self-consciousness, intelligence, and sentience of many nonhumans. I am thinking of humans with severe and irreparable brain damage, and *also of infant humans;* [emphasis added] to avoid the complication of the potential of infants, however, I shall concentrate on permanently retarded humans" (p. 253 et seq.). Thus, he starts to approach the issue of justifiable infanticide, but backs off at the last instant, on a trivial excuse for not discussing this type of atrocity. Clearly, then, he feels that the deliberate killing of an infant, any infant, is of little consequence, especially if the act is contrasted to the killing, of, for instance, a fully capable rat. I interpret this to imply that the use of infants, any infant, in a laboratory experiment would also be ethically acceptable by Singer's set of morals.

An appeal to morality — Singer continues, "The core of this book is the claim that to discriminate against beings solely on account of their species is a form of prejudice, immoral and indefensible in the same way that discrimination on the basis of race is immoral and indefensible. I have not been content to put forward this claim as a bare assertion, or as a statement of my own personal view, which others may or may not choose to accept, I have *argued* [his emphasis] for it, appealing to reason rather than to emotion or sentiment." To this reader, it seems that Singer uses very little logic in his arguments, basing his contentions on ideas he has picked up by reading or consulting some little known oracle of his own choosing, then applying intuitive processes to select dicta that fit into his view of animal liberation. He has few new ideas, it is merely the blatancy and extremism of his views that have attracted attention.

Singer implies his morality is superior to other persons' morality. Also, " . . . if you take morality seriously, you must try to eliminate speciesist practices from your own life, and oppose them elsewhere. Otherwise, no basis remains from which you can, without hypocrisy, criticize racism and sexism" (p. 256). So, we learn that one benefit we would receive from embracing cockroaches as brothers (and, presumably, as sisters) would be that we could criticize racism and sexism with a clear conscience. What a glorious prospect!

The Singer manifesto — "We ought to consider the interests of animals because they have interests [!] and it is unjustifiable to exclude them from the sphere of moral concern; to make this consideration depend on beneficial consequences for humans is to accept the implication that the interests of animals do not warrant consideration for their own sakes." On the other hand, to make this consideration without considering its malificent effect on human beings is to accept the implication that humans do not have the right to make judgements as to what affects their welfare.

He equates his battling of "speciesism" with the environmental movement, with the emancipation of slaves, etc. He may be right, in that speciesism is intended to be another rallying point for the discontented and the disoriented.

Although we may not be able to decide whether or not Singer actually believes all of the stuff he publishes, we do know that he has profited greatly as a result of advocating the bizarre principles of what he describes as Animal Liberation, and his views are no doubt colored by reflections from the shekels (as are most people's).

More Monkey Business

There seems to be an epidemic of simian uplift. Professor Stephen Wise, a Harvard professor and animal rights crusader, says both his son and a chimpanzee can communicate using language and both have "a sense of self," which qualifies the chimp for the same Constitutional rights as humans. Of course, Prof. Wise has written a book about this topic, and, no doubt, is available for duty on the lecture circuit. The Wall Street Journal (Anon. 2002C) seems to believe that the lawyers are starting to set up the people and companies who use monkeys in, e.g., medical research for heavy damages. If the lawyers can convince courts that the chimps are being maltreated in the labs (or, perhaps in circuses and zoos), lawsuits asking for compensation would be appropriate. Anything is possible in the courts of today.

Zoophilism

Zoophilism is different in its scope and assumptions from the narrower concept of "animal rights." For most (but certainly not all) of the adherents to the latter philosophy, all (or most) animals have the same rights as mankind, they are to be protected by humans, and where possible they are to be given all the advantages possessed by, or claimed by, humans. The zoophilist, however, exalts all other animals above man. Non-human animals are to be protected and given advantages even though such privileges may result in substantial harm to some or all humans. For example, to a zoophilist, a vicious (or even rabid) dog should not be restrained, certainly not killed, even though a failure to neutralize the animal may result in some humans dying horrible deaths. Furthermore, animals must be given "respect;" they must be given precedence — I presume they are to walk on the pavement while humans must walk in the ditch.

For those persons who have had little experience with the ravings of the compassion merchants, the above description of zoophilism may seem fantastic; impossible to credit. Yet, zoophilists have been around since ancient times. The worship of specific animals undoubtedly precedes the historical record, and the giving of special status to certain classes of animals is also a very old and very widespread practice. In modern times, the practice can still be found, although it is not widely present.

An editorial entitled"Zoophilism and Degeneracy," was printed in the Journal of the American Medical Association more than a hundred years ago. The article was reprinted by JAMA in 2001. It is reproduced below because there are many points in the text which bear on the present discussion of Animal Liberation. Readers may find the old editorial is politically insensitive on several counts, but it does tell us that Animal Liberation, under other names, has been around for a long time, and that its current practitioners have few, if any, new ideas. The article is reproduced below; a few small deletions of irrelevant and dated material have been made. Quotation marks have been omitted.

Zoophilism and Degeneracy

Undue love for animals (zoophilism) such as so frequently finds expression in antivivisection fanaticism, has frequently been found associated with various forms of degeneracy and especially with mental expressions in connection with suspicional and persecutory conceptions.

[T]he suspicional world-betterers whose cruelty marred the French Revolution were all of them zoophilists whose love for animals contrasted markedly with their severities toward human beings. The fanatics who were guilty of such brutalities during the East Indian mutiny were intensely opposed to the taking of animal life. Very frequently their suspicional ideas are especially extended toward blood relatives. The mother of Savage, the poet, who persecuted him with such malignity, was very fond of cats and lap-dogs.

The fifth (or "wicked") Lord Byron, the immediate predecessor of the poet, was notorious for his dueling propensities, his disregard of major and minor morality, his cruelty toward his kin, and for his brutality toward his servants . . . the old man used to lie on the ground and gossip with the crickets, whom he loved far more than his descendants. When the crickets were troublesome, he used to whip them with a wisp of hay.

The same feature appears in the wife and daughters of Claude Bernard, the French physiologist. According to the recent life of Claude Bernard by Sir Michael Foster, the physiologist married a woman of degenerate stock, descendant from the French aristocracy of the pre-Revolutionary epoch. This woman had suspicional and persecutory ideas of that systematized type which so often occurs in degenerates prior to the full development of paranoia. After making Bernard's life miserable, his wife took her daughters and left him, alleging as a reason his experiments in vivisection. One of the daughters carried her antivivisectionism so far as to interrupt physiologic lectures, and was arrested therefor more than once, but the offense was condoned because of the manifest mental disorder present in her. There was evidence to show that her zoophilism took at times a sexually abnormal direction. In a will, which was subsequently modified by the court as in violation of the French laws governing wills, she left large sums for a hospital and asylum for cats and dogs.

Commenting on her procedures, the *Chicago Chronicle* remarks that on the theory of heredity, this daughter's performance reflects more suspicion on the father's sanity than anything he ever did himself.

The *Chronicle* comments severely but logically anent the antivivisectionists. The curious thing about these pranks is that motive never seems to have any weight with them; it would not surprise one if they some day object to the study and destruction of bacteria as cruelty to animals. This erroneous view of bacteria — whose zoologic position is not settled, whence the name "microbe" — has already been taken by zoophilists in New York, Boston, Philadelphia and Chicago, who have denounced the experiments in this direction for the reason stated by the *Chronicle*.

In New York a curious inconsistency has occurred. Some years ago experiments in vivisection made by Spitzka, for the purpose of demonstrating the nosolgic limitations of hydrophobia, were approved by the New York Society for the Prevention of Cruelty to Animals, on the ground that they tended to prevent cruelty to dogs wrongly suspected of having hydrophobia. Some thirteen years later the Society, having obtained the spinal cord of a dog which had bitten several people, refused to allow this cord to be used in Pasteur experiments for the purpose of allaying the fears of the persons bitten. Experiments in vivisection for the benefit of animals were praiseworthy, but the same experiments for the benefit of human beings were atrocious brutalities.

          — end of JAMA article —

Current Status of Zoophilism

What was true in this field a hundred years ago is also true today. The stories of people, courts, and legislative bodies that have given the welfare of animals more weight than the health, safety, and livelihood of humans are far too numerous to list completely in this chapter.

Zoophilism is a rejection of the human spirit and a negation of the instinct for self-preservation. It is anti-realism and anti-human, and in these respects could be considered a form of insanity, as is clearly stated in the JAMA editorial. Because persons afflicted by this disorder might be persuaded to disrupt, destroy, and kill (i.e., commit terroristic acts) for their "faith," they can be made into useful tools for Reds. Making them co-conspirators fits in nicely with the other disruptive tactics of the Red tactics of divide, disrupt, and destroy.

Zero population growth, so desirable for the human race (we have been told), is for some reason not to be considered a valid practice for any other species of animals. Thus it is satisfactory, even desirable, to kill unborn babies (by abortion), but not ethically acceptable to kill mosquitoes or wolves, or members of any other species.

Modern Lycanophila

One of the most curious aberrations found in the zoophilic coterie is an inordinate concern for the welfare of wolves. When their passion is in full flower, sufferers from this mania do not hesitate to affirm that, in a contest for survival between *Canis lupis* and *Homo sapiens*, the wolves would have the ethical right to prevail. Some examples of more or less extreme cases will be quoted below.

Singer (1975), in his book, *Animal Liberation*, informs us that, in addition to their other merits, wolves are faithful and affectionate spouses for life. We don't have a Kinsey report about wolves, so we haven't a source on which to base our disagreement with Singer's point, but we would like to see some data supporting his conclusion, as well as for several dozen other dicta he provides absent experimental or observational data.

The sensitive Paul Brooks asked his readers, in the book *The Pursuit of Wilderness* (1971), " . . . would the senseless poisoning and shooting of wolves be tolerated by the public if wolves were not still associated with evil?" As we have seen in other quotes and discussions of this author's works, Brooks seemed to have a type of adoration for wolves. Several times he uses them as examples of the beauty of the wild which, he says, is being threatened and must be preserved. See, for example, on page 86, he describes wolves as, "These much maligned animals . . . " And, on page 180: " . . . many otherwise rational persons still think in terms of 'good animals' and 'bad animals'; they cherish the dove and the deer, they hate the hawk and the wolf."

Carlton (2002) described the work of Gordon Haber, who receives about $150,000 a year for alleviating the problems of Alaskan wolves. Most of this money seems to come from Friends of Animals, a tax-advantaged foundation headed by Priscilla Feral — some cynical readers might want to know if her last name has been assumed for business purposes to replace a less appropriate "Butcher" or "Hunter.". Ms. Feral lives in Darien CT, where she can look at pictures of wolves in library books. According to Carlton, "Mr. Haber became passionate about wolves as a teenager growing up in Michigan, after he read the wilderness classic, 'Arctic Wild,' a memoir by the late Lois Crisler on how she and her husband lived with some Arctic wolves in the 1950s."

Haber received a Ph.D. in zoology from a Canadian university. A bachelor, he is said to live in a one-room cabin near Denali National Park in Alaska, but his ascetic judgement permits him to have a private plane that has been especially outfitted for wolf watching. He appealed a $190,000 judgement levied by a jury which heard a case involving Haber's interference with the legal hunting activities of the inhabitants of an Inuit village.

Gordon Haber blames the government for allowing "persecution of an animal he considers more gentle and intelligent than popularly portrayed. He objects to the use of the term 'pack' to desribe wolf groupings, preferring to call them families...He is trying to get people to respect wolves for their inherent worth." Apparently, he thinks wolves' hunting skills are learned, and fears that the encroachment of humans will interfere with the passing down of the skills from father to pup. Carlton points out, "Rival scientists dispute that...arguing that the wolf is an instinctive hunter."

According to Midgely (1978), ethologists "watch wolves systematically and have found them to be, by human standards, paragons of steadiness and good conduct...and extremely seldom kill anything that they do not need for dinner." This sensitive prose goes on and on in a similar vein. Sapontzis (1987) agrees, and finds that wolf behavior is an example of being rational and acting morally, areas in which *Homo sapiens* has so often disappointed him.

Strassel (2002) relays a report by Bruce Vincent who learned that an environmentalist was going to give a talk to a class in a Montana middle school, at the end of which the students would be asked if they would like to adopt a wolf. Now, we can reconstruct this scenario: the environmentalist is interested in getting contributions for his (or her) organization. Merely asking the kids for donations to a rather amorphous cause will very likely result in low returns. But, asking them to "adopt" a wolf puts them on the mailing list, allowing the organization to "bill" the children (or their parents) for the support of an individual (likely fictitious) animal. The billing will continue as long as contributions can be wrung from the parents. We can expect that the fictitious animal will have an attractive name (perhaps Alaskan Jim). Each contributor will be provided with a picture of their wolf (washed, brushed, and in soft focus) obtained from an agency specializing in wildlife images. We hardly dare to suggest that the contribuors will actually receive a "thank you" letter from the animal, signed with a paw print — but who knows?

The significance of this story to our lycanophila theme is that the so-called environmentalists who running these scams carefully choose as the subjects of their sales pitches animals thought to appeal to the greatest number of the group of potential contributors that is being targeted — choosing in this case, wolves. Perhaps lycanophila is more widely spread than we thought.

A SPECIESIST'S MANIFESTO

It is right and proper to use all of the earth's surface for the subsistence and enjoyment of mankind. People do not exist for the benefit of the land.

Lower animals (as well as the earth's vegetation and minerals) are justly exploitable for the use of man. Humans do not exist for the comfort and convenience of other things or beings. If the organism (whether anthrax bacillus, mosquito, snail darter, peregrine falcon, or poodle) serves no useful purpose, as determined by humans, then it is occupying space that can be put to better use. If animals interfere with the welfare of humans, they should be removed. If they can be used for the benefit of humans, including as food, they should be so used.

The desire of some persons to gain spiritual or esthetic pleasure by the viewing of vast empty spaces once every few years, to the exclusion of persons who could live comfortably and safely in those areas, raising families and doing productive work the year-round, is an arrogant, selfish presumption which should be given no weight at all in deciding what to do on or in any area or region.

With the preceding as a basis and justification, we speciesists offer the following Statement of Rights:

1. Vegetation does not have citizenship rights.

2. Snail darters are not entitled to equal representation.

3. Neither mushrooms, trees, nor falcons, nor any organism other than man have souls. Even your dear little doggy or cute little pussy doesn't have a soul. If you believe that elephants or butterflies have souls, it is up to your god and their god to protect them, not my God.

4. The use of public moneys (including tax-advantaged donations and the like) to preserve, "restore," or otherwise enhance a particular scenic site should not be permitted.

5. The more people who gain a pleasurable experience by viewing or travelling through a scenic area, the more that area is fulfilling its only reason for being. Charging visitors for maintaining services and the like is an equitable way of financing the scenic area as a source of human enjoyment/entertainment.

6. Only persons with extremely perverse imaginations can reach the conclusion that a swamp, bog, mudhole, or the like is beautiful, or should be preserved for esthetic reasons. If they believe differently, let them pay all of the costs of acquiring and preserving the spot and of adding features that prevent it from endangering or inconveniencing other people.

7. The recreational possibilities of an area should not be the only factor controlling the use of an area. As *one* of the factors, recreational use should be carefully evaluated by neutral administrators because of the emotional appeal of such areas to certain types of interested parties.

8. Insofar as a space is uninhabited and unused by humans, its full potential for human good is not being achieved.

9. "Scientific" data allegedly supporting an environmentalist position should be carefully examined. The investigation should include interrogation of the originator of the data to determine the statistical significance of the data and the conditions surrounding its acquisition.

10. In fine, you may believe you are entitled to advocate the "holiness" of empty spaces, i.e., wildernesses, but do not expect others to accept the burden of the restrictions upon land use that your god demands or of the expenditure of tax money needed to further your religious and/or spiritual beliefs.

A Motto for speciesists — Kill a wolf and save 1,000 cute little bunny rabbits from horrible deaths. Send in a contribution and we will shoot a wolf with a bullet having your name scratched on it.

chapter twelve

PROTECTING BIODIVERSITY

Closely allied with zoophilia is the mania which can be described as "Protecting Biodiversity." In some ways, the idea of maintaining populations of all the existing types (species?, varieties?) of not only animals, but of the whole biota, is even more extreme than the goals of the zoophilists. At least, the latter do not specifically state that all types of organisms must be rescued even though the normal processes of evolution and survival of the fittest are driving them to extinction. This principle is, howevever, paramount in the bible of the biodiversity saviors. It sets an impossible goal.

The definition of "species" is crucial to this discussion. Unfortunately, the word is somewhat plastic. The standard definition, as the word is used by biologists, goes something like this:

species — (n, sing. & plural) *Biol.* A category of classification lower than a genus or subgenus and above a subspecies or variety; a group of animals or plants which possess in common one or more characters distinguishing them from other similar groups, and which do or may interbreed and reproduce their characters in their offspring, exhibiting between each other only minor differences bridged over by intermediate forms (e.g., subspecies) and differences ascribable to age, sex, polymorphism, individual peculiarity or accident, or to selective breeding by man; a distinct kind or sort of animal or plant.

Until the acceptance of the theory of evolution, members of a species were regarded as being the offspring of a single specially created ancestor or pair; hence, each species was considered definitely separated from other species, and usually as unchanging from one generation to another. Individuals intergrading between two supposedly distinct species were commonly considered as hybrids or as abnormal individuals whose peculiarities approached the normal characters of other species.

The theory of evolution, however, involves the conception that species are not unchanging, but that they have developed from pre-existing and different species, also that this process is in many cases still going on. With the abandonment of the doctrine of separate creation of species, the term *species* lost much of its theoretical importance. In the case of closely allied groups, the prevailing practice is to recognize as a distinct species a group of living things whose members are not known to, or are assumed not to, intergrade with some other species, even if the characters distinguishing them are very slight. Groups which intergrade are regarded only as subspecies.

At one time, and in some taxonomic circles, a specifically described organism was said by the authorities to be a separate species if its members did not mate with any other approximately similar organisms, or, if such matings did occur the offspring were sterile. This is perfectly clear if we are deciding whether or not elephants and butterflies constitute distinct species, as regards to one another, but when one's interest is, for example, microbes, then we are faced with the necessity for determining species level by finding out, e.g., whether or not two cultures of yeast cells can utilize a particular carbohydrate or whether a bacteria is an obligate or facultative anaerobe. And, will they mate, assuming some of the organisms achieve a sexual phase, which may not have been observed, or at least not reported in the literature.

The problem of interchange of parts of the genetic apparatus rather than the whole chromosome(s), poses yet another difficult question in determining whether a distinct species exists. The status of microsomes in the taxonomic scheme might be considered of some importance by a few specialists. Viruses are generally not regarded as living organisms, even though they pack a considerable amount of genetic material (they do not reproduce but cause other organisms to replicate the various components and then assemble the virus). Prions are definitely not living organisms and they do not contain genetic materials and do not mate, so they are outside the topic we are discussing.

Once we abandon "no crosses," or "no fertile offspring from crosses," as the criterion denoting a different species, we find there is a necessity for random and arbitrary designations or tests for deciding whether an organism constitutes a species distinct from another superficially identical culture. It is reasonably clear that an organism belongs to the same species as another organism if their genetic constitutions are exactly alike. But when, in fact, does this ever occur? And is there any realistic test to determine precise equivalence of the genes and their arrangement in chromosomes? In spite of the all the mapping of chromosomes and allied studies, much remains unknown.

The genetic material, consisting of an assemblage of chemical compounds existing in vivo in some kind of very complex and unique spatial arrangement, is capable of so many permutations that we can conceive of a vast number of alternatives varying perhaps only in seemingly minor details. In fact, it is the apparent similarity between two organisms' genetic material that should cause amazement, not the occasional (apparent) exact duplication of phenotype.

This may be true even with microorganisms. Would each small but detectable spatial difference in the arrangement of genes in a chromosome result in a different species? We could go to the extreme and say that every individual (even of *Homo sapiens*) is a species in and of itself. Furthermore, if uniqueness of the genetic material in a individual, or group of individuals, is the key to determining a species, then we are faced with all sorts of problems, among these the curious fact that the genetic material of males is certainly different from that of females of the same species.

If we accept the criterion of the sterility of crossbreeds, when crossbreeds occur, as proof the parents are of different species, then we come to a curious situation in which a living, breathing, and copulating organism belongs to no species at all. The offspring resulting from the crossing of a horse and a donkey, resulting in a mule or hinny, is usually sterile. Does this mean that the offspring is not a member of a species? What force does the modifier, "usually," have in this case? In rare cases, the animal resulting from the cross does turn out to be fertile — does this mean it constitutes a new species?

When dealing with microorganisms, failure to conjugate or failure of the conjoined cells to subsequently divide into separate cells that are viable, may be very difficult to determine, and may depend upon such things as the availability of a certain nutrient, the temperature of the medium, or many other factors.

There are other problems with the definition of species. For example, lines of dogs (*Canis familiaris*) which breed true to type, include such extremes as the tiny chihuahua and the giant Saint Bernard, as well as hundreds of variations in other physical features such as hairiness, general body conformation (e.g., greyhound vs. dachshund), temperament (aggressiveness vs. timidity), etc. And many of these varieties ("breeds") have verified genealogies for a hundred generations or more recorded with the American Kennel Club, which testifies to the stability of their distinguishing characteristics. Of course, there is no doubt that fertile crosses can occur between many, if not most, of the "breeds."

"New data emerging from microbial genome sequences are so perplexing that 'we can no longer comfortably say what is a species anymore,'says Daniel Drell, who manages the Department of Energy's microbial genomes program. Two bugs in particular, described at a recent meeting, seem to have nabbed enough genes from other organisms that they no longer resemble their supposedly closest relatives — raising fascinating questions about how and why thye obtained these new traits" (Pennisi 2001).

Although it may be politically incorrect to point it out, the human species (*Homo sapiens*), has dozens, perhaps hundreds, of varieties which breed true to type, from the Australian aborigines to the Nordic race, from pigmies to Masai, etc. There are hundreds, or thousands, of crosses occurring daily, and many of them undoubtedly yield fertile offspring, though it is not clear that *all* of the possible crosses would yield viable or fertile offspring.

Mankind's Responsibility

The axioms of the diversity-protectors are much the same as the rules adopted by most zoophilists, but with the added fillip that we must act to preserve species which seem to be on the verge of dying out. If any of them vanished, there would be less biodiversity in the world, and that would be bad — very bad.

The advocates of "Protecting biodiversity" have at least two major criteria for judging whether or not a species/race/type/variety/strain of organism needs our assistance to survive:

(1) If a "species" is threatened with extinction throughout the world, it should be protected.

(2) If there are pockets or enclaves where a rare species exists, then the populations in each of these places should be protected.

Both plant and animal species are thought to be deserving of protection by most biodiversity advocates. The necessity of protecting microorganisms is a subject of debate.

It should be noted before we continue our discussion that protectors of diversity do not want to hear about setting up artificial enclaves (zoos, herbariums, aquariums, etc.) in which the threatened species will be coddled and encouraged to reproduce. Instead, they want each species to flourish where it is presently located; and, generally, in *every* place where it currently exists. The latter goal overlaps the aims and purposes of the Habitat Preservation coterie, whose program has been discussed elsewhere in this book.

The Extinction Epidemic

Inadequate obeisance to biodiversity is another form of heresy that eco-doyen Paul Ehrlich would like to blot out. An extensive review of this man's history and oeuvre appears elsewhere in this volume. The following quotations are from *The Population Explosion* and relate to biodiversity preservation. "The planet's plants, animals, and microorganisms are now threatened with a colossal extinction epidemic." We must be sure to protect those plague bacilli, they are an essential part of the grand scheme of things.

He says, "As humanity destroys biodiversity in tropical forests and elsewhere, it reduces the pool of genetic variability needed to stay in the game of high-yield agriculture." No, it doesn't. If we consider food plants as the field of interest, I am not aware of any race of rice, wheat, corn, or sorghum in wide use that contains a gene that originated from a cross with a tropical forest plant. So far as "elsewhere" is concerned, many races of maize have been lost from among the numerous sports that occurred during the domestication and spread of this grain. Undoubtedly, many similar losses occurred during the history of the development of modern races of rice, wheat, barley, etc. The inferior strains were abandoned and disappeared from the face of the earth because all of their good traits were combined in the high yielding, relatively climate tolerant strains that formed the food which allowed the human population to achieve its present level. Loss of these strains did not delay the success of the Green Revolution, which was built upon gene pools that were already successful and only needed fine-tuning to increase food production to an amazing degree. The idea that geniuses such as Borlaug scramble around trying to resurrect some offbeat strain on which to base their developments is just plain wrong.

The same argument aplies to any group of species one wishes to consider. Opening up the argument to all species on earth, whether they are known or unknown, unnecessarily complicates the argument.

Elsewhere, Ehrlich has written, "About a third of all prescription medicines are either plant defensive chemicals or chemicals modeled on them." No citations of sources or actual data are given, but if he is implying that the newest medications are based on the analysis of some witch doctor's magical brew, he should put his evidence on record.

An Impossible Goal

A United Nations'estimate shows a total in excess of 12 million estimated species (see Table 12.1). To call this figure an educated guess is to credit the UN administrators with a characteristic to which they are may not be entitled. Going back to basics discussed previously, the definition of a species is in doubt, so the value of such estimates is even more dubious than it appears on the surface.

Even if we could count all of the species in existence at any given time, which is of course impossible, the job would not be done, because, within seconds after the polls were closed, a species would vanish forever, and another species would emerge. Nature has no interest in official deadlines.

Table 12.1

ESTIMATES OF NUMBER OF SPECIES[1]

Group	Identified	Estimated
Viruses	4,000	400,000
Bacteria	4,000	>1 million
Fungi	72,000	1.5 million
Protozoans	40,000	200,000
Algae	40,000	400,000
Plants	270,000	320,000
Nematodes	25,000	400,000
Crustaceans	40,000	150,000
Arachnids	75,000	750,000
Insects	950,000	8 million
Mollusks	70,000	200,000
Vertebrates[2]	45,000	50,000
Others	115,000	250,000

[1] Includes all life forms. Source of data: Global Biodiversity Assessment, UN Environment Program, as presented by Bank (2002).

[2] As the term is used here, "Vertebrates" includes certain allied organisms.

New Species Constantly Being Reported

There are ornithologists specializing in the bird species living on the Galápagos Islands. They classify them as species if they have small differences in beak conformation, habitat, food preferences, etc. The concentration of interest is due to what seems to be evidence of evolution within an isolated area.

"The change in character of the [Galápagos] archipelago resulted, in part, from global cooling that started well before the onset of the recent ice age about 2.8 million years ago and has continued to the present. The amplitude of temperature oscillations — and probably of precipitation — has increased in the past million years" (Grant and Grant 2002).

The experts have decided there are dozens, if not hundreds, of species on this small group of bleak rock outcroppings in the Pacific Ocean, possibly 3000 square miles in total area. And, the researchers seem to find additional varieties or species on each return visit to the area. Who can say that a similar concentration of effort applied to any square mile in the world (land or ocean) would not turn up dozens of new species of plants or animals? There are certainly attempts being made to proceed in this

Organizations have been formed for the specific purpose of seeking out hitherto unreported "species." For example, Bank (2002), tells us, "A model for the global effort is already under way at Costa Rica's biodiversity institute, familiarly called InBio, which occupies a sprawling campus on a former coffee plantation. InBio researchers discover, on average, one new species each day. Local residents are trained and sent into the field to collect insects and worms." It is not beyond the realm of imagination to project this kind of activity to 1,000 research posts, covering the globe, with a corresponding yield of 1,000 new species per day. How could the world possibly support the manpower and facilities needed to protect all of these new species in addition to the species now thought to require "preservation?"

Cui Bono

What is the motivating force behind the campaign to "preserve diversity?" There is not much difficulty in discovering the persons who profit the most from increased activity in this discipline. These fall mainly into three groups:

1. Academics who have, or expect to obtain, publicly or privately funded research projects dealing with some small aspect of the alleged problem. Perhaps they even dream of ultimately founding a college department of, e.g., "Biodiversity."

2. Capitalists who believe they will be able to benefit by selling goods or services that are compatible with the biodiversity concept: take a line through Ben and Jerry's ice cream.

3. The thinktank mob who expect to gain grants and gifts that will enable them to investigate or promote some small fraction of the biodiversity gag. Among the largest tax-advantaged organizations in this group are Conservation International, the International Union for the Conservation of Nature, and the World Wildlife Fund, all of which seem to obtain without difficulty all the funding they need.

Politicians can be expected to join the movement if there seems to be enough public interest to justify a vote-getting campaign based on a biodiversity preservation theme. It is more likely, however, that the politicians who are supporting the grant gatherers in their search for funds would just as soon not get a lot of publicity on the contributions they receive from this particular pork barrel. Several national and international agencies are active in the field, dispensing many millions of dollars in grants. Among these are the World Bank, Inter-American Development Bank, Global Environmental Facility, the European Community, and the US Agency for International Development (Simpson 1999).

That is not to say there are no true believers to be found in the biodiversity preservation ranks. Causes of this sort will always attract a certain fraction of the discontented, restless, "unfulfilled," "unappreciated" men and women who dimly recognize the utter futility of their lives, and who believe they deserve more appreciation, more recognition, a chance to "do something worthwile." Once within the web, these victims will often, though not always, develop an emotional attachment to the goals, or purported goals, of the cause.

It is from this same subset of humanity, the discontented failures and parasites looking for a cause to justify their futile existence, that the Reds obtained the major part of their recruits. Consequently, reds have been very active in the biodiversity movement.

Natural Medical Miracles

It is curious that biodiversity protectors, who show so little concern about human life or human values when judging whether or not to legislate or implement a procedure that may put people at danger, jump at any chance to claim their policies will, at some distant time in the future, improve human health.

The Taxol Story — A linchpin in the promotional efforts for biodiversity projects, current or proposed, is the taxol story. A very brief review follows.

A substance was found in the bark of Pacific yew trees which, after years of investigation, proved to be a suitable raw material for the manufacture of a medication that was helpful in alleviating (curing, reducing the effects of, or halting growth) of breast cancer and some other neoplasms. This story is supposed to justify the preservation of every kind of plant and animal, because, "You never know, maybe the next cancer cure will be found in a fungus that is being crowded out of the Amazon rain forest." The curious part of this story is that the person(s) collecting the bark of Pacific yew trees was probably endangering a scarce variety of plant, and, had the collectors been observing biodiversity tenets, they would never have taken the samples which eventually came to the attention of medical researchers.

The following commentary is based, in part, on material in the book, *The Story of Taxol: Nature and Politics in the Pursuit of an*

Anticancer Drug, by Goodman and Walsh (2001).

In the early phases of the development and commercial exploitation of pharmaceuticals containing taxol, the only known source for the compound was the bark of a tree *Taxus brevifolia*, which was a survival-threatened component of old-growth forests in the Pacific Northwest. Although other parts of the plant contain some taxol, the bark has the highest concentration, and, after the initial promising tests, Food and Drug Administration regulations made it much simpler for investigators to continue with that source of raw material.

As Goodman and Walsh pointed out, collecting the bark " . . . put severe pressure on the tree, which gave rise to tensions between conservationists anxious to preserve the old-growth forests and the endangered northern spotted owl that lives there . . . "

" . . . environmentalists first exploited the Pacific yew's potential as both the source of a cancer therapeutic and an ecosystem anchor to change its legal status and then used it as a rallying point in the debate over deforestation in the US. This activism resulted in the passage of the 1992 Pacific Yew Act, which limited the harvesting of *T. brevifolia* on federal lands to the needs of the medical community. In the end, however, federal legislation and environmental concerns aside, the tree was abandoned by a pharmaceutical industry weary of controversy."

It was eventually discovered that paclitaxel (generic name for the active compound) could be semi-synthesized starting with the more readily available 10-deacetylbaccatin III, so the remaining Pacific yew trees are no longer threatened by selfish people who are only interested in saving human lives.

The story of the political, academic, and bureaucratic maneuvering that took place after the commercial value of taxol and its derivatives became known is very curious, and seems to merit a thorough investigation. Very large sums of money seem to have been made by persons and companies who performed only minor work, if any, in the early phases of development.

Can We Depend on Nature?

The taxol example has been used as the justification for spending vast sums of money searching through libraries of cultures collected by taxonomists, etc., but there are a number of questions which seem never to occur to those persons who believe Mother Nature, or God, has provided humans with a library of compounds which would heal every illness if we would only spend enough time and money looking for them.

There are quite a few problems connected with depending upon Nature's "universal pharmacopoeia" for our medical needs. Among the questions to be considered are:

1. Would not the energy and money spent on collecting, isolating, identifying, and determining the clinical value of the small fraction of one percent of all plant constituents that might be effective medications be better used to determine the basic causes of diseases and then develop "designer" drugs (pharmaceuticals synthesized from readily obtainable raw materials) to cure a specific problem?

2. Are we to await the adventitious discovery of suitable natural raw materials before we proceed with the development of new pharmaceuticals? The structure and activity of taxol was known 20 years or more before its clinical activity was announced. A lot of basic research on disease causes and disease cures can be done in 20 years.

David Kingston, who has worked on the chemistry of paclitaxel since the early 1980s, says, "The story reminds us of the bounty nature provides us with, but also of the perseverance and, yes, good luck needed to take advantage of that bounty" (Kingston 2001).

Property rights — Vandana Shiva, director of the Research Foundation for Science, Technology and Natural Resource Policy, headquartered in New Delhi (India) is working to prevent "biopiracy," which seems to be defined as the discovery, improvement, and merchandising of native or traditional medications, the knowledge of which is at present confined to a relatively small area. It's apparently OK with Vandana if the information has never been, or never will be, widely disseminated (and the rest of the world's population deprived of its benefits), but patenting it in preparation for wide distribution is anathema to Shiva.

She says (Willis 2002), "Contemporary patents on life [sic] seem to be of a similar quality. They are pieces of paper issued by patent offices of the world that basically are telling corporations that if there's knowledge of living material, plant, seeds, medicines which the white man has not known about before, claim it on [their] behalf and make profits out of it." Further wisdom from Shiva can be found at: **www.vshiva.net**

Supporting the viewpoint of such proscriptionists as V. Shiva, were the persons who met in Rio de Janeiro in 1992 at a shindig called the First Earth Summit. They generated, or approved, a document called *Convention on Biological Diversity*, a proposed treaty which would place restrictions on botanical prospecting and other methods of improving medical care for the world's inhabitants. Further details can be found at: **www.biodiv.org**

The net effect of the biodiversity protection hysteria is to place additional bureaucratic hobbles on bioprospecting while at the same time generating grants to nonprofit organizations and providing employment for academics. Your present author believes the most efficient way to develop new pharmaceuticals is not by searching for witch doctors' potions in all corners of the world as a guide for the design of chemicals which can cure diseases. After all, Viagra was not developed on the basis of an analysis of powdered rhinocerous horns — but on knowledge obtained from the study of the biochemical basis of the disorder the horns were supposed to correct. These are approaches which have achieved remarkable successes and which will continue to work if they are not hampered by government regulations.

Genetically Modified Plants

Selection, hybridization, and other agronomist's techniques have been used since the beginning of agriculture to improve the yield, product quality, disease resistance, and other properties of plants that are useful to man. In the last few decades, another approach has been under investigation: this is targeted genetic modification of the germ plasm of plants, sometimes called gene-splicing. For some reason, this has become a bête noire of the biodiversity lynch mob. Hysterical attacks have been made on persons who provide seeds or grow crops utilizing the new techniques.

European nations have been particularly rigid in their refusal to accept bioengineered foods. This is just another way they attempt to restrict imports to protect their farmers who have grossly inflated costs of production.

Ross (2002) wrote, " . . . the brewing biotech-food contretemps in Africa illustrates yet another example of the callous disregard of prosperous first world 'environmentalists' toward human life in the undeveloped world. Despite seven-plus years of widespread use, there is not a shred of evidence of adverse health effects in humans from the new food technologies represented by the rubric 'genetically engineered.' Despite shrill alarums from anti-capitalist groups pitching their unscientific agendas under the guise of friends of butterflies and nature, there has never been any reliable evidence of adverse impact on the environment from these agricultural products . . . the alarmists in Europe would sacrifice the great potential for lifesaving improvements in nutrition on their altar of genetic purity."

There seem to be no such superstitions in China, and agriculture in that country has benefited substantially from use of genetically modified plants. The following is a summary of an article from the journal, *Science*. "A survey of China's plant biotechnologists shows that China is developing the largest plant biotechnology capacity outside of North America. The list of genetically modified plant technologies in trials, including rice, wheat, potatoes, and peanuts, is impressive and differs from those being worked on in other countries. Poor farmers in China are cultivating a greater area of genetically modified plants than are small farmers in any other developing country. A survey of agricultural producers in China demonstrates that *Bacillus thuringiensis* cotton adoption increases production efficiency and improves farmer health" (Huang, et al. 2002).

Ehrlich urgently advises his readers to do everything they can to reduce the population, because (he says) we can never grow enough food to support the number of people he expects will inhabit the earth in 30 years (beginning about 1970). If we hamstring the scientists and technologists who are working to increase productivity, quality, and adaptability of crops, Ehrlich's prophecy may eventually come true.

Fukuda-Parr (2001) said, relative to a UN report summarized and reviewed on the editorial page of the Wall Street Journal, that Western-based environmental groups are impeding efforts to alleviate starvation in Third World nations by blocking the development of bioengineered foods. She challenged opponents of these new foods to produce evidence that modified foods threaten the environment or public health. A supporter of this report, Mark Malloch Brown, insisted that the need for widespread use of genetically modified rice, millet, and cassava is urgent and could alleviate malnutrition for up to 800 million people.

Abuse of Authority

With all the moral power and legal authority given to government agencies to enforce green superstitions, and the nearly complete lack of oversight into these agencies' baneful effects on law-abiding citizens, it is small wonder that there are abuses of power so absurd as to cast doubt on the sanity of some of the participants. Space is available here for only a few examples.

Federal pampering of pests — In an internet publication attributed to the Glacier National Park administration, we learn of the efforts that have been made over many years to get a few more animals of four different species that are on the endangered list. Apparently, this refers only to the "Crown of the Continent Ecosystem."

•Grizzly bear-*Ursus arctos horribilis*. In 1975, the grizzly was listed

under the Endangered Species Act and a Grizzly Bear Recovery Plan
was written. After more than 15 years of study, researchers are still
struggling to develop practical methods of monitoring grizzly bear
population trends so that managers can both assess whether recovery
goals are being met and determine whether those goals are valid in the
first place.

•Northern Rocky Mountain wolf-*Canis lupus irremotus.* The northern
Rocky Mountain wolf is one of 32 subspecies of gray wolf. From 1984 to
1992, the wolf population in the Glacier area has risen from 7 to as high
as 30 wolves.

•Rocky Mountain Bighorn sheep-*Ovis canadensis canadensis.* In
Glacier National Park 9 or 10 winter ranges support from 5 to 60
individuals each. These animals are very subject to disease, and the
population seems to fluctuate wildly from year to year.

•Westslope cutthroat trout-*Onchorhynchus clarki lewisi.* "The pure
westslope cutthroat trout populations in Glacier represent the last
stronghold for this subspecies; their protection is of the utmost
importance both to the park and to other agencies that may in the future
use transplants from Glacier to reestablish population in the trout's
former range."

We can only speculate on the amount of money spent coddling
these four useless animals, but it must at the very least be in the
hundreds of millions of dollars. And what is the result?

The author of the newsletter from which the above material has
been excerpted (Karen J. Schmidt) says, "Perhaps the biggest lesson to
be learned from the case studies above is that there is still a great deal
we do not understand about the complex web of interrelationships and
processes that support single species, let alone entire ecosystems . . . conducting population viability assessments is difficult,
costly, and extremely time-consuming . . . "

A grisly future — During his last days in office, Bill Clinton
used the National Endangered Species Act to finance transport of grizzly

bears to Idaho. Grizzly bears (*Ursus horribilus*) are not on the list of Endangered Species. The governor of Idaho said that government agents advocated the experiment even though it was opposed by all the state's congressmen, the state Legislature, and the state Fish and Game Commission. Governor Kempthorne revealed that the Clintonites estimated the introduction of these dangerous animals would cost the US Treasury between $4 million and $10 million for each human killed. Annual costs were amortized at between 80 and 200 thousand dollars (Anon. 2001M).

The governor could have counterattacked by declaring open season on grizzly bears, and selling hunting licenses for $100,000 or so. We predict there would be several plutocrats who would jump at the chance of securing a trophy which would be nearly unique. What a talking point at the cocktail and coke parties. A stuffed grizzly in the party room! And, there would be a chance of profit from the sale of videos of the hunt, the kill, and the preparation of the trophy.

As a side benefit of this promotion, the governor would be giving the state's bank balance a little boost, and he would forestall those lawsuits we anticipate being filed by people whose spouses, children, or livestock were killed by these ugly, worthless beasts (in this case, meaning the bears not the bureaucrats).

The Next Leap Forward

Plans are being made to "catalog the planet's biodiversity." A possible cost of three billion dollars has mentioned. Since the biota is constantly changing, and since there are unknown numbers of existing species as yet unidentified, there is, in fact, a potential for unlimited expenditures continuing forever. But wait — why limit the preservation to living organisms? If this kind of money is going to be available, there will be efforts to extend the "diversity protection" label so as to enable workers in other disciplines to get some of the gravy. The boundaries are already being tested.

An article by John J. Miller (2002), subtitled, "Languages die. The United Nations is upset about this," informs us that Daniel Nettle and

Suzanne Romaine have written of "biolinguistic diversity," which in their lexicon is defined as "the rich spectrum of life encompassing all the earth's species of plants and animals along with human cultures and their languages." And one of their conclusions from this amazing bit of insight is that, "the next great step in scientific development may lie locked up in some obscure languages in a distant rainforest."

And, for an endowment of a few million, I have no doubt that Dan and Suzanne will be willing to set up a foundation to study ways in which we can save all the earth's languages.

Words fail us.

Nature's "Plan"

If, for some reason, it is decided that all species/races of life, from unicellular organisms to man, in existence at a given time must be preserved forever, at whatever cost to the human race, either for spiritual or other reason, one alternative may be to preserve frozen embryos of the endangered species for, essentially, eternity. In this way we could give future generations the ability to reconstitute species which have no known living representatives.

But, before we consider spending the trillions of dollars such a program would cost (and it would never reach completion) we should consider the following:

Nature has no plan to preserve for eternity all the species existing at one moment of time. Since life has first appeared on earth it has clearly been a result of nature's operation to randomly supply innumerable modifications to existing genera with the undoubted results that some of the preceding organisms, and most of the new varieties, will fail to compete successfully and will completely disappear. It is no plan of mindless nature to preserve either humanity, cockroaches, or anthrax bacilli for all eternity, or even until tomorrow.

Suffice it to say that there are millions of species, and some of them become extinct every year. The great majority of these lost species were not known to man, and never will be known because they leave no traces.

Nature has no interest in preserving species, it does *seem* to have an interest in creating new species, some of which will survive and become dominant in their particular environment, which may be a very small niche indeed. Only a bizarre, and illogical kind of nature worship can lead a devotee to look upon the loss of a species as anything other than the normal functioning of evolution, which has been operating on the same principle since the first gene appeared in the primordial soup.

All living beings are programmed to survive and produce as many offspring as possible even though they may drive to extinction one or more competing species. There are countless examples in evolutionary history of species which disappeared because they had to compete with species that were more efficient in their survival and reproductive abilities. If these losers left any traces, they were merely mineralized bones or coprolites.

Only *Homo sapiens*, of the millions of species that have appeared on earth, is capable of *knowingly* providing for anticipated changes in the environment, and for making tools that maximize the value of resources that do exist at any given time. In the absence of the benefits provided by science and technology, a few isolated bands of *Homo sapiens* (if any specimens had managed to survive) would be fearfully hiding from tigers and cobras and wolves, and would be subject to attack from every parasite able to feed on them. And they would be dying in droves after every major change in the climate.

New Disguises for Biodiversity

There must be scores of "Green" organizations looking for ways to position their groups so that they can escape blame for the senseless and harmful biodiversity preservation programs they have been responsible for instituting over the past 3 or 4 decades. The more fanatical greenies will, of course, stay the course, welcoming the abuse they receive for the disruption they create in business and employment, because it gives them a sense of power and an opportunity to become martyrs.

When the more reasonable directors see a marked decline in their contributions, donations, and grants, they will, like any good commercial person, attempt to find a marketing ploy that will keep them in business. The duller wits, who were able to make a living of sorts in the burgeoning compassion market of the '70s and '80s, and for part of the 90s, will simply continue to mail out their old brochures to their aging mailing lists, until the time comes when the donations do not pay their rent.

In a Wall Street Journal article titled "A quiet truce in the Green wars: Former foes unite to create eco-friendly employment in the hard-hit rural west.," Carlton (2001) explains, "thousands of loggers have lost jobs" in one small section of Oregon, because of environmental actions.

A nonprofit group called Sustainable Harvest, "is trying to revive local economies with eco-friendly projects." In five years it has helped to create "about 100 green jobs, paid for in part by the federal government." About 400 jobs had been lost due to extreme restrictions on logging in the surrounding national forest. For every job created by government subsidy, four productive, self-sustaining, jobs were lost. Not a very efficient operation, but probably typical of the usual government community assistance program.

"In Arizona, the Sonoran Institute is helping ranchers to diversify from cattle grazing on public lands to pursuits such as hosting eco-tours. In California's Monterrey County ... farmers ... work controlling soil runoff ... Sustainable Conservation, a San Francisco group that helped start the erosion project."

Carlton applauds the "so-called sustainability movement, a compromise-minded faction of environmentalists that tries to turn grass-roots foes into allies by offering them incentives, *such as jobs* [emphasis supplied] to go green." However, he points out the new jobs are far fewer in number, and many don't pay nearly as well as the former jobs.

"The sustainable-development movement began in the developing world, where indigenous peoples were encouraged to work as tour guides and park rangers ... Living in the shadow of the 10,000 foot peaks of the Wallowa Mountains, the 7,000 residents of Wallowa County have paid dearly for protection of the Chinook salmon. After the 1993 Chinook listing, the county's three mills shut down and unemployment shot to 15%, the highest in the state." Some residents thought the town wouldn't survive.

Then Martin Goebel came to the rescue. He is the president of Sustainable Northwest, and he had received $150,000 (probably more than the average family could make in several years) so that he could find a solution. Mr. Goebel is a city boy, but he knows all about sustainability because he has been to college. He started a nonprofit group, Wallowa Resources, "to carry out job-development programs." He figured the grant would enable him to hire a director and a staff of 10. They've already used most of the money in projects that didn't work. However, they've developed a brand name, "Healthy Forests, Healthy Communities," and sell a little lumber to an Oregon home developer. The very pattern of a sustainable enterprise — it looks as though this one is going to sustain Mr. Goebel for the rest of his life.

chapter thirteen

MOSQUITOES VS. MANKIND

This chapter is devoted to the case history of a movement which used "sensitivity" to the welfare of all animals (indeed, of the whole biota of the planet) as a justification for a program that has led to the deaths of millions of people who otherwise might have survived to old age in reasonable comfort. This choice of targets for compassion (lower animals before people) is an easily predictable result of the reds' hatred of mankind, but it has further interest for us in that it also involves the manipulation of public opinion in a manner intended to benefit a few industrialists. There is nothing surprising in this. Financiers and entrepreneurs of a certain type have always worked hand in glove with reds — in fact, they are willing to cooperate with Reds of the greatest doctrinal purity, if the cooperation *seems* to further their own interests. In a few cases, their cooperation has led to disastrous results for the deluded capitalists.

DDT

This little lesson in Red strategy, tactics, and goals begins with a scientific discovery and a technological success story and ends with politicians, money, and death — a pattern very prevalent in history.

Discovery

The chemical compound, DDT (dichloro-diphenyl-trichloro-ethane), was first prepared by a German chemist, Zeidler, in 1874. About 65 years later, Paul Mueller discovered DDT was extremely toxic to certain insects. This led to use of the compound as an insecticide for protecting American troops against insect-borne diseases during World War II, and it was subsequently adopted world-wide as a destroyer of many species of pests that adversely affect the comfort, health, and life spans of many hundreds of millions of human beings.

The author first encountered this substance as the active ingredient in pressurized insecticide applicators (predictably called "bombs") that were distributed to the US Armed Forces in World War II, an exercise in which the author was reluctantly participating. He can testify from personal observations and experiences that this insecticide was sprayed on clothing, bedding, buildings, tents, rooms, and each other by soldiers who had access to the bombs. They had no doubt as to the efficacy of the material, and no one complained of unpleasant side effects, not then, not ever (so far as the author knows).

After WW II, DDT was made available for purchase and use by the general public. Its very low level of human toxicity, its obvious effectiveness in killing and repelling insects, its low cost, and its lack of any major negative features led to rapid acceptance of the substance as the insecticide of choice throughout the world. This single scientific development and its commercial application resulted in an improved level of health and comfort for hundreds of millions of people.

Potential

Using DDT to kill the mosquitoes that serve as vectors not only for the trypanosomes causing malaria, sleeping sickness, and nagana, but also for the viruses causing yellow fever, etc., is the only practical way of controlling these diseases. Other insecticides are either too expensive, have too many undesirable side effects, or are too difficult to use. Often they have a combination of these defects, as well as others not named.

DDT had the possibility of permanently controlling, and perhaps virtually abolishing these deadly diseases. It was well on its way to performing this miracle, when persons to whom such an occurrence was unacceptable began a campaign to de-legitimatize the substance. An intensive search was started to discover undesirable side effects, however insignificant or rare they might be.

One of the complaints about DDT made by the establishment flacks was that it persisted in the soil and ground water, either in unchanged form or as its breakdown products DDE and DDD, for many months or years. Its stability was found to depend on temperature, presence of catalysts, etc., as is usually the case. In the following discussion, the triumvirate of DDT, DDE, and DDD will be comprehended within the term DDT, unless otherwise indicated.

It must seem to the unbiased observer that persistence is a very good thing — apply the product once and you've got the job done. Many other insecticides are broken down fairly rapidly into smaller compounds by animals and microorganisms, or by chemicals naturally in the environment that come into contact with them, so they have to be applied repeatedly if control of the insect population in a given area is to be maintained.

There are other possible advantages of the stability of DDT. If the compound does not break down into other substances as a result of either physical or chemical reactions with the materials it contacts (including water), then we do not have a group of degradation products rapidly increasing in the environment, with effects on the health and welfare of humans that are difficult to predict.

The property of persistence, which was an economic benefit and a convenience advantage to the consumer, was not, however, appreciated by the manufacturers and sellers of insecticides. Their idea of a good compound was one that had to be applied early and often in considerable amounts.

Early Acceptance and Opposition

About five decades ago, the Rockefeller Foundation began advocating the use of DDT (which they described as, "the most effective synthetic pesticide ever created") to wipe out mosquitoes. So effective was this program that, by the end of the 1940s, there were very few new cases of malaria being reported in the US, and by 1965 malaria had been substantially eradicated from the developed countries of the world, though it was still rampant elsewhere. However, an intense publicity campaign was put into operation to discredit the substance in the minds of the public. Rachel Carson's book, "Silent Spring," attacked the use of DDT in passionate, almost hysterical terms, and gave the initial impetus to a well-coordinated crusade led by "sensitive" and "compassionate" persons working to ban the chemical.

Carson and her accomplices were amazingly successful in gaining "public" support for outlawing DDT and as a result this pesticide was eventually taken off the market. Malaria then began to re-assume its age-old role as a deadly, world-wide plague. The disease affected more than 300 million persons in the year 2000. Nice going Rachel!

There are other pesticides of course, but some of them cost up to 20 times as much as DDT, most of them are not as effective as DDT, and all of them have other problems as well.

The Doyenne of DDT Bashers

Of all the propaganda pieces ever foisted on an unsuspecting populace, the one which had the strongest impact on the health and welfare of the human race (if we except religious books) is, arguably, *Silent Spring* . This book was first published in 1962. The putative author was Rachel Carson, but she had plenty of help. Portions of the book were first published as a series of articles in *The New Yorker,* that well-known scientific journal.

Never before had there been a book on environmental subjects that had such a rapid and catastrophic impact on public opinion and on the health and welfare of millions of people. The publishers claimed it was (The/A) "Number One Bestseller." They described it as "The World-Famous Bestseller about the Man-made Pollutants that Threaten to Destroy Life on this Earth."

Rachel Carson's *Silent Spring* has been used ever since its publication as a bible for the nature-conservation movement, but its real thrust was zoophilic. Although Carson gave some space to her belief in the necessity of preserving plants, streams, rocks, etc., she was mainly concerned about man's influence on other animals. She seemed to believe these effects were uniformly harmful. This concept is inherent in the title of the book, which indicates she envisions a hateful world where no birds sing, no chipmunks chatter, no monkeys scream, and no fish splash — a world where the sounds are mainly motorboats, automobiles, and screeching kids, with an occasional atomic bomb explosion.

Although Carson's concept overlaps somewhat that of "nature conservationists," the latter generally show less concern for animals and more for inaminate manifestations of nature.

There can be little doubt that Rachel Carson was sincere in her belief in animism, even before she began to gain substantial profits from her advocacy of a return to a "simpler" lifestyle. *Silent Spring* is far more a religious screed than a scientific discourse. Carson became an avatar or apotheosis of environmentalism. Her name and her oeuvre were of inestimable value to the econuts.

Here are some of the blurbs from the covers and endpapers of the 1970 paperback edition of Carson's book:

•"I recommend *Silent Spring* above all other books." N. J. Berrill, author of *Man's Emerging Mind.*

•"Certain to be history-making in its influence upon thought and public policy all over the world." Book-of-the-Month Club News.

•"Miss Carson is a scientist and is not given to tossing serious charges around carelessly. When she warns us, as she does with such a profound sense of urgency, we ought to take heed. *Silent Spring* may well be one of the great and towering books of our time. This book is **must** reading for every responsible citizen." Chicago Daily News.

•"Miss Carson's cry of warning is timely. If our species cannot police itself against overpopulation, nuclear weapons and pollution, it may become extinct." The New York Times.

•"A great woman has awakened the Nation by her forceful account of the dangers around us. We owe much to Rachel Carson." Former Secretary of the Interior Steward L. Udall.

•"It is high time for people to know about these rapid changes in their environment, and to take an effective part in the battle that may shape the future of all life on earth." The New York Times Book Review (front page).

•"It should come as no surprise that the gifted author of *The Sea*

Around Us can take another branch of science . . . and bring it so sharply into focus that any intelligent layman can understand what she is talking about. Understand, yes, and shudder, for she has drawn a living portrait of what is happening to this balance of nature as decreed in the science of life — and what man is doing (and has done) to destroy it and create a science of death." Virginia Kirkus Bulletin.

•"When you read *Silent Spring*, you will know why Justice William O. Douglas called it, 'The most important chronicle of this century for the human race.'" Unattributed.

•"Not war, but a plethora of manmade things . . . is threatening to strangle us, suffocate us, bury us, in the debris and by-products of our technologically inventive and irresponsible age." Margaret Mead.

•"The 1970s absolutely must be the years when America pays its debt to the past by reclaiming the purity of its air, its waters, and our living environment. It is literally now or never." Richard M. Nixon.

•"If man is fortunate enough to survive his undeclared war on nature, an ample share of the credit will go to a gallant lady, Rachel Carson." Paul R. Ehrlich.

•"Should be read by every American who does not want it to be the epitaph of a world not very far beyond us in time." Loren Eiseley.

In this brief summary of some of the compliments given to Carson we find her described as, "scientist," "great," "gifted," and "gallant," while we are told the book is "certain to be history-making," "great," "towering," "must reading," "forceful," "the most important chronicle of our time [!]," and "should be read by every American." Much of this stuff is the customary rubber-stamped praise produced on demand by the advertising and public relations departments of the big publishers, but a considerable amount of creativity is evident in the choice of purported endorsers.

This list of admirers shows us that a great amount of influence and money went into the promotion of *Silent Spring*. Although some of the usual suspects, Paul Ehrlich, Margaret Mead, and Stew Udall, are among the crowd, we find others who must have had been offered a considerable incentive to join the parade. We also see that the people involved range across the political spectrum, another sign that very heavy pressure was being brought to bear to promote the anti-DDT theology.

Review of Silent Spring

Because of the historical importance of Carson's book and since it reveals the type of thinking characteristic of the "Green" movement and of naturists in general, considerable space will be devoted at this point to an extensive review of *Silent Spring*.

The cover art shows the skeleton of a bird resting in a human hand. This sets the tone of the text. The first chapter of *Silent Spring* is, "A fable for tomorrow." This short "fable" tells of a town where all the wildlife had died. Many, if not all, of the other animals had also vanished. Many, perhaps most, of the plants had followed their example. Unfortunately, some of the humans still survived.

Of course, this holocaust was mostly due to DDT, but other evils of humanity, such as the practice of growing food crops, contributed to it. Miss Carson is particularly sad about the wildlife — although she was Encouraged by the thought that humans were also on the brink of destruction. The chapter titles suggest the bias of her magnum opus:

1. A Fable for Tomorrow
2. The Obligation to Endure
3. Elixirs of Death
4. Surface Waters and Underground Seas
5. Realms of the Soil
6. Earth's Green Mantle
7. Needless Havoc
8. And No Birds Sing
9. Rivers of Death
10. Indiscriminately from the Skies
11. Beyond the Dreams of the Borgias
12. The Human Price

Examples of the Carson Wisdom

Carson believed the *ultimate* danger to "life on earth" is not DDT, it is the human race, per se. Her words leave us with the feeling that Carson would have thoroughly approved of a potion which would have the same effect on people that DDT has on insects. For example, Carson does not appear to regard insect destruction of crops as "environmental damage," while considering destruction of the insects by humans as "environmental damage."

Scientific proofs of most of the points she attempts to make in her book are markedly lacking, but she does not seem to consider these lacunae as a fault. In her "List of principal sources," Carson cites over 500 publications, or parts of publications (with many duplications), but her citations usually are not tied to specific statements or bits of data cited in the text. As a result, the original authorities on which her claims are based are difficult, if not impossible, to identify. Examples of the style of her citations are:

"Page 26 — Hueper, *Occupational Tumors*"
"Page 31 — Laug et al., 'Liver cell Alteration.' "

The final chapter, "The Other Road," includes Rachel's precepts for our future conduct, based on her regard for the little fishies and other nice things that she saw in her early career as a dabbler in water.

It is certainly possible, that Carson did not have the original idea for *Silent Spring*, but had been sought out by the public relations experts who had been hired to get DDT banned. She was known to be emotionally dedicated to a theory they wanted the public to accept and she had a reputation which guaranteed that her recommendations would be given credence by the popular press and the green movement.

The author of the book you are now reading does not object to the idea of humankind as an integral part of "nature" or to the philosophical (or spiritual) proposition that humans should make an effort to improve the welfare of other animals (unless such action leads to harm to humans), but he objects to Carson's approach, because a mutually dependent web — benefiting man as well as other animals — does not seem to be in accord with her worldview. She appears to regard the very existence of humanity as a threat to "Nature," and even to suggest (perhaps unintentionally) that Nature would be a helluvalot better off if mankind wasn't around to interfere with it.

Enter Paul Ehrlich

The Introduction to the *Silent Spring* paperback edition of 1970 was written by Paul R. Ehrlich, whose extravagant praise for the book has been noted above. Ehrlich deserves more space than is available here, because his comments clearly reveal the thrust of the publicity program that was in progress. He was a darling of the leftist media, having written *The Population Bomb*, a book about the imminent demise of the human race, which was highly praised by all the establishment press. Before he joined this crusade, he specialized in Lepidoptera — thus progressing from saving butterflies to saving the world in less than 10 years.

Proving his adeptness as a master of hyperbole, Mr. Ehrlich pulled no punches in his praise for Carson's tour de "farce." Twice in two pages he calls Carson's book, "beautifully written." He also says, "If man is fortunate enough to survive his undeclared war on nature, an ample share of the credit will go to a gallant lady, Rachel Carson." He berates pesticide producers and users. He attributes effects to pesticide use which are contrary not only to published scientific results, but to reason and common sense. Programs to eradicate fire ants are described as "insane," an opinion which might be shared by fire ants but is hard to justify on a broader ecological or sociological basis.

Ehrlich cautions us that "... the load of DDT stored in their tissues *may* [his emphasis] have already cut years off the life expectancy of every American child born since 1945." Strangely, population studies have not yet reported this effect. He claims that, "Over the last decade or so, people in the US have averaged some 7-12 million parts [of DDT] in their body fat." No reference is cited, and there are no descriptions of the cohort, analytical procedures, etc. for this astonishing claim.

He acknowledges that the acute toxicity of DDT is quite low, but he claims that prolonged exposure to the chemical has very deleterious effects. For example, "... DDT exposure has been shown to reduce the learning ability of trout and to make previously trained trout naive again." Not nearly as naive as some of Ehrlich's supporters, one might suggest.

Following a few pages of vitriolic prose devoted to bashing every person who disagrees with him, Ehrlich asks us to sympathize with Carson because she was subjected to a "vicious campaign of vilification" and "preposterous abuse." Translation: A few independent scientists proved that Carson didn't know what she was talking about. After concluding that DDT would have destroyed the planet, had not he, and other heroes like him, directed attention to our predicament, Ehrlich notifies us that polychlorinated biphenyls are "virtually world-wide environmental contaminants" which ought to be abolished.

Ehrlich acknowledges that, if DDT is banned, "The synthetic organic phosphate insecticides which lack the persistence of chlorinated hydrocarbons will doubtless come into wider use." He also admits that these new insecticides (such as parathion, TEPP, and Azodrin) "tend to have very high acute toxicities." But, the active molecules have shorter lives after they are applied to the soil, vegetation, etc. This is the main reason Ehrlich gives for advocating their use in preference to DDT, apparently disregarding the cumulative effect of the decompositon products.

But, the very resistance of DDT to chemical changes under normal conditions of use suggests that it is not utilized by the body. There is no indication it substitutes for a normal reactant in any body process and it does not act as a hormone. If it is not transformed into other compounds by physiological processes, then it is difficult to see how it will affect animal physiology, when present in a concentration likely to be encountered by any human. On the other hand, the greater reactivity of DDT replacements, and the need for applying them in greater quantity than DDT, and more often than DDT, indicates there will be an accumulation of reaction products in the biosphere which will have results that are unknown but which are certainly not beneficial. The ultimate conclusion an unbiased observer would reach is that all of the replacements mentioned by Ehrlich are likely to be more dangerous than DDT.

The true Red Guard spirit is evoked by Ehrlich: "It is too bad that Miss Carson cannot see the youngsters marching with 'Ban DDT' banners or hear the folksong written about that chemical . . . a chemical which has become symbolic of the willingness of men to destroy the environment for profit." And, "They [the environmentalists] will not be satisfied until the . . . people of the entire world, have learned to respect their environment, to live in harmony with it rather than try to attempt the impossible task of dominating it with brute force." He is glad to know that there is a burgeoning movement (circa 1970) all over the world for people to "respect" their environment (we will all pledge allegiance to Mr. Environment. Or am I thinking of Big Brother?). "Nothing less will suffice," is the way Ehrlich expresses it.

But, they are not marching to his drummer in the malaria-ridden tropics. It has been estimated that 300 millions of Africans and Asians are infected with malaria each year and about 1.5 million die, most of them children. And the disease is starting to revive in the US: in 1998 there were 1,540 cases. Every one of these victims had been injected with trypanosomes by mosquitoes, insects which could have been readily and cheaply eliminated by DDT. But this insecticide has not been available to those who need it most — it has been banned by an international authority as a result of econut activism, thanks largely to Dr. Ehrlich and Miss Carson.

Preventive medication, for those who can afford it, depends on about four drugs, chloroquine, doxycycline, mefloquine, and malarone. In WWII, Atebrine was used. All of these have frightening side effects (including psychosis) in some users, are often very expensive, and do not afford complete protection.

Further examples of Ehrlich's intemperate and ill-considered language are given below.

page xvi: "The pesticide industry . . . began a campaign to protect their profits . . . a campaign unparalleled in its distortions, outright lies, personal abuse of opponents, and, above all, stupidity."

page xviii: "We are slowly beginning to realize . . . that the load of DDT stored in their tissues may already have cut years off the life expectancy of every child born since 1945." There has been no increase in death rate in those generations, except for the increase due to AIDS, malaria, and violence.

page xix: " . . . while DDT . . . does not have high acute toxicity (that is, you do not drop dead if you eat a teaspoonful) the evidence is piling up that continuous exposure over the long term may be fatal." There never was any valid evidence that long term exposure to DDT, in the amounts present in the environment, had increased the death rate anywhere.

page xx: "In 1967, a study was published indicating that a small group of men who had been working a number of years for a DDT manufacturer showed no obvious ill effects. The group was too small [no details given], the time period of exposure too short [no data given to support this claim], and the examinations too cursory [no details given] to permit any conclusions to be drawn. In addition, the design of the study was incompetent" [no justification given for this conclusion].

page xxi. "It is impossible to say exactly what the long term direct effects of the chlorinated hydrocarbon load in the human population will be." Clearly not impossible for Ehrlich, since he spells out the consequences he foresees throughout his publications, while implying a high deal of certainty for his prophesies. For example, on the same page:

"Since 1962 the evidence has steadily mounted that chlorinated hydrocarbon poisoning of ecosystems is generating a massive ecocatastrophe." Also, on the same page, "DDT and its relatives are very poisonous, very persistent, highly mobile, and highly fat soluble. It is these four characteristics [which he has stated he knows exist] which make chlorinated hydrocarbons such a potent threat to the ecological systems of the Earth." He had previously stated (page xix) that DDT did not have high acute toxicity.

On pages xxii and xxiii we find the rather famous claim that the egg shells of wild birds were getting thinner because of DDT. Many researchers who are not economically involved in the outcome have questioned these results. He continues, " ... the omelet-laying dickey birds are a symptom of a much more serious and possibly fatal sickness in the sea." Surprisingly, the sharks and whales still live.

At the end of his lengthy introduction to *Silent Spring*, Ehrlichman gets in a plug for the book, *Population, Resources, Environment: Issues in Human Ecology*. The authors are Paul R. and Anne H. Ehrlich. Chutzpah is the word that springs to the lips.

Alternative Approaches

Since no reasonable person would propose that the insect vectors of numerous diseases that kill millions of people every year should be allowed to proliferate freely, with no type of control, the sensitive environmentals sought to provide us with alternatives to DDT.

Rachel has the answer — Carson wrote, "A truly extraordinary variety of alternatives to the chemical control of insects is available." Sure there are! One can swat mosquitoes, step on caterpillars, and incinerate moths, but such pests have the advantages of much greater numbers and much more rapid reproduction than are characteristic of human beings, so it is fairly obvious that, even if the persons residing in the malaria zones spent every waking moment combatting their culturally deprived little opponents on a one to one basis, we would never be able to keep their populations within acceptable bounds.

Nonetheless, our famous author is sure she has the answers. "Some [of the alternatives] are already in use and have achieved brilliant success. Others are in the stage of laboratory testing. Still others are little more than ideas in the minds of imaginative scientists, waiting for the opportunity to put them to the test. All have this in common: they are *biological* solutions, based on understanding of the living organisms they seek to control, and of the whole fabric of life to which these organisms belong."

It would be interesting to question the experts allegedly working on these pest controls. We would begin by asking them, "Tell us how you are testing your results against 'the whole fabric of life to which these organisms belong.'"

Rachel has reservations — At some time, there appeared to Ms. Carson, through the vapors surrounding her, a vision which convinced our courageous scientist that some people, however green they might be, would like to have access to a method for killing insects. It is intriguing to speculate that one of her backers discovered that an investment in, e.g., a posh resort, was going down the drain because of bedbug infestation, and called on Rachel for help. Whatever her motive was, Carson agreed there might be a valid reason for reducing the population of insects in a carefully targeted area, using Nature's way.

She described the potential of biological control, "In America it had its obscure beginnings a century ago with the first attempts to introduce natural enemies of insects that were proving troublesome to farmers, an effort that sometimes moved slowly or not at all, but now and again gathered speed under the impetus of an outstanding success." She means such ideas as the introduction of large numbers of insect-killing animals. That is, if you are bothered by ants, you bring in a few dozen aardvarks; if mosquitoes are the problem, you rent a bevy of bats.

Contrary to her assertion, there were no outstanding successes. Some tests showed early promise in limited laboratory experiments, but unexpected (to Carson) problems quickly arose in the field tests. Among these were (1) development of resistance by the targeted insects and (2) adaptation of the added predatory insects or viruses to different hosts. These adaptations by host and predator caused major losses to farmers. Above all, the concept of fighting insect pests by distributing organisms that preyed upon them foundered on the rock of testing by unbiased experts using controlled tests. Incidentally, previous attempts (no connection with Carson) to control plant or animal pests by introducing non-indigenous predators had led to disastrous effects in whole countries.

More from Rachel: "Some of the most fascinating of the new methods are those that seek to turn the strength of a species against itself — to use the drive of an insect's life forces to destroy it. The most spectacular of these approaches is the 'male sterilization' technique developed by the chief of the US Department of Agriculture's Entomology Research Branch, Dr. Edward Knipling, and his associates." It is worthwhile, in order to cast more light on Carson's reliability, to explore this comment further. We examine below not only the "sterile male" concept, but also the "artificial cow," and the "bednet" methods of combatting insect vectors of disease.

Sterile males — Carson's fascination with biological methods for insect control led her to express a somewhat premature enthusiasm for a ingenious but poorly validated concept which involves three (or more) steps. These are:

1. Large numbers of insects of the targeted species are grown in a laboratory setting.

2. The males are sterilized by radiation, chemicals, or other agent.

3. The supposedly sterile males are released into the fields where the pests are causing a problem.

In theory, the sterile males will mate with the wild females, leading to unfertilized eggs, and (of course) to a failure of the eggs to hatch, so there will be no more of the insects — after the existing generation dies off.

There are some negatives to the male sterilization approach which are obvious at the outset. For example, the target population (i.e., the predatory insects which are already in place chewing up the crops) will always include the usual proportion of fertile males. Since the females normally lay many eggs, one successful mating with a fertile male will offset many female matings with sterile males. Furthermore, the cost of this approach is prohibitive and its inflexibility relative to time and place of application would make it an unacceptable choice to most agriculturalists.

In the first practical tests of this compassionate, sensitive theory, there were cases in which the treated males were *not* infertile, contrary to the assurances of the scientists who provided them, so that runaway proliferation of the pests resulted when quantities of the test insects were released in the fields. And then, of course, the enormous population of predatory insects ruined the farmers' crops for the test years, and perhaps their progeny infested the fields for many years after that.

The enthusiastic and unquestioning approval given by Carson to biological methods for controlling insect pests suggests to this author that she was getting some monetary assistance (by way of grants, etc.) from companies that expected to profit from a movement away from chemical means of insect control. Unfortunately, no one has ever investigated this connection, so far as this author knows.

A recent news report (Cho 2002) describes some experimentation being done with bollworm moths, the pests that spoil cotton crops. "For years, USDA and California officials have released millions of irradiated, sterile bollworm moths to disrupt the mating practices of fertile females. But the releases aren't efficient, some 60 irradiated moths are needed for every wild one because the lab-bred moths compete poorly in the field ... [Scientists are planning] ... to release hardier, genetically engineered bollworms that father stillborn young. But first [the scientists] ... will test mutants that produce a fluorescent jellyfish protein making them easier to track as they compete for mates."

Bednets — Another environmentally friendly, biodiversity sensitive, politically correct method for controlling those nasty mosquitoes requires the use of insect-resistant bednets sprayed with some sort of preparation based, we may suppose, on an organic, holistic vegetable extract such as pyrethrins. Citizens of third-world countries who can't even afford a bed are supposed to buy treated bed nets, most of them undoubtedly imported.

Not only must they buy the nets, but it is likely they will have to frequently replenish the insecticide (or insect repellent) coating with, e.g., an aerosol spray — purchased with their spare funds. And, of course, the inhabitants must retire to their netted beds whenever they see a mosquito, this in areas where mosquitoes (often clouds of mosquitoes) are present at all hours of the day in all seasons. It is noteworthy that this so-called solution to the malaria problem leaves the most economically deprived members of the population at the greatest risk.

Artificial cows — If this report reads like something clipped from a Dave Barry column, don't blame this author. An expanded version of the following discussion can be found at the Daily University Science News site: **http://unisci.com/stories/20013/092001.htm**

"Dr. Stephen Torr of the University of Greenwich's Natural Resources Institute," reported that "In total, around 2,900 tons of DDT have been used in Zimbabwe. This pest control policy has now been abandoned in favor of more effective and environmentally friendly alternatives such as artificial cows."

"Developed by an international group of researchers including scientists from the University of Greenwich in the UK, the artificial cows attract tsetse [flies] by using kairomones (a blend of chemicals emitted by one species and detected by another) to mimic the smell of real cattle. The fake cattle are *impregnated with insecticides* that kill the tsetse attracted to them." Four artificial cows are usually placed per square kilometer of land. The tsetse flies often carry trypanosomes which infect the cattle the flies feed on. One type of organism causes the disease, nagana, in cattle, while another variety causes sleeping sickness in humans. "There have been three severe epidemics of sleeping sickness in Africa over the last century, with the last one beginning in 1970 and still in progress." *Silent Spring* was first published in 1962.

The basic problem with this approach is that the breeding places of the mosquitoes are not eliminated, therefore swarms of mosquitoes will still be present in areas occupied by humans, and, of course, the insects will continue to serve as vectors of sleeping sickness.

A Flicker of Light?

Advocates of the use of DDT to kill trypanosome-carrying mosquitoes have been getting a bit of favorable publicity recently. A report dated November 29, 2000, and entitled "DDT still has role to play in fighting malaria" can be found at: **http://unisci.com/stories**

Excerpts follow: "For many malaria-affected countries, responsible DDT use is a vital strategy for preventing malaria transmission and controlling epidemics. Countries continue to use DDT primarily because they cannot affort reliable alternatives and do not have the capacity to develop them."

"In order to ensure that treaty restrictions on DDT will not result in an increase in malaria deaths, WHO and the Roll Back Malaria partnership (RBM) are encouraging the negotiators to support time-limited exemptions for the public health use of DDT."

"WHO recommends that DDT should be used only for indoor residual spraying and every step must be taken to prevent DDT from being diverted to agricultural uses," says Dr. Heymann. "Projections suggest that the amounts of DDT needed for malaria control are a very small fraction of what has been used in the past for agricultural purposes." We see here an attempt to keep the major share of the insecticide market (the agricultural applications) as a monopoly for the producers of the more expensive insecticides.

A recent UN report described by Fukuda-Parr (2001) contained some unexpected support for mosquito control by chemical means.

Amazingly, the UN (that citadel of political correctness) saw fit to attack the ban on DDT. In 2000, the UN brokered a new Stockholm Convention on Persistent Organic Pollutants (POPs) that resulted in a provision for the continued use of DDT for malaria control. Also, to keep the money flowing to establishment favorites, the UN mandated increased spending for the evaluation of alternatives. It seems their goal is still the ultimate elimination of DDT.

The acceptance by the UN of the continued use of DDT came after much pressure had been exerted on the bootless bureaucrats of that massive scam by countries who were seeing vast numbers of their workers die from malaria ostensibly "controlled" by other (natural?) means, such as bed nets sprayed with pyrethrins.

Behind that curtain — The concealed motive for banning DDT, and the reason the campaign to ban it (starting with the promoting of Carson's book) was put into play, is that large corporations had developed patentable insecticides which would never have achieved wide use had not the cheap, effective, persistent (and patent-free) DDT been propagandized out of existence. Vast profits were made from these patented insecticides, some of which cost up to 10 times as much as DDT would have cost. And, none of these pesticides were ever tested by independent laboratories to see if they were free of the problems alleged to be caused by DDT (such as causing wild birds to lay eggs with thin shells). Nevertheless, the anti-DDT propagandists continue to pursue their disinformation campaigns.

For example, Liroff (2001), the Director, Alternatives to DDT Project, World Wildlife Fund, mentions some of his environmentally sensitive ideas for replacing DDT, although he says it is a "myth" that environmentalists want DDT banned regardless of its usefulness in combatting malaria. This statement is breathtaking in its effrontery — ever since *Silent Spring* the environmentalists have wanted DDT banned regardless of its benefits to humanity.

Liroff then states that the World Wildlife Fund wants reduced reliance on DDT for malaria control because of the hazards to health created when it is sprayed indoors and the demonstrated success of alternative approaches. The alternative approaches have already resulted in the deaths of millions from malaria, and no one knows what will be the ultimate results on human health of the residues of the alternatives that have been applied during the ban.

Dr. Liroff says that Mexico and Vietnam are among the countries that "have controlled malaria while eliminating DDT." The citizens of these countries will be interested to know that the malaria-like symptoms they are suffering from, or that their relatives and neighbors have died from, are really due to some other disease. And besides, this author knows for a fact that DDT products can be bought over the counter in Mexico, regardless of the legal status of the substance in that country.

Liroff mentions a report in a recent issue of *Lancet* which suggested that DDE (a breakdown product of DDT) is "associated with" preterm deliveries and low birth weights. But, haven't we been told that one of the "problems" with DDT is its stability, that it does not break down readily?

Liroff also explains that the World Health Organization's "Roll Back Malaria" program "emphasizes use of bed nets treated with other chemicals." So, we are to have the poor citizens confined to their beds behind their stinking mosquito netting during the entire period that mosquitoes are abroad. This solution is typical of the propagandizing and maneuverings of red-oriented organizations such as WHO.

Ingenious Ways of Avoiding the Obvious

Many roundabout ways have been suggested for preventing insect-borne diseases without killing the insects. The ingenuity used in conceiving and elaborating some of these scenarios is quite remarkable, but they all ignore the obvious simple solution, because there is no money in it. A few of the ideas will be discussed briefly in the following paragraphs.

Chagas disease — American trypansomiasis, or Chagas disease, is caused by a protozoan parasite (*Trypanosoma cruzi*) that is carried by triatomine bugs, which feed on blood. About 18 million people are infected annually. The disease is frequently fatal, and neither effective drugs nor vaccines are available. The bugs can be killed by a number of different insecticides. Wouldn't you say that lives could be saved and much suffering prevented by applying an appropriate insecticide in sufficient amount in all the places likely to be occupied by the bugs? But, that isn't the way we do things around here.

Cohen and Gürtler (2001) mention (without approval) the suggestion of diverting bugs from humans by using animals not susceptible to the trypanosome. "In three rural villages ... in ... northwest Argentina" they studied the animal and human households. " ... The median household ... had five people, about three infected dogs, no more than one cat, and 8 to 27 chickens and ducks." Cohen and Gürtler developed a mathematical model which showed that householders could greatly reduce the risk of disease by "excluding domestic animals, especially infected dogs, from bedrooms, removing potential refuges for bugs from walls and ceilings, and ... " intermittently using insecticides.

Mild mosquitoes — We learn from a news item by Milius (2002) that genetic engineers have built a mosquito "that's wonderfully bad at transmitting malaria in lab tests." These transgenic pansies is only 20% as likely to infect mice with trypanosomes. Researcher hope that some day they can deploy the antimalarial gene into wild populations of mosquitoes. Research continues.

River blindness — This disease is caused by a nematode (*Onchocerca volvulus*) transmitted by several species of Simuliid flies that breed in moving water. According to Kennedy (2002), the World Health Organization has, *for 25 years,* been working on black fly vector control in West Africa. "Another program, the African Programme for

Ochocerciasis, emphasizes annual treatment with the antifilarial drug ivermectin ... A third program, the Onchocerciasis Elimination Program of the Americas, promotes twice-a-year ivermectin treatments ... " Guinea worm disease in Africa is a similar problem. They are working on the basics. In another 25 years, and after another billion dollars or so, they are pretty sure they'll have a grasp on treatment — not prevention, treatment. But, no bugs, no blindness — kill the bugs.

As Al-Olayan, et al. (2002) says, "For over a century, a major objective of malaria control programs has been to block parasite transmission by mosquitoes." These researchers then present their development of a method to culture the trypanosomes in vitro. No doubt a very fine achievement, but if we killed all the mosquitoes, we wouldn't have to do all this work, would we?

In 1991, the US National Institute of Allergy and Infectious Diseases awarded $9 million to Celera Genomics Group of Rockville MD to elucidate the genome of the mosquito (*Anopheles gambiae*), the primary carrier of the malaria trypanosome in sub-Saharan Africa. The idea is to get information on which to base anti-malaria strategies such as vaccines and drugs. Apparently, scientists are working on at least four different kinds of malaria vaccines: (1) targeting the sexual stages of the parasites, (2) making the mosquitoes resistant to infection, (3) preventing clinical manifestations in infected persons by immunizing against sporozite antigens, and (4) targeting merozoites.

In 2002, it was announced that scientists from Wellcome Trust, the Institute for Genome Research, and Stanford U were close to being able to publish the entire DNA sequence of the malaria organism (*Plasmodium falciparum*). At least $30 million has been spent on the project this far. That would buy a lot of DDT.

Better off dead — A book by Desowitz (1992) is the source for the following: "Population control advocates blamed DDT for increasing third world population. In the 1960s, World Health Organization authorities believed there was no alternative to the overpopulation problem but to assure that up to 40% of the children in poor nations should die of malaria. As an official of the Agency for International Development stated, 'Rather dead than alive and riotously reproducing.' "

For the Birds

As previously mentioned, a major talking point in the battle to make the use of DDT illegal was the claim that the peregrine falcon population of the world was being greatly reduced by the build-up of the insecticide's residues in the environment. Part of the supposed mechanism of this avian holocaust was the thinning of the birds' egg shells by some poorly explained mechanism. Photos of broken eggs in falcons' nests (though not necessarily placed there by the birds) were prominent exhibits in the propaganda campaign. Tables, graphs, and reams of discussion were published (mostly *not* in scientific journals) to support the claim that there were fewer peregrine falcons in the world today than there were before DDT came into use.

The peregrine falcon scam has been thoroughly debunked by a number of writers, of which none have been more comprehensive and direct in their rebuttals than Dr. J. Gordon Edwards, professor of entomology at San Jose U, and Steven J. Milloy, of *Junk Science* fame.

Some of the points made by Edwards and Milloy in their article, *100 things you should know about DDT*, can be found on the Internet at: **www.junkscience.com/aug99.falfall**

This site should be consulted by those readers interested in identifying the original references. Following are edited excerpts from the Edwards and Milloy compilation.

• Peregrine falcons were uncommon and were deemed undesirable in the early 20th century. Dr. William Hornaday of the New York Zoological Society referred to them as birds that "deserve death, but are so rare we need not take them into account."

• Falconers were blamed for decimating western populations by trapping falcons either for their personal use in hunting other birds or for sale to other falconers.

• In 1966, scientists impaneled by the UK government concluded: "There is no close correlation between the declines in populations of predatory birds, particularly the peregrine falcon . . . and the use of DDT." [Milloy's ellipsis]

• Many experiments on caged birds demonstrate that DDT and its breakdown products (DDD and DDE) do not cause serious eggshell thinning, even at levels many hundreds of times greater than wild birds could ever accumulate.

• After seven months of testimony during 1971-1972, an administrative judge in the Environmental Protection Agency concluded that DDT had no deleterious effects on wild birds. He was overruled by EPA administrator William Ruckelshaus, who decided to ban DDT even though he never attended any of the DDT hearings and had never even read the hearing transcript.

• Stress due to intrusion of humans into the falcons' nesting grounds (as by environmentalists seeking evidence of DDT poisoning) could account for at least some eggshell thinning, if any occurred.

• Declines in the US peregrine falcon population occurred long before the DDT years, as did declines in the numbers of many other wild birds. Habitat changes clearly account for most of these, and probably account for nearly all.

• Widespread declines in the populations of birds other than falcons during the DDT years is a myth.

• Gas chromatography was universally used for pesticide analysis in the mid-1960s. But it often failed to differentiate between DDT residues and other chemicals. Furthermore, published articles suggest there was accidental intra-laboratory contamination of some of the samples.

Scrambled data — A famous graph of data (perhaps a computer-generated chart) said to have been derived from tests on peregrine falcon eggs, shows a dramatic drop in the shell thicknesses of peregrine falcon eggs beginning around 1970. This diagram was much used (and is still being used) as "proof" of the effect of DDT on the environment. It must have occasioned much uneasiness on the part of any experimental scientist who took the time to study it.

The graph shows what appears to be a relatively large amount of data entered each year for several years, which indicates that, for some reason, a person or a team was spending a great deal of time collecting (and, perhaps destroying) eggs for the purpose of determining the shell thickness, even though the lack of substantial change in years preceding the introduction of DDT would have seemed to suggest to the person who designed the study that he wasn't getting anywhere. Yet, this indefatigable investigator proceeded with his thankless task up to several years after the time DDT was first introduced, when, lo and behold, the whole mass of data shifted downward. Frankly, this is rather suspicious, although it is true there is no accounting for the vagaries of the environmentally sensitive.

Even if the graph turns out to be substantially correct, and that is, of course, a possibility, we are left with some critical questions about the study. Such as:

• Where is the proof that the peregrine falcons that laid the fragile eggs had ingested *any* DDT?

• The drastic change in shell thickness was first observed in eggs laid in about 1970 or 1971, long after DDT had come into use.

• What were the other causes that were considered and eliminated in fixing the responsibility for eggshell thinning on DDT ingestion?

• There are suggestions in other literature that peregrine falcon eggs were a favorite target of egg collectors and, as this relatively rare specimen became even rarer, the collectors increased their efforts to collect the eggs. In fact, the birds themselves were favorite targets of hunters who wanted stuffed specimens to exhibit. Were these factors considered?

• The sudden influx of frantic egg measurers into the habitats of the very few peregrine falcons in the US, which seems to have started immediately after someone suggested that DDT was the cause of eggshell thinning, may have convinced these birds to migrate to other locales, leading to a drop in the bird count, or to complete absence of the species, in their old nesting area. Remember, these birds are not committed to a given spot, they are perfectly able to relocate when dissatisfied with their previous nesting spot, and they are known to choose areas which experience the least human intervention.

• What is the statistical probability that the observed decline in shell thickness (if it was observed) was the result of random variations in the small sample base? Were all the data obtained using the same protocol and standardized instruments? Were the raw data used in the study of egg thickness subjected to a rigorous statistical analysis to determine the possibility of inadvertent experimental bias in the form of variations in test procedures, sample selection and preparation, and the instruments used? Do the data show bias in selection, retention, and rejection of data?

The First Question That Should Have Been Asked

No one in the literature relating to peregrine falcon populations that this author has reviewed, has ever asked the simple question: "Should we devote *any* time, money, or even thought, to the preservation of this carnivorous feathered rarity?" A few of the points we should consider:

1. The peregrine falcon requires hundreds of square miles of free range before it is comfortable with its surroundings. We are speaking of wild birds, who were raised in a traditional family, not those birds hatched in the laboratory of some academic, birds who think it is perfectly reasonable to perch on the window sill of a New York City skyscraper and eat the pigeons who are themselves fed by the kindly parkbench-sitters.

2. Falcons kill hundreds of other birds each year. They never ask whether or not their prey is on the Endangered Species List. Many of their favorite targets are song birds, or other animals thought by some to be attractive additions to the biota. If one sample of some of the species they kill and eat on a routine basis were to be found in the game bag of a human hunter, that person would be liable to fine and imprisonment,

and would be vilified in the press. And, if someone should suggest that this killer bird be exterminated so it does not interfere with, for example, carrier pigeons, he would be thought to be terribly cruel, and possibly insane.

A Fable for Our Times

Mr. and Mrs. Peregrine were flying high above the river that runs through their 200,000 acre ranch.

Seeing a small speck far below, Mrs. P says, "Ooh look, isn't that a meadowlark?"

Hubby responds, "Yes. You may recall they are on the Endangered Species List."

Mrs. P. "Yes, and don't they taste good!"

Mr. P. "I'll knock him down and tear his head off."

Mrs. P. "No fair! It's my turn to tear the head off. You know that's the best part!"

To conclude our discussion of this idolized feathered pest, we offer the following modest suggestion:

Kill all the peregrine falcons and save   millions of songbirds from gruesome deaths.

Exposing the Disinformation

In view of the many fallacies clearly present in Carson's work, it is astounding that the establishment was able to blacklist and censor virtually every attempt to bring the public's attention to the truth about DDT. Among the books, essays, and scientific articles which dissected *Silent Spring*, Rita Beatty's volume, *The DDT Myth: Triumph of the Amateurs* (Beatty 1973), stands out. This book was one of the most valuable summaries of the literature available at the time of its publication. As might be expected, Beatty's remarkable achievement received little or no attention from the establishment media. There were few attempts to rebut its conclusions or even to review it — the book was simply ignored.

A dedicated researcher who could devote a lot of time to the project should be able to trace the threads of the anti-DDT campaigns back to the providers of seed money, and thus reveal the identity of the persons or companies who expected to benefit on a large scale from the demonization of this useful insecticide. This project could result in a very useful book, a primer on how public opinion is manipulated by the newspeak managers.

We suggest that the chief beneficiaries of the DDT bans were the companies who manufactured, or who owned patents on, insecticides that would have sold poorly, if at all, as long as the cheap, effective, and persistent insecticide DDT was available to the public. In addition to their other flaws, the new insecticides were often much more toxic to humans than DDT. Many of them degraded relatively quickly in the environment, requiring more frequent applications in order to protect crops throughout the growing season, so that larger quantities of them could be sold. Of course, the degradation products themselves remained, to cause unknown amounts of unknown kinds of damage.

A product (whether medicine, cosmetic, food, or insectide) that lasts a long time is anathema to manufacturers and marketers. Ideally, it should be necessary to use a product daily, or even more often, to get the desired results. DDT doesn't meet this requirement.

An even more deeply hidden motive may have been the desire to kill off millions of human beings who could have been saved by DDT. See the Desowitz quotation above.

Analogous Programs

It is instructive to examine other methods used by companies who either wish to introduce a new product into a market segment presently dominated by a competitive item or to destroy a currently successful product in order to make room for their new, somewhat similar, item. Two case studies illustrating these procedures will be given at this point. These compounds and programs do not directly impact environmental goals: it is the product-killing technique that is being shown here.

Demonizing saccharin — The campaign to demonize DDT resembled in many respects the scenario that was followed in the anti-saccharin campaign of the 1970s. The latter program was closely followed contemporaneously by the author. It was obvious at the time that the producers of Aspartame, a dipeptide-based low calorie sweetener which had been patented by a large corporation, could develop only a very limited market if their product had to compete with saccharin on a level playing field.

Aspartame was considerably more expensive than saccharin, when sweetening power per dollar was considered, and it was less stable under conditions existing in many foodstuffs (in carbonated beverages, for example). Furthermore, it had potential health problems of its own, possibly more than those alleged for saccharin.

However, a tightly focused, heavily financed, and ruthless media campaign extending over many months succeeded in getting the FDA to ban saccharin from most foodstuffs. As time went on, and as financing for the media campaign and bribes for legislators tapered off, it was decided by the regulatory authorities that saccharin was not poisonous after all, and it is being used again in large amounts.

Delegitimatizing metolachlor — A market-control program dependent primarily on patents must constantly be refreshed, as the old protection expires, with newly patented products of the same general type. A company called Sygenta patented a herbicide called "racemic metolachlor" in about 1976. This chemical was very useful in controlling landscape weeds such as yellow nutsedge and crabgrass, and so became especially popular with the landscape managers attached to golf courses, sod farms, and football and baseball fields. In 1999, the company introduced a single-isomer version of the active compound (called S-metolachlor), and ceased production of the racemic product, which no longer had patent protection.

Whereupon, other companies announced their intention to manufacture their own versions of the original product and sell them in competition with the new *S*-metolachlor. The prices of the competitive items will undoubtedly be substantially below that of *S*-metolachlor. Sygenta, which had an legally enforceable monopoly as long as the original patent was alive, will now have to market its goods in a strongly competitive market with consequent loss of sales, higher advertising and promotional costs, and reduced profits.

Sygenta is trying to preserve its monopoly by appealing to the EPA to cancel the registration of the original material, which Sygenta sold for more than 20 years with full approval of the EPA! The argument being used by Sygenta is that the single-isomer material can be used in smaller quantities, to achieve the same goal, and this minimizes the threat to the environment (Watkins 2002). Such an appeal may, in fact, prevail because the EPA developed something called the "reduced risk initiative" in the early 1990s. This program gives preference to new herbicides, and the like, which can be used in smaller quantities or which pose less of a threat to the environment for some other reason.

This is but a single example of hundreds of such strategies practiced by manufacturers of beneficial chemical substances, as aided by their attorneys, public relations consultants, and politicians, who manipulate public officials of all types to secure commercial advantages.

SUMMARY AND CONCLUSIONS

Stripped to its basics, the DDT story is this:

• Diseases for which mosquitoes are vectors kill millions of persons every year.

• Many potentially fatal diseases (including malaria) are caused *only* by organisms carried by mosquitoes from one human to another.

• Mosquitoes can be killed by any number of chemical compounds which are relatively inexpensive to produce and easy to apply. If the bugs become resistant to one chemical, another can be substituted. The much-studied chemical compound DDT can kill most, if not all, varieties of mosquitoes on contact.

• DDT is inexpensive, easy to use, and easy to manufacture. It is also chemically rather stable, and is nearly odorless. Even when insects in a certain population become tolerant to normal concentrations of DDT (which seems to be a rather uncommon occurrence), the compound continues to repel the insects.

• DDT has very low toxicity for humans. There are no recorded cases of humans being killed by DDT under normal conditions of manufacture or application.

• Substituting other insecticides for DDT leads to problems such as: increased cost, increased difficulty of application, rapid loss of potency after application, insufficient toxicity to insects, and unacceptable toxicity to humans.

• Cost per insect killed (including the combined costs of the chemical itself and the application method) is one of the most important factors affecting use, because the greatest need is in the most poverty stricken countries in the world. DDT wins this point hands down.

The answer should be obvious: Save as many people as possible by killing as many mosquitoes as possible, using the best insecticide available. DDT is the "best" insecticide presently available, all things considered. Future developments may give us a "better" insecticide, perhaps even a "greener" insecticide, but we should not delay action until that happens.

Since the transmission of Plasmodium organisms to humans absolutely requires the presence of mosquito vectors, the simple process of destroying all of these useless bugs by DDT (or some other equally effective insecticide) will prevent the transmission of every one of these diseases. New cases will drop nearly to zero in every locale from which mosquitoes have been eradicated.

The cost will be relatively nominal, possibly as low as a few dollars per person. The killing or inconveniencing of a few hundred or several thousand animals which suffer side effects from the insecticide should be given absolutely no weight compared to the saving of the lives of millions of people or to the elimination of intense suffering in many additional persons who would be infected but manage to survive. And, a high level of value should be attributed to the saving of food raw materials that would be lost if insects that interfere with crop production and storage are not destroyed. Of course, mosquitoes don't directly affect plant crops, but they do sicken and kill animals that are being grown for food, fiber, milk, eggs, etc.

How simple is the answer when the problem is reduced to the basics!

section 5
DESTABILIZING THE GOVERNMENT

Since the very first of the "Internationals" came into being, the Reds have attempted to destabilize existing governments, even when it appeared unlikely that the ensuing regime would be a full-scale Communist tyranny. They sought out discontented but unorganized persons as well as loosely organized groups of many types in every targeted country.

They established militant "workers' councils," "teachers' unions," and other groups which could be dominated by a small cadre of highly disciplined but covert communists. Any group having a unifying characteristic that might be attractive to a considerable number of susceptible partisans was fair game for the communist strategists. And, of course, they initiated new groups which were specifically dedicated to promoting "friendship" with Russia.

In the US, Red intelligence agencies initiated the formation of associations supposedly dedicated to furthering the aims of various ethnic groups whose members thought they had been victimized by Christian, patriotic, conservative, and middle class citizens. The Reds' greatest success in the United States, and in many other countries of the world, has probably been in the Hispanic and Jewish communities.

Considerable success was also obtained in some parts of the Negro community of the US, especially in the early days of the Red campaign — that is in the 1920s through the 1940s. Subsequently, however, many blacks moved into so-called Islamic groups and into organizations devoted to black nationalism. The majority of the blacks were never comfortable associating with people who had difficulty speaking their idiom and who advocated causes that were not directly connected with the blacks' immediate welfare.

The chapters in this section deal with Communist efforts to enlist African-Americans, Hispanics, and Jews in their battle to destroy democracy.

chapter fourteen

BLACK POWER

During the years leading up to the decline and eventual collapse of the Soviet Union, the Communists attempted to divert to their own purposes the widespread discontent and turmoil in the American Negro community. The Reds had some success in founding various Black Power organizations, but all of these groups exhibited a tendency to drift away from the pure doctrines of Marx and Engels, Lenin and Stalin. Their apostasies ultimately led to complete independence from Communist control of some, perhaps most, of those Negro organizations. In one form or another, this independence has persisted to the present time. A brief history of these developments and their significance to American politics will be given in this chapter.

No Honkies Need Apply

It has been the custom in some milieus to describe multiracial movements as "rainbows," but the rainbows apparently envisioned by Black demagogues such as Jesse Jackson, tend to be strongly oriented toward one color: green — as in currency. As a practical matter, however, these so-called multiracial movements are usually devoted to mobilizing and victimizing brown ("Hispanic") and/or black ("African") peoples. The bronze (Amerindian or "Native American") and the yellow (Oriental) components of our culture also come into play intermittently, but seldom as strongly as the Africans or Hispanics.

The American Communist Party had officially announced as early as 1958 that it would not support blacks who were aiming for separatism. The latter group included the Afro nationalists, Black Muslims, and other cultists who advocated withdrawal of people of African ancestry from the general population, not only in the US but in all countries. The reasons for the Communist position were obvious enough — the black segregationists were introducing concepts which were quite alien to the stated goals of Marx and Lenin and they also interfered with Moscow's control of their policies.

It is interesting to note that Angela Yvonne Davis, the famous academic star and jailbird, had been exposed to Red influences from early childhood, but suffered major disappointments in trying to reconcile Black goals with Red principles. She never completely resolved this difficulty, having become intricately linked with Black power icons before she decided that the Red avenue led to a brighter future, i.e., a future in which she would be alive. High points in the Angela Davis biography have been covered in another chapter.

The official Soviet policy did not, however, prevent Red agents and their social allies from providing financial and administrative support to some of the most rigid black power leaders; as always, the existence of division, disruption, and chaos was thought to facilitate the development of a workers' paradise, vide Russia in 1917. We see the results of this clandestine cooperation in the relative immunity of criminals of the black power structure from imprisonment. Of course, this immunity was not total, so some of the more violent operators were chased out of the country or even jailed, for a time. And, some were killed.

There were internecine conflicts in the Black community. A significant percentage of its leaders were violent, even paranoid, criminals who sought to establish their own little kingdoms within the community, so that they could have unlimited supplies of drugs and sex, expensive cars and clothes, lots of gold chains, and other amenities sought by all moronic dictators. Such persons were incapable of accepting orders from the Communist party or any other authority. Neither God nor Marx had any influence on them.

A few clever individuals, who could be seen circling around the edges of the roiling masses of the Negro community looking always for opportunities to profit, were far from being paranoid, but instead were cold, calculating, and smooth demagogues who managed to benefit largely by blackmailing the total American population with a curious combination of threats and appeals to sympathy: Such persons as Father Divine, the Reverend Doctor Martin Luther King, Jr., Reverend Jesse Jackson, and Reverend Al Sharpton.

Table 14.1

LEADERS AND INITIATORS OF EARLY BLACK POWER GROUPS

Republic of New Afrika [sic] — (All black)

Robert F. Williams

Milton R. Henry

Richard Henry

Herman Ferguson

Joan Franklin

LeRoi Jones

Ron Karenga

Betty Shabazz (widow of Malcom X)

Student National Coordinating Committee (SNCC)

(Originally had many white members; became all black)

James Forman

H. Rap Brown

Philip Hutchings

Revolutionary Action Movement (RAM) — (All black)

Robert F. Williams

Maxwell Stanford

Black Panther Party (Exclusively Black)

Huey P. Newton

Bobby George Seale

Eldridge Cleaver

Kathleen Cleaver

Franklyn Jones

David Hilliard

Donald L. Cox

Stokely Carmichael

George Mason Murray

Ivanhoe Donaldson

Early Red Efforts to Co-opt Negroes

According to Benjamin Gitlow, who had been a trusted and prominent Communist leader, the Comintern furnished the Party with money to establish a special Negro department. This group created a number of Negro organizations, issued Negro papers and periodicals, and used other means to attract Black agitators into the Communist party. In addition, there were continuous efforts to penetrate the existing Black power organizations and to play a role in their demonstrations, whether those displays were organized or not. "Yet in spite of our efforts and the large sums of money spent on that sort of propaganda, we made very little headway among the Negro masses. The Negroes in the United States refused to flock into the Communist Party and gave little credence to our promises" (Gitlow 1968).

In spite of Gitlow's gloomy retrospect, the Communists did have limited success with their National Negro Congress in the 1930s. The Reds had been working against the National Association for the Advancement of Colored People and the Urban League almost since the founding of these organizations. The Reds said these racially mixed groups had bourgeois goals and did not show the proper anticapitalistic venom. The biases of the NAACP and the UL should have been no surprise, since these two groups were largely managed, from behind the scenes, by "liberal" whites (mostly Jewish social workers, politicians, educators, and capitalists).

The infiltration came about in the following manner. A Joint Committee on National Recovery had been formed by the NAACP for the ostensible purpose of ameliorating the effects of the New Deal depression. The JCNR was supposed to work with government agencies to accomplish its goals.

Communist organizations were not invited to join the JCNR, but CP members and commie sympathizers were among the individuals serving on the Committee. A National Negro Congress was formed as a conduit for transmitting the views of members to influential people in the Roosevelt administration. Communists had obtained effective control of the NNC by about 1938. At the time the German-Russian cooperation treaty was announced, the NNC began to denounce "antifascist movements." This program provided an excuse for ejecting anticommunists from the Congress, which then began issuing dicta such as claiming that the administration and its supporters "insult the negro people by brazenly asking us to support this war in order than we may further enslave ourselves and [other] oppressed peoples throughout the world."

The Reds in the Committee had been premature with their moves, however, and when Hitler invaded Poland and eventually declared war on the Communists' spiritual home, Russia, the Congress lost its value as a front for the Reds. Since that time, the Communist Party and its many open and clandestine affiliates have adopted a cautious attitude about cooperating with Negroes. Of course, they never neglect an opportunity to goad the black community into violence and rebellion, and they undoubtedly have (or had) undercover agents operating within all of the African-oriented gangs and societies of appreciable size.

Black Muslims

The Nation of Islam (Black Muslims) has an interesting and instructive history which lack of space prevents us from examining in detail. See *Black Nationalism*, by E. U. Essien-Udom for a relatively neutral and quite detailed report of the method of operation of this organization and the attitudes of its members and leaders.

This author wrote, "In its ideology the Nation of Islam is political: its objective is expressed both in terms of a Negro homeland and in the wishful image of the post-apocalypse Black Nation. The former, improbable as its realization may be, lies within the realm of human experience and is therefore theoretically possible. The latter is a paradise located outside of society in some sphere transcending historical experience. In practice, however, the Nation of Islam is apolitical. If it has political aims of a practical kind, they are not clear."

As a practical matter, the real control is vested in the leader and a very few close associates, and they profit considerably from the operation of the group. They have become fairly conservative in their outlook, and no longer believe in burning down buildings for fun or killing people in a moment of pique. Their rhetoric is occasionally quite extreme, however, since they figure that is what it takes to keep the troops happy.

It is believed the leader(s) of the Nation of Islam currently have little interest in being affiliated with Bolshevik activities. Their mode of operation does, however, have strong socialistic overtones, actually showing some similarities with the Israeli kibbutzim, but with more emphasis on religious or quasi-religious rituals and fewer restrictions on geographic movements.

In spite of the name, their religion shows many significant differences from Islamic practices in the Muslim Arab nations of the Middle East.

Black Panthers

The Black Panthers began as a black nationalist group which had as its main tenet the use of violence to destroy white civilization. Later, it began to add Marxist overtones to its basic tactics of indiscriminate murder, mayhem, and destruction.

The Panthers were idolized by many persons in intellectual circles and academia, and heavily publicized by the news media. This group became the most popular object of attention by masochistic dilettantes overcome by nostalgie de boue. Although the members seldom had funds of their own, many of them having never worked at any productive job, there always seemed to be enough money coming in from undisclosed sources to support the leaders in a lifestyle that met their refined requirements.

According to evidence presented at a meeting of the Permanent Subcommittee on Investigations of the Senate Committee on Government Operations, in June of 1969, literature distributed by the Black Panthers included a leaflet entitled, "Primary Objective of Our Party: To Establish Revolutionary Political Power for Black People." It contained the following statements [in the following text, "the enemy," means all ethnic groups except African, but especially "white people"]: "The Black Panther is an armed body for carrying out the political tasks of the revolution. Especially at the present, the Black Panther Party should certainly not confine itself to only fighting; besides fighting to destroy the enemy's military strength, our Party must also shoulder such important tasks as doing propaganda among the masses, organizing the masses, arming Black people, helping them to establish revolutionary political power and setting up party organizations. The Black Panther Party defends itself with guns and force not only merely for the sake of fighting but in order to conduct propaganda among the masses, organize them, and help them to establish revolutionary political power. Without these objectives, fighting loses its meaning and the Black Panther Party loses the reason for its existence.

CARDINAL RULE: Have Faith in the People and Faith in the Party."

Planning for death and destruction — A leaflet entitled "Urban Warfare Duty" was exhibited to the Senators. It told the true believers exactly what was expected of them in terms of actions during rioting and other violent demonstrations conducted or incited by these thugs. Some extracts follow [emphasis by capitalization is present in the original]:

"We should keep in mind that an overall strategy would include simultaneous ATTACKS on suburban areas and urban areas . . . "

"Your particular mission might call for the use of wire cutters, electrical gloves, or small detonation devices, and the other teams might call for light or heavy automatic weapons, molotov fire bombs, rifles with scopes. All of this must be planned in advance the same way you would proceed to play a game of football, each man having a specific job and a specific time to do it . . . "

"In setting up an ATTACK the GUERRILLA must realize one important aim, the destruction of his target. Be it man, building, electro plant, train, what have you. The destruction of this target is of prime importance for many reasons. First of all the psychological effect of destroying the enemies [sic] complex within his own area will be devastating. The enemy will start to second guess himself. He will start to double check his security if not just increase it. And finally he will make that fatal mistake of becoming more rigid. The Imperialist getting rigid in his own mechanical society is something that will aid the GUERRILLA . . . "

"The enemy will always be able to muster troops to one point and another. But that takes time. Therefore he cannot be where the GUERRILLA is at the same time as the GUERRILLA because you will maintain the initiative. This is maintained by constant ATTACKS at varied spots in the city. You will employ AMBUSH on AMBUSH. This means that an attack on a [sic] avenue that the enemy is known to use will just be a trick to get him to stop and attack you. Once he has stopped he exposes himself to the main AMBUSH which is meant to destroy his . . . vehicles . . . "

"Brothers, these tactics are not games: they are being used today in cities where the people are ATTACKING the system. We must no longer play, but plan . . . "

"Reviewing the above, let us look once more at the necessity of planning your missions down to the smallest detail. This also includes one or all of the above items. Timing, who will be where at what time, to do what job? How long will it take the enemy to react from his barracks or police stations? What will be the enemies most likely route to our target, and how will we delay him? How many and what type weapons will we use, and for what purpose? And last but not least, what will be the reaction of our people to this attack and how will the enemy be destroyed by this action?"

Planning arson — The material presented to the Senate committee also included a description of how to make a fire bomb, and its method of use. Some extracts from this material follow.

"The Guerrilla in the city is essentially a street fighter. His main aim is to surprise the enemy, hit him where he is weakest, and to vanish into the cities maze of buildings, cellars and alley ways . . . Therefore the arms tht this type of GUERRILLA carries will have to be adapted to the physical structure of the city . . . "

"Now, fire is a prime weapon of the GUERRILLA in the city. With fire he cause [sic] the significent [sic] and insignificent building . . . to become targets because of their direct relationship to things around them or close by. A fire will spread and cause much damage to the peace and tranquility of a given area . . . And if by chance the enemy should decide to guard his fire equipment with police or army troops, we the GUERRILLA will immediately put them under automatic fire. This becomes a problem for the enemy. Because he cannot protect all of his fire equipment with police or national guard detachments for they are needed to fight or rather try to combat the GUERRILLA . . . "

"Now Molotov fire bombs can be used for all the above targets mentioned. Furthermore the fire bomb can be made, carried, and even, in some cases, even thrown without anyone noticing . . . Now fire bombs can be used against people as shock treatment. For example, whereever there is a crowd of people, there is the potential of panic. In some cities five o'clock or five thirty in the evening is the rush hour. It is also the hour of mass hysteria . . . "

"Now in a crowd like this one must make his fire bomb with a lot of petroleum. This will give the fire a napalm effect and thereby stick to the skin and clothes of the enemy . . . "

The evidence before the Committee, if supported in a court of law, would surely have been sufficient to justify conviction on charges of treason and rebellion, and would, in the author's opinion, have fully justified death sentences for all concerned in the plot. Our weak-kneed congressmen and the fanatical reds on the Federal bench would never dare to proceed to such a conclusion — instead, they managed to gloss over the evidence, and delay any meaningful decision, desperately hoping that they could get through another election, or perhaps until retirement, without being forced to take action.

The role of China — If more evidence is needed to convince the reader that violent and catastrophic rebellion was the intention of at least some Black Nationalist, we have the following message from Mao Tse-tung to the black activists:

"I call on the workers, peasants and revolutionary intellectuals of every country and all who are willing to fight against U.S. imperialism to take action and extend strong support to the struggle of the black people in the United States! People of the whole world, unite still more closely and launch a sustained and vigorous offensive against our common enemy, U.S. imperialism, and against its accomplices! It can be said with certainty that the complete collapse of colonialism, imperialism and all systems of exploitation, and the complete emancipation of all the oppressed peoples and nations of the world are not far off.

[signed] *Mao Tse-tung*"

The above message was printed in the November 1968 issue of the Crusader, the monthly newsletter of the Republic of New Africa (Afrika), a fictional nation dreamed up by (apparently) Robert F. Williams. He was living in Peking at the time, where he had sought refuge from charges of kidnapping and other felonies in the U.S.

Claude Lightfoot, a negro who had a leadership position in the Communist party, described his position on violence: "Throughout the Smith Act trials we communists never renounced force and violence per se. We said that at certain historical moments the necessity for armed struggle may be present. But we held that we were not guilty of a conspiracy to employ force and violence, nor were we guilty of teaching and advocating the necessity of the overthrow of the government by force and violence."

Traditional Communism and Blacks

The Communist Party always had trouble recruiting blacks. When American Negroes saw the white faces on the Red leaders here and in the Soviet Union, they tended to reach the reasonable conclusion that influence by black people on Communist party actions would be diluted by persons having agendas of little interest to them. A few of the more intellectual blacks were co-opted into the Communist Party by giving them honorary titles or other attentions that were attractive to certain types: for example, Charlene Mitchell was the Communist Party's candidate for President of the U.S. in 1968. Other renegades, such as Angela Davis, operating essentially independently or uncontrollably, also served the communist cause by promoting general unrest and violence.

Some unsophisticated negroes joined the party because recruiters had led them to believe it was a kind of labor union that would help them get jobs or improve their working conditions. Most of these dupes became inactive almost immediately when they got an inkling of the real agenda of the party, but others were propagandized into believing the Red story and became active members, more or less (Hoover 1958).

Another consideration reducing the compatibility of Communist recruiters and black leaders was the extreme tendency of the latter toward committing violent and destructive acts to gratify their sadistic instincts, i.e., for pleasure. These tendencies, which were exhibited by most of the disaffected Blacks who were potential candidates for membership in the Communist Party, and the unwillingness of the Blacks to accept Party discipline must have eventually caused the Communist leaders to exercise extreme caution in recruitment campaigns carried out in the black community.

In the event, Blacks formed a number of organizations which varied principally in the amount of bloodshed and vandalism they were willing to acknowledge as being necessary for (1) the eventual triumph of the Negro race and the (2) reduction to servitude (or extinction) of all other races. Several of these groups claimed to adhere to Communist principles, more or less, and of these reds some preferred the Russian brand of socialism while others looked to Maoist China's paradise for guidance and inspiration. The general tendency seemed to be a gradual but erratic movement away from pure Marxism/Communism to a deviant version of Stalinism/Bolshevism.

On the other side of the coin, very few, if any, white persons were recruited for membership in the Black organizations. Stokely Carmichael said, disapprovingly, "Communism is white." Of course, he and his comrades were willing to accept donations from members of any race whatever, and the evidence seems to indicate that Moscow was providing funds to certain Black organizations, but only occasionally and for specific purposes, as for legal assistance to murderers.

As a result of their belligerent and self-promotional attitudes, exhibited both as tactics for gaining complete control of their own little groups and as a method of freeing themselves from outside direction, the various Black commanders had a tendency to fight among themselves. This general drive for independence by the figureheads was another feature that was distasteful to the highly disciplined Bolsheviks who ran the American Communist Party and its satellite organizations.

As a matter of policy, or philosophy, the Black figureheads seemed to gradually push out members of other ethnic groups once their organization had established a more or less stable power strucure and, perhaps, a program. Tolerated as hangers-on were a few Jews who contributed money which must have been the sole source of income to many of the Blacks, except for the money coming in from thefts and drug dealings. And, these blacks-of-convenience also provided access to legal advice and representation, when it served a purpose — generally a Communist purpose.

Hispanics created something of a philosophical problem for the black nationalists. Obviously, they were not out-of-Africa, but they were not "whites," which brought them part of the way toward acceptance. A big problem in forging an ongoing intimacy was that Hispanics, most of them, had an agenda of their own, and it did not include the elevation of Blacks above Browns. The next chapter will deal with Hispanic tactics, especially in relationship to Bolshevik programs.

Whitey was the main foe, always, but, when on the warpath to loot and burn down white-owned shops and homes, Oriental and Hispanic footsoldiers were temporarily accepted. Jews, as always, circled around the camp, giving dimes, and taking dollars, and diving for the trenches when the shooting started.

Initially, Fidel Castro's Cuba was attractive to Blacks. They tended to identify with him, possibly in part because of Castro's love of killing, or because of the glamor with which he was invested by the American media. Raymond Johnson was a Black Panther who hijacked an airliner and forced it to go to Cuba. After he spent some time immersed in the Castro paradise, he told a reporter from the U.S. that he and other black exiles were unhappy in Cuba. He also said, "We would like this information to reach the Black Panther Party in the United States, so the Party will know the unrevolutionary. way we are being treated." He eventually recognized that there was racial discrimination in Cuba.

Eldridge Cleaver also went to Cuba when he faced imprisonment in California for violating his conditions of parole. Cleaver and other exiled Panthers were prevented from mixing with the Cuban people. Castro had no intention of letting these loose cannons talk to his subjects about the Negro brand of rebellion. It is quite possible that, if the exiles had not decided to voluntarily leave Cuba, they would have expired quietly from some convenient disease within a few months, thus removing an embarrassment from the Cuban paradise.

It is important to remember, also, that the black power exiles were a total loss to the Cuban economy, since they were not only inherently incapable of doing any productive work, but required constant supervision, making them a drain on the Cuban economy. And Castro was not in a position to support such luxuries.

After spending a total of about eight years in Cuba, China, and Africa, Robert Williams, another black rebel, returned to the U.S. to face charges of kidnapping, etc. Possible jail in the US seemed better to him than a life in any of the socialist paradises — probably much better for one's health and longevity, too.

Communist fronts — The traditional, Soviet-style Communist and Communist-front organizations who claimed they were concerned with negro "rights" also had a predominant ethnic group — the Jews. Leadership roles in these groups, and their offshoots, seemed to be composed of about 50% to 60% Jews. And these people were in the most influential positions. Membership rolls also seemed to have a much higher percentage of Jews than were found in the general population of the U.S.

Horowitz (1997), another honkie who was immersed in the black power movement, provides a view of the liberals' love affair with the Panthers. "Over the course of twenty years, the Panther myth had been firmly planted in the literary culture by radical scholars and journalists. The silence of the witnesses — Hayden, Scheer, Kenner, and the others — left the mythmakers with no serious challenge, and made its construction relatively easy . . . The Panther myth was propagated in the academy by tenured radicals who made them icons. Panther veterans had been hired to teach in African-American studies departments, and even Warren Kimbro, the convicted murderer of Alex Rackley, had been matriculated at Harvard as an affirmative action student, and became a dean at a Connecticut college. The myth was also spread through campus speakers' programs, which were generally controlled by the Left and whose stars often were Panther enthusiasts like 'Professor Griff,' and Angela Davis — who commanded $10,000 fees and received official university honors."

The Curious Story of The People's Temple

The People's Temple episode is brought into the picture at this point because it is considered to be an example of the use of red strategies to establish a dictatorship using appeals to ethnicity and religions which have are not related to the critical hidden goals of the organization. The Jones congregation was predominantly black and, in his proselyting and publicizing literature he strongly emphasized equal treatment of all races — this was true, he treated his entire congregation like slaves, regardless of color. He was very successful in convincing both blacks and whites, and some orientals, that he would take care of them.

His approach had similarities to the system of Father Divine.

The horrific finish of "Reverend" Jim Jones and the congregation of his People's Temple is remembered by nearly everyone who was around when hundreds of people were poisoned in a mass "suicide" in the jungles of Guayana in September of 1978. What they tend to forget, however, is that the Temple was a 100% communist organization which (allegedly) found its model in the Soviet Union and that Jim Jones was (allegedly) a strong supporter of black power.

The reason these aspects of that colossal con game have been forgotten is that the media conveniently neglect to allude to them when they speak of Jim Jones and the People's Temple — indeed, the media experts almost always try to show that Jones was a Christian preacher (which he was not) and that the Temple was a Christian organization (which it was not).

Jim Jones was a dictator in the classic red style. It is not clear from the information available to the present author whether or not he had contacts with any Soviet intelligence agency, but, if he did not, the Soviets were uncharacteristically lax in failing to take advantage of a terrific opportunity to increase their power within the US.

For more information about Jonestown, see Kerns' (1979) *Peoples Temple Peoples Tomb* and Layton's (1998) *Seductive Poison* for survivors' description of Jim Jones and his philosophy, Dieckmann's (1981) *Beyond Jonestown* for a no-holds-barred comparison of Jones' methods of group manipulation with sensitivity training and some aspects of Synanon and Zionism, and Lane's (1980) *The Strongest Poison*, an explanation of how another of Mark's clients wound up dead.

And the Band Played On

The collapse of the Soviet Union, and the resulting diminution of financing and guidance flowing from its intelligence and subversion branches, led to only minor changes in the Afro terrorist/activist groups worldwide. Their leadership had, in general, been independent of effective Red control for a long time, and the Black leaders continued to pursue their highly idiosyncratic courses after the fall. Except for the complexions of their members and the generally more erratic programs pursued by the black cults, their programs could be compared to those of the Mafia, i.e., gangsterism refined by an ethnic justification.

The Symbionese Liberation Army (SLA) could be considered an aberration from, or at least a partial and temporary exception to, the general pattern of Black freedom from both Red domination and white interference. The SLA was a particularly vicious black and white terrorist organization which had at least some philosophical connection to Communism, and it was certainly supported by leading Reds within the US when it or its members came into conflict with the law.

Gurr (1990) said, "In 1973-4 the SLA enjoyed a brief but spectacular career based on the exploits of a dozen members, white radicals of middle-class origin who had joined with black ex-convicts. The SLA echoed, almost parodied, the revolutionary rhetoric of the 1960s by advocating the 'unity in love' of all oppressed people, redistribution of capital, dismantling of the prison system, and so forth. But the SLA's first revolutionary action was the 1973 murder of Oakland's black superintendent of schools, Marcus Foster, because he had cooperated with police in planning a school identity card system.

This action was followed in early 1974 by the kidnapping and brainwashing of Patty Hearst, and in May of that year by the fiery shootout in Los Angeles in which six SLA members died.

Gurr continued, "Shortly before SLA's fatal denouement, *Ramparts* magazine, a journal of the New Left, wrote what seems in retrospect an epitaph for revolutionary action in the US. It attributed the emergence of the SLA 'to the collapse of the organized left at the end of the sixties, and its continuing failure to regroup itself and survive.' The SLA itself was criticized as as 'self-appointed vigilante group' and its murder of Marcus Foster as an act of 'desperate violence.' Although a few violent acts of would-be revolutionaries continued until 1985, there is little doubt that by 1974 events had helped discredit both revolutionary objectives and violent means for virtually the entire left."

The bestial sadistic violence so characteristic of the SLA, was sometimes applied to a situation when it served no practical purpose or even when more sensible options would have been easier to implement and probably more productive. These were typical examples of pure undiluted red anarchical terrorism as implemented by sadistic psychopaths.

chapter fifteen

RED HISPANICS

The preceding discussion covered the relationships of various African-American groups with the overt and covert organizations dominated by Communists before, during, and after the breakup of the Soviet Union. We will now devote some space to the connections between Hispanic activists and the Reds.

Many of the violent Hispanic organizations, and even some of the less destructive ones, had a tie-in with Fidel Castro, whose agents are completely ruthless and willing to resort to murder or any other sort of terroristic action in order to destabilize local governments and, they hoped, national agencies as well. As usual, the liberals who predominate in the nation's judiciary and in some parts of the law enforcement agencies, found excuses for these treasonous outbreaks, or ignored them, thus placing their constituents, and indeed all Americans, at risk.

Black and Brown Rivalry

The Hispanics, as a group, seemed to have more interest in, and greater success at, merging into the white community than did the black African component of the population, although the usual clannishness of a distinctive group and the misunderstandings and damaged egos deliberately sought out and manipulated by politicians and other crooks gave plenty of opportunity for the development of Latino clubs and other organizations having various degrees of potential for treason.

Nearly all of the Hispanic groups had red tendencies, at least philosophically, although personal political success and big money were always the ultimate goals of the La Raza demagogues. The success of Castro in overthrowing the government of Cuba while waving the red banner also made Bolshevik goals more acceptable to the members of this ethnic group.

Another factor in predisposing Hispanics toward acceptance of far-left flags was their familial connections to the Roman Catholic Church. Some priests and friars of the church were expert at using the tenets of

Liberation Theology (another communist ploy) to fortify the appeal of Red doctrine.

Such factors made the brown/tan power groups, the southwest secessionists, and their ilk, more amenable than the black community to control by Marxists. We also find Communist infiltration was facilitated by the constant efforts by Castro to gain control of as many Spanish/Portuguese speaking people as possible using exported terrorists to destabilize existing governments.

There did not seem to be a strong tendency among U.S. Hispanics to abandon their hard left organizations after the fall of the Soviet empire. Many of their leaders continued to have ties to Castro, who retained an emotional appeal for those Spanish speaking citizens who felt a sense of racial compatibility with the bearded one. During the same period, however, Castro has come under increasing economic pressure due to loss of Russian subsidies and the inevitable complete failure of his Communist system to provide the basic amenities to his subjects. This makes him somewhat less of a hero and role model

Mexico

The communists have been interested in getting control of Mexico ever since they conceived the idea of an Internationale. Mexico is very appealing to them because its long, relatively unguarded border with the US opens up all sorts of opportunities for importation of men and materials to be used in subverting the American government. In addition, the country is well worth annexing to the communist list because of its potential natural resources, particularly oil and raw materials for narcotics. This Red interest has led to an almost continuous program designed to install ever more "liberal" governments.

A land of revolutionaries — According to Donovan (1962), "The Mexican Revolution [of 1910] is frequently called the first of the twentieth century Latin-American social revolutions." The publicly announced reason for this rebellion was the need for agrarian reform.

There were even some moves in this direction in the earliest stages. However, corruption, violence for the sake of violence, chaos, and destruction, which are the inevitable end points of Mexican revolutions, soon reduced the movement to nothing more than a battle for power among different factions.

Of course, the 1910 revolution occurred before communists took over the Russian government, but the Marxist philosophy and its practitioners were abroad in the world long before Lenin assumed power. Donovan believed the revolutionaries had the goal of raising Mexico's standard of living and improving working conditions. So thought many others. But, as is usual in these communist upheavals, working conditions were not improved and, in fact, many of the old jobs simply disappeared because marketing networks were abolished and credit of any kind became unavailable.

In addition, looting and senseless destruction permanently removed production equipment and raw materials from existence, and no one would or could supply new goods to replace them. The new masters had no idea how to implement methods for improving agriculture or industry; not a clue as to ways to protect peasants, craftsmen, and small shopkeepers so they could add to the stock of consumer goods. As a result, few or no goods were offered for sale, and the lot of the "common man" became worse than ever, while his chance of getting killed in some random imbroglio became much greater. In other words, there was another victory for the haters of humanity.

Donovan continues, "Prior to World War I there was a small Socialist Party, which became the nucleus of the Mexican Communist Party. An American draft dodger, Linn Gale, fled the US in 1917 and became a member of the party. There was competition between Gale and an East Indian, M.N. Roy, to see who would lead the Party. Roy, a nationalist who had turned Communist, was working with a Russian named Borodin representing the Soviet Union in the US.

"Roy bested Linn Gale and had the American expelled. The Indian then renamed the group *Partido Comunista de Mexico*. Unable to

convince the members of the new party that they should join the alien
direction of the Comintern, Roy himself was expelled. Shorty after Roy's
expulsion his faction formed a second group, also called the *Partido
Comunista*. The pattern seems never to vary from country to country.

"Another draft dodger from the US, Charles Phillips, then became
a power in the nascent Mexican Communist Party. In the early years of
the party, Phillips and the other top Mexican Communists managed to
draw a number of members of the Mexican Revolution into the Party,
but few remained with the Communists for any length of time . . . "

The Mexican Communist party attracted flamboyant artists. Diego
Rivera, José Clemente Orozco, and David Alfaro Siqueiros were among
the most prominent painters who were active in the Communist Party.
Perhaps the most famous of these was Diego Rivera, whose cartoon-like
works were highly praised and exhibited the world over, a treatment
similar to that accorded the dada-esque output of the Spaniard Pablo
Picasso.

Rivera was ultimately expelled from the Party and joined the
Trotskyite movement. He was responsible for getting the Mexican
government to give Trotsky permission to come to that country as a
refugee. Trotsky signed his own death warrant by this ill-advised move.
Very likely Rivera had received the assignment to set him up for the
assassination, which took place several months later.

After several months Trotsky and Rivera had a violent disagreement, and Rivera returned to the Stalinist fold, which meant he was, of
necessity, a deadly enemy of Trotsky. The artist Siqueiros led an attack
on the refugee's new residence, but it failed. Records available to this
writer do not show what complicity any of these artists had in the fatal
attack on Trotsky by an assassin who had insinuated himself into the
victim's household, but it is hard to believe that they were not
participants in the planning phase.

Communism and the economy — The Communists have had
occasional setbacks in program for acquiring national influence in

Mexico. After a president elect, Obregon, was assassinated before he could be inaugurated, General Ortiz Rubio took over, and he violently repressed the Party. But General Lazaro Cardenas legalized the communist Party in 1935, and rapidly and harshly implemented land reform with the complete support of the Reds.

Cardenas also nationalized the oil industry in about 1938. The petroleum complex had been planned and built largely by persons from the US, and companies from the States financed the drilling, transporting, and refining facilities. Cardenas simply stole this US property without a hint of compensation. As might be expected, Roosevelt (who was president at that time) took no action supporting the US interests. This should not have been a surprise — FDR never saw a communist he didn't like.

By utilizing funds received from sale of the stolen oil, some industrial growth was attained, but, as is inevitable in this culture, an ever increasing percentage of the oil money was diverted to various Mexican plutocrats and criminals, so that modernization of the economy essentially ground to a halt, and the technological base of the country declined markedly.

Gradually, some money started to come into the country from agricultural exports (fresh fruits and vegetables), and from manufacturing plants that were financed and built (largely by US planners with US money) close to the US border so they could benefit from free trade provisions that had been enacted into US law. In addition, many legal and illegal immigrants into the US sent money back home from the low-paying jobs they were able to get. Ultimately, this source of Mexican income will decline and decay, ruined by endemic graft and corruption, and hampered by the general technical incompetence of the labor pool and managers.

The Church and communism — A very large part of the Mexican people are nominally Roman Catholics, but the majority of them ignore the parts of church doctrine which do not suit their convenience. Few of them would consider their church obligations as being inconsistent with activities of a Communist nature.

The church administrative structure in Mexico, such as it is, has been irreversibly tainted by the liberation theology spirit, and priests imbued with this philosophy can be regarded as nothing more than tools (whether they know it or not) of international communism.

A safe haven and transfer point — For many years, Latin-American political refugees have gone into exile in Mexico City, and Communist agents have often fled to the Mexican capital on their escape route to Moscow or to their next assignment. For example, two National Security Agency cryptographers, Bernon F. Mitchell and William H. Martin, fled to Mexico City to make contact with Russian agents and then proceeded to Moscow in 1960.

"Shortly afterward, a US Army deserter, George John Gessner, left his post as a nuclear technician at Fort Bliss TX, the Army guided missile center, and made his way to Mexico City. According to American authorities, the 25-yr old technician turned over restricted nuclear missile secrets to Soviet agents at the Russian embassy in December of 1960 and January of 1961" (Donovan 1962).

Mexican Politics in the US
The US has not been free of Hispanic attempts to profit from religious bigotry and domination. Pauken (1995) observed many of these maneuvers during his political career in Texas and Washington. The following commentary relies heavily on his book.

Separatist politics — La Raza Unida was an attempt at a separate Mexican political party. It grew out of a meeting, Chamizal Conference, in south Texas in 1967. From the public announcements and general attitudes of the leadership of this group, it seems to have had a strong pro-Communist orientation, although Pauken could not say whether or not it was dominated entirely by Communists. There is very little doubt that, if this party had shown any signs of vitality, it would have been targeted by the Reds for complete domination by Communists hard-liners.

The failure of the 1968 et seq. attempt based on Chamizal, was probably due to an understanding by the prospective members that the party would draw votes away from the Democrat party, which would then, very likely lose elections to the Republicans. The left-wing Hispanics, who are (in this author's opinion) the majority of all Spanish-speaking voters) were not prepared to make this sacrifice.

At the present time, however, the accumulated Mexican immigrants, and other left-wing Hispanic types, make up such a large proportion of the voting public, and, more importantly are in control of such a large part of the vote-counting officials, that a pure Hispanic Party, La Raza Unida or whatever it would be called, would have a good chance of filling many posts in a three-way race, i.e., Democrat, Republican, and La Raza. This could very well lead to a resurrection of the 1967 idea, with bad results for the Democrats. In fact, the whole state would suffer.

The likelihood is very high that any conceivable Hispanic political party would trend steadily toward the left, and would soon end up under the complete control of Communist-indoctrinated thugs.

Interfaith — Thomas W. Pauken, who was very active in Texas Republican politics during most of the 1965-1994 period, describes his experiences when he attempted to offset the influence of a group called Valley Interfaith. This group was apparently created by a Saul Alinsky organ called The Industrial Areas Foundation, thus in philosophy Valley Interfaith was an arm of the Communist Party, though perhaps not so in a managerial sense. The area of interest was the Rio Grande Valley, as it had been for the Chamizal Conference, the reason still being that the greatest proportion of voters, and inhabitants, were recent immigrants, many of them illegal immigrants.

An additional incentive for IAF to concentrate on the Valley, was that the area was undergoing a sharp depression in commerce due to record low temperatures that had destroyed many citrus groves, and a plunge in the value of the peso (one of many) had reduced the buying power of cross-border (Mexico into the US) shoppers to essentially zero. The economic health of the Valley then, as now, was heavily dependent on expenditures by shoppers who cross from Mexico into the US.

The following passage is a quotation from the book, *The Thirty Years War* (Pauken 1995). "Valley Interfaith was a classic example of a New Left organization all dressed up for the eighties. Its founder was Ernesto Cortes, a sixties activist, who was acknowledged to be the most successful Alinsky-style organizer in the Southwest. Cortes had been part of a contingent of former radicals who met with Sam Brown and Marge Tagankin during the early days of the Carter administration to chart a new direction for VISTA. During the seventies, Cortes had organized a grass roots organization in San Antonio known as C.O.P.S. At one time it became the most powerful political organization in that city. With the success of C.O.P.S. behind him, Cortes decided to establish a network of similar local organization throughout the state with particular emphasis on border communities with a substantial Mexican-American population.

"Cortes enjoyed the active support of the Catholic archbishop of San Antonio and Catholic bishops in El Paso and Brownsville. All of Saul Alinsky's hard work in recruiting religious support from within the Catholic church was now paying off as the dioceses threw their weight behind Cortes's organizational efforts. The Alinsky organizers even had their own training institute in San Antonio to educate the clergy and civilians on 'social justice' issues. Cortes was one of the instructors at the Mexican-American Cultural Center (MACC) which was directed at that time by Fr. Virgil Elizando, another Alinksy disciple. The curriculum at MACC emphasized the principles of 'liberation theology' and the development of 'base communities' in the barrios and depressed neighborhoods ... The base communities were the organizational vehicle through which the liberation theologians would try to create a society based on the principles of 'Christian Marxism.' The model for this 'new society' was the Sandinista regime in Nicaragua which used base communities to establish a so-called popular church independent of the Catholic hierarchy."

"As had been the case in San Antonio, Cortes was able to elicit the enthusiastic backing of the local Catholic bishop, Bishop Pena, for his project. Local Catholic churches in El Paso were 'encouraged' to join as dues-paying members of this new community-based organization called E.P.I.S.O. What was represented to be an interfaith alliance of churches and local leaders to improve the conditions of the people in the poorest predominantly Hispanic neighborhoods in El Paso was in reality the nucleus of what Cortes and his associates hoped would be the most influential political force in this Texas border city.

"While E.P.I.S.O. enjoyed some initial success, there was tremendous opposition from local Catholics who resented their churches and funds being used to support a secular, political movement. Consequently, IAF organizers did not achieve the degree of influence in El Paso that they had enjoyed in San Antonio.

"It was then that Cortes and his cohorts launched Valley Interfaith. Jim Drake, a Protestant minister who had been one of Cesar Chavez's closest advisers in California, was brought into the Valley to run the operation. Again Cortes was able to get backing from the local Catholic bishop."

Idealistic Money Makers

Some of the most news-worthy Hispanic agitators are more interested in money than violence. The late César E. Chavez, who received amazing amounts of favorable publicity during his career, and whose memory is still revered by some Hispanics, falling just a tad below Francisco *Pancho* Villa (1877-1923) as a role model, was in reality nothing more than an extortionist. His favorite gambit was to take his entourage to a highly visible location, and hire some day workers to stand at intersections and in front of food supermarkets and the like waving placards denouncing the grape growers of California for exploiting the Hispanic grape pickers, many of the latter being illegal immigrants. Occasionally, they would wave bunches of grapes to give photographers a bit more variety.

The establishment news media never reported that the grape pickers who were being "exploited" were mostly undocumented aliens who earned about ten times more in California than they could make anywhere in their homeland of Mexico, and who used every subterfuge at their command to avoid going back to Mexico, even though they were being "exploited" in Chavez's somewhat biased view of the situation.

Of course, there were always reporters and cameramen on the scene to give Chavez the publicity he thrived on, even though the story was old and repetitious, besides being of no interest whatever except to the liberals who could feel as though they had accomplished something worthwhile because they hadn't bought any fresh grapes that week.

The advantages to Chavez of these demonstrations included:

(1) The publicity generated by them led to increases in donations to Chavez's group by leftwingers who believed Chavez could play a decisive role in destabilizing government.

(2) The publicity as well as the personal contacts made in the locales being picketed may have led to the recruitment of new members, although Chavez did not seem (at least in his later years) to be particularly interested in adding more of the proletariat to his rolls.

(3) The grape growers sometimes made direct or indirect contributions to Chavez in order to get him to take off the heat.

(4) In some cases the local stores in the targeted area would make cash payments to Chavez so he would remove the demonstrators who were interfering with customer traffic.

(5) It is said by some, though the author cannot verify this, that Chilean grape exporters were behind some of the efforts to damage the image of domestic table grape producers in the U.S.

Cesar Chavez was a prime example of a crude extortionist, or blackmailer, who used the cover of a Latino equality proponent. His specialty was intimidating grape growers and other farmers who needed field help on a seasonal basis. As a matter of convenience and/or necessity, most of these workers were Hispanic, and they were selected largely from illegal Mexican immigrants.

Colombia

Especially in Mexico and Central America, but also in other parts of the world, Reds have become capitalists of a sort, by specializing in the production and smuggling of narcotics. This situation is particularly important in Colombia, where the guerrilla (ELN) leadership describes its strategy as "the combination of forms of struggle." Their full-blown narcotics operation is supplemented by kidnapings, extortion, torture, and murder. Religion is no longer the opium of the people, cocaine is the opium of the people.

To baffle law enforcement officials, the ELNs turn "human rights" into a political and judicial campaign intended to flood military officers, the police, and other opponents with masses of paperwork and multiple court appearances.

The effectiveness of this well-organized campaign is described by Mendoza (2001), who tells us about tragic occurrences at a town called El Carman de Chucuri, which had been under guerrilla control for 30 years. Then, a young captain named Pataquiva was assigned to lead the small army garrison in the town. At first, the captain attempted to mollify the citizens by doing good and constructive works. He also made friends with the mayor. As a result, the rebels called the mayor to a meeting, then tortured him and killed him. This was too much for the townspeople to endure — they rose up against the terrorists.

In retaliation, the FLN "blew up the town's waterworks and bridges, burned the cocoa bean trucks, and planted mines on the farms." The latter tactic was particularly effective as the explosives killed and maimed many of the farmers who were trying to make a living. Even terrorist acts such as these failed to make the region's populace return to the ELN.

"When terror failed, the guerrillas initiated a judicial war against the town's leaders . . . Local NGOs, such as Justicia y Paz [Comision de Justicia y Paz], mobilized false testimony to inundate the government oversight office, the prosecutor, the public defender, and all sorts of international organizations." Captain Pataquiva has been accused of 147 murders, numerous acts of intimidation, terrorism, torture, and disappearances. He was arrested and interrogated by hooded prosecutors. "He has been cleared in ten investigations. *Yet international reports still present the original charges as truth.* Every indication is that international NGOs have given credence to the reports from Justicia y Paz, which claims that two of the town's elected mayors, Jairo Beltran and Timoteo Rueda, as well as retired General Valencia Tovar, newspaperman Manuel Vicente Pena, and I [i.e., Mendoza] are paramilitary operatives. Yet none of us has ever had any association with any paramilitary organization . . . The ELN, for its part, tried to assassinate me by sending me a book bomb on March 29, 1999." The ELN tried to justify this action by calling it "punishment by military action."

It is noteworthy that priests of the Catholic Church fully cooperated with the criminals, even fighting with the rebels in battles against government troops and helping to torture and kill opponents within the town. Priests are still trying to destroy Mendoza.

Moreno was the executive secretary of CJP in 1992, and he remains in Colombia to this day, bearing the red banner. Another Jesuit, Alejandro Angulo, who is the General Director of Centro de Investigacion y Educacion Popular (CINEP), an institution "not financed *only* by the Jesuit order." He claims (Angulo 2001) that CINEP is not composed of priests devoted to Liberation Theology, and furthermore, that it is not true that Liberation Theology "posits that poverty legitimizes revolution; rather, it affirms that revolution comes out of the despair of poverty." A truly Jesuitical differentiation.

In a news release of late September 2001, it was reported that Colombian police found the body of the attorney general's wife a week after the biggest rebel group kidnapped her.

Further from Angulo (2001), "The Archbishopric of El Salvador is accused of doctoring army releases to imply that the military admits brutality against peasants. One report mentions a Fray Beto (presumably a Franciscan) as Castro's religious adviser. In reply to my request for more information about him, I am told that he is the link between Castro and the Workers Party (PT) of Brazil. He has written *Horizonte Perdido nos Bastidores do Socialismo* (1993) and publishes a review, *America Libre*."

At the present time, Red guerillas are terrorizing the countryside in Colombia. As is the wont of such creatures, they seek out less terroristic leveller movements in order to first demoralize, then torture and kill those who might appeal to the populace by offering gentler, kinder programs. The Colombian thugs call themselves the Liberation Army, as is so often the case.

Ramírez (2001) wrote, "The zone at El Carmen de Chucuri has been subjected to bloody attacks against the populations by the terrorist Army of National Liberation (ELN). Thousands of peasants, many of them children, have been mutilated by landmines built and placed by the ELN. These crimes, as well as the kidnapings and extortions committed by the guerrillas, are not denounced by Justicia y Paz or by CINEP with the intensity with which they accuse the Colombian state in their reports.

About the same group, Posada (2001) stated, "Jesuit priest Javier Giraldo has attempted to discredit journalist and author Plinio Mendoza. Several years ago, Mr. Mendoza earned the highest award possible for a communications professional in Colombia: The Simon Bolivar Lifetime Achievement Award. He is a rigorous and expert investigator who also has the courage to say what others are afraid to say.

O'Grady (2001) gives a description of the tactics of the ruthless Colombian Armed Revolutionary Forces (FARC). The legally constituted national government tried for three years to negotiate a peace agreement with FARC. They ceded a large part of the country as an act of good faith. "The guerillas responded by using the demilitarized territory to build their army through the forced recruitment of boys, to bulk up on arms, to traffic in illegal narcotics, and to launch strikes agains civilians in other parts of the country. Recently, they invited in bomb-making experts from the Irish Republican Army. They also expelled or killed anyone living within the territory who didn't agree with them."

O'Grady points out, " . . . human rights groups, ever distrustful of the military, insist that the armed forces are a key source of the evil in the country." This is a key tactic of Reds, they know that once the military has been discredited, the way is opened to the chaos and destruction which set the stage for a Soviet-style dictatorship.

Cuba

This small island nation, insignificant in so many ways, has been a giant thorn in the side of the US for several decades. It illustrates the expertness of Reds' use of satellite populations, as well as the weakness and vacillation of the US when its foreign relations options are restricted by the Red-collaborating legislators and judges who infest the federal government.

The case of Castro — Fidel Castro, the murderous despot who bears responsibility for the present degraded condition of Cuba, has become the premier star in the galaxy of heroes of Latin American communism. Because of his long reign, Castro's methodology has been looked upon as a pattern to be followed by the liberation theologians. See, for example, Boff and Boff (2001), who state, " . . . the socialist revolution in Cuba stood out as an alternative leading to the dissolution of the chief cause of underdevelopment: dependence."

However, Castro's Cuba is a total disaster. He managed to put up a good front when he was receiving hundreds of millions of dollars in subsidies from the USSR, and when he could rent Cuban soldiers to do the bidding of tyrants in Africa, and when the useful idiots in Canada supported him because they thought there was some commercial advantage in doing so. Now, all these sources of income have dried up and he has to depend on cigars, sex, and drugs as sources of foreign exchange.

This is not so good — there is a lot of international competition in these markets, except perhaps for cigars. But this source of income is, after all, rather limited. Even the sugar crop, a mainstay of the Cuban economy for centuries, can no longer be depended upon, and recent news reports confirm that many of the old cane processing plants have deteriorated to the point where they can no longer be operated.

Longevity and the clinging to a dead idea like a barnacle to the hull of a wrecked ship are Castro's chief claims to fame — that, and his apparent defying of a craven US government. Not much, yet it is more than many another Communist leader has been able to achieve.

But, the negative results are obvious and typical. Whenever and wherever such criminals have assumed power, the same results have been seen: intense repression of the populace with loss of all individual freedoms, grinding poverty without hope of relief, constant propagandizing and indoctrination of the populace, and the assuming of quasi-royal power by a group of thugs. Also seen on the international front is the elevation of the "hero" of the revolution to demi-god status by the media, academia, and certain political groups.

Cuba as a progaganda source — Describing the situation existing several years ago, but applicable for the most part to recent conditions, Donovan (1962) wrote, "The posters, pamphlets, newspapers, films, and radio broadcasts with which Cuba inundates Latin America are proof of the goals held by Castro, Khrushchev, and Mao. Described as the 'Free Voice of Latin America,' Castro's foreign broadcasts are programmed for 22 hours a day in French, Spanish, English, and Portuguese, from six powerful transmitters.

" ... One of the founders of the FPCC, the ex-CBS newsman Robert Taber, is said to have 'figured in Castro's English-language broadcasts.' Yet another radio propagandist for Communist Cuba is Robert Williams, a North Carolina Negro, who denounces the US over the airwaves for its racism. Williams fled the US to escape kidnapping charges."

"Documents seized by anti-Castro Cubans from the Cuban embassy at Lima revealed that at least 15 journalists were on Castro's payroll in Cuba alone. Payments varied from a minimum of 2,500 up to 20,000 soles — a sizable sum in Peru. These men were employed by the largest and most important papers in Peru, many of them militantly anti-Communist in editorial policy. Rather than betray their source of revenue, or break their cover, these men maintained a convincing anti-Communist pose." (Donovan 1962).

Narco politics — It is widely acknowledged that Cuba is using the narcotics trade to obtain funds for subversion in the US and elsewhere. Their main activity seems to concern cocaine. In terms of quantity, more marijuana is smuggled into the US, but most of this drug comes from Mexico and its total value is probably considerably less than that of the cocaine coming through Cuban routes.

According to Donovan (1962), cocaine traffic had been insignificant before the Fidel Castro regime came to power in 1959. A US drug control official stated that the US had been free of cocaine addicts for 20 years until the Cuban traffic began.

In August 1962, the president of the Cuban Revolutionary Council charged that more than 5,000 military volunteers from Soviet bloc countries had been shipped to Cuba in five Russian vessels. José Miro Cardona said that the large military detachment was part of a Russian plan to dominate Latin America and said that the US and other American countries would have to act immediately 'against Communist invaders.

JFK does his part — Castro owes his life and power to US blunders. Perhaps "blunders" is the wrong word, because the two events which led to the consolidation of his power and insured the continuation of it, were (in this author's opinion) carefully and shrewdly orchestrated by Bolshevik agencies, and enabled by a weak and vacillating president (JFK) and his treasonous advisers. These events were the Cuban missile crisis and the Bay of Pigs invasion. Space is not available for a complete review of these gross errors of US policy, but brief summaries will follow.

The idea of US support of an invasion of Cuba by expatriates who were strongly opposed to Castro was accepted by some elements in the government during the presidency of Dwight Eisenhower. Preparations, which included the collection and training of persons who would be in the invading force, and the accumulation of weaponry and transports, were underway at the time JFK took over the administration. What seemed to be missing were a definite timetable and the coordination of the various elements. There is also evidence of internal sabotage and other activities by Red agents.

Leaks of information about preparations being made for the invasion were so bad that newspapers were able to print articles about the rebels being trained in battle techniques at a base in Guatemala months before the actual attack. *The Nation* and the *Miami Herald* broke the news in November of 1960, and the *New York Times* published an extensive account of the operation (with photos) in January 1961.

On April 15, various targets in Cuba were attacked by B-26 bombers manned by what were claimed to be defecting Cuban air force pilots. During the actual invasion, which started on April 17, 1961, just about everything that could go wrong did go wrong. Ships were wrecked, troops were lost, materiel failed to arrive at battle points, etc. When it became apparent that the patriot forces were in deep trouble, JFK was urged by some of his advisers to send in heavy air support, but in the end he drooped his way to a weaker course, and inaction.

The net results were death for the Cuban patriots who had depended on US promises, humiliation for the United States, and an immense boost in prestige for Castro.

The second event which was of inestimable value to Castro was the missile crisis. This was a very illuminating example of one upmanship as practiced by an adroit Soviet intelligence agency against the administration of JFK. They won, though enough crumbs were left on the plate to enable the liberal press to claim (as a disinformation ploy) that the Democratic administration had managed to salvage half a loaf.

The missile crisis had so many ramifications that a summary including only the crucial points, with a short explanation of each, would easily fill a chapter the size of the present one. Following are a few points thought by the author to be among the most important.

• In October of 1962, aerial photographs made by US show missile launchers and what may be intercontinental ballistic missiles on Cuban soil. IL-28 planes are also in Cuba.

• November 1962. After a tremendous turmoil in diplomatic circles, the missile sites are broken up and the missiles placed on ships for Russia.

• The net effect is that Soviet IL-28 planes are left in Cuba, the US missile bases in Turkey are turned over to the host country, and the Italian bases scheduled for closing.

A very extensive chronology of the missile crisis can be found on the Internet at: **www.gwu.edu/~nsarchiv/nsa/cuba_mis_cri**

Two things must be emphasized: There never was any proof that workable rockets or rocket launchers were present in Cuba, and there was only the most flimsy pretense that nuclear warheads were there. What we saw here was a Potemkin-launch site created for the purpose of demoralizing the US and gaining tacit approval for arming Cuba with conventional weapons. There may have been a disinformation facet which we have never been able to discover.

The net effect of these two defining events — the Bay of Pigs disaster and the missile crisis — was to give the island kingdom of Castro immunity from direct attack for four decades. From this safe haven, agents of destruction departed for locations all over the world, though their major direct impacts were found in South and Central America and Africa. Furthermore, funds for Castro's operations were supplemented by income from narcotics transshipment, from South American (and perhaps Asian) manufacturing plants to US and other sales regions.

chapter sixteen

JUDAISTS

The essence of rabbinical study is casuistry.
Israel Bruna *Responda* (15C) 1798, #100

If you can't cut off your enemy's hand, kiss
it and appease him.
Amram *Noam Haddidot* 1854, #12

Zionism means one man persuading another man to
give money to a third man to go to Palestine.
A. Koestler, 1952. *Arrow in the Blue.* p. 114.

Judaism is not a religion, but a law religionized.
Moses Mendelssohn (fl. mid-18th century)

Jews were very prominent in all of the left wing movements of the 19th and 20th centuries, first in Europe and the US, then throughout the world. The best known of all, a co-author of the *Communist Manifesto* and the author of *Das Kapital*, was Karl Marx. He was an ethnic Jew but, he claimed, not a religious Judaist.

During the last two hundred years, there have been very few terrorist or subversive organizations anywhere in the Western world that did not have at least a leavening of radical Judaists, and many (perhaps most) of these were of the Yiddish-speaking Ashkenazim variety. Possible exceptions to this general rule were the areas dominated by Islamic forces and philosophies, although some commentators claim to be able to detect the hidden hand of Judaism in the highest levels of these organizations. Certainly, such influences have become apparent in the hierarchy of the Catholic Church and in the leadership positions of virtually all Protestant denominations.

The acquisition of power in radical activist organs of the left by Jews seemed to have begun at about the time of the French Revolution. Ever after, persons of this persuasion can be found in the policy-making cadres of all European and most Western Hemisphere "revolutionary" movements. Of course, their presence as an effective force in all kinds of social and cultural organizations, including the Christian Church, began much earlier.

Marxism, communism, socialism, anarchism, and many other violent, or potentially violent, social movements which flourished in the nineteenth and twentieth centuries, and perhaps earlier, attracted a disproportionate number of Jews, and particularly of Ashkenazim, in both their theoretical and enforcement branches. It is hardly likely that the doctrines of Communism would have received such wide acceptance by the restless intellectuals and the bred-in-the-bone terrorists of this era if the Jew Karl Marx had not been such an indefatigable and ruthless worker for their success in the earlier phases.

Therefore, it seems somewhat naive to ask if there has been a continuing effect of Communism upon the international Jewish community — they are interlaced parts of a whole system, but, while the Bolsheviki have suffered many serious setbacks, the Jews have continued to increase their influence in most nations.

It is very probable that, without the financing supplied by New York City Jews, the Russian Bolsheviki would have not been able to subvert the largely peaceful development of a representative government in Russia during the 1917-1918 period. With these funds, the radical and violence-prone minority was able to overcome their less well-financed opponents, leading to the complete triumph of the Red conspirators, and to the eventual murder of millions and enslavement of tens of millions of people. Although we have been told that neither Lenin or Stalin were Jews, the predominance of this ethnic group in the Bolsheviki was obvious, with Trotsky being, perhaps, the most prominent Jew in the early development of the Red government.

This phenomenon was recognized by many observers and commentators, but most of them averted their gaze and kept their silence. Even the redoubtable J. Edgar Hoover acknowledged the omnipresent Jewish influence in Communist circles. He wrote (Hoover

1958), "It is a matter of record that numerous Communist Party leaders call themselves Jews and claim a Jewish origin. This does not, however, make them Jews ... Typical of the Communist claims which have led to the false myth indicating that Jews have an affinity for communism are the remarks of Paul Novick, the editor of *Morning Freiheit*, a communist paper published in Yiddish in New York City. Novick said, 'The development of Yiddish literature in the US went hand-in-hand with the growth of the Socialist movement at the beginning of this century [1900s] and of the Communist Party after the October Revolution.' "

Hoover had a rather unique explanation for his claim that there were few if any Jews in the Communist Party, in spite of all the evidence to the contrary. He explained it this way, "A true follower of the Jewish faith, like those of other religions, cannot embrace communism." Thus, if you have been an observant Jew all your life, but decide to join the Communist Party, you are no longer a real Jew. Thus, there are no Jewish communists — there are, however, a lot of ex-Jews who are communists. Of course, this is mere persiflage — Hoover knew, and no doubt expected his more sophisticated readers to know, that he had to insert this obeisance if he ever expected to get his book published in the US. He surely knew, as we all know, that to nearly all Jews, their Jewishness is a racial, inherited trait. They are of the family of Abraham by blood line (and, if they wish to so regard it, by genetics) and nothing can change that fact — they could have been willing followers of Adolf Hitler, and they would have remained Jews. To suggest otherwise, would be regarded by Orthodox Jews, and by a large percentage of other Jews, as a mortal insult. Another facet of this problem is that there are many Jews today who, in spite of all the facts regarding the bestial nature of Marxism-Bolshevism still regard themselves as spiritual communists while at the same time observing most of the Mosaic rituals. They have made no excuses for their strenuous efforts to overthrow the American democracy, and they never will.

As the concept of internationalizing the Red terror developed,

Jews were very active at all levels in the implementation of the program. It is interesting to note that many of those agents who were not Jews had Jewish spouses, and that the spouse sometimes survived and remained at liberty even after husband (nearly always the more publicized member of the marriage) had been killed, imprisoned, or exiled.

Stalin had one or more Jewish wives, the second one being shot to death in a mysterious episode officially described as a suicide. His offspring also had a curious propensity for marrying Jews. In fact, we find that Jewish women were very prominent at all levels of the Soviet government. They proved to be among the most effective agents in the various spying and disinformation tasks assigned by the KGB and other agencies of the Russian government, but they seldom came to the kinds of sticky ends reserved for their husbands.

In the USA, the Communist party was founded, funded, and operated principally by Jews, most of them immigrants (some legal, some illegal). Not all of these leaders came from Russia. Persons selected from other ethnic groups were sometimes found useful as figureheads in public functions or to perform other non-critical duties. They were also expected to do missionary work among their particular group.

In addition to the Communist party itself, many front organizations were set up by the Communists to appeal to various dissatisfied elements in the population. Not all of these had Jewish officials, although most of them were controlled by a Jew who may not have had any title at all.

The strong predominance of Jews in the group of Soviet spies operating in the US, particularly immediately before and during World War II, has been well documented in numerous studies. We are justified in asking, "What was the cultural, or genetic, factor that caused this curious relationship?" Some students have blamed Judaism.

What is a Jew?

Even the most fervent Jew might find it difficult to frame a non-rebuttable answer to this seemingly simple question — but this doesn't keep many of them from trying.

One of the problems is that the word "Jew," or its equivalents in other languages, had different meanings at different times and in different places. Some of the generally accepted elements in its origination and the fluctuations in its meanings over the centuries will be dealt with in this section.

We can resort to the dictionary preferred by the author, where we find:

Jew — Heb. *Yehudhi, one belonging to Judah.* Orig., one belonging to the tribe or kingdom of Judah; after the return from the Babylonian captivity, any member of the new Hebrew state; hence any person of the Hebrew race or people or any one whose religion is Judaism. The Jews of today do not uniformly reveal a pure Semitic type, but show evidences of intermixture of various countries where they dwell. As a rule, they are shorter than native populations, and, especially in northern Europe, more brunet.

This is from what might be considered by some as a goyish dictionary, though the editors undoubtedly had much input from Jewish sources. Very likely, the quoted definition would not be completely satisfactory to all Jews, especially to the Orthodox variety.

It might be useful to examine how learned Jews have defined their own ethnic group. A possible unifying factor would be the conscious practice of some of the rituals of Judaism; another would be membership in a family that can be genealogically related to forebears who had belonged to a definable group that practiced Judaism. For this, we need to agree upon a definition for "Judaism." This is not as easy as it may seem.

The clarification we are seeking is made immeasurably more difficult by the disagreements among those who want to be declared Jews (or those who do not want to be so labeled) as to what the specifications for this ethnic group should be. A generally accepted formulation is: "A Jew is the child of a Jewish mother." This is very unsatisfactory from several standpoints: to begin with, it merely takes the uncertainty back one generation — what is a Jewish mother?

For example, there are those who say that only those persons who can trace their descent from Abraham are truly Jews, while at the other extreme there are those who say that anyone who considers himself to be a Jew should be accepted as a member of the group.

Both positions are absurd, of course. No one can possibly trace their descent from a person who very likely never existed and, if he did exist, left no trace whatever in contemporary records, or in *any* verifiable written record for more than a thousand years after he supposedly flourished, so that any geneology relating a person living today to Abraham is certain to be fictitious. And, at the other extreme, universal acceptance of the self-designation criterion would reduce the whole clique to the level of exclusiveness of the average bridge club.

In observing the attitudes and behavior of members of the world "Jewish" community, it seems that, as a practical matter, a continuum exists, running from (1) the extremely Orthodox Jew with highly specialized clothing and food requirements, totally immersed in ritual and the Talmud, who proclaims rigid adherence to "the law of Moses," and who despises goyim and those Jews who associate with goyim, to (2) the Jew who often professes to look with a certain amount of humor and condescension on their more observant brethren and who eats pork and shellfish, breaks the Sabbath without a qualm, intermixes freely with the goyim in virtually all venues, sings Christmas carols with a clear conscience, and, in extreme cases, forgoes circumcision of their male offspring.

Zionism

After the Soviet empire collapsed, many of its zealous supporters were left without an excuse for using terrorism to express their hatred of the US and their envy of its loyal citizens. Most of them soon found another raison d'etre. The Jews had a ready made cause which was even dearer to their hearts than Communism — this was Zionism.

Zionism had already been in existence for several hundred years before conditions seemed to be maturing for its realization. Indeed, the

Old Testament (and parts of the Talmud) can be read as *commands* for the followers of Moses to return to Palestine. But the idea was not received with wild enthusiasm by most members of the Diaspora. Many of the Jews living in North America and Europe, particularly, did not relish the idea of relocating to the Middle East.

The first thing it is necessary to know in order to understand Zionism is that it has the same relationship to Judaism as the Spanish Inquisition had to Christianity and the second thing we need to know is that it has exactly the same relationship to Palestine as the Third Reich had to Germany. Zionism, at its core, is a program, many centuries old, having as its mission the establishment of a protected enclave from which to direct a program of enslavement and impoverishment targeting the whole world for the benefit of a limited number of Ashkenazim. This process will be considered complete only when all the goyim have been deprived of their property and are cowed subjects (in essence, slaves) of the master race. These characteristics seem to justify our description of Zionism as a psychopathic conspiracy willing to use any kind of terrorism to obtain their God-promised rewards. Of course, not all members of Zionist organizations are psychopaths. Perhaps, even some of the leaders are not.

The Zionist movement did not disappear when the nation of Israel was formed, its devotees merely became permanent activists for promoting the interests of the new nation without regard to the effects of their actions on the country in which they were residing at the time. In a like manner, many of them did not abandon the tenets of communism even though there might not be any more secret messages or little packets of currency from Moscow. What they found particularly appropriate, however, were causes which attracted donations from foundations, government agencies, and wealthy donors.

For those Jews who did not wish to relocate to the Middle East, or who wanted to join a more cosmopolitan type of movement, there was a wide choice of causes not involving religion, as such. Anarchism, socialism, atheism, environmentalism, black power, Hispanic power, gay rights, animal liberation, feminism, anti-military, peace, save the earth, libertarianism, abortion rights, free speech, harassing Holocaust deniers and aged camp guards, and many other causes. And there are permutations and mixtures of these which spring up and last for a time, then either take fire and grow or gradually fade away.

Activism Has Its Charms

Young Jews seemed to be attracted to programs giving the prospect of a considerable amount of violence and destruction, while older members of this cohort often thought it was more prudent to restrict their efforts to destroying, by one method or another, the reputations and careers of selected goyim. If it became necessary to choose a cause, a philosophy, which gave the true believers a justification for denigrating, embarrassing, and harassing competitors, there were many such causes to choose from — some of them will be discussed later in this paper.

Perfection Not Yet Achieved

Zionism has not yet lived up to the aspirations of some of its most fervid proponents. The true believers feel this is due to a lack of dedication on the part of other Zionists.

Jacob Neusner, who is committed to the interests of Israel, finds some problems in that country which he cannot understand, but he quickly learns that advice, or even commentary on failings of the people or government, is not welcome (Neusner 1981). "I once asked why the newest and most modern apartment houses invariably have obvious and malodorous garbage cans in the front entry, instead of at the back door, and was accused of being a Jewish anti-Semite or an assimilationist."

"And for the average Jew, the chief Jewish issue is phrased in wholly ethnic terms; whether children marry Jews is more important than whether they build Jewish homes, whether people live in Jewish neighborhoods matters more than whether the neighborhoods in which they live are places of dignity and commonplace justice."

"Nearly all American Jews are not only supporters of the State of Israel. They also regard their own 'being Jewish' as inextricably bound up with the meaning they impute to the Jewish state. Within that simple fact we find the explanation of why nearly all American Jews are, plain and simple, Zionists."

"Halpern offers the insight that until American Jews perceive themselves as strangers at home, they will be out of touch with the fundamental self-conception of the Jewish people through history."

"Common to all Israeli thought about Israel's place in world Jewry is the metaphor of the circle, with Jerusalem conceived to be the center and the *Golah* to be the periphery."

Maintaining Jewish Identity

Prell (1999) is mostly interested in Jewish identity. "Children's loathing for their Jewish parents and Jewish women's and men's loathing for one another are some of the legacies of Americanization."

"Prell looks at the 'Ghetto Girls,' Yiddish-speaking women from the East Side of Manhattan whose pictures often appeared in the socialist, working-class newspaper, the *Jewish Daily Forward*. The stereotype was of someone embodying not simply vulgarity but unregulated desire ... "Then in the 1960s and 1970s ... came the Jewish American Princess as a 'ubiquitous stereotype of Jewish life.' The mirror image of the Jewish Mother, she too was insatiable in her demands while reluctant to do anything herself. In a highly entertaining but non-PC chapter, Prell records some of the classic jokes, such as, 'What does a Jewish American Princess make for dinner? Reservations.' "

Choosing to Flee

Many of the so-called Holocaust survivors, and their descendants, owe the rest of the world an explanation of why they left Europe (and especially Germany, Poland, and Russia) at a critical time in apparent disregard for their coreligionists and family members. Typically, they abandoned their parents, children, spouses, and, in general, the elderly, the handicapped, and the poorest members of their ethnic group, leaving them to endure as best they could the tender mercies of their oppressors.

In many cases, the absconders appear to have smuggled most of the family's money out of the country to ease their transition — perhaps they also followed Moses' advice to the Jews who were fleeing Egypt, i.e., the night before you leave, borrow everything you can from your neighbors (Exodus 12:35-36 "And the children of Israel did according to the word of Moses; and they borrowed of the Egyptians jewels of silver, and jewels of gold, and rainment: And the LORD gave the people favour in the sight of the Egyptians, so that they lent unto them such things as they required. And they spoiled [i.e., despoiled] the Egyptians.")

In many cases, it is quite apparent that the persons most capable of staying and fighting against their oppressors, preceding and during World War II, were exactly the persons who found a way to escape to safety. The record also seems to show they depleted their families' funds to such an extent that those persons they left behind never had a chance to emigrate but had to stay and accept the consequences. Many of them were killed, or died of privation.

If all the Jews had remained in Germany and fought an underground battle against the Nazis, as many other ethnic groups did when their countries were occupied by Germany, or Russia, or China, or Israel, it is entirely possible that hundreds of thousands of non-Jewish casualties would have been prevented, and the war significantly shortened. But the European Jews did not seem to fight against the "Holocaust" at all, except perhaps for the Warsaw ghetto uprising, which involved probably only a few hundred, at most a few thousand, individuals and was, in the event, a miserable failure.

Instead, the fittest of the Jews fled to save their lives and, particularly, their assets. Tender solicitude for their own welfare continued after they established residence in the U.S. and elsewhere. Very, very few Jews volunteered to serve in the Allies' armies. Indeed, most men of draft age found some means to avoid the draft.

Contrast this lack of desire to fight against the Axis powers to the rush by Jewish Communists to get to Spain to fight in the Spanish Civil War. Indeed, contrast it with the influx of militant Jews (and their lackeys) into Russia when it became obvious that the Czar was about to lose his power in about 1915.

The Holocaust Survivors' Industry

The shakedown of various European countries, principally Germany, of course, by Jews for "reparations" for the "Holocaust" and other alleged war crimes, is developing into an industry which gives signs of continuing forever in a constantly increasing series of demands.

In an interesting twist, Sher informs us, in an article titled "Israel Banks 'not credible' on dormant accounts," that some repositories don't want to let the collected funds be dispersed. A lawyer representing Israei Holocaust survivors is pressing for a public inquiry into unclaimed accounts held by Israeli banks. Claiming that survivors have been lied to by the banks and the custodian of absentee property, he says that even Bank Leumi, which in mid-January made available a list of 12,959 accounts that have been dormant for 45 years or more, hasn't satisfied the demand for full disclosure.

"Leumi has set up a search facility at four branches and on its website, allowing interested parties to look up the names of the account holders. The bank says that the deposits, many of them of just a few dollars or pounds would today have a total value of no more than 8 million shekels ($1.95 million).

The appetite of certain Jewish groups for additions to the Holocaust myth appears to be insatiable and shameless. Chutzpah is not a strong enough word for it. Boudette (2001) reports, "An organization representing Jewish victims of Nazi Germany may soon take ownership of a piece of one of the most provocative symbols of the Third Reich — the vacant lot where Adolf Hitler killed himself in a Berlin bunker . . . the Jewish Claims Conference recently moved a step closer to taking possession of the land as a result of a ruling by the Berlin authority responsible for settling restitution cases ... If the German government, the properties' current owner, lets the ruling stand, the Claims Conference would sell the land and give about 80% of the proceeds — perhaps several million dollars — to a half dozen or so descendants of the Wertheim family, the former owners of one of the largest fortunes plundered by the Nazis." Gary Osen, an American attorney represents two Wertheim heirs. Will the Jews who obtain the property be willing to pay back taxes, say to 1950, on the property. If not, why?

Perhaps any reparations should be directed toward benefiting the soldiers, sailors, and Marines from the US, Britain, etc., who did the work for the Jews by fighting and dying in WWII while Jews who fled from Europe did little or nothing to win the European war, but took over the arts, finance, and civil service jobs vacated by the GIs, even though these interlopers should have known better than anyone else (including Pope Pius) of the anti-Jewish trend of events. But no, these slackers, and their families out to the fourth and fifth generations, must be rewarded while the surviving GIs and their families can only regard with fatalism their lost opportunities which fell into the hands of the immigrant Jews.

It will be said, there were some Jews in the US Armed Forces. Yes, there were some, I met a few during my 1943-1946 service — they exhibited a strong tendency to seek out office jobs and apply for transfers to the Quartermaster Corps. As one visits the cemeteries in Europe holding the bodies of GIs who fell in battle, one is struck by the strong preponderance of crosses as compared to the number of stars of David, a proportion far out of the expected range when we compare the percentages of Christians versus Jews in the US population at that time.

And, perhaps the Poles, Czechs, Austrians, and other ethnic groups which suffered under both Nazi and Communist occupation, with the usual accompanying massacres and expropriations, should consider the possibility of levying damages on the international communist conspirators who were equally responsible for their sufferings.

The Genetic Composition of Modern Jews

It is ridiculous to pretend that the modern jew is a pure, undefiled genetical counterpart of that mythical itinerant goatherd, Abraham, who might have lived sometime in antiquity, somewhere in the Middle East, possibly traveling under another name.

The Jews of today are a mixture of races, adulterated by genetic contributions from the many ethnic groups they contacted in their dispersion among and agglomeration with, other genetic types. A comparison of a Sephardic Jew and an Ashkenazic Jew, whether they consider themselves typical of their preferred ethnic affiliation or not, will give a quick answer to this question.

Indeed, there are many Jewish authorities who agree (at least in part) with the theory that most modern Ashkenazim are descended from a Turkic race, or other type of ancestor, rather than a Semitic one.

In recent years, the use of DNA testing to establish Jewish origins has achieved considerable attention. Preliminary results have been downplayed by the media, particularly after one set of data showed that a tribe of short black people (who practice a form of Judaism) living in southern Africa have a higher frequency of the "Cohen" (priestly) gene than do present-day Jewish individuals in Israel.

It is reasonably certain that the Ashkenazic Jews are a mixed race, carrying genes from some Middle Eastern ethnic group that might possibly be called Semitic, mixed with adventitious interlopers from other gene pools — sort of a pousse-café of a race.

The problems the so-called Jews have had in their relationships with other ethnic groups almost uninterruptedly throughout their history, result not so much from their chromosomal architecture and chemistry, but from their adherence to an ethos based on the Old Testament, interpreted in such a way by the rabbis (as in their Talmud) that relationships of . . . select group (Chosen People) to ethnic groups distinguished from them by genetic or philosophic differences is basically that of master to slave, with the latter having no rights unless they are specifically granted by the master race. This attitude naturally arouses opposition from the goyim, opposition which is characterized by the Jews as pogroms, hate speech, holocausts, etc., and is used as further evidence of the need to bilk, suppress, and destroy *all* opposition to the Chosen People.

It is clear enough, even though some Christians refuse to acknowledge it, that the Old Testament is full of examples of, not only justification but glorification, of adultery, thievery, swindling, deception, and murder (including human sacrifice), and, yes, even pogroms and holocausts directed at the enemies of the presumptive Semites. The rabbis have concentrated and modified these examples so as to remove any doubt that the current day Jews are justified in any procedure whatsoever that is necessary to exploit, demonize, and degrade the goyim.

Blacklisting

Goys should not mention Jews or Judaism in relation to any negative comment whatsoever, so say our friends among the Chosen People. In fact, many of these natural aristocrats believe that even *neutral* mention of this ethnic identification should be avoided. Consider the following extract from a discussion of early 20th century mystery novels, selected as an example specifically because it *is* so trivial. "What these apologists forget is that while it may be acceptable and even necessary for an author to show that such views [ethnic identifications] were commonplace at the time . . . , the authorial expression of such views is never acceptable. Take for example, Bruce Hamilton's 1930 English mystery, *To Be Hanged* (much praised by those two great snobs of crime fiction, Jacques Barzun and Wendell Hertig Taylor) in which a very minor — and very disagreeable — character is offhandedly described in the narrative as a 'little Jew.' "

We are left to wonder if Hamilton's book would have been less objectionable if the character had been described as "large," or "average," or "a little J_w." We know, of course, that it would have been perfectly satisfactory, even admirable, if Hamilton had referred to a disagreeable character as, "a little Christian/Protestant/Catholic/Seventh Day Adventist," although, of course, it would have been preferable to say he was "a little goy." We are also unsure whether or not Barzun and Taylor would have been described as "great snobs" if they had thought to crucify Hamilton for his use of the term, "a little Jew." Just a touch of paranoia, there.

Jews Are Conspiratorial by Training

Various psychopolitical theories are advanced as to why Jews seem to be in the ruling factions of nearly all radical organizations, especially in violent radical groups such as the Communist organizations operating under various names. See McKinney (2001) for a review of some of these rationalizations. However, a simpler explanation is that the Jewish religion glorifies the Old Testament stories of betrayal, spying, treachery, genocide, and the like, all justified by being performed for the sake of advancing Mosaicism.

According to Barrett (1996), "One of the cult-watching organizations once gave the remarkable statistic that a quarter of recruits to the more recent alternative religions are Jewish by birth. This may or may not be accurate, but it does become understandable when the profile of new members of alternative religions is examined. They tend to be intelligent, well-educated young people who have often had a religious upbringing (the members of the Jesus Army are very much an exception). They have been brought up to accept the importance of religious belief, and they have been taken to church or synagogue since childhood, but they often become disillusioned with the religion of their parents. They see their parents as having an unquestioned set of beliefs; when (as normal teenagers) they begin to question what they have been taught, this is discouraged, often with horror at what the parents see as the youngster's rejection of God's truth." This comment is very pertinent to the preceding discussion.

Longing for Discrimination

Jews, as well as many other ethnic groups, tend to look for discrimination in many places, even in the most unlikely ones. Although it is known without a doubt that Jews adopted Christian names for business purposes or to improve their children's opportunities for blending into the goyisch population, we find that some representatives of this ethnic group claim their ancestors were forced to alter their names by the evil goyim.

The author was presented with one of these fables by a friend who claimed that his great grandfather, when he came to this country, told the official who interviewed him on arrival that his name was "Heiligman," but the official either misunderstood or deliberately altered the name to "I. Litman." This was said to explain why my friend was forced to bear the name "Irving Litman." The story seemed specious at the time, but credulous as the author was (and is), he was willing to accept it, only wondering why, in the 50 or so years since the time of the re-christening (you should pardon the expression), the family members had not taken the opportunity to change their name back to "Heiligman."

It turns out that the basic story of "forced renaming" has had thousands of replications and variations over the last century or so. It is one of those curious urban legends we hear so much about. According to Ann Lewis (2001), "Sure, immigrants changed their names or their names were changed by someone, somewhere along the road to assimilation, but not at the whim of some Ellis Island bureaucrat. His job, in the vast majority of cases, was simply to check off names on passenger lists generated by the steamship company itself."

Ms. Lewis bases this conclusion on evidence uncovered by New York film maker Alan Berliner, "who backed into it unsuspectingly while researching" the origins of his own name. The Chief Historian of the Immigration and Nationalization Service (Marian Smith) told him that at Ellis Island there was not a name-changing room, table, station, form, rule, regulation, or law. Ms. Smith further said, "I have yet to see any evidence that the government issued every single person a piece of paper with a name on it. Unless they were detained for further questioning, the only documents immigrants had were those issued by the shipping company."

"Why that's paramount to denying the Holocaust, sputters one indignant women on the street to Mr. Berliner." Yes, very much the same.

Not just Jews, but many ethnic groups, especially those whose members were largely illiterate, voluntarily or inadvertently took their names through a number of spelling changes and even more radical alterations during their lifetimes, for several reasons: To avoid debts and other legal problems, to hide from relatives including unwanted spouses, to blend in with the dominant ethnic group, etc.

And there is the ever-popular, "for business reasons." Fictional books of the early part of the 20th century often include references to moneylenders with Scottish names who advertised easy credit, leading to the surprising discovery, when the applicant visits them, that Mr. MacDougal appears to have just returned from the synagogue.

One would think descendants would be grateful granddad was received in a new country without undergoing lengthy tests and expenses and was not faced with a demand for verification of the claimed birth name. But, gratitude is not a prominent part of the Jewish personality. There's no money in it.

The Intolerances of Jews

Jews enjoy being different. They often find it difficult to establish a rapport with their neighbors and co-workers, and are gratified to be able to consider this as being due to persecution. Their paranoia makes it seem justifiable to treat their goyisch customers and clients harshly, to make sharp deals, to cheat if necessary.

Intermarriage — The prejudice of many, if not most, Jews against marrying goyim is widely recognized. Few Jews would attempt to deny this prejudice exists, though they might say, "It's only the orthodox who feel that way." On the other hand, any tendency of whites to decry intermarriage with African Americans, or vice versa, will be described by the Jewish media, and Jews in general, as a disgusting manifestation of racial intolerance.

If the white person happens to be a Jew who tries to keep his or her child or other relative from marrying a black person, however, there is no bigotry, merely a desire to conform to the holy traditions.

Avri Shafran, Director of Public Affairs, Agudath Israel of America [NYC], is a rabbi who is willing to explain this seeming contradiction to us. He says, "There may indeed be a large demand for Jewish clergymen to officiate at marriages between Jews and non-Jews, but the claim that 'nothing in the Bible forbids such unions' is very misleading. The Jewish religious tradition has never been confined to the literal words of the Bible. Both the intent of the Bible's verses and a large host of additional instructions reside in what Jews call the Oral Law. And that corpus of law clearly prohibits Jews from marrying non-Jews. That there are Jewish clergy entirely willing to ignore that fact speaks of a different Jewish tragedy every bit as painful as intermarriage."

Richard Kraus, also of New York, agrees. "I am writing in response to the claim made by Joanne Kaufman in her piece 'Tying the knot with a gentile? Call Rabbi Fishbein . . . that 'nothing in the Bible forbids such unions (intermarriages).' Miss Kaufman must have an interesting, not to mention non-halachic interpretation, of the commandment 'You shall not intermarry with them: do not give your daughters to their sons or take their daughters for your sons.' (Deut. 7:3, JPS translation, 1999/5759). While it is of course entirely permissible to marry a convert to Judaism . . . it is not permissible to marry a gentile."

Jews and Terrorism

The records of Jewish terrorism are not restricted to Biblical examples. An excellent discussion by Nackman Ben-Yehuda is *Political Assassination by Jews: A rhetorical device for justice* (1993). In the section, "Actual Cases," the chapters are:

Political assassinations by Jews in the Bible, the Sicariis, and in Europe.

Political assassinations by Jews in Palestine between 1882-1918 — the Turkish period.

Political assassinations by Jews in Palestine between 1919-1948 — the British period.

Political assassinations by Jews in Israel between 1949-1988 — the Israeli period.

Political executions.

Political assassinations, terror, and tangential cases.

There are about a hundred cases, some of them involving multiple victims, and in some cases, the intended victim was not killed.

In one of the discussions, the author states: "Two clear 'reasons' for the assassinations are salient: (a) revenge and a warning signal; (b) prevention of, or interference in, a process of social or political change represented or proposed by the victim. The fact that many cases occurred after the potential victim did something, was warned, and that therefore most cases were considered as revenge as well as a warning sign implies that there is an alternative system of 'justice' in operation here."

UN Documentation of Jewish Terrorism

An official report of the United Nations prepared in 1948 for Dr. Ralph J. Bunche, who was at the time UN Mediator for Palestine, listed numerous cases of Zionist terrorism in the Near East during the period 1944-1948. The list begins with the assassination of Lord Moyne, British Resident Minister in the Middle East (and his chauffeur) on November 6, 1944, and ends with the murder of Count Folke Bernadotte, UN Mediator for Palestine and French Colonel André Serot, chief of France's contingent in the unarmed UN truce-observer team. Bernadotte was killed because he had ordered 8,000 Arab refugees to be returned to the villages from which they had been driven by attacks of Jewish terrorists.

"August 5, 1947, Palestine. Striking at dawn, British security forces arrested 35 leading Zionists and sent them to the Latrun detention camp in an attempt to wipe out the Irgun Leadership. In reprisal, Igurists blew up the Department of Labor in Jerusalem, killing three British constables . . . All those arrested except the three mayors were Revisionists. Among many papers confiscated was correspondence from Soviet Russian agents in Italy and Bulgaria and extensive plans to poison the water supply of the non-Jewish parts of Jerusalem with botulism and other bacteria. Bacteria was supplied by Soviet sources through Bulgaria."

In an August 16, 1947, "British military authorities, citing captured intelligence and statements from Jewish defectors from terrorist organizations, state that it now appears that Jewish terrorists are beginning to attack Arabs where ever they are found because Jews wish the Arabs to be driven out of Palestine entirely."

In late 1947, the UN was saying, "The Arabs, initially living in peace with the Jewish minority, have been increasingly victimized by the Jews who, now that the British are leaving, are turning their savage behavior against them." Also, "It appears that the Soviets have been sending weapons, mostly captured German pieces, to assist the Zionists and accompanying these clandestine arms shipment the Soviets have also sent a very sizable contingent of instructors and advisors to Palestine in months past. As many of the Zionists are Russian or Polish in origin, these Communist Russians have been received very gladly by the Jewish extremists and quickly blend in with the local populations. Soviet interest in Middle East oil and an overriding interest in obtaining warm-water ports are a prime factor in their interest in a Jewish state in Palestine."

"January 28, 1948, Jerusalem. Rabbi Hillel Silver, chief of the Jewish Agency's American Division . . . [campaigned] for American public support of armed Jewish backing for partition and eventual Zionist control of all Palestine."

"January 31, 1948, London. British foreign office officials revealed that over 1,000 Soviets, all Russian-speaking Communist military technicians, had been intercepted on . . . on two immigrant ships."

On March 5, 1948, "The Jewish Agency stated that . . . arms shipments were . . . destined for the arming of Jewish partisans in Palestine to 'fight and drive out' the Arab population of what the Agency stated 'was eternal Jewish land' that could not be occupied by either the British or the Arabs."

On March 11, 1948, in New York City "Communists and their left-wing labor unions turned out over 10,000 persons in a protest rally against US betrayal of partition."

March 12, 1948, "An Arab Higher Command paper . . . charged the Jewish Agency with massing Soviet trained and equipped illegal immigrants in Eastern war service in Palestine and had set up laboratories for bacteriological warfare."

April 30, 1948. "Jewish extremists threatened to dynamite the Arab Dome of the Rock Mosque unless all Arabs immediately evacuated Jerusalem . . . Haganah . . . insisted all Arabs and Christians must leave Jerusalem . . . [and] overran the Christian Arab quarter in southwestern modern Jerusalem . . . In Katamon, Haganah captured St. Simon's Greek Orthodox Monastery, drove out the monks and vandalized the building . . . "

"Safad, capital of Upper Galilee and normally a city of 15,000 Arabs, was reported by the Jewish Agency as having been 'cleansed' of Arabs by May 6 [1948]. The only remaining inhabitants of the town were 2,000 Jews. Haganah announced that all Arab property had been confiscated from the owners and would be given to Jewish settlers."

May 4, 1948, Tel Aviv. "The Stern gang resumed direct war against the British for protecting the Arab population of Jerusalem. Seven British soldiers were killed near Nethanya. At the same time, the Stern gang took credit for a letter bomb which killed the young brother of a British army officer in England."

May 6, 1948, Jerusalem. "Haganah was redesignated as the Jewish State Army and reported that 200 aircraft, later revealed by

British authorities as having come from Czechoslovakia, whose new communist government is almost entirely composed of Zionists and who have been pouring weapons into Palestine, are slated to reinforce the new army."

May 22, 1948, Jerusalem. "Thomas Wasson, US Consul General in Jerusalem and a member of the Council's Truce Commission, was fatally wounded by a Stern gang sniper near the US Consulate. Two other Consulate members were also assaulted, one dying the next day."

September 17, 1948, Jerusalem. "Angered by his order to readmit 8,000 Arab refugees driven from three villages near Haifa by attacks of Jewish terrorists, the Stern gang assassinated Count Folke Bernadotte, UN mediator for Palestine. Also killed in the attack was French Col. André Serot, chief of France's 100-man contingent in the unarmed UN truce-observer team."

Jewish Presence in US Terrorist Movements

Rothman (1978), is an ex-Jewish Weatherman of the 1960s who, later, tried to make some sense of his experiences and the experiences of those around him: 'A lot of the Weatherman leadership was Jewish and had never been tough street kids, and I really believe that a tremendous amount of what they were doing was overcoming their own fears about their masculinity ... Most of them ... had been intellectually aggressive, but all of a sudden they were trying to be tough street kids ... I think there was a lot of self-hatred going on' " (Rothman 1978).

Horowitz (1997) and Halevi (1995) gave firsthand descriptions of life in the modern American milieu of Jewish communists. These two members of the intelligentsia published frank descriptions of their indoctrination into groups that were dedicated to overthrowing and subjugating their host country. This at a time when American soldiers were fighting for the Jewish cause in World War II and the American Jews were living safely and in comparative luxury in the United States.

Halevi's story is particularly compelling. Brought up in Brooklyn, living in middle-class comfort, he engaged from his adolescent days in various disruptive and destructive tactics targeting virtually every other ethnic group in the city, all justified (really, necessitated) he thought, because he was preventing another Holocaust. Imagine this story repeated a thousand times in New York City, and many times that throughout the country, and we have a clear picture of the effect of Jewish psychopaths on the culture of the nation.

Although Halevi was bitter about other nations' failure to do anything for the European Jews during the World War II period, his own father did nothing for them. The father was too busy protecting his own delicate Jewish body. Here are Halevi's own words: "When the Nazis invaded Transylvania and the Jews of my father's town . . . were sent to the cattlecars, he didn't go. Instead, he fled to the forest, dug a hole, and lived in it until the end of the war."

Other ethnic groups may have had their freedom fighters, while the Jews had hole sitters. They were waiting for someone else to fight for them. I had friends and relatives who were killed, many others who were badly injured, and very many others (including myself) who endured dreadful living conditions for years as members of the Allies' Armed Forces, all to fight the Jew's battle for them. But, of course, we did not do enough for the Jews — no one can ever do enough for the Jews.

HOW TO ELIMINATE A PREDATORY SPECIES

Among the measures reds regard as essential is the restricting of the numbers of humans present on the planet — preferably by markedly reducing the current population, but in any case avoiding an increase in the earth's inhabitants. The pronouncements by some enthusasts seem to indicate that their desired end point is not zero population growth but zero population.

Many reds seem to regard the mere presence on earth of any appreciable number of humans as an affront to Nature. If this is not the case, it is hard to understand why so many of the policies undertaken, or advocated, by red organizations can be expected to lead to a serious reduction in the total number of humans. These policies generally take one of the following approaches: (1) encouraging attitudes and practices that diminish the number of babies born, and (2) creating situations which lead to the death of large numbers of people, as by: (a) encouraging wars (including civil wars) and other armed struggles, (b) allowing conditions to develop which are favorable to the occurrence of famines, epidemics, etc., and (c) carrying out mass indiscriminate executions.

In pursuance of their goal, the people haters give us books and articles on zero population growth, the population bomb, the population explosion, the rape of the environment, etc. We learn that families should have no more than two children — one is better and zero is best. Decreasing the birth rate can be approached in various ways: e.g., reducing the opportunities for normal sexual intercourse, promoting means for blocking conception, providing free abortion, and acquiescing in infanticide. Abstinence from sexual acts goes against the grain of liberals, however, so it is seldom, if ever, recommended or even mentioned as an alternative. And, homosexuality is very much OK — many of the reds seem to practice what they preach.

One can hardly avoid reaching the conclusion that a large percentage of those who advocate population restrictions show great antipathy to the normal family structure (father, mother, children) because they are obligate homosexuals, and they wish to bring everyone into their fold. Or, motivated by jealousy and envy of normal families, they wish to deprive everyone else of the experiences they will never have.

chapter seventeen

SEXUAL POLITICS

Either there has been a deliberate attempt to Balkanize the moral landscape, or the numerous campaigns undertaken by the media and academia (among other cultural elements) to promote that sort of compartmentalization of the electorate have in some miraculous manner assumed such a position without there having been a conscious attempt to do so.

By Balkanization of sexual morals for political reasons, the author means the intentional separating of the population into groups which make their political and social decisions primarily on the basis of sexual matters. For example, many homosexuals will vote for homosexuals regardless of a candidate's other qualifications, many women will automatically vote for the female candidate, pederasts will vote for the person they think will allow them the greatest freedom in practicing their perversion, and so on. This allows the villains to pursue their much larger goal of breaking down the financial and political structure of the country so they can obtain absolute power over the masses, without spending large sums of money on perverting the electoral process via advertisements, bribes, and the like.

The reds hate humanity, or perhaps it would be more correct to say that they hate those cohorts (the largest part of humanity) which they do not regard as part of their own extended family, the latter term meaning in this case those individuals who share some particular behavioral trait or racial identification with the supermen who want to make all the rules. This naturally leads to a desire to limit the number of persons not approved by them, a limitation which approaches an asymptote of zero. Since a frank expression of this attitude would hardly be politically correct, and might, in fact, arouse considerable annoying (or even dangerous) opposition from the rest of the population, they pretend to be in favor of reducing the total number of people in order that those who remain will have a better life. This means they must somehow convince the victims that they will be part of the favored few.

Most of the cliques appealed to, and affected by, this fragmenting and polarizing of the electorate include only people who are not interested in forming relationships that result in offspring. Their attitude is very much favored by bosses on the Red side of the political spectrum. They do not see any point in encouraging the reproduction of persons who do not fit into their quite narrow definition of fitness (or of "humanity"). Therefore, the promotion of sexual deviations has a two-fold (i.e., electoral and survival) advantage for reds.

In this chapter we will examine the use made by Reds/reds of sexual tactics in gathering recruits, energizing members, soliciting donations, and increasing their power. Because of the intricate and intertwined relationships between different branches of the overall strategy (i.e., the diverting of sexual drives into political energies), no single existing word or phrase of common currency seemed adequate to cover the subject, so the recently developed neologism, "sexpol," will be used in the following discussion.

Sexpol is Not a New Concept

In a review of E. M. Jones's book, *Degenerate Moderns*, Schafly (1994) states, "Jones argues persuasively that a causal relationship exists between private behavior and intellectual product that is presented to the world as 'science' or 'economics' or 'psychology' or 'art.' The thesis of the Jones book is that the theories expounded by many enormously influential modern intellectuals are simply rationalizations of their own sexual misbehavior. Their so-called intellectual and scientific breakthroughs were the result of their own sexual desires . . . [for example] Biographers of the 1980s admitted what earlier biographers had concealed: that [John Maynard] Keynes was a homosexual, and so were [other members of] the Oxford-Cambridge elite of which he was a central figure."

Many utopian dreamers had as one of their principal creeds that marriage (or monogamy) was sexual exploitation (of men, women, or both) and that any man should be able to use any woman, and vice versa, in their idealized communities. However, homosexuality and other types of sexual deviance were looked upon with disfavor by many of the dreamers, and by leaders in those communes which came into being.

This concept allows us to understand why socialists, communalists, communists, anarchists, and the like have founded communities which seemed to have little economic, philosophical, or social rationale. Perhaps they were founded specifically for the purpose (or as one of their purposes) of allowing the originators to increase their opportunities for varied sexual experiences.

Free love was the reef on which some of the utopian communities foundered, since virulent jealousies were invariably created in such partner-swapping environments, and these antagonisms led to unrest, defections, and violence. It is inevitable that, over a period of time, emotional attachments form between at least a few couples, and they strongly resent the attempts of others to mate with their partner.

The demonization both of humans (as a species) and of many human activities which are intended or designed to reduce suffering and provide better lives to humans, is done routinely by dedicated environmentalists. For example, it is beyond doubt that an appreciable number of extremely naive and mentally disturbed persons who call themselves environmentalists really do believe the Earth has a personality and a form of consciousness, and that it is disturbed by what careless and selfish humans are doing to it. It is useless to provide evidence contradicting "revealed truths" such as these — logic and reason have no part in the beliefs of these fanatics, faith alone is the justification.

Sexual Warfare

There are several methods for accomplishing the major red goal of fragmenting society into warring cliques based on the preferred form of sexual expression. Nearly all of these lead, perhaps only as a collateral result, to a reduction in the birth rate. Among the tactics are:

1. Dissuading women from having sexual relations with males, and even inducing in them a feeling of revulsion toward every normal male.

This is the intent, or result, of the "Womyn's" rights movement, called by some of its critics the feminazi troops. There can be little doubt that many of the leaders of this movement are obligate homosexuals.

2. Encouraging homosexuality in men. This has at least two desirable outcomes for the enemies of civilization:

(a) Fewer women will have an opportunity to get pregnant.

(b) The well known prevalence of promiscuity in homosexual men leads to a higher incidence of venereal infections, and this causes increased death rates.

(c) Simple homosexuality can be diverted into even more extreme forms of sexual expression — sadism for example.

3. Advocating restrictions in the number of children generated in normal marriages or bisexual companionships. The reasons the reds suggest for such a stance include:

(a) The world would be better off if there were fewer people. Thus the childless couple can regard themselves as being superior to normal families.

(b) Children are expensive, troublesome, and unrewarding.

(c) Normal families are crass, square, and unsophisticated.

(d) It is unfair to bring children into a world like this.

4. Encouraging governmental policies which lead to increased deaths, such as:

(a) The campaign against use of DDT in the fight against malaria.

(b) Educational trends and social customs which lead to behavior favoring the transmission of AIDS virus. "Gay rights" is either an announced goal or a concealed plank in the program of every red organization.

Female activists of less extreme orientation, who ostensibly seek only a policy of equal pay for equal work, or some other rational goal, may simply intend to help their own career by espousing a cause that has general approval. Or, they may be using this approach to begin indoctrinating their recruits into the the more extreme sexual movements.

Creating Discontent

Many people, perhaps most people, like to believe that their true merit is not being recognized because of unfair or misguided opposition to their advancement. "Jealousy in high places," is the old saw which applies to their view of the basic reason for their lack of success in their chosen careers. That is, they have talent, but it is not being put to use because they are women, homosexuals, black, Jewish, or old/young, and the people who are doing the hiring are men, straight, white, Christian, or young/old.

But, there are, very likely, valid reasons for their failure to get the job(s) they want. When push comes to shove, no one with any degree of foresight will hire a person whose talents are so limited (or whose behavior is so bizarre) as to endanger the organization which pays the recruiter's salary. In some cases, these trouble makers, these non-producers are hired because the decision-maker does not have the courage to reject them. The misfit will then, almost immediately, begin to complain that he has not received the proper treatment and that compassion for his innate problems has not been forthcoming.

Of course, sometimes the complainers are correct, and they have indeed been discriminated against because of inborn characteristics supposedly not connected to their ability to perform a job. This is unfair, but the eternal truth is, people will always tend to hire persons with whom they feel more comfortable. A Jew will often tend to hire a Jew, a black will often tend to hire a black, a homosexual will often tend to hire a person of the same sexual orientation, etc.

Reds understand very well how to turn resentment based on a person's lack of achievement into a jihad against "the establishment." They are also familiar with the need for gradualism in implementing the more extreme principles of their program. They may start out with simple, seemingly innocuous demands or requests, and gradually escalate into a full-scale destruction of the existing civilization, using the most ardent and active supporters of the previous step as the nucleus for the following stage. The gains from the earlier programs are then considered as the base, but as an inadequate base which must be expanded to arrive at the final truth. And so on, ad infinitum.

Quite often, the creators of discontent will try to convince persons who have not advanced as fast as they think they should have that the reason for their failures are due to their supervisors' objections to their "sexual preferences."

Sodom and Gomorrah Redivivus

The fragmentation and weak discipline in the community of protestant Christians offers many opportunities for take overs by determined and callous cadres of reds. They use many strategies to fragment and dishearten their opposition. Among the most effective of their methods are the mobilization of sexual perverts already in the church and the infiltration of the organization by additional sexual deviants. Homosexuals are by far the most active group in this regard.

Homosexual influences in Christian churches — A rumor that up to 25% of the persons working at the New York headquarters of the National Council of Churches (NCC) were homosexual, led Beck (1993) to investigate the role of deviant sex influences on Protestant executive offices. He confirmed that a network of homosexuals did exist in the NCC headquarters. Staff members told him that "a veritable decathlon of homosexual couplings" occurred in the restrooms.

"Deprived of the issue of war and peace, the Protestant Church has now taken on homosexuality as its burning question.

"*Presbyterians*: The Presbyterian Church USA did not allow the Rev. Jane Spahr, a lesbian, to be ordained. So a church in Rochester hired her as an 'evangelist,' and she now conducts missionary work to the heathens in the pews who might still harbor doubts on the blessedness of homosexuality . . .

"Presbyterians for Lesbian and Gay Concerns (PLGC) lobbies for ordination of homosexuals and acceptance of the gay lifestyle. The group finds strong support in the Presbyterian bureaucracy. One worker at the denomination's Louisville headquarters was selling PLGC buttons and advertising through PLGC Public, an electronic bulletin board on the Presbnet system.

"In 1991, the PCUSA's' Special Committee on Human Sexuality released, 'Keeping Body and Soul Together: Sexuality, Spirituality and Social Justice,' a study that baptized the gay agenda as an admirable ethic of 'justice love.'

"*Episcopalians*: 'Integrity' is the Episcopalians' official pro-gay organization, active since the late 1970s and counting 57 chapters in four regions of the US, along with chapters in Canada and Australia. While there is no official policy on gay ministers, they do operate in the church. Members see Bishop Spong of New Jersey as a key advocate for gay concerns.

"*Lutherans*: 'I support your intention to lift the ban on homosexual persons in the armed forces,' wrote Bishop Herbert Chilstrom of the Evangelical Lutheran Church in America to President Clinton last February. The bishop cited the 'enormous problem' of 'sexual misconduct of heterosexual persons in the military.' He concluded, 'Please be assured of the prayers of our church as you wrestle with many complex issues.'

"The Lutherans ordain gays but expect them to be celibate. 'Lutherans Concerned,' the denomination's gay caucus, is trying to change that policy, which some San Francisco clergy have already done. There have been several resolutions calling upon the church to 'recognize the dignity, value, and giftedness present, by the grace of God, in the lesbian and gay community.' TAGS (Teen Age Gays of St. Paul) meets at St. Paul Reformation Lutheran Church. This is the gay version of Sunday school and youth ministry. There have also been various Lutheran task forces on 'Homosexuality, Homophobia and Ordination.'

"*Methodists*: The Methodists have not yet approved the ordination of homosexuals but there was a case of a marriage ceremony involving two men. Several years ago Methodist clergy in Denver refused to dismiss a pastor who dumped his wife and children for his boyfriend. The Methodists' caucus for lesbian homosexual and bisexual concerns is

'Affirmation.' The organization recently issued a resolution calling the United Methodist Church, 'a moribund institution drained by its idolatry of heterosexual norms,' and threatened to split off into a gay sect.

"Clerical signers of a letter in support of lifting the military's ban on gays included Methodist bishop Melvin Talbert, a longtime anti-military stalwart. Steve Beard of the traditionalist Methodist group Good News points out the contradiction: 'You have these left-wing clergymen campaigning to have homosexuals be able to participate in everything these homosexuals have always hated.

"*Unitarians*: The United Church of Christ is led by the kind of people who drive you out of town by burning a question mark on your front lawn. The UCC has been ordaining gay clergy since the late 1970s and denominational staffers work with the Gay and Lesbian coalition. The UCC approves homosexual marriage but there is no official rule on the practice. The UCC's Inter-Instrumentality Task Force on the Right to Privacy shows up at synod meetings and demonstrates for the overturning of anti-sodomy laws."

Advantages of targeting churches — One of the main reasons, if not *the* most important reason that left-wingers of all types seek to maximize the number and influence of unconventional, weak-willed, or nontraditional persons in Christian church organizations is that such people often lack interest in day to day operations. This allows the more doctrinaire, better organized, and less lawful group (the reds) control of the money. While the perverts are hanging around the rest rooms, the reds are writing checks and issuing their press releases. Many of the old-line churches have access to large, reliable incomes and vast endowments.

Add to this tempting prize the easy targets afforded by the decrepit, weak, and often senile officials who have drifted to the top of the administrative pile over the decades and whose only real interest is the preservation of their own power, pensions, and privileges, and you have ready-made candidates for takeover by vicious, determined, and committed reds of any hue.

The utilization of sexual perverts as front persons (things?) in the destruction of traditional Christianity has several advantages for the Reds. Firstly, the tunnel vision of homosexuals and other deviants (i.e., their near-total absorption in the practice of their particular perversion) obliterates all normal moral guides, so that the destruction of Christian beliefs and practices can go on all around them without arousing their fear or resentment.

Secondly, though the perverts may be interested in the money that can be diverted to communist causes or personal use by gaining control of the organization, this is not a principal — often not even a major — factor affecting their actions, so that the reds are able to divert large sums of the church's money to subverting political processes and bribing the media.

Thirdly, the "social" activities of perverts often lead to the breaking of laws, which makes them subject to blackmail, and thus turns them into dependable servants regardless of their other motivations, eliminating the need for expending money in bribes, salaries, etc.

A homosexual Christian is a homosexual first, last, and always, and a Christian only insofar as the restrictions and practices of that religion can be fitted into the facilitation and concealment of his or her sexual acts. Teaching and socializing within the framework of the church's programs allows the homosexual to contact potential victims and converts, so the adopting of a Christian camouflage is recognized by these deviants as a worthwhile strategy.

Few, if any, of the homosexual activists have difficulty understanding that the practices, and even the mental tendencies, concomitant with the homosexual mindset, cannot possibly be made to conform to Biblical teachings. So these people become bitter enemies of Christianity and want to destroy it. Their attitude fits in nicely with the Red program.

Women's Liberation Movements

Activists seeking to prove the equality or supremacy of women in the battle of the sexes often appeal to socialist theory as the basis of their demands. It is certainly true that many socialists, both the academic or theoretical variety and the utopian experimenters wanted to abolish family life and other facets of what seemed to them to be the enslavement of women. However, in the communes where any woman could be used by any man, it soon became obvious that the rule of the harem prevailed, and none of the women and few of the men had any rights at all.

None of this history makes the slightest impression on the female homosexuals and the viragos who operate on the basic principle that all men are hateful and need to be taught a lesson they won't soon forget.

One of the contributors to the web site, Workers Power Global www.workerspower.com puts it this way. "For women to achieve full political, economic and social equality with men, the social and economic basis of their oppression must be destroyed. The existence of the family as a privatised sphere of labour must be ended. This can only be achieved by the full socialisation of child-rearing and household labour."

Continuing, "For this reason we reject Stalinism's idealisation of the 'proletarian family' which is in reality a replica of the bourgeois family in which privatised domestic labour is maintained, in this instance in the interests of the bureaucracy."

"The tasks of providing food, shelter and comfort necessary for the reproduction of labour power must be undertaken collectively by society, ending the individual responsibility of each separate family to try and cope. Only when relieved of this domestic slavery can women be drawn into socialised production fully and equally alongside men.

"However, this socialisation will only have a really socialist character if it is accompanied by the destruction of the gender-specific division of labour (and the corresponding roles) in socialised production. Women will not be the only historical subject for this special transformation, the deliberate dissolution of the bourgeois family and the overcoming of gender-specific forces, although they will be the most forward pushing section of the working class on this matter."

The Workers Power Global site includes a fairly extensive history of the women's power movement as related to developments within the Bolshevist government over the years.

There is also a movement called "AnarchaFeminism," aka "Anarchist Feminism." Its principal interests seem to be abortion rights, prostitution rights, and divorce (the web originator lives in Ireland, where divorce is not easy to obtain). She coins the phrase, "Better dead than wed," which certainly goes a long way to clarifying her point of view. A 14-page pamphlet, "Sex, class and women's oppression," being a collection of anarchist articles railing against the oppression of women, is free for the downloading. She provides photos of seven female anarchist heroes, including such freaks as Emma Goldman — a nastier looking bunch you are not likely to see this side of Hell.

The Traditional Family is the Enemy

The basic cultural group of man and wife and their children, if any, is the principal target of the enemies of civilization that call themselves Reds, liberals, etc. — what the author has denominated, "reds." Dalrymple (2001) tells us of the BBC television producer who wanted to make documentaries showing the devastating effects on society of the atomization of family life that was taking place in England. His superiors at BBC rejected the idea completely.

"But why so insistent a denial of the obvious by the very class of people whose primary function, one might have supposed was to be what the Russians called truth bearers ... They [liberals] saw their society as being so unjust that nothing in it was worth preserving; and they thought that all human unhappiness arose from the arbitrary and artificial fetters that their society placed on the satisfaction of appetite ... they could not see the possibility of deterioration. And so if family life was less than blissful, with all its inevitable little prohibitions, frustrations, and hypocrisies, they called for the destruction of the family as an institution. The destigmatization of illegitimacy went hand in hand with easy divorce, the extension of marital rights to other forms of association between adults, and the removal of all the fiscal advantages of marriage. Marriage melted as snow in the sunshine. The destruction of the family was, of course, an important component and consequence of sexual liberation, whose utopian program was to have increased the stock of innocent sexual pleasure, not least among the liberators themselves. It resulted instead in widespread violence consequent upon sexual insecurity and in the mass neglect of children, as people became ever more egotistical in their search for momentary pleasure."

Dalrymple also said, "Every liberal prescription worsened the problem that it was ostensibly designed to solve. But every liberal intellectual had to deny that obvious consequence or lose his Weltanschauung: for what shall it profit an intellectual if he acknowledge a simple truth and lose his Weltanschauung? Let millions suffer so long as he can retain his sense of his own righteousness and moral superiority. Indeed, if millions suffer they are additional compassion fodder for him, and the more of their pain will he so generously feel."

Academia Fosters Sexual Antagonisms

According to Billingsley (1992), who reviewed the history and status of "Women's Studies" programs in institutions of higher education, these disciplines (if they can be called that) were unknown prior to 1969, "when the first official program began at San Diego State University . . . By the end of the '70s there were over 100 women's studies programs at schools across the country. By 1977 there were 276 [and by 1982] . . . 350 programs and over 30,000 different courses." Billingsley estimates that there were 530 programs in 1989 and 620 in 1992.

When such an amazing proliferation comes into view, the first thought of the seasoned observer is, "Where does the money come from?" The second thought is, "Who is the on-site controller?" The third thought is, sometimes, "How can I get a piece of the action."

These startling increases in women's studies programs and associated devilry are said to have been financed by philanthropic organizations, and in particular, the Ford Foundation. Billingsley puts a major part of the blame at the feet of Mariam Chamberlain, who was, for a time, a program officer in the Ford Foundation's Department of Education and Culture. She became "Founding President" and resident scholar of the National Council for Research on Women — in other words, she became a spender of the funds she once had a hand in allocating.

Genetic Factors

In a "compassionate" and wealthy society such as the US during the last 100 years or so, many persons of extreme sociological aberrancy have mated and had offsrping who would have, in other places and other times, been killed at an early age — accidentally or intentionally. Premature deaths of these aberrant specimens might have been caused by execution, by police actions, or by fights with other persons of the same bent. Or they might have been removed from the pool of potential mothers and fathers by diseases that interfere with reproductive success, or would have, at least, been deterred from reproducing by the difficulty of finding a suitable mate, i.e., one who would accept their aberrant behavior and/or appearance as being within the range of acceptability when choosing a mate.

They might have recognized their own problems and realized they might be carried into their offspring, so, in some cases, they might have preferred not to incur the burden of children, especially defective children, and would have submitted to sterilization procedures or aborted their children. They might have killed their infants in a fit of pique. If their children survived to adulthood, they would have had, under conditions of normal competitiveness, poor chances of having offspring. So, proliferation of the genes of negative survival value would have been curtailed.

But, much of the survival-of-the-fittest pattern has been in abeyance during the past several scores of years, and we have developed a large pool of persons who have survival-impacting inheritable diseases (physical and mental), but who managed to survive to adolescence and were able to reproduce. Thus there has been, and there continues to be, a pollution of the gene pool with genetically determined traits, including complexes of multiple traits, which yield humans that would not be able live to adulthood without extensive medical services and almost continual assistance in their daily routines.

It gets worse. In today's world, we have homosexuals who take advantage of clinical procedures to create embryos using both sperm and eggs from homosexually oriented persons, although this creates an off-spring who would, probably, be homozygous for homosexuality — if there is such a gene, which this author regards as unproven and, indeed, unlikely. Surely, it is obvious that in the type of community existing even 50 years ago, persons with homosexual tendencies would have been much less likely to conceive children, and so, the genetic contribution to homosexuality, if there is one, would have been kept at a very low level.

Male homosexuals and bisexuals are currently having their reproductive opportunities reduced by the effects of AIDS, which is killing off many of them before they have an opportunity to sire children by any means, either by natural intercourse or by clinical methods. Once a cure for this disease is found, another barrier to the conceiving of children not fitted to survive in a highly competitive environment will have been eliminated.

Changes Have Already Occurred in the Gene Pool

A general tendency toward a decline of civilization has been noticed by other students. Anthony Daniels is an English psychiatrist who has worked in a hospital in Birmingham (England), in prisons, and in various Latin American venues. Most of his patients seem to have been either prisoners or persons who had serious survival problems. His remarkable and insightful book, *Life at the Bottom*, was published under the pseudonym, Theodore Dalrymple (2001). The present author has studied this book and strongly recommends it to persons who are trying to understand the reason for the present state of civilization.

To provide an analysis of of "Dalrymple's" treatise by an establishment deep thinker, we will quote from a review by Philip Terzian (2002), and then provide the present author's viewpoint of some of the major points presented by Daniels.

Terzian wrote, "Over his years of practice ... [Daniels came] to the conclusion that the underclass is not just pervasive but growing in numbers, representing the slow, inexorable unraveling of traditional Britain ... [It has been] replaced by a constant whine of excuses, complaints, and special pleading ... [Daniels] is interested to know how these wretched people became who they are, how they view their circumstances and what they intend to do — if they intend to do anything — to pull themselves out of the slough of despond ... they seldom blame themselves for their dire predicaments and are eager to hold a faceless social system responsible for their troubles. They lie, they lounge about all day, they have lost their inhibitions and expect to be treated with deference, or pity.

"They see little point in self-improvement, and seldom experience remorse or shame; they are alternately violent and passive. Girls still 'love' and crave the approval of the boyfriends who beat them routinely. Career burglars are indignant that they should be punished for plying their trade. Hooligans stomp innocent bystanders because its fun, and addicts indulge their fatal habits because it feels good."

Terzian asks if all this is " ... really caused by contemporary standards ... and a liberal ideology that pleads for victimhood and excuses misbehavior? ... It is unquestionably true that our popular culture is much coarser than it used to be, and we tend to tolerate behavior that would have been forbidden in the past ... Dalrymple [Daniels] is right to note that in the past half-century, the intelligentsia in Europe and America has twisted itself into knots to explain away human misery and violence: Poverty causes crime, crime is essentially a social construct, punishment is invariably cruel and unusual . . . There is indeed sickness on the lower fringes of society, but the virus is older than the doctor suspects."

Certainly it is older than either the author or the reviewer acknowledges. It is the "virus" of the beast-like behavior of the uncivilized animal covered with a thin veneer of humanity: the ape within the cape. And the disguise continually becomes more transparent as more humans are born with replications and combinations of the genes that, in some fashion largely unknown to us at present, cause behavorial patterns that are inconsistent with what is generally regarded as civilized society, and indeed are inimical to survival unless the individual is constantly monitored and supported.

Group Sex and Random Sex

The facilitating of varied sexual experiences involving numerous partners is another strategy for preventing the development of normal families. The persons behind the leftist programs of the 1950s and later understood this principle very well. The prospect of easy and inexpensive sex attracted students who were basically apolitical to communes where they could be indoctrinated. And, the cost for establishing and maintaining these groups was nominal. Campus-based institutions of higher education are among the major sources of this disease.

A basic and ever present characteristic of the gipsying communes like The Weatherman and The Weather Underground was the orgies featuring every kind of sex combination imaginable. Revell and Williams (1998) gave a summary of a raid conducted in the course of an investigation of one of the robberies conducted by the Weather Underground. Susan Saxe, Katherine Ann Powers, and two male accomplices killed a Boston police officer while robbing a bank. The two "girls" later moved to a location near Bryn Mawr in the Philadelphia area. The description of the situation in the building raided by the FBI gives some indication of the kind of home life preferred by these two whores and their compatriots. Revell states, "We obtained a search warrant for the apartment, and arrest warrants for the women ... We arrived at the four-story apartment [sic] at around one in the morning. We came so late because we believed it was our best chance to find the wanted women there. The evening was quiet, the traffic had died down. After scouting the area, I ordered the power to the building cut so that we would be the only ones with light. As we came in, we announced ourselves in customary fashion. Everywhere kids were smoking pot and using various drugs. In one room a couple were having sex. We told them we were FBI, that we had a search warrant, and to sit down and be quiet.

"This didn't work so well. The students, or ex-students, began haranguing and spitting on us. Some continued to run around the apartment nude. The scene was altogether bizarre. Eventually, we ran across a professor, who began shouting, challenging our legal right to be here. He became so belligerent that I decided we should interrogate him as a possible conspirator, an aider and abettor of fugitives. Clearly, he was impeding the lawful execution of our search warrant. A radical distortion of this story would appear just a few months later in the *Washington Post*."

"In the end [we found that] Saxe and Powers were not there, and we left empty handed. Reports later came in that the girls had split. Powers apparently wanted to separate herself from Saxe, finding her too stridently militant."

Sexual Blackmail as a Red Tactic

Soviet agents were expected to use sexual tactics if these were necessary in order to advance the intelligence-gathering program. Many of these spies became experts in entangling their targets in situations which left them powerless to withstand   · .der given by their controllers.

Some sources say the KGB had specialized in the sexual entrapment of Western diplomats and visitors to Moscow at least as early as the 1930s.

Not a nice picture — The following tale of life among the queer Brits, as related by Bittman (1985), gives some interesting details about the methods used by the Reds to involve informers in sexual crimes so as to insure their loyalty.

"The British police did not realize that Geoffrey Arthur Prime was one of the most important Communist spies of the post-World War II period when they arrested him on June 28, 1982, on three charges of molesting children. For nine years ending in 1977, Prime worked for the British secret electronic eavesdropping center ... in southwestern England. At this time, the center employed more than 10,000 officers around the world ... where they listened 24 hrs a day to radio, television, and satellite communications of foreign powers and transmitted them to the center ... Translators and cryptologists then decoded the messages and determined their intelligence value ... "

Unlike many other prominent Soviet spies in Britain, Prime had attended a small technical college in Staffordshire rather than Cambridge U. He was recruited by the Russians in the early 1960s when, as a member of the Royal Air Force, he was stationed in West Berlin ... At the center "Prime was considered an unusually quiet, private ... and nobody suspected his strange sexual escapades or contacts with the Russians ... Many decisions of serious consequences for the defense of Western Europe and the US were based on deliberately distorted information by Soviet intelligence experts. After leaving the agency in 1977 for reasons not quite clear, Prime supported himself as a taxi driver and later had a job selling wine to restaurants and hotels, but until the end, he stayed in touch with the Soviets. In November 1982, he pleaded guilty to spying for the Soviets for a period of 15 years and was sentenced to 35 years in prison for espionage and an additional three years on the morals charge that led to his arrest."

Sexual deviants rule society — It is generally known that the most famous group of British traitors in modern history, the Magnificent Five, included obligate homosexuals, bisexuals, and sadists. Andrew

and Mitrokhin (1999), in their book describing the "secret history" of the
KGB, say, "Burgess was one of the most flamboyant figures in
Cambridge; a brilliant, gregarious conversationalist equally at home
with the teetotal intellectual discussions of the Apostle, the socially
exclusive and heavy-drinking Pitt Club and the irreverent satirical
reviews of the Footlights. He made no secret either of his Communist
sympathies or of his enjoyment of the then illegal pleasure of
homosexual 'rough trade' with young working class men. A more
doctrinaire and less imaginative controller than Deutsch might have
well concluded that the outrageous Burgess would be a liability rather
than an asset. But Deutsch may well have sensed that Burgess's very
outrageousness would give him good, if unconventional cover for his
work as a secret agent... Late in 1935, he became personal assistant
to the young rightwing gay Conservative MP Captain 'Jack' Macnamara.
Together they went of fact-finding missions to Nazi Germany, which
according to Burgess, consisted largely of homosexual escapades with
like-minded members of the Hitler Youth.

"Burgess built up a remarkable range of contacts among the
continental 'Homintern'. Chief among them was Edward Pfeifer, chef de
cabinet to Edouard Daladier, French war minister from January 1936 to
May 1940 and prime minister from April 1938 to March 1940. Burgess
boasted to friends that, "He and Pfeifer and two members of the French
Cabinet... had spent an evening together at a male brothel in Paris.
Singing and dancing, they had danced around a table, lashing a naked
boy, who was strapped to it, with leather whips."

"A trip by Burgess to Gibraltar and Tangier in the autumn of 1949
turned into what Goronwy Rees called a 'wild odyssey of indiscretions':
among them failing to pay his hotel bills, publicly identifying British
intelligence officers and drunkenly singing in local bars, 'Little boys are
cheap today, cheaper than yesterday.' Burgess was surprised not to be
sacked on his return to London. Once back in the Foreign Office,
however, he resumed his career as a dedicated Soviet agent, supplying
large quantities of classified papers."

"In 1938 Burgess recruited one of his lovers, Eric Kessler; a Swiss journalist turned diplomat on the staff of the Swiss embassy in London . . . Probably in 1939, Burgess recruited another foreign lover, the Hungarian Andrew Revoi, later leader of the exiled Free Hungarians in wartime London . . . he was described in his KGB file as a pederast; the same source also claimed that he had homosexual relations with a Foreign Office official."

Andrew and Mitrokhin also describe a husband and wife team who apparently compromised dozens of high, low, and mid-level diplomats, secret service agents, and the like. "The Koechers may also have been the most sexually active illegals in the history of Soviet Bloc intelligence, graduating from 'wife-swapping' parties to group orgies at New York's Plato's Retreat and Hell Fire sex clubs which flourished in the sexually permissive pre-AIDS era of the late 1960s and 1970s. With the blessing of the StB [Czechoslovak security and intelligence service], the Koechers later revealed some of their colorful careers to the Washington investigative journalist Ronald Kessler. Karl Koecher's KGB file, however, reveals that he withheld important details. In 1970 he was summoned back to Prague [but he was] . . . too attached to his swinging lifestyle to leave New York, refused to return and for the next four years broke off contact with the StB. In 1971 he succeeded in becoming a naturalized US citizen; his wife was granted citizenship a year later . . . Sex in Washington struck Koecher as even more exciting than in New York. In the mid-1970s he later claimed nostalgically, Washington was 'the sex capital of the world.'

Imagine the havoc that could have been created had the Russians been capable of infecting "Mrs. Koecher" with a venereal disease that had delayed fatal effects. It would seem that a very large part of the State Department and the UK intelligence team (both queer and straight) and their second, third, and fourth level contacts would have been finished off with very little expenditure of money. And a very good thing it would have been, too.

chapter eighteen

DECREASING THE BIRTH RATE

The Bolsheviks were at their base ingenerate enemies of the human species, and many of their policies had the unmistakable intention of reducing the numbers of human beings. They did not seem to have in mind an end point to this process, leaving us free to conclude that their utopia was a unpeopled earth. Thus, zero population growth could be considered a way point in the trip to zero population.

It is not generally realized that most anarchists are opposed to the traditional family: a mother and a father and their children. This attitude is generally de-emphasized in the public pronouncements of anarchist groups. But in a few cases, it is clearly stated. " . . . the family acts as a very important enemy in the hands of our controllers. Children often learn from their parents . . . ideas of male superiority, racism, patriotism and the necessity for domination and obedience. The ways with which people get on with each other often reinforce personal oppressions which need to be challenged" (burn.uscd.edu).

It has been remarked before that the ranks of communists in general, and anarchists in particular, seem to include a relatively high proportion of sexual perverts, with homosexuals being the major component of this subset. Their lifestyle bias is clearly evident in some of the websites. Very likely the bias against families, which seems to be inconsistent with some of other purported aims of anarchists, is due in part to the envy (and the hatred derived from that envy) felt by the homosexuals for normal families.

This hatred of humanity did not expire with the Soviet Union — in fact, it did not even originate with the Reds. Throughout history we can find persons, some with great power, who appeared to be at ease only when they were killing as many persons as possible. The Bolsheviks offer the clearest and most recent example of the institutionalizing of this genetically influenced suite of traits.

A Criterion of Civilization

A basic tenet of Western culture in general, and of American democracy in particular, holds that the decision to create offspring is a prerogative of the prospective father and mother — the choice lies with them, not with the state or any other group. The decision to conceive and bear children works both ways: having babies is a right, not a duty. This right is everywhere considered a freedom to be jealously guarded, but reds have never regarded it as being of any importance whatsoever.

Some religions and perhaps a few governments frown upon the use of any method of birth control other than the obvious one of abstaining from copulation, while a few extreme authorities say, or imply, that it is a spiritual or philosophical duty to have as many children as possible. The latter policy would seem to violate the couple's freedom to regulate this essential function of their life as much as the limitation of family size by government fiat does.

Reds have been at the forefront of the propaganda campaigns designed to cause couples to limit their families to no more than two children, preferably only one, and best of all — none. In this section, the author discusses the various approaches to population control that have been suggested by Reds and their allies and successors, and explains why restricting the number of births is a cause which is inherently attractive to reds.

The use of methods of birth control which are based on preventing conception is now very widely accepted, and has been for many years. Very few people object to such practices. Abortion used as a post-conception method for preventing births solely because of a desire to limit family size (as opposed to other reasons, such as endangerment of the woman's life by a continuation of the pregnancy, for example) has become legal in all of the United States only during the last few decades. Infanticide, although it seems to be practiced a great deal, has not yet become popular with the American public, though, if current trends continue, this method (though loathed by man and God) will become accepted as a cultural norm.

Strangely, the simple strategy of permanent sterilization, that is vasectomy for males or tubal ligation for females, though widely practiced, is not in fact strongly emphasized by reds. They seem to be more interested in promoting abortion, although there is a financial motive as well — pharmaceutical companies, condom manufacturers, and surgeons can expect continuing income from some of the methods.

A 1995 Survey of Family Growth by the National Center for Health Statistics showed that American women (ages 15 to 44) relied upon the following methods of birth control (i.e., prevention of conception, including those methods used by the male partner): tubal sterilization 27.7%, pills 26.9%, diaphragm 1.9%, vasectomy 10.9%, condom 20.4%, and "other" 12.2%. In over 30% of this panel, the woman depends on the male to take measures for preventing conception — a risky decision.

A Pioneer of Population Control

The pressure groups conducting population limitation propaganda owe a great deal to Hugh Everett Moore (1887-1972). He was one of six children born to his parents. Moore was a native of Kansas who had the idea of manufacturing disposable drinking containers — Dixie Cups to replace the then ubiquitous arrangement of community dipper (or cup) and barrel (or faucet). At an early age he became a backer of socialist-anarchist causes, Unitarianism, and violent labor-union tactics.

Journalism, of a sort, was Moore's first career choice. He attended Harvard for one or two semesters, then quit to establish the company which eventually brought him a very considerable fortune. He married at the age of 30, and had two children. When he became 70 he retired from business and began a second career as a chronic do-gooder, working for international peace, the League of Nations, the United Nations, etc.

The cause he seemed to promote with the greatest energy and the most money was population control. He became chairman of the board of Population Reference Bureau and vice president of International Planned Parenthood Federation. He was co-founder of the Population

Crisis Committee, and established the Hugh Moore Fund for International Peace, which funded organizations promoting birth control. His pamphlet, "The Population Bomb," which includes the basic principles of his crusade to limit births, was published in 1954. He was one of the first, if not the earliest, to use the term, "The Population Explosion." Dr. Paul Ehrlich appropriated both these names as titles for his own publications: actions which were perfectly legal, of course.

Among the currently functioning organizations which owe their initial funding to Hugh Moore is *The Louise and Hugh Moore Population Project*, described as "an initiative of the General Board of Church and Society — The United Methodist Church," the latter being an allegedly religious organization which is described in more detail elsewhere in this book. The "Project" has a mission statement: " . . . to call the United Methodist Church to faithful witness to the biblical [yes, lower case 'b'] and theological vision of health, wholeness and justice for God's entire creation so that we, and future generations, may live healthy and fulfilling lives through responsible/sustainable development."

The UMT proclaimed, in its *2000 Book of Resolutions, The UMC,* . *377* , "Programs aimed at reducing population growth should not be ends in themselves, not substitutes for other measures necessary to eliminate hunger and poverty. The church supports population programs as needed to move toward its goal of a just and humane world order."

If we sift through this mush in an attempt to find some sort of concrete program statement understandable by those of us who are unanointed, we seem to find that they do not intend to limit themselves to controlling parents' choice of family size, but intend to control everyone's choice of everything. As has been stated elsewhere, this is a church any red could love.

Zero Population Growth

The organization, *Zero Population Growth*, describes itself as "a national nonprofit membership organization based in Washington DC that works to achieve a sustainable balance of population, resources and the environment. ZPG was founded in 1968 by Richard Bowers (a Connecticut lawyer), Professor Charles Remington, and Paul Ehrlich. This is combination found rather often as the management team in non-profit organizations: a lawyer (obligatory), a figurehead professor, and the sparkplug publicizer. The organization got a big boost from the many appearances of Ehrlich on the Johnny Carson, an extremely popular late night television show. Carson gave Ehrlich practically unlimited opportunities to promote his organization (and books).

ZPG is the nation's leading grassroots-based population organization. They say, "Through education and advocacy we address a variety of population-rated concerns, including family planning, status of women, and growth of local communities."

From their "History," we learn, "ZPG's early mission was relatively straightforward: raise public awareness of the link between population growth and environmental degradation and, in turn, encourage people to have smaller families. Thus, the corresponding message was simple: Stop at Two [children]. ZPG's focus concentrated on reducing desired family size and ensuring the means and rights of human reproduction." They claim a peak membership of more than 35,000 members. The valuable assistance obtained from the leadership of women's liberation movements is acknowledged, as well as help from such outstanding disruptive red organizations as the American Civil Liberties Union.

The ZPG operates (or operated) vasectomy clinics. They hand out condoms. They facilitate or encourage abortions. They targeted the white middle classes, because [unsaid by them] this group is, or was, the backbone of our culture, and its voluntary reduction would make the task of involuntary obliteration easier. They also concentrated initially on the US, for the same reason.

One of the most dangerous operations of ZPG is its attempt to penetrate into every branch of the educational establishment, starting with kindergarten. They offer to provide teaching tools — books, teachers' supplies, program guides, etc., to all kinds of schools. They conduct "Teacher's Workshops"which are " . . . tailored to the professional needs of the participants." The workshops include:

•Up-to-date information on global and US population trends and their impacts.

•A showing of their "award winning" video, *World Population.*

•Games, quizzes, role-playing simulations, cooperative learning exercises, and problem solving challenges.

•Complimentary teaching materials.

•Follow-up assistance through a quarterly newsletter, phone contacts and correspondence.

And, other mind-bending techniques, as needed and appropriate.

A successful business — ZPG received about $3.7 million in contributions in 1999, as well as about $1.5 million from "other" sources. They list expenditures as: Program services, $3.9 million; administration $821 thousand; and "other" at $237 thousand. They started the year with about $1.2 million in cash, and about $2.23 million in total assets. They maintain an office at 1400 16th street NW, Suite 320, Washington DC 20036.

The Changing Horizons of Dr. Paul Ehrlich

Dr. Paul Ehrlich is such an icon in the population limiting field that it should be worthwhile examining him and his philosophy in considerable detail.

I would not call Dr. Paul Ehrlich an intentional Red; perhaps he is no kind of "red" at all, at least not consciously. But his programs certainly parallel the population control line that is so dear to the hearts of red activists. The following comments include quotes taken directly from "The Population Bomb," 1968 copyright, 19th printing (May 1970), with page numbers as indicated. Perhaps we should be careful not to give too much weight to someone who has "shamelessly pirated their [his colleagues'] ideas without crediting them individually." [p. 221] " . . . it is important for you [us] to consider that I [he], and many of the people who share my [his] views are just plain wrong, that we [they] are alarmists..." [p. 197]. Ehrlich admits he has published erroneous material in the scientific literature [p. 197] "...wrong answers...I've published a few myself, as some of my colleagues will gladly testify." [p. 197]

Ehrlich acknowledges that he appropriated the phrase, "Population Bomb" from a pamphlet published by Hugh Moore in 1954. This affirmation can be found on page iii, unnumbered, facing the title page. The term, "The Population Explosion," was similarly appropriated.

Dr. Ehrlich's prescription — The back cover of the paperback lists "Mankind's Inalienable Rights" as discovered by Paul R. Ehrlich, Director of Graduate Studies for the Department of Biological Sciences, Stanford University.

1. The right to eat well.
2. The right to drink pure water.
3. The right to breathe clean air.
4. The right to decent, uncrowded shelter.
5. The right to enjoy natural beauty.
6. The right to avoid regimentation.
7. The right to avoid pesticide poisoning.
8. The right to freedom from thermonuclear war.
9. The right to limit families.
10. The right to educate our children.
11. The right to have grandchildren.

On the other hand, *The Environmental Handbook Prepared for the First National Environmental Teach-in. April 22, 1970,* by Garrett De Bell, tells us that Ehrlich has discovered, in the less than two years since the Bomb appeared, four other inalienable rights. In addition, several of the originals have been modified considerably (asterisks indicate "rights" not found in the Bomb):

1. The right to limit our families. [Notice that "our" has been inserted to somewhat blunt the universally applicable statement in the

original which the perpetrators must have feared would expose their true agenda of forcing families to limit the number of children].

2. The right to eat [Paul has decided we don't have to eat "well."]

*3. The right to eat meat. [Yes, it really does say that].

4. The right to drink pure water [he's holding fast to this one].

5. The right to live uncrowded ["decent" and "shelter" aren't in the picture anymore].

6. The right to avoid regimentation [unless, of course, it is regimentation by Ehrlich and his crew].

*7. The right to hunt and fish [what traitor sneaked in this one?]

8. The right to view natural beauty [we must view it, but not necessarily enjoy it].

9. The right to breathe clean air. [Another unmodified right].

*10. The right to silence. [Others must keep quiet].

11. The right to avoid pesticide poisoning [Other kinds of poisoning are OK, and if they are natural poisonings (as by cobras or Clostridium botulinum) you don't have the right to avoid them].

12. The right to be free of thermonuclear war.

13. The right to educate our children.

14. The right to have grandchildren.

*15. The right to have great-grandchildren [another new one — why stop at this level, why not great-great-grandchildren, etc.]

Anyway you look at it, this is a very curious list. The right to eat meat and the right to hunt are totally unexpected in this context. In all other respects, it is a predictably litany from one of the establishment's favorite econuts.

The Population Bomb — The 'Prologue" to Ehrlich's famous book, *The Population Bomb* is, in many ways, the most damning part of the volume because it summarizes the kernel of Ehrlich's philosophy without the questionable statistics and other bits of misinformation which he uses to pad out the rest of the text. The following quotations from the "Prologue" are taken from a 1969 printing of the book first issued in 1968. In later versions of the book revisions were made to accommodate historical trends which made Ehrlich's predictions seem not only poorly thought out, but downright silly.

Following are excerpts from the "Preface."

"The battle to feed all of humanity is over. In the 1970s the world will undergo famines — hundreds of millions of people are going to starve to death in spite of any crash programs embarked upon now. At this late date nothing can prevent a substantial increase in the world death rate, although many lives could be saved through dramatic programs to 'stretch' the carrying capacity of the earth by increasing food production."

Comment: Over three decades have passed since Ehrlich wrote these words, and nearly a quarter of a century has gone by since the vast famines prophesied by him should have occurred. In fact, nothing of the sort has happened, population has continued to increase, and the average levels of health and nutrition have increased although they remain appalling in some isolated areas because of political interferences with market forces. Ehrlich made no provision for the human benefits of technology, and this is no surprise, since he has little acquaintance with applied science or technology, his scientific specialty having been the watching of butterflies.

Ehrlich also wrote, "Population control is the conscious regulation of the numbers of human beings to meet the needs, not just of individual families, but of society as a whole ... Our position requires that we take immediate action at home and promote effective action worldwide. We must have population control at home, hopefully through a system of incentives and penalties, but by compulsion if voluntary methods fail. We must use our political power to push other countries into programs which continue agricultural development and population control."

Comment: Notice the emphasis on compulsion and immediacy. These urgencies are expressed everywhere in the utterances of environmental activists. We must FORCE people to do this, we must force them to do it NOW. The reader might be interested in comparing

Ehrlich's commandments for population control to the dicta issued by the global warming propagandists.

And Ehrlich is, of course, satisfied that we could alleviate the horrendous plagues of starvation that he predicts by, not only mandating abortion and other means of population control worldwide, but also forcing the people into "agricultural development." Now, agricultural development doesn't mean to Paul what the knowledgeable reader of today might think, because pure Paul doesn't believe in insecticides, herbicides, improved species of plants, better storage and distribution policies, and other benefits of technology and free markets. No, we must get back to Nature's principles, so while we are killing off infants we must be careful not to disturb any of the butterflies or, especially, peregrine falcons.

Ehrlich is a shameless user of scare tactics. In the Preface, he tells us, "Since 1968, at least 200 million people — mostly children — have perished needlessly of hunger and hunger-related causes . . . The size of the human population is now 5.3 billion, and still climbing . . . Each hour there are 11,000 more mouths to feed; each year, more than 95 million. Yet the world has hundreds of billions fewer tons of topsoil and hundreds of trillions fewer gallons of groundwater with which to grow food crops than it had in 1968." The Ehrlichs wrote this in July 1989 at the Rocky Mountain Biological Laboratory in Gothic CO — a pleasant place to spend the summer thinking about all those starving, unenlightened peasants, especially when the government is footing the bill.

On page 19, they give us some insight into their orientation: "One might ask whether feeding 40 billion people is a worthwhile goal for humanity, even if it could be reached. Is any purpose served in turning Earth, in essence, into a gigantic human feedlot? Putting aside the near-certainty that such a miracle couldn't be sustained, what would happen to the quality of life?" Well, of course, even now, most of us can't afford to spend the summer in Gothic, Colorado — the government doesn't finance us. Maybe most people regard the quality of life as perfectly satisfactory if they have a happy family, even though they have more than 1.5 children — and, even if some professor tells them this is wrong.

Ehrlich was wrong. He was devastatingly wrong, so fantastically wrong in his predictions that one can only wonder why he did not become the laughing stock of the world. But, quite to the contrary, many millions of his books were sold, he achieved great success in academia (no surprise there), his presence was desired at all special convocations of econuts throughout the world, governments listened to him, and he was awarded one of those super-plums reserved for the pre-eminent freaks of the world, a MacArthur foundation "genius" award.

An interesting question is: did Ehrlich really believe the hogwash he promoted, or was he clever enough to see a unfilled market need and proceed to fill it? This author is inclined to think a combination of these factors was involved. The cleverness with which Ehrlich promoted a thesis that is clearly wrongheaded without any apparent fear of future discreditation is more the approach of a dedicated marketing man than of a fanatic, as shown by the rewards he has obtained, but there are elements in his life that suggests he may, in fact, hate people as a class. It appears from his biography that he is married and that his wife bore a child, but his public persona is more that of an embittered homosexual who hates all normal families — indeed, hates mankind as a whole. This could also be a role he played to gain the favor of a large segment of the arts and media crowd.

Mr. Econut

In Ehrlich's book, *Human Ecology:Problems and Solutions* (1973), we find the following. "In the first part of this book, we attempt to present the essence of demography, man's utilization of resources, the world food problem, and man's assaults on his own health and on the health of the ecological systems upon which his existence depends. Our discussion of problems ends with an analysis of the interrelationships of population growth, 'affluence' (or standard of living), and technological errors as causes of what is coming to be recognized as the most serious crisis ever faced by *Homo sapiens*.

"In the second part we look to solutions. Having established the need to halt population growth, we turn to what is now being done about other aspects of human behavior. How can the demands of individuals on resources be reduced? How can each individual's deleterious impact on his or her environment be minimized? How can people be made aware that man's many problems are inextricably intertwined and that, therefore, ecological problems will not be solved unless racism, poverty, exploitation, and war are tackled at the same time?"

After a couple of hundred pages spent dancing around the subject, the authors finally get down to brass tacks: they present the case for "Involuntary Fertility Control," that is, forcing people to reduce their family size. As in Red China of today. On page 256, we find, "The third approach to population control is that of involuntary fertility control. Several coercive proposals deserve discussion, mainly because societies may ultimately have to resort to them unless current trends in birth rates are rapidly reversed by other means. Some involuntary measures may prove to be less repressive or discriminatory, in fact, than some socioeconomic measures that have been proposed."

Some of these approaches are:

• Forcing fathers of more than three children to undergo vasectomies.

• Compulsory sterilization of women who have two (or three) children.

• Compulsory implantation of birth control steroids *at puberty*, with removal for child-bearing by official permission, perhaps combined with baby licenses (shades of *1984!*)

• Ensuring that the means of birth control, including abortion and sterilization, are accessible to every human being on Earth within the shortest possible time.

The book is loaded with imperatives: we *must* do X before Y happens, (Y nearly always being "the end of 'The Earth' as we know it") and we must do it *"immediately."* And, there is no need to discuss the alternatives because there are none — the Ehrlichs have decided, and the longer the delay, the thinner the eggshells of the peregrine falcons become.

Another deep thinker weighs in — In one of the jacket blurbs for the Ehrlichs' book, *The Population Explosion* (Ehrlich and Ehrlich 1990), the eminent scientist Al Gore is quoted as saying, "...our numbers threaten the ecological system that supports life as we know it...The time for action is due, and past due." The first chapter of this book is entitled, "Why Isn't Everyone as Scared as We Are." Well, Paul and Anne, I guess the canaille just haven't received the same revelation as the chosen people. We can only hope for better luck in the future.

Looking Back at Dr. Ehrlich

In his 1968 best seller, "The Population Bomb," Dr. Paul H. Ehrlich confidently asserted that in the 1970s and 1980s hundreds of millions of people will starve to death. Also, "I have yet to meet anyone familiar with the situation who thinks India will be self-sufficient in food by 1971... India could not possibly feed 200,000,000 more people by 1980." But, the Green Revolution of genetically altered crops was already underway when these predictions were made, and improved insecticides and other agricultural advances helped the emerging nations feed their people. Pakistanis saw wheat harvests rise from 4.6 million tons in 1965 to 8.4 million tons in 1970, while India's total crop rose from 12.3 million to 20 million in the same period. In 1999, India harvested a record 73.5 million tons of wheat, up nearly 12% from the preceding year.

Dr. Ehrlich had a solution to all this static: He removed his Doomsday predictions from subsequent editions of "The Population Bomb." Oh well, even Nostradamus probably needed to use the Wite-out occasionally.

Dr. Borlaug of the Green Revolution had a more meaningful answer. Over thirty years ago, he wrote, "One of the greatest threats to mankind today is that the world may be choked by an explosively pervasive but well camouflaged bureaucracy."

Other Voices

The following is an extract from a Robert Conquest speech made in 1992 to a San Francisco CA meeting of the *Independent Institute*. "We all know the economic and ecological disasters of the Soviet era. What has perhaps not been stressed enough is the moral and intellectual collapse of the regime. One reason for this is that, for more than half a century, the whole system had as a major characteristic falsification on an enormous scale. History, production figures, census results — all were faked. Even more demoralizing, the whole sphere of thought was controlled and distorted.

"As truth penetrated it became increasingly the case that only the stupidest and most abject could really accept this delusional world. One of the most difficult things to convey to a Western audience is how disgusting the rank and file of the old Soviet ruling class really were — how mean, treacherous, shamelessly lying, cowardly, sycophantic and ignorant. (Unfortunately, these concepts are unknown to 'political science.') Thus the Soviet system underwent a long process of stultification . . . "

"For if the Soviet ideology is now dead in its homeland, we must ask, has the lesson been learned over here in the West? For the mere existence of the USSR, and its ideas, distorted the way in which many people over the whole world thought about society, the economy, human history. A not inconsiderable number of members of the West's elite were to one degree or another deceived, or self-deceived, about the communist regime. Some saw it as a great exception, in all essentials more advanced than ourselves. This view was mainly held by 'idealists.' Others argued that the USSR was a normal state, one like any other, and that it should be treated as such. This view was mainly held by the 'pragmatists.' Both were wrong: Far from being advanced, it was based on an armchair fantasy; far from being normal, it was a revolting aberration."

And, Conquest also says, "Historians with little knowledge of history believed Soviet documents. Demographers with little knowledge of the Soviet Union believed Soviet census figures ... It was precisely at this juncture that Moscow started to make the real facts public, and the whole enterprise collapsed amid general contempt.

"Or so you would think. But this would be to underestimate the obstinate survivability of dead ideas, particularly in the minds of those who have invested emotional capital in them. We still find, especially in parts of academe, the damaging notion that everything is a struggle for power, or being empowered, or hegemony, or oppression; and that all competition is a zero-sum game. This is no more than a repetition of Lenin's destructive doctrine. Intellectually, it is reductionism; politically, it is fanaticism.

"How does fanaticism and dogmatism of, or resembling, the Soviet type arise? Often at the age of 18 or 20 a student meets some such glittering general idea and, far from feeling any responsibility to submit it to serious questioning, henceforward follows it like a duckling imprinted with its mother. Is this adequately discouraged? Is the student induced to think, to aim for intellectual responsibility; to seek knowledge and practice judgment; to avoid formulas?

"I am afraid that much of the education we now find does not, to put it mildly, even approach these criteria. Indeed, it is an educated, or half-educated, stratum whose minds are still infested with what in computers we would call viruses, which distort their calculations."

One Hand Washes the Other

David Brower, in a foreword written for one of Ehrlich's books, gives some history of his organization's adopting of the population limiting agenda. "It was Professor Raymond Cowles who shook us loose with a provocative address before a Sierra Club conference, 'The Meaning of Wilderness to Science.'

"What in the late fifties had seemed heretical soon was not so. For the complaints that I had received about mentioning population problems in early speeches, there were more vociferous complaints if I forgot to mention the big problem. In just two or three years it became possible to question growth, to suggest that DNA was greater than GNP, to predict that man had enough genius to require that science and technology be put to good purpose. He could limit his numbers. He could limit his heretofore unslackened appetite for destroying wilderness. He could go back over the nine-tenths or so of the earth that had already felt his touch, sometimes a gentle touch but too often brutal, and do better where he had been. He could start with Manhattan, or Los Angeles.

"Whatever resources the wilderness still held would not sustain him in his old habits of growing and reaching without limits. Wilderness could, however, provide answers for questions he had not yet learned how to ask. He could predict that the day of creation was not over, that there would be wiser men, and they would thank him for leaving the source of those answers. Wilderness would remain part of his geography of hope, as Wallace Stegner put it, and could, merely because wilderness endured on the planet, prevent man's world from becoming a cage.

"The good predictions could be entertained — the notion of predicting a more and more desirable future, not just a more and more crowded one."

chapter nineteen

INCREASING THE DEATH RATE

Without mercy, without sparing, we will kill our enemies by the scores of hundreds, let them be thousands, let them drown themselves in their own blood. For Lenin and Uritskii . . . let there be floods of blood of the bourgeoisie — more blood, as much as possible.
Krasnaia Gazetta (Red Gazette) September 1, 1918.

The most important democidal force in the history of the world has been Communism, or if you prefer, Bolshevism. An unbiased reader with the uncensored reports of their crimes in front of him, can hardly doubt that Lenin, Stalin, Trotsky, and their henchmen enjoyed killing people, whether personally or by proxy. It was sort of a hobby with them. As long as they had to rely on the occasional assassination performed at a distance by some lunatic supporter, they felt unfulfilled. Once they could command armies, intelligence agencies, and other groups of murderers, they really got into the swing of things. There was literally no limit to their ambitions, if they had lived long enough, and retained their power, they would have depopulated the whole earth.

DEATH BY VIOLENCE

The total death count of innocent persons killed in one way or another by government actions undertaken by the Red nations of the world during the 1900s far exceeds the murder record of Nazi governments. The German effort, however, receives far more publicity, for reasons that are no doubt clear to any thoughtful reader. Bean counting, when it is numbers of deceased human beings we are comparing, could probably be considered poor taste and perhaps shows lack of compassion. Even so, it is reasonably clear that killing two people should be considered more reprehensible than killing one person, and so on.

It is true that the mind boggles at the higher numbers and our stock of pity is exhausted long before the first hundred are examined in detail. This is the reason that propagandists seeking to elicit an expression of outrage from their audience will often seek out a victim having characteristics to which the intended audience can relate, and then publicize that person's "sufferings" to the utmost, even though there are many others far more worthy of our pity — Anne Frank comes to mind immediately. The same psychological principle is effective when heroes are chosen — there is little doubt that many war heroes are chosen for public adulation because they fit the establishment's specifications more closely than other candidates who may have achieved much more and exhibited greater courage. Vide JFK.

If we think in terms of *percentages* of specific ethnic groups killed, and expand the temporal limits of our search, we can find accounts of massacres that exceed those of either the Reds or the Nazis. Consider for example, Moses — if we are willing to concede that Moses was a *historical* figure. This rough customer ordered his merry band of cutthroats to kill every man, woman, and child in some of the city-states he had selected for takeover — and they did. You can't do better than 100%.

Credible Enumerations of Victims

The credit and honor for being the first to bring to the public an unvarnished account of the mass murders committed by Stalin and other Red sadists go to Robert Conquest, whose book, *The Great Terror*, was published in 1968. This work has been revised, and is now available as *The Great Terror, A Reassessment* (Conquest 1990). The later book includes new evidence which became available as a result of Glasnost revelations.

Conquest's achievement was lauded by Nobel Award winner Czeslaw Milosz, who said (Anon. 1992B), "The achievement of Robert Conquest becomes most obvious when we view it together with the behavior of his contemporaries, writers in the same genre, whether they are English, American, French, or Italian. For many decades of the twentieth century, the great majority of them observed certain rules, which seemed to them so obvious that they became their second nature.

To act against these rules would be to violate powerful taboos. Not that the existence of these taboos testified to open political choices. The choices were there, but not avowed, and the penalty for conformity was not political but societal, as it entailed a loss of status in the community. I have in mind, of course, an injunction forbidding anyone from speaking the truth about the Communist system in the Soviet Union. Being a poet myself and having lived in the fifties in Paris, I am able to visualize the risk assumed by a poet who would transgress against what was then considered as politically correct. At that time, Jean Paul Sartre was leading a hideous campaign against Albert Camus, who dared to mention, in his book, 'The Rebel,' the existence of concentration camps in the Soviet Union. Robert Conquest's London must have been not very different in this respect from Paris."

Also very valuable as a reference on the death toll resulting from red activities is *The Black Book of Communism* (Courtois 1999), a collection of essays by several authors, which offer somewhat different views on the Communist holocaust(s), mostly arranged by geographical occurrence. Both the Conquest and the Courtois volumes were preceded by various other books on this same subject, but the earlier books were not quite as comprehensive and/or as wide ranging.

A very worthwhile predecessor was *The Secret History of Stalin's Crimes* by Alexander Orlov, but it deals mostly with individual murders, often conducted under quasi-legal gloss, such as the death by shooting of one of Stalin's wives — also, the executions of Yagoda, Bukharin, and hundreds of other enemies of Stalin. Not, strictly speaking, terroristic incidents, merely the day-to-day sanitizing operations of a government such as that of Stalin.

We should not spare fellow travelers in the US and other Western countries who eagerly accepted all of the propaganda spread by the left-leaning press, those persons for whom it was impossible to believe that "Uncle Joe" could do anything wrong. It is very important to realize that persons calling themselves "liberals, " or "moderates," or "friends of the Russian people" bear a great deal of responsibility for the millions of untimely deaths that resulted from Red activities all over the world.

"It is here that the true *dvoeverye* — double belief — of the party moderates lay. It explains as nothing else can, the horrified resistance of many who had cheerfully massacred the Whites, and at least uncomplainingly starved and slaughtered the peasantry, to the execution of prominent party members, to 'shedding the blood of Bolsheviks.' It reflects a double standard of morality comparable to the attitude of sensitive and intelligent men in the ancient world to slaves or of the French nobility of the eighteenth century to the lower classes. Non-Party people were hardly more taken into account, even by the better Old Bolsheviks, than slaves were by Plato. They were in effect, non-men" (Conquest 1990).

The attitude of the Western intelligentsia to the Communist Holocausts, so predictable and yet so difficult to believe, was caricatured by Orwell (1975): "Consider for instance some comfortable English professor defending Russian totalitarianism. He cannot say outright, 'I believe in killing off your opponents when it is necessary to promote or maintain tyranny.' Probably, therefore, he will say something like this: 'While freely conceding that the Soviet regime exhibits certain features which the humanitarian may be inclined to deplore, we must, I think, agree that a certain curtailment of the right to political opposition is an unavoidable concomitant of transitional periods. . . . ' "

A Grand Summary of Deaths from Red Terror

The following passage is taken from the Foreword of the Black Book of Communism, with minor editorial modifications:

page x. " . . . a basic problem remains: the conceptual poverty of the Western empirical effort.

"With such fables now consigned to what Trotsky called 'the ash heap of history,' perhaps a moral rather than a social, approach to the Communist phenomenon can yield a truer understanding — for the much-investigated Soviet social process claimed victims on a scale that has never aroused a scholarly curiosity at all proportionate to the magnitude of the disaster. *The Black Book* offers us the first attempt to determine, overall, the actual magnitude of what occurred, by systematically detailing Leninism's 'crimes, terror, and repression' from Russia in 1917 to Afghanistan in 1989.

"This factual approach puts Communism in what is, after all, its basic human perspective. For it was in truth a 'tragedy of planetary dimension' (in the French publisher's characterization), with a grand total of victims variously estimated by contributors to the volume at between 85 million and 100 million." The authors included in these numbers not only the victims in Europe, but also those killed in Red China, North Vietnam, and Cambodia.

    If we consider only Soviet victims, we find the following:

•The execution of tens of thousands of hostages and prisoners without trial, and the murder of hundreds of thousands of rebellious workers and peasants from 1918 to 1922.

•The famine of 1922, which caused the death of 5 million people.

•The extermination or deportation of Don Cossacks in 1920.

•The murders of tens of thousands in concentration camps, 1918-1930.

•Liquidation of almost 600,000 people in the Great Purge of 1937-38.

•The deportation of 2,000,000 kulaks (and so-called kulaks) in 1930-32.

•Destruction of 4,000,000 Ukrainians and 2,000,000 others by means of an artificial and systematically perpetuated famine in 1932-33.

•The deportation of hundreds of thousands of Poles, Ukrainians, Balts, Moldovans, and Bessarabians from 1939 to 1941, and again in 1944-45.

•The deportation of the Volga Germans in 1941.

•The wholesale deportation of the Crimean Tatars in 1943.

•The wholesale deportation of the Chechens in 1944.

•The wholesale deportation of the Ingush in 1944.

    Grigori Zinoviev: speaking at a meeting of Communists in September 1918, said [some editing and paraphrasing has been done for the sake of clarity]: The use of terror as a method of controlling or neutralizing the internal enemies of Communism began a few weeks after Lenin seized power in 1917. For several years, probably until about 1934, the major effort was directed toward destroying, or at least completely neutralizing, the kulaks. This resulted from a conscious decision, first by Lenin, then by Stalin, to eliminate this class which was perceived as being composed of inveterate enemies of Soviet power who would without exception sabotage collectivization. This democidal operation was carried out by all elements of the state, as necessary, but more or less directed by the OGPU, who were primarily the persons responsible for ejecting the kulaks from their land. The kulaks who objected were shot on the spot, the remainder became prisoners of the OGPU and were sentenced to forced labor under the harshest conditions, as in lumber camps or coal mines.

Table 19.1
DEATHS IN RUSSIA DUE TO COMMUNISM[1]

Historical Event	Number of Persons Killed
Deaths related to the civil war, 1919-1921	9,000,000
Deaths resulting from the Great Famine of 1921	5,000,000
Executed or died in prison camps during 1919-1923	500,000
Executed during the Stalin terror	2,000,000
Died in prison camps during pre-Yezhov period (1930-36)	3,500,000
Died in camps during Stalin-Yezhov terror (1936-38)	12,000,000
Died in programmed famines during forced collectivization of the thirties	3,500,000
Total of the above	35,500,000

[1] Collected and modified from various sources, see esp., Anon. (1970).

The show trials were not legitimate jurisprudence, but merely another method of inspiring terror and, probably, of adding public humiliation to the physical tortures applied to the defendant.

Prior to 1934, the victims of OGPU (later NKVD) were mainly White Guards, persons thought to be members of the bourgeoisie, political opponents, private traders, members of the intelligentsia, and kulaks. Some writers claim that many of these persons were held under relatively humane conditions. There seemed to be an abrupt change at the end of 1934, possibly as a result of the assassination of Kirov, a prominent government figure. It is very likely that Stalin arranged the assassination so as to have an excuse to apply terror more widely. In later years, Stalin never bothered about setting the stage in such a relatively elaborate manner. He simply decided to kill or torture or imprison someone, or some group, and issued an order to that effect.

In addition to the hundreds of people who were arrested and shot almost immediately after Kirov's assassination, tens of thousands of Leningrad inhabitants were arrested and deported to Siberia in the spring of 1935. They were called "Kirov's assassins."

The pace of internal terror accelerated and some prominent Party members became victims to instant retirement from life or were subjected to the show trials grisly farce, in which confession was not enough; agreement to all sorts of ridiculous charges became necessary in order for the defendant to have some little hope of escaping with his life. Very few of them did: to be arrested was to be found guilty.

The year 1970, date of the records consulted for the preceding table, didn't mark the end of Soviet massacres, but the internal cleansing was on a much smaller scale thereafter. Some other Communist countries still had not reached their peak of genocidal frenzy.

Readers will see that the previously quoted data indicate the Chinese Reds killed many more people than their Russian comrades did. Of course, Mao's crew had a larger population base to work from, but it was still a remarkable "achievement." The figures in Table 19.2 (data mostly from Schwarz 1972) help us to understand the enormity of their crimes.

Table 19.2

DEATHS IN CHINA DUE TO COMMUNIST ACTIONS[1]

Event or Program	Number of Casualties [2]
First Civil War (1927-36)	375,000
War with Japan (1937-45)	50,000
Second Civil War (1945-9)	1,250,000
Land Reform pre-Liberation	750,000
Political[3] liquidation	22,500,000
Korean War	880,000
GLF[4] and Communes	1,500,000
Struggles with minorities	750,000
GPCR[5] and its aftermath	375,000
Forced labor camps, etc.	20,000,000
Total of above medians	48.430,000

[1] Adapted from *The Three Faces of Revolution* (Schwarz 1972).
[2] Medians of maximums and minimums given in original article.
[3] Campaigns of 1949-1958.
[4] Great Leap Forward.
[5] Great Proletarian Cultural Revolution.

Table 19.3 includes data on Communist-caused deaths for the world, classified according to countries or regions. In referring to these mortality Tables, the reader needs to keep in mind the different years in which the material was published. And, of course, it is again necessary to point out that there are no independently authenticated written records to verify many of the estimates. They are in fact, adjusted combinations of data from several sources which vary, as is always the case, in reliability and quality of the provenance. However, the data are generally accepted as the best available at this time.

Table 19.3
WORLD DEATHS DUE TO COMMUNISM[1]

Location	Number of Persons Killed
The Soviet Union	20,000,000
China	65,000,000
Vietnam	1,000,000
North Korea	2,000,000
Cambodia	2,000,000
Eastern Europe	1,000,000
Latin America	150,000
Africa	1,700,000
Afghanistan	1,500.000
Other	10,000
Total of the above	94,360,000

[1] Adapted from *The Black Book of Communism* (Courtois 1999).

From the preceding table, we learn that approximately 94 million deaths throughout the world are attributed to Communist action up to, perhaps, 1995 or 1996. Although the cut-off dates may be slightly different for the various geographical divisions, the death rates in China and Russia can be expected to have tapered off to relatively low levels in recent years, so large additions are not likely to originate with the most prolific producers. Africa and North Korea may be different propositions.

Kill the messenger — The editor of *The Black Book of Communism*, Stephane Courtois, wrote of the adverse reaction of most of the establishment media to the publication of his work: " . . . the Communist record offers the most colossal case of political carnage in history. And when this fact began to sink in with the French public, an apparently dry academic work became a publishing sensation, the focus of impassioned political and intellectual debate.

"The shocking dimensions of the Communist tragedy, however, are hardly news to any serious student of twentieth-century history, at least when the different Leninist regimes are taken individually. The real

news is that at this late date the truth should come as such a shock to
the public at large. To be sure, each major episode of the tragedy —
Stalin's Gulag, Mao Zedong's Great Leap Forward and his Cultural
Revolution, Pol Pot's Khmer Rouge — had its moment of notoriety. But
these horrors soon faded away into 'history'; nor did anyone trouble to
add up the total and set it before the public.

"The full power of the shock, however, was delivered by the unavoidable comparison of this sum with that for Naziism, which at an estimated 25 million turns out to be distinctly less murderous than Communism. And the volume's editor, Stéphane Courtois, rather than let the
figures speak for themselves, spelled out the comparison, thereby making the volume a firebrand. Arguing from the fact that some Nuremberg
jurisprudence has been incorporated into French law (to accommodate
such cases as that of Maurice Papon, a former minister of Giscard
d'Estaing tried in 1997-98 for complicity in deporting Jews while a local
official of Vichy), Courtois explicitly equated the 'class genocide' of
Communism with the 'race genocide' of Naziism, and categorized both as
'crimes against humanity' What is more, he raised the question of the
'complicity' with Communist crime of the legions of Western apologists
for Stalin, Mao, Ho Chi Minh, Fidel Castro, and indeed Pol Pot who,
even when they abandoned their idols of yesteryear, did so discreetly,
and in silence."

A mild disclaimer may be appropriate with respect to Courtois'
claim that no one had previously attempted to add up the number of
dead attributable to Reds and to Nazis, compare the two figures, and
draw the logical conclusion — i.e., the Reds were more horrible than the
Nazis. Various students on the right side of the political spectrum had
been doing similar exercises for years, and had reached the correct
conclusion in their publications. But their articles appeared in books and
journals the establishment media managers avoided like poison, so the
general public never heard of them. They were usually tagged with
epithets such as *Holocaust Deniers*, *Fascists*, and *Rednecks*. However,
The Black Book of Communism appeared at a time when and at a place
where a slight opening to the Right occurred, due to the more or less
complete demoralization of the leftists who had had their saints recalled

for repair. Its publication and subsequent popularity must have struck the leftist media controllers like a particularly unpleasant bolt of lightning. Conquest, for example, though he was not noticeably rightist and did not emphasize the comparison of Nazis and Communists, received little encouragement from the literary establishment, and his book, *The Great Terror*, was allowed to go out of print.

THE SILENT KILLERS

The murder of millions of people by the methods employed by Bolsheviks, Mao Zedong, Pol Pot, and the like was a time-consuming and messy process, accompanied by heavy costs and perhaps arousing considerable resentment or even a desire for revenge among those who survived the extermination projects. What was needed was a process that, once started, was self-sustaining and for which the citizens had no defense. In addition, it was be desirable that the international press would not be able to show that the Red icons were involved in the process in any way. Something like the Black Plague would be nice.

In the following paragraphs, we will discuss two quite different types of plague — malaria and AIDS, the depredations of which might have been accentuated by Red agents. The author readily admits that no smoking gun exists. But the smoke is there: who was the man you saw holding a gun?

Malaria

In a preceding chapter, it was suggested that the deaths from malaria of millions of Africans, Asians, and South Americans occurred because an inexpensive and safe means of killing mosquitoes (i.e., spraying with DDT) was denied to them, perhaps by machinations of persons who wished to sell insecticides that were more profitable. The author did not suggest, and he does not believe, that active malice towards the potential victims was a motive behind the campaign to ban DDT. The promoters of the campaign were neutral, they did not care whether the people who could not afford their insecticides lived or died.

If the enemies of DDT could sell their products in ever-increasing quantities at highly profitable prices, they were perfectly contented with the prospect that all the impoverished natives would continue to exist until their miserable lives were terminated by hunger, violence, or venereal disease. If, however, they died from malaria — so what?

On the other hand, the campaign to ban DDT, and other activist projects having as their goal the criminalizing of the use of many substances that could improve the health and lifestyle of various fractions of the population, *might* have been facilitated, or even originated, by persons who had an active hatred for human beings as a species. Perhaps they would have preferred to explain their attitude as a desire to reduce the damage to the environment caused by "excessive" numbers of people.

Even so, Desowitz (1993), quotes an official of the AID Office of Policy Development and Analysis who . . . "said in effect, on behalf of AID, 'better dead than alive and riotously reproducing.' This was malaria and the Big Bang all over again: freedom from malaria lowered the crude death rate with sustained high fertility, which caused the rapid population growth, which led to the decline of economic development. The Third World would be well advised to return to the condition it enjoyed before embarking on the campaign to eradicate malaria."

Along the same lines, we have a National Security Study Memorandum No. 200 (NSSM 200), written by none other than Dr. Henry Kissinger, who was at the time the US National Security Adviser. This memo originally had a "top secret" classification, but was declassified in 1990, and can now be viewed in the National Archives. It reads in part, "De-population should be the highest priority of US foreign policy towards the Third World . . . Reduction of population in these states [i.e., Third World Nations] is a matter of vital US national security . . . The US economy will require large and increasing amounts of minerals from abroad, especially from less developed countries." Perhaps Henry was thinking about introducing family planning into Africa — or was it something more sinister?

The many objections environmentalists bring up to prevent the implementation of effective anti-malaria methods which have relatively modest costs have been discussed earlier, and those details will not be reproduced at this point. As a brief summary, it can be said that there now exist, and there have existed for decades, simple and very effective methods which could be employed anywhere in the world to virtually eliminate malaria *as well as many other diseases which depend on insects for their transfer to humans.* These methods require only the repeated spraying of insect breeding areas with cheap, non-poisonous, and very effective insecticides. DDT is a typical example of these bug killers, but it is not the only one. There is nothing magical about such measures, and nothing about their safety or effectiveness remains in doubt after 60 years or so of their use. They are safe, effective, and cheap.

Why does the establishment fight so savagely to prevent the implementation of such obviously effective measures? There are at least four reasons:

1. If the problem is solved, the many tens of millions of dollars being paid to environmentalist investigators, researchers, think tanks, nonprofit organizations, etc., will no longer be available.

2. If a cheap insecticide is the answer, the more profitable patented insecticides will not be needed. Other high profit items such as vaccines to prevent infection when people are bitten and medications to treat active cases of malaria will not be required.

3. Hospitals and doctors will not receive fees for treating malarial patients.

4. Not as many people will die from malaria.

AIDS

The first signs that a new plague was taking form began to be noticed in about 1970. The AIDS virus was identified around 1982. The disease rapidly became a worldwide scourge, and the death toll from it now stands at about 8,000 per day (Anon. 2001A) — and it seems to be increasing.

Origin and proliferation — Current estimates show us that about 75% of HIV victims are in Sub-Saharan Africa, where the epidemic apparently got its start. It is claimed that about 2.2 million Africans died of AIDS (or complications) in 2001, and about 28.5 million were infected as of 2002.

The method by which the AIDS virus spreads is somewhat unusual in that it requires the transfer of blood (or certain other body fluids) directly from one person's circulatory system to another's. However, an intermediate vector such as a mosquito or flea is not involved in this process as it is in malaria or bubonic plague.

It is possible even a single virus particle would be sufficient to start a new case, so that very small amounts of blood can serve to transfer the disease. This means persons in rather early stages of AIDS, perhaps without visible symptoms, can be sources of infection. Although it does not appear that the AIDS virus passes through the placenta, between a quarter and a third of infected mothers pass the virus to their babies either by blood transfer during labor or while breast feeding.

Among the nonsexual modes of blood (or plasma) interchange which can result in AIDS infections are blood transfusions for medical purposes, use of a single hypodermic needle by two or more narcotic injecters, and blood transfer during fights or violent assaults.

It quickly became obvious to the medical community, however, that the principal means by which AIDS virus moves from one human to another is transfer of blood during sexual interactions. Furthermore, most researchers now admit that normal heterosexual coitus is an inefficient way of spreading the disease, although it is possible for the virus to be transmitted in such activities.

Although other means of infection are certainly possible, most AIDS cases result from homosexual intercourse, and these are in large part the result of "unprotected" anal intercourse. By far, the greatest number of victims in the US have been male homosexuals or bisexuals. Estimates of annual new HIV infections by risk category in the US (Carens 2002) show 42% are "men who have sex with men," 33% are self-described as "heterosexual" men and women (we have to assume some of these are actually primarily homosexuals or bisexuals), and 25% acquire the disease from "injection drug use." In sub-Saharan Africa, where the percentage of persons suffering from this disease is the largest in the world, most of the *newly reported* victims seem to be female (Schoofs and

Zimmerman 2002). Other sources claim there are strong intimations that the virus transfer occurs even in these cases as a result of anal intercourse, which is used as a form of birth control in some of these African cultures.

The founding fathers — A major problem confronting students of AIDS — and there have been many scientists and large amounts of money devoted to the elucidation of every conceivable aspect of the disease — is "how did it originate."

Occasional cases of this disease could have been occurring for decades if not centuries before it was recognized by the scientific community that a new virus was had appeared. Especially in localities where there are few doctors and very little interchange of information with the outside world, the deaths of people from AIDS could have been attributed to some other cause, and would have failed to attract the interest of either the scientific or medical communities. If there was no money in it, there would have been very little incentive to determine the true cause of such deaths.

At some time, whether it was 40 years ago or 4,000 years ago, the first unit of AIDS virus came into being. There are several possible mechanisms by which this new form of infective particle could have originated. Some of these are:

1. A virus much like AIDS had been endemic in some other animal (chimpanzee?) for centuries if not millenia, and a chance mutation adapted it to the human host, transfer then occurring to humans by contact with chimpanzee blood, as from butchered animals.

2. A virus nearly identical to AIDS, but not causing the symptoms of AIDS, or any symptoms, had been present in humans for a long time without being detected or recognized, and it mutated to the much more lethal form characteristic of AIDS.

3. A virus identical to, or almost identical to, AIDS had been present in restricted populations (say African pigmies) for millennia, but new routes of transmission opened up so that the virus was spread throughout the world.

4. An evil scientist, of the fantasy fiction type, deliberately modified an

existing virus so as to destroy mankind.

5. That ever popular villain, the CIA, originated the virus for some nefarious purpose of its own, probably at the instigation of rich Texas oil millionaires, most of whom were named Hunt.

In this connection, we learn it is generally agreed there exists in wild chimpanzees an immunodeficiency virus that has been named SIVcpz. It closely resembles the human virus HIV1 (there are said to be three subtypes of HIV-1, namely M, N, and O). The chimp virus may have infected man and then mutated to its present form over an unknown period. Some other less obvious connection may exist.

Not all persons are equally at risk. Persons who want to prevent infection need only to avoid receiving into their body blood or plasma originating from another person. Males who avoid homosexual contacts and who do not use "recreational drugs" should not be at risk. Finally, a break for the "straights!" None of the other great plagues allowed perfect protection by such convenient methods.

If AIDS is a "designer plague," as some have claimed, i.e., if the virus was somehow developed by scientific experimentation for the specific purpose of killing large numbers of the human race, then the originators (and others "in the know") would have wanted to have a reliable method for avoiding death at the "hands" of their invention. It was to be Frankenstein's monster on a leash.

We can conclude, then, that the person(s) who developed the AIDS virus (if there was such a group) knew very well how to avoid dying from the disease and followed the necessary precautions without fail. It is also possible, though not a necessary precondition, that the organization which developed the virus (in this case, it would have to be an organization because of the complexity of the experimentation which would have been required) also developed a vaccine to prevent infection. Possibly, there was also developed a medication which cured the disease once it began to spread, or which could be used if one of the illuminated happened to become infected.

A tremendous advantage of having a treatment available before the disease began to spread was that the value of such a medication would be enormous, especially if it could be revealed after the disease had spread throughout the world and everyone had become aware of the dangers it posed. If we believe the "man-made plague" scenario, then it is logical to take the next step and accept the possibility that the development of a cure began as soon as the development of the virus prototype went into its final stages of refinement and fine tuning.

Some other groups of suspects who would benefit in terms of power and money from the spread of AIDS include:

1. Health care operations — persons and organizations that would benefit greatly from increased number of patients. Trillions of dollars would be in the potential pot for this game.

2. Academics, think tanks, non-profit agencies, and all other persons and groups that could expect to get billions of dollars to "study" this disease and then suggest ways to study it some more.

3. Pharmaceutical manufacturers — the greatest number of dollars in profits would lie here, especially if a sure cure became available after the virus has spread throughout the world.

4. Heads of state, especially in Africa, Asia, and South America, who would see in the AIDS virus a simple way to reduce their excess population, thereby eliminating unproductive persons who cause so much annoyance by asking for food and shelter when the limited amount of available money is urgently needed for offensive weapons, palaces, yachts, harems, bodyguards, and the like.

At this point, the author must enter a disclaimer. He does not believe there is solid evidence that the AIDS plague resulted from an engineered virus. He does believe that such a course of events is possible, though at a low level of probability. If the disease is "man made" then we have to look at the list of persons and organizations who benefitted, and we find there not only the Red behemoth but all those persons who are interested in reducing the numbers of the human race to the least possible amount, with zero population as the asymptote.

Many deaths that go into the statistical record as being due to other diseases are an indirect result of AIDS, the victims being weakened and/or their immune systems being damaged so much by AIDS that supervening infections quickly lead to death. Tuberculosis is one of these collateral diseases. The World Health Organization estimated there were over a 700,000 new cases of tuberculosis that have been   facilitated by prior HIV symptoms and over 200,000 deaths by tuberculosis of HIV sufferers (Naik 2002).

It is also possible that many doctors certify deaths as being due to other diseases in order to save face for relatives. On the other hand, it is very unlikely that a physician would record HIV as "cause of death" unless it is very clear that such is indeed the case. The point is, the actual number of deaths from AIDS is probably substantially greater than official statistics indicate. Offsetting all this, however, is the possibility that persons who would benefit from a public perception of AIDS as being even worse than it actually is are inflating the statistics.

What of the future? — Representatives of the UN AIDS program estimated, early in 2002, that the two-decade toll (2000-2020) "among the hardest hit countries," will be 68 million deaths. That would be five times the number of dead officially recorded for the first 20 years of the epidemic. The UN also said that $9.2 billion per year will be required, beginning in 2005, just to provide an expanded "response" to HIV/AIDS in low and middle income countries — $4.8 billion for prevention and $4.4 billion for "treatment and support."

The promise or presence of this kind of money attracts researchers, activists, condom manufacturers, and drug producers like a corpse attracts buzzards. Consequently, they are frantically convening meetings, conferences, symposia, etc., trying to determine how to divide the jackpot. A Barcelona conference held in July of 2002 was estimated to have attracted 10,000 AIDS researchers, activists, and physicians (Zimmerman and Schoofs 2002).

A major division has occurred among the potential recipients of the funds, and among some of the donors as well, as to the percentages of the available money that will be spent on prevention of new cases vs. amounts which should be spent on treatment of existing victims. There has been an estimate that preventive measures (defined as "condom use, behavioral changes, voluntary testing and counseling, vaccine and microbicide research, and methadone and needle-exchange programs") are 28 times more effective than one of the most praised types of treatment. This alone should make prevention a non-starter among the academics and the producers of pharmaceuticals who want to see the grants, awards, and profits continue to increase indefinitely.

Disinformation projects — An agent of the East German (Communist) secret police (KGB), Dr. Jakob Segal, claimed that AIDS was the result of a US germ warfare program. In 1986, Jakob (at the time, professor of biology at Humboldt U in East Germany) and his wife Lilli, published a pamphlet, *AIDS: USA Home-made Evil*, describing their theory. Basically, the idea was that the evil Army scientists at Fort Detrick MD spliced two viruses (Visna, which kills sheep, and HLTV-1, a leukemia virus) to get AIDS. He also claimed the first AIDS cases originated in the US, from prisoners the government had infected with the virus as a test. Apparently, there is convincing evidence that Segal was carrying out orders of the KGB when he concocted his story and promoted it throughout the world.

Another person who uses basically the same villains, but with a slightly different playbook, is Dr. William Campbell Douglas, a physician. He claims that the World Health Organization infected Africans with laboratory created AIDS virus, using their smallpox vaccination project as a cover.

There are others, but the fact that no one has fingered the Reds as the villains in an AIDS-spreading program is rather interesting. Seems as though they would have been the most likely source, given their long-time role as democidists.

The Role of Environmentalism

The category of "environmentalist" includes persons who, we must conclude from a review of their statements and actions, hate humanity and all (or nearly all) of its activities and all the results of those activities. They may proclaim an interest in returning to "a simpler time," a desire to "become a part of nature," a need to "stop the exploitation," but at the core of their agendas the careful reader will detect a more-or-less concealed wish to decrease the total population and to devolve the more advanced cultural groups. They are quite willing to endanger humanity for the benefit of plants and sub-human animals. For example, there is a fairly large segment of the public which strongly promotes the view that population increases must be prevented, and total populations reduced drastically from present levels in order to "save the planet."

Persons having this type of mindset would tend to favor any phenomenon, practice, or policy that reduces the numbers of humans, and so they would look with disfavor on any program that had as its goal the prevention or curing of malaria, AIDS, or any other plague.

section seven
CONCLUSIONS AND RECOMMENDATIONS

In this, the final set of chapters, the author will provide an analysis of the lessons which can be learned from the data appearing in the preceding text and will suggest ways for neutralizing those enemies of civilization which we have called "reds."

In the first chapter of this section, the author attempts to answer the question: What does aging do to a terrorist? Do old terrorists pack high explosives in their incontinence appliances, with the detonator switches concealed in hearing aids, before boarding planes filled with the hated bourgeoisie? Or does the graying Red become a terrorist tycoon, running a string of agents from a mansion on the Riviera? Perhaps the young buzzards grow into birds of paradise, whose gaudily feathered exterior conceals a taste for death which has been present since birth.

The penultimate chapter deals with psychological profiles of terrorists. We will find that psychopathy, envy, and sadism are possible facets of their personalities. Answers are sought to the questions of the origin of these personality defects and the possibility of modifying them so that the terrorist can become a useful and trustworthy citizen. The possibilities of inheritable flaws and deliberate personality modification are discussed in considerable detail. In the end, we are forced to admit that the tag, "once a terrorist in deed, always a terrorist at heart," is often applicable.

In the final chapter, we recommend methods for neutralizing terrorists and resolving terroristic episodes. The futility of trying to deal with such people in a humane and rational manner (as proved by numerous examples) forces us to come to the unpleasant conclusion that, at times, the best terrorist is a dead terrorist. But, we suggest that the spoiled brats who were attracted only by the dope, broads, and easy money of the terrorist milieu may mature sufficiently to become at least marginally useful citizens.

Perhaps our most significant finding is that the foci of the terrorist plague can be found in our institutions of higher education, and that their nutrient stream comes from a network of nonprofit organizations, religious institutions, and foreign agents who are red to the core.

chapter twenty

WHERE ARE THEY NOW?

"We're against everything that's good and decent."

John J. Jacobs, Weatherman leader (1970)

It is instructive to compare the present status of aging terrorists with their actions and life styles during their heyday, and to examine their activities in the intervening years. There appears to have been certain more or less consistent differences in the later careers of the subjects that is related in some way to their ethnic affiliations and their original devotion to communism. Although the pattern is not entirely clear, it seems to the author that the following tendencies can be found.

•Former black supremacists — most of these are dead or in prison. A few have managed to escape major legal penalties and the casual violence of their murderous colleagues, and now eke out an existence in various ways, some of them honest. A few have adopted some deviant version of Mohammedism, and these types are especially apt to retain their old propensity for committing major felonies.

•Former black communists — many are now doing moderately well in various roles; some occupy positions on univerity and college faculties; several have achieved moderate successes in Democrat politics.

•Former white gentile hippies — most of these apolitical specimens are either dead or struggling to survive in relatively low-level jobs, but a few have done fairly well. Some of them are still facing legal problems of significant magnitude.

•Former white gentile communists — typically found on college faculties or running nonprofit civil rights and environmental organizations. Several have done exceedingly well in politics.

•Former Jewish communists — members of this group seem to have been the most successful of the terrorists in their post-treason existence. They are now writing books, running businesses related to amusement media, representing class action plaintiffs, occupying high level positions in government as appointed or elected officials, or resting as professors emeritus. Many have become very wealthy.

A closer view of the lives and accomplishments of some of the most celebrated revolutionaries of the 1960s tends to support the author's theory that those radicals who accepted direction from Communist masters did very well after they "matured," while those persons who supported causes antagonistic to international communism (e.g, Black Power) tended to have bad luck in their post-60s careers. Persons with Jewish backgrounds tended to do very well indeed. Some readers may reach different conclusions.

In researching the literature for the preceding information, we find that fewer revolutionaries have died than the author thought would be the case and not nearly as many are serving time as their history seemed to justify. Some have disappeared completely. A rather high percentage of violent revolutionaries who were active during a part of the 1950s, 1960s, and 1970s are still alive and out of prison. It is not necessary, or even desirable, to give space in this book to a large number of such specimens, because many of their life histories are very similar in the major events, and so do not teach us any new lessons. And, at any rate, such histories would not fit the plan of this book, which is more concerned with broad trends.

Any budding authors who are searching for a writing project might consider developing a book in which the life histories of scores or hundreds of the old terrorists are compared. A novel and revealing approach would be to apply concrete numerical data to the creation of profiles of their backgrounds, personalities, and actions. It might be possible to trace the threads of money and influence behind the red organizations all the way back to the original sources. Many interesting movers and shakers should be discovered.

SELECTED HISTORIES

As mentioned in the introductory section, the wealth of information found in the public records of red terrorists made it necessary to be highly selective in order to get a representative sample which would fit the available space. This necessarily means that some of the readers will find their favorite red, say Jerry Rubin or Mark Rudd, has been omitted.

H. Rap Brown — H. Rap Brown was very prominent in the extortion and terrorism stunts of the Black Power movement in the 1960s. He has continued his murderous activities into the new millenium. Now in his late 50s, he is posing as a Muslim holy man and has changed his name to Jamil Abdullah Al-Amin.

When sheriff's deputies of Cobb County (Georgia) tried to serve Rap with a warrant on March 16, 2000, this cleric shot them down with his consecrated assault rifle. One of the officers was shot three times in the groin with a holy 9 mm handgun as he lay bleeding from a previous shot — he subsequently died.

This occurrence was followed about two years later by a true miracle: Brown was convicted of murder and a few other crimes by a Cobb County jury consisting mostly of Blacks. This verdict was rendered despite an imaginative defense which included contentions that: (1) The witnesses (including the surviving deputy) were mistaken in their identification of Brown as the assailant, and (2) Government conspirators framed Brown because the Black Panther outrages in the 1960s for which he was largely responsible included attacks on law enforcement officers.

The Reverend Brown was sentenced to life in prison without possibility of parole, which probably means it will be about 2 or 3 years before he gets out on bail while awaiting a retrial on the basis of newly discovered evidence.

Tom Hayden — Thomas Hayden became famous for a number of outrageous antics during the 1960s, including marrying Jane Fonda. He was exceedingly prominent in the anti-Vietnam protests and he used his wife as an attention-getting prop in these demonstrations and in fund raising activities.

In later years, Tom succeeded in getting himself elected and re-elected to the California legislature where he found a very congenial coterie of freaks. He had raked in plenty of money as he pursued his Red-ward way to fame. One jackpot was the large settlement he had stripped from Jane Fonda when they were divorced.

Hayden remains an icon of the extreme left but he has found the going a bit tougher in the 2000s. There is no money flowing in from his overseas masters, and the wealthy eccentrics who once adored him need younger, fresher meat to titillate them.

After deciding the electoral scam was petering out, and with no other stupid rich broads willing to share their fortune with him, Hayden had to look for new fields to exploit. He discovered that a significant fraction of the public was willing to spend money for books by clapped out terrorists. As a result, in early 2002 we were treated to not just one, but two new publications from this great intellect. One of these, *Irish on the Inside: In Search of the Soul of Irish America,* is said to show us that, " . . . the most independent Irish consciousness is rooted in the North of Ireland . . . where the ancient and enduring conflict between Irish nationalism and British neocolonialism is most stark." *Ancient British neocolonialism?*

A reviewer, McCourt (2002), comments, "When he says the 60s made him Irish, he refers mainly to the Kennedys, particularly Bobby, the more Irish of the two dead Kennedys." Their surviving siblings will be interested to hear about this novel view of Kennedy geneology.

Anyone who pays the asking price of $25 for this book has a very strange sense of values. Twenty-five cents, maybe.

Not just one, but two publishers were convinced that Hayden had something to say, or were directed by a behind-the-scenes power to help this terrorist make a little money. In addition, it was thought desirable to establish Hayden as a member of the "intelligentsia." The second item in this propaganda explosion, which we fear is only beginning, is *The Zapatista Reader,* a collection of about 60 separate articles bearing on the terroristic activities of Subcommandante Marcos. This man was a sadistic murderer who led a gang of guerillas around the Chiapas area of Mexico beginning in 1994. His group of red criminals destroyed, pillaged, and burned large areas in the name of Communism.

Among the collaborators (meant in the broadest sense) given disinformation opportunities in Hayden's book are Regis Debray, Adolfo Gilly, Enrique Krauze, Carlos Montemayor, and John Ross.

Also putting in an appearance in this distinguished retinue is the ubiquitous Saul Landau, who seems to be a sort of bagman or deal-maker for propagandists of the Hayden type. Saul has made many TV films and written several books, all promoting the extreme left, and he has been a major apologist for Castro from the start. In mid-2002, he posted an internet list of the world's most important terrorists, among whom he included Dr. Kissinger and Oliver North: but there's nary a Red (or even a pale pinko) in the lot.

Reavis (2002) says of *The Zapatista Reader*, " . . . the essays are laudatory, many of them without any content except fascination for masked man Marcos and the Indian troops of the Zapatista Army of National Liberation, whose Spanish initials are EZLN."

Angela Yvonne Davis — Angie has been a dedicated, even servile, member of the Communist apparatus for decades. Her creden-tials in the international conspiracy were so firmly established that Castro invited her to Cuba so she could write her autobiography in peace. The Soviets then financed a trip to Russia, and treated her like a celebrity. Somehow, the conditions were not quite right in these utopias, however, so she returned to the US, determined to tough it out.

Davis was, and probably still is, a fanatical promoter of Communism, violence, sexism, and racism. Her most newsworthy exploit in these causes was her facilitation of the 1970 failed escape attempt at the Marin County GA courthouse by Black-power convicts. In this terrorist episode, her lover's brother, striking another blow for peace and co-existence, shot off the head of Superior Judge Harold Haley. Among several pieces of evidence connecting Angela with this murder, was the proof that she had owned the shotgun used to kill Haley (Collier 1995B). She was imprisoned for a time and then went to trial for her part in this brutal crime. She was acquitted by a jury consisting mostly of Blacks.

The 1995 appointment of Davis to the "prestigious" Presidential

Chair at the University of California Santa Cruz campus is one of the most extreme examples of academic arrogance and leftist influence ever to be reported in the public press. Her position paid not only the same salary as a professor would receive, but $30,000 extra for three years. There were also research assistance and other perquisites.

What did Angela do to deserve this scholarly recognition? She sapiently doesn't call herself either a teacher or a scholar, preferring the appellation, "political activist." That is certainly a title which she can reasonably claim, in the same way that H. Rap Brown is entitled to it. She has been a popular and well-paid ($10,000 a crack) speaker at campus convocations across the country (Collier 1995A), and she frequently travels abroad to spread her message — but she doesn't have time to go to Africa.

A charming couple — Bernardine Rae Dohrn (aka Ohrnstein) and William Charles Ayers have been married for some time. They entered the holy state of wedlock after a decade or so of wholesale sexual experimentation with friends, strangers, and whoever was around at the appropriate time — gender optional.

Dohrn and Ayers were present at the founding of The Weatherman (sometimes incorrectly given as "The Weathermen") in 1969. They were also prominent in its successor group, The Weather Underground.

Among the many other crimes this relatively small group of criminals (The Weather Underground) planned and conducted were bombings of public places. Several deaths resulted directly from their actions, and many more from crimes committed by individuals and groups who were moved to act by the "glamour" the media attached to the crimes committed by Weather Underground.

Dohrn served seven months in jail for her refusal to testify about the robbery of a Brinks facility during which two members of the Black Liberation Army killed two police officers. As a member of the Weatherman, she gained a listing on the FBI's Ten Most Wanted list. She went into hiding for several years, living during this time with

William Charles ("Bill") Ayers, also a violent radical.

Ayers is the son of former Commonwealth Edison Chairman Thomas Ayers (Swanson 2001). No doubt Bill has had access to family funds over the years. This may have something to do with his success in avoiding negative responses to a past that would seriously hamper a less well-endowed individual. It would also help to answer the question as to why his companion is facing a long prison sentence and he is not.

The gross indecency of Angela Davis' appointment to the faculty of the University of California (described in prior paragraphs) has been equaled, if not exceeded, by the appointments of Bernardine Dohrn to a faculty position in the Northwestern University School of Law and Bill Ayers to the faculty of the University of Illinois.

According to an editorial comment in the Wall Street Journal (Anon. 2001J), Northwestern University has shown "contempt for the law ... by [placing] on its faculty someone who could not pass a character and fitness test and who could not be admitted to the bar. The university's representatives point out that membership in the bar isn't a requirement for the law faculty. Dean David Van Zant issued a statement on academic freedom, saying that the law school's ability to understand and relate to controversial views was one of its strengths and that Ms. Dohrn, *director of a family law center*, channeled 'her energy and her passion into making a difference in our legal system.' " Yes, creating a climate which encourages the killing of policemen does make a difference in our legal system. Notice the radicals never advocate killing lawyers.

As the WSJ pointed out, Ms. Dohrn is an unrepentant lawbreaker who never took responsibility for her own crimes. One of her paramours, later her husband (the aforesaid Bill Ayers), managed to get his memoirs published, which, considering the character and political orientation of the US book publishing industry, is no surprise at all.

At the party this lovely and soigné couple gave to celebrate Ayers' official entry into the ranks of the intelligentsia, they gave out stick-on tattoos of the Weatherman symbol. Some of the guests thought this was quite humorous — would they have thought it humorous if she had passed out swastika stickers? If not, why not? What is the difference?

When Ayers was asked if he had regrets about the several bombings in which he had some complicity, he said "no." He also said he did not want to discount the possibility that he might commit more bombings. We are entitled to extrapolate: if he had been asked if he had regretted the deaths resulting from his comrades' actions, he would have said, "No." And, if he had been asked if he was willing to kill people who disagreed with his sociopolitical views, he would have answered, "Yes."

Bill and Bernie, a modern day version of Bonny and Clyde, though without their panache, should have been convicted of their crimes and executed years ago. Instead, they now have prominent positions in the academic field and are feted as celebrities. Their standard of living is apparently quite comfortable, if not lavish. No doubt they have grants from tax-advantaged foundations and income from various welfare plans in addition to their other income. And they have their pick of invitations to social soirees held by rich and famous degenerates who are in the throes of nostalgie de boue.

In addition to the other lessons the Ayers-Dohrn story provides, we are given one more proof of the sheer unbridled arrogance of the educational establishment, members of which not only make the most disgusting appointments to the faculty and staff of their institutions, but viciously attack anyone who publicizes or criticizes such outrages. They defend their moves as being noncontroversial or run of the mill, and apparently have no fear of oversight, review, or retaliation from the governing boards or even the alumni of their institutions.

It is clear to the present writer that the cause of this problem is the saturating of institutions of higher education with administrators and faculty members who despise and even hate, normal, ethical, and responsible human behavior. They are, indeed, "reds," and, as such, dedicated enemies of the human species. Academia in the US — in the world — is old, rotten, and worthless. It is worse than worthless, because it is an active agent for evil.

By the way, Bill and Bernie are members of the United Methodist Church — if you remember our comments about this quasi-spiritual organization in the chapter about Religion you will not find this surprising.

Patty Hearst — The daughter of the millionaire newspaper publisher, William Randolph Hearst, was kidnapped by members of the Symbionese Liberation Army in 1974. The SLA threatened to kill or maim their captive in the process of extorting large sums of money (ransom) from her father.

The gang was apparently able to brainwash Patty to the extent that she participated in at least one of their crimes. They beat her, raped her, and imprisoned her in a closet for months . . . yet the government attorney who led the prosecution team at her trial said, "She did everything voluntarily."

This author believes that the gang deliberately targeted W.R. Hearst because he was a publisher on the right side of the political spectrum and was a patriot who told the truth about red terrorists. The SLA (and the people who were behind this gang of Communist thugs) were determined to both punish W.R. Hearst and inactivate him. It is also possible that competing newspaper publishers in California, or perhaps malcontents in his own firm, wanted Hearst to be discredited and driven out of the newspaper business. These people could easily have contacted the SLA and financed the abduction.

Whatever the reason, Patty Hearst was selected from hundreds of possible targets as the best choice to serve the needs of the communists.

After her release, Patty was tried, convicted, and imprisoned for the bank robbery, while her captors remained at large! Of course, this group of murdering thugs — who have escaped punishment for all these years — knew where the political bodies were buried. The fear that they might implicate their behind-the-scenes conspirators has motivated and funded the coverup that has protected Emily Harris, William Harris, Sara Jane Olson, and Michael Bortin for nearly three decades.

Patty Hearst eventually recovered from her ordeal, married, and had two daughters. She wrote a book about her abduction and some of the events that followed it. She obtained a full pardon from Bill Clinton.

Kathleen Soliah — Now known as Sara Jane Olson. This woman remained in hiding for 24 years after participating in a series of crimes with other members of the Symbionese Liberation Army. She married a Harvard-educated doctor (Gerald F. Peterson), and was happily raising three teen-age daughters in an ivy-covered Tudor home in one of the better neighborhoods of St. Paul MN when the FBI finally caught up with her.

Investigators located and identified her in 1999, but she remained free on bail until her trial for the attempted killing, by pipe-bomb, of Los Angeles policemen in 1975. In 2001, Soliah pleaded guilty to the charges. In an impromptu press conference held shortly after the court recessed, she told the reporters she was in fact innocent, but had pleaded guilty for other reasons. The judge, learning of these comments, called Soliah back to court and demanded that she explain her remarks. Soliah said she was in fact guilty, but meant (in her remarks to the reporters) that she wasn't exactly guilty. Subsequently, this wavering lady changed her mind again and filed a motion to withdraw the guilty plea. This was denied, and the judge sentenced her to two consecutive terms of 10 years to life.

The mills of the gods grind slowly, yet they grind exceeding small, as the poet has told us. Soliah could say, "Amen," to that. In mid-January of 2002, Olson (and four other SLA members) were charged with the killing of Myrna Opsahl in a 1975 bank robbery. Mrs. Opsahl, a 47-year old mother of four children, was killed by a blast from a shotgun. Surely we are justified in describing Kathleen/Sara as a typical red — a sadistic psychopath, even though she was not the trigger person in this particular crime.

Michael Bortin — This man was a member of the Symbionese Liberation Army. He married the sister (Josephine) of Kathleen Soliah. When Soliah/Olson was arrested in 1999, he announced that people should *not* draw a distinction between that lady's past and present behavior, saying, "It's who she is — just the same Kathy. She was just as wonderful then."

Bortin was charged with possession of explosives in 1972, and spent 18 months in jail. He said (Anon. 2002A), "I was about to bomb a building over the Vietnam thing. I never denied that."

For about the last 20 years, Boortin owned and operated a hardwood flooring company in Portland OR. In late April of 2002, he waived extradition to California. He was in the bank with Emily Harris, Sara Jane Olson, William Harris, and James Kilgore when Emily shot Myrna Opsahl, who was waiting in line to deposit offerings collected at the church she attended.

Bortin was arrested in 2002, at which time his wife told reporters, "We're just two middle-aged, middle-class,, hard-working people. We were not expecting this" (Anon. 2002A). Her attitude seems to be: Just forget about it folks — it's all water under the bridge. Besides, we're capitalist pigs ourselves now — doesn't that make it all right?

A privileged character — One member of the bank-robbing gang, James Kilgore, disappeared from public view, and it seems that no one knows where he is. His good fortune is suspicious. Is he dead? Is he in Cuba, China, or Russia? Is he being protected by persons even more powerful than the backers of Olson et al.?

William Harris — This bank-robbing member of the SLA divorced his wife Emily, then remarried and had two children. He is a former Marine, and has been employed as a private investigator in San Francisco. Here is another suspicious case of non-prosecution. To what or to whom does he owe his exemption from due legal process?

Emily Harris — Now in her mid-50s, this member of the bank-robbing team has been working as a computer consultant in the Los Angeles area. She calls herself Emily Montague and lives, or did reside, in Altadena CA. Pattie Hearst said Emily was the person who shot Myrna Opsahl. After the robbery, Emily told her comrades it didn't matter, "She [Opsahl] was a bourgeois pig anyway."

The 47-year old mother of four children, was killed by a blast from a shotgun. Patty Hearst testified that Emily Harris carried the loaded gun into the bank, her finger on the trigger. The murder was "an accident," Emily said. Consider this sequence: steal or buy gun, steal or buy shells, load the gun, carry the loaded gun into bank, place finger on trigger, point gun at victim — presumably all in preparation for a little joke. Then — surprise! — the finger accidentally presses the trigger! Never could trust that finger!

So all those little coincidences leading up to the murder of the harmless and unassuming mother were just an unfortunate concatenation of circumstances. Do you believe that? Does anyone believe that? Incidentally, one of the other bank robbers kicked a pregnant woman in the stomach, for no apparent reason, and the woman had a miscarriage and nearly died. But, we can't blame him — his foot slipped, and anyway he didn't know it was loaded.

David Horowitz — Here is a nice, or maybe not so nice, Jewish boy who learned at an early age to always land on his feet, running. His father and mother, and some other members of the family, immigrated to America, and, while enjoying the ambience and opportunities of the US, they evaded their responsibilities to the country and acted as agents of Soviet Russia. Gratitude is not a strong point of the Jewish ethic. Naturally, Dave wanted to follow in his parents' footsteps, so he also associated with Communist front groups from an early age.

Eventually, Horowitz became closely connected with *Ramparts* magazine, a sort of *National Enguirer* of the red activist network. He was mixed up to some extent with the Black Panthers and other Afro-power gangs, mostly on the West Coast. After a time, he began to distance himself from his violent Black acquaintances, probably because he concluded that there was not much money to made from them. Also, he may have started to suspect that he was on the list of honkies designated to be "offed" when the time was ripe. The murder of one of his friends, a lady who was the accountant for a Black group Horowitz was promoting in his magazine, may have had something to do with his disillusionment. The lady was about to inform the police about highly illegal actions of the Black thugs she worked for, but those civil rights activists of a darker hue beat her to death before she could reach the police.

Horowitz eventually deviated from the pure Communist line, and began publishing descriptions of his experiences in the Red milieu. Surprisingly, he started to support some relatively middle-of-the-road causes. He is a facile writer and his style and attitude, though brash and self-indulgent, is often appealing. And, his open and critical approach to the violent activities of the black gangs (some of which he observed at first hand) is important from a historical standpoint.

The Horowitz autobiographical memoir, *Radical Son*, is useful as a source of information about the attitudes and customs that led to the selection of Communism as the religion of choice for many of the Central European Jews who poured into American cities during the 1930s and 1940s. The autobiography also describes in a relatively objective manner the radical activist milieu, especially as it existed in New York City and California during the postwar years.

In collaboration with his long-time friend, Peter Collier, Horowitz published the journal *Heterodoxy*, which carried fiction as well as supposedly factual material critical of the left-wing world. It also carried in some issues, a fairly lengthy article, appearing in every way to be a factual account of a ludicrous left-wing situation, which was made up out of whole cloth. These fictional articles were apparently smart aleck attempts by our cynical Jewish genius to embarrass and denigrate those readers who were not "clever" by his standards; not "in the know."

This practice was clearly unethical, and in violation of every journalistic standard. It shows Horowitz in, what I believe is a true light and tells us that he is, at heart, a true red now as always, with an undiminished contempt for the "squares."

It appears this journal is no longer available in hard copy, but it is carried on the internet. Horowitz also helped establish the Center for the Study of Popular Culture, a nonprofit organization that seems to be devoted mostly to exposés of people in the entertainment industry.

His Web-site gets much attention from people who seek out controversy. He posts comments that are critical of his work as well as the favorable stuff. This leads to an interesting cross-section of current thought among the intellectually deprived segments of several countries.

His books seem to have been quite successful. He is now engaged in writing about and speaking against reparations for the descendants of slaves, which should gain him a lot of white supporters and confirm the opinion of the surviving Black Panthers that they should have offed this honky when they had the chance.

One factor in Horowitz's continuing success and relatively favored position in society (i.e., he is not in jail or even under indictment) is that he kept clear of active participation in the violence of organizations such as the Symbionese Liberation Army, and confined his role in the red activist world to observing the action, and writing and publishing about what he saw.

These tactics, or perhaps "strategy" is a better word, kept him free of the legal entanglements that are even now troubling poor, misunderstood benefactors of humanity such as William Ayers and Bernardine Dohrn. It is also undoubtedly true that Horowitz has communications skills, or talents, that few if any of his old associates possessed. Having an able collaborator such as Peter Collier must have helped a lot, too.

Recently, Horowitz has had some nasty things to say about Noam Chomsky, another Jewish phenomenon, relative to Noam's expressed reservations concerning the truth of some generally accepted details of the Holocaust. As if this weren't enough to make poor Noam a pariah to all left-thinking people, he also suspects some merit might be found in

The Protocols of the Learned Elders of Zion. The Protocols is a document that seems to be the current bête noire (or, one of them) of the intellectual establishment. Your present author suggests that readers might be interested in reading the Protocols and making up their own minds as to this document's validity. The Protocols, in whole or part, can be located on several web sites.

Bobby Seale — This Black Panther has moderated his advocacy of violent negro supremacism, at least if his website content is indicative of his present philosophy. "All Power to All People," is his current motto (or, one of them). This is a very inclusive statement, but a bit difficult to understand — it seems to approach an anarchical viewpoint.

Bobby informs website visitors that he was the co-founder (along with Huey Newton) of the Black Panther Party, but he has now transferred his attention to Reach, Inc., which he also founded. If you wish to purchase BPP memorabilia, he has a nice stock. Books about the BPP and Bobby's career are also available, and he indicates a willingness to speak at gatherings anywhere in the US. He proposes to make films under the aegis of Reach Cinema Productions. Interested parties can learn more at **www.bobbyseale.com.**

John Buttny — This man attended the 1969 War Council in Flint MI where it was decided to disband The Weatherman and create the Weather Underground. The Underground was intended from the start to be a violent, subversive organization consisting of only the tried and true members of the original group.

Buttny's FBI file shows he trained in guerrila warfare methods abroad and received an assignment to infltrate the government. By his own account, he was arrested 15 times during demonstrations.

At the time of this writing, it appears that Buttny is a deputy to Santa Barbara County Supervisor Gail Marshall. This woman is, or was, caught up in a recall movement initiated by citizens who accuse her of opposing a salute to the flag at a community meeting.

John Gregory Jacobs — He was also known as Barry P. Stein and Gary C. Witzel, and, doubtless, by many other aliases. He was arrested several times in the few years from 1966 when the SDS/Weatherman/Underground criminal activity was approaching its peak. Some of the charges were aggravated battery, mob action, resisting arrest, assault, possession of drugs, unlawful possession of a weapon, mob action, conspiracy, and violation of the Federal Anti-riot Act.

Jacobs was the son of wealthy left-wing parents (Douglas and Lucille Jacobs) residing in the eastern part of the US, and graduated from a prep school. He was a close friend of Mark Rudd, who may have recruited him into the treason game. Castro and Che Guevara were his role models.

He was said to be the boy friend of Bernardine Dohrn, but that is hardly a distinguishing feature — just a face in the crowd. At one time, he lived at 4943 Winthrop ave., Chicago. He disappeared from public view sometime about 1971. Rudd says Jacobs was voted out of the Weather Underground after the famous bomb explosion on March 6, 1970 which killed three members of the Weather Underground. It was rumored that he had gone to Canada.

On October 19, 1997, paramedics were called to a Vancouver BC (Canada) basement apartment to treat a seriously ill individual known as Wayne Curry. This man, though in the terminal stages of myeloma, was in a fighting mood. He did not want to go, and struggled with the paramedics, who called the police. They found a bottle of whiskey and a half gram of cocaine beside his bed.

He was being led from the house when a woman detective patted him on the back as a comforting gesture and got slugged in the face as a reward. The police strapped him to a stretcher and took him to a hospital, where he died about 18 hours later. It was learned that he had made a living by selling marijuana and working at blue-collar jobs.

Within a rather short length of time after his death, it became known that "Curry" was, in fact, John Jacobs, the fighting Weatherman.

chapter twenty-one

PSYCHOLOGICAL ASPECTS OF BOLSHEVISM

In the preceding chapters we have attempted to present some of the evidence bearing on the fallacies and phony-ness underlying Red/red pretensions. We have listed some of the mental and emotional characteristics of the people who became activists in these groups, and speculated on the motivations of persons who enriched themselves at the expense of genuinely concerned — though misled — contributors to Communistic and Communist-front organizations.

The question inevitably arises — how could so many apparently intelligent and certainly successful (in material ways) people be misled by such transparent frauds? The answer is: Very few of them *were* deceived. They saw Bolshevism for what it really was — an immensely successful con game which could be used to advance the careers and fortunes of knowledgeable participants in the scam. They saw that intelligence, job skills, productivity, educational attainments, industriousness, and the like were not essential to success in the Red universe, so it was truly an equal opportunity environment — any psychopath could succeed. They also realized that the outlaw mentality of the movement gave gave the illuminati unparalelled access to sex, drugs, travel, and excitement.

The undeniable facts that violence and destruction as well as the wounding and killing of innocent people were the invariable concomitants of Red activity made absolutely no difference to such people. So, we have to ask ourselves, "What kind of person could be so callous, so indifferent to the suffering of their victims?" We will explore some possible answers to this question.

Many Reds are Psychopaths

Reds in all hues of their manifestations are the greatest force promoting reaction and savagery in the world today, and they have been playing this role for more than a century, perhaps for more than two centuries. They are mostly unseen and unrecognized but they work diligently and constantly to destroy complex and beautiful structures which they have not made in order to build from the broken down residue ugly and shapeless structures whose only purposes are to conceal and protect their own kind — replacing order with chaos, beauty with filth, and culture with instinct. We could call them "The termites of civilization."

If the above description is correct, we are faced with the possibility that persons who seek out red organizations and become members of them, well as those who are active in promoting such organizations' agendas even though they are not members themselves, are not normal productive members of society. Instead, they are part of a subclass of humanity that differs in a significant way from useful (or at least harmless) human beings. This difference could be described as a pathological hatred of humanity.

In fine, the author suggests that most of the active members of Bolshevist groups, whether they resided in Russia or in other parts of the world were, in fact, psychopaths. Of course, we are not saying that all psychopaths are Communists — there are other roles such people can play which give them similar kinds of satisfaction without the necessity of conforming to a set of rules which some psychopaths might find too restrictive.

The Useful Idiots

There are red followers and there are Red activists. Overlap of the two categories may exist, but in practice it seems to be rather slight. It is true, however, that yesterday's infantryman may become today's captain and tomorrow's general. Behind the two publicly visible categories — followers and leaders — we have behind-the-scenes controllers and instigators, who manage and finance the movement's activities and establish the policy and the agendas that govern them and who coordinate the various manifestations of terrorism.

Accidental idiots — Some of the persons who show up at meetings and participate in non-violent demonstrations do not have a clue as to what it is all about and do not fall into any of the categories described above. Among these innocents are the casual members, who have stumbled onto a red organization while searching for a hobby or a pastime, as one might blunder into a meeting of poodle fanciers while searching for a restroom in a hotel lobby, and who might, in their struggle against loneliness and boredom, continue to attend meetings in spite of their lack of understanding of the group's goals. They may never achieve any substantial insight into the organizers' character and, as long as they get some fellowshipping, however minor, from other members, or if they like the snacks, they will continue to attend meetings.

And, there are members' boyfriends and girlfriends who attend boring meetings so they can enjoy the company of their more committed companions, but who have no desire to promote any significant change in the social status quo. There are spouses, sons, daughters, and other relatives of Red activists who are more or less forced to participate in party activities by the family Communist, but, who, if they eventually achieve a measure of independence, quickly distance themselves from their troublesome sponsors. The same pattern can be seen in all activist organizations and in most lodges, unions, and religions.

Less innocent in their motivations are those persons who believe it is good for their careers to associate with party members, but who have a deep cynicism about the philosophical basis of communism — most academic reds would probably fall into this category. Many of these people would even attend Mass if they thought it would help them get grants, career advancement, awards, etc. But anyone who eagerly participates in Communist activities after learning the true agenda of the leaders can hardly be considered normal. Are we not justified in concluding that there is some type of innate fault in the reasoning ability or emotional drives of Reds/reds?

Volunteer idiots — The Spanish Civil War presented Communist sympathizers in the US with an opportunity to put up or shut up. Rather surprisingly, about 3,300 Americans actually took steps to place themselves in what was obviously a dangerous position. Although only a few of these volunteers became battle casualties, quite a few were killed by their "comrades" in the purges conducted by agents of the Russian secret police.

The Americans who went to Spain to kill for the Communist cause constituted what was, for practical purposes, a 100% hardcore Bolshevik contingent. Possibly, a few participants were merely borderline Communists who had only a tenuous grasp on reality. This segment included such upperclass misfits as the famous author Ernest Hemingway, who finally had to commit suicide, years later, to reach the goal he had been seeking during most of his life.

Then there was Eric Blair/George Orwell, who may have thought the opportunity to gain literary fame justified risking his life in the Spanish conflict. Orwell went to the war zone as a journalist, but he joined the Loyalist (Red) militia soon after arriving. According to his account, he was very nearly caught up in one of the numerous purges the Bolshevik commissars conducted, but he managed to escape execution. This experience soured him considerably on Marxism as a life style, and no doubt established the prejudices which were so pungently exhibited in his polemical novels, "The Animal Farm" and "1984."

The literati were especially attracted by the Soviet efforts in the Spanish conflict, and many of them attempted to assist the propaganda efforts by poems, articles, plays, movies, and the like. W. H. Auden, in his literary effusion, "Spain 1937," demanded, "Intervene!" — somewhat blunting the manly force of this command by adding the detailed instructions, "O descend as a dove or a furious papa or a mild engineer, but descend." Auden himself couldn't make it to Spain, due to the pressure of other business — and cowardice.

Readers interested in expanding their knowledge of international communists' influence and participation in the Spanish Civil War would be well advised to consult Radosh (2000) and Ybarra (2001). These two publications contain much information on the participation of Americans in the Spanish Civil War, and their subsequent careers, if any.

Psychopathy and Reds

Some authorities have suggested that all, or a considerable proportion of, terrorists are psychopaths. Two useful references are: Cooper's *What is a Terrorist*, and K. J. Pearce's *Police Negotiations* (Psychiatric Association Journal 22). However, Reich (1990) contends that, although the terrorist groups operate on the fringes of society and so might bring in the occasional psychopath, " . . . the proportion is not strikingly high." He refers to the "mentally ill," a category in which he seems to include psychopaths. Some authors, and apparently most judicial authorities, do not regard psychopaths as being legally insane/mentally ill. I interpret Dr. Hervey Cleckley's writings (see below) to say that he does not consider psychopaths as being legally insane.

Diagnosing psychopathy — It is interesting to compare the behavior of reds in general, and Communists in particular, with the famous list of 16 points thought to be characteristic of the behavior of psychopaths, which was included by Dr. Cleckley in his book, *The Mask of Sanity* (1964). This list is reproduced below, preceded by Dr. Cleckley's introduction to it.

"Before going on to the perhaps still unanswerable questions of why the psychopath behaves as he does or of how he comes to follow such a life scheme, let us . . . attempt to say what the psychopath is, in terms of his actions and his apparent intentions, so that we may recognize him readily and distinguish him from others. We shall list the characteristic points that have emerged . . . :
1. Superficial charm and good 'intelligence.'
2. Absence of delusions and other signs of irrational thinking.
3. Absence of 'nervousness' or psychoneurotic manifestations.
4. Unreliability.
5. Untruthfulness and insincerity.
6. Lack of remorse or shame.
7. Inadequately motivated antisocial behavior.
8. Poor judgment and failure to learn by experience.

9. Pathological egocentricity and incapacity for love.

10. General poverty in major affective reactions.

11. Specific loss of insight.

12. Unresponsiveness in general interpersonal relations.

13. Fantastic and uninviting behavior [with and sometimes without alcohol consumption.]

14. Suicide is rarely carried out.

15. Sex life is impersonal, trivial, and poorly integrated.

16. Failure to follow any life plan."

Practical problems with classification — If we try to match Cleckley's characteristic points with the behavior of individual Reds, we are usually confronted by an paucity of reliable data. No one has recorded, in any publication available to the author, observations adequately detailed and sufficiently reliable to enable us to make a comparison of *any* person's behavior with *all* of the points above.

It is true there are some autobiographical and semi-autobiographical accounts which give us a great deal of information about certain individuals, enough perhaps to permit a yes/no choice for each of Cleckley's factors, but the question then arises, can we depend upon the accuracy of these accounts? The answer is: "No'" — not for a final diagnosis that would be acceptable in court. But it is very likely that in some cases we can arrive at an evaluation suggestive of a psychological category fitting the individuals which we are discussing.

We could, perhaps, even construct a hypothetical "typical Communist" and compare his behavior with Dr. Cleckley's list of traits of psychopaths. But this would leave the author open to possible criticism for making prejudiced choices of data, and, in any case such an exercise is not essential for the present discussion.

Although outward manifestations of the radical activist phenotype may vary from individual to individual in seemingly unpredictable (and often unexplainable) combinations, much of their apparently erratic behavior and attitude can be explained when one understands they have a deep and abiding fear of and distaste for humanity, not based on experience or logic, but on an innate and unreasoning hatred for all persons, perhaps even including themselves.

True Believers

Generally speaking, the old radicals (and some of the new ones) are not amenable to, or even capable of, changing their positions when they are presented with data showing the shortcomings of their philosophy. There may be several reasons for this, but it is certain that one of the reasons is that some of these people, though originally cold and calculating dissimulators, have become emotionally committed to, and true believers of, the Bolshevik tenets through their constant iteration of the beliefs of the communist system.

This phenomenon is not new, it is in fact older than history, being a method for indoctrinating converts that has been practiced by every cult leader from the beginning of civilization. The acceptance as truth of constantly repeated *dicta probantia* is so universal that we are tempted to regard it as a genetically determined trait, or set of traits.

We might say that people behaviorally oriented in this manner act and think as though they have become converted to a supernaturally revealed mission. As a result, any attempts by others to bring to light their past transgressions and call them to account for their crimes, will cause the converts to believe they are being persecuted by devils, by satanic forces, by the CIA or the FBI.

This conclusion is used by them as a justification for assuming the even more destructive roles of martyrs and bombthrowers. They are willing to sacrifice themselves in a battle to bring down the whole of civilization as a symbol of their frustration with society's defects (as they see them). Even from the earliest times, most radical activists have had more Bakunin and de Sade than Lenin and Stalin in their make-up, not that there was much difference in the operating principles established by these four enemies of civilization.

A Psychodynamic Interpretation

In a note appearing in Rothman's *Group Fantasies and Jewish Radicalism: A Psychodynamic Interpretation* (1978), there is an interesting bit of speculation on the causes underlying an individual's expression of rebellion, the latter including attacks made on various aspects of the social order with which the subjects have come into contact. Some of Rothman's material seems to be applicable to the theme of the present book, and so will be reproduced below.

"Most psychoanalysts (and many social scientists) feel that calls for a radical re-orientation of basic societal structures must spring from underlying psychological and social changes. Thus they would say that the emergence of the 'new left' with its call for radically altered sexual practices and communalism must reflect basic personality changes on the part of those making the demands, and should be correlated with social and cultural changes or changes in child-rearing practices (the Dr. Spock permissiveness thesis)." That is, the commentators believe a new type of person (or at least, an new type of personality) must have developed to cause the extreme changes in activity which are observed.

Rothman takes a position contrary to such opinions. He believes, "... that a variety of alternative fantasy solutions of personal problems are available in the unconscious of most individuals, but are kept in check when such individuals mature in an environment charac- terized by a self-confident authority structure. When such authority is weakened, these fantasies beome public. Thus political revolutions with purely political causes can result in radical changes in social, cultural and family life. Of course, the most primitive fantasies are never institu- tionalized because they are incompatible with an organized social order. Thus, every modern revolution from the Puritan to the Russian has produced radical ferment with calls for free love and the end of the family, as well as, often, of the glorification of polymorphously perverse sexuality. Once the new revolutionary elite consolidates its power these more 'radical' elements are suppressed."

Rothman insists that most major revolutions involve crises in both social and political values and norms. He does not believe that all major political upheavals have to be explained as resulting from underlying personality, social, and/or cultural changes. I take this to mean there is, or can be, in his view, a basic philosophical foundation for at least some major cultural changes.

They Do It Because It Feels Good

The following extract from Post (1990) is very important, and his entire paper is valuable in establishing what seems to the present author to be the simple principle that terrorists commit their dastardly acts because they like to plan them, to do them, and to view the consequences, and no other position, except that of the professional assassin, would give them as much satisfaction, as great a thrill.

Post wrote, " ... *political terrorists are driven to commit acts of violence as a consequence of psychological forces, and ... their special psycho-logic is constructed to rationalize acts they are psychologically compelled to commit. Thus the principal argument of this essay is that individuals are drawn to the path of terrorism in order to commit acts of violence, and their special logic, which is grounded in their psychology and reflected in their rhetoric, becomes the justification for violent acts.*"

"Considering the diversity of causes to which terrorists are committed, the uniformity of their rhetoric is striking. Polarizing and absolutist, it is a rhetoric of 'us vs. them.' It is a rhetoric without nuance, without shades of gray. 'They,' the establishment, are the source of all evil, in vivid contrast to 'us,' the freedom fighters, consumed by righteous rage. And if 'they' are the source of our problems, it follows ineluctably, in the special psycho-logic of the terrorist, that 'they' must be destroyed."

Post continued, "Doubts concerning the legitimacy of the goals and actions of the group are intolerable ... The person who questions a group decision risks the wrath of the group and possible expulsion. Indeed, the fear is even more profound, for, as Baumann has stated, withdrawal was impossible 'except by way of the graveyard.' *The way to get rid of doubt is to get rid of the doubters.*" Extreme pressure to conform has been reported by all who have discussed the atmosphere within the group. Baeyer-Kaette has described the first meeting of a new recruit to the Heidelberg cell of the Red Army Faction. The group, which previously had targeted only identified representatives of the establishment such as magistrates and policemen, was discussing a plan to firebomb a major department store. Horrified, the new recruit blurted out, 'But that will lead to loss of innocent lives!' A chill fell over the room, and the new recruit quickly realized that to question the group consensus was to risk losing his membership in the group. What an interesting paradox, that these groups, whose ideology is intensely against the dominance of authority, should be so authoritarian and should so insist on conformity and unquestioning obedience . . . "

The facade is designed to fit the inner need.

Light Brown, Like Me

When we are discussing the visible characteristics of truly dangerous persons, those sadistic terrorists who are able to dissemble their true character, multiple examples tempt us to conclude that the female is the more vicious sex. Examples abound, but Bernardine Dohrn and Angela Yvonne Davis come to mind immediately. Dohrn has been extensively discussed elsewhere in this book, so in the following paragraphs, we will attempt to cast some light on the career of Davis.

The author believes that this lady provides us with a useful case history of psychopathy, sadism, and envy combined. The main events of her career can be traced through numerous media reports, records of law enforcement agencies, and comments made by her associates and victims over the past 30 or 40 years. We also have the story of a life, possibly hers: *Angela Davis: With My Mind on Freedom*. This book (Davis 1974) is an alleged autobiography, but it very likely contains massive contributions by her editor, Toni Morrison, who has participated in several other outrages of roseate hue.

Davis edited (so she claims), an earlier anthology containing the work of several contributors. When the publishers printed this book, *If*

They Come in the Morning, they displayed Angela's name as *author,* and the book was promoted quite successfully on that basis. Angela says this was done without her knowledge. The book is still being promoted, over 30 years later, as having been written by Angela Davis. Evidently, Angela hasn't managed to find the time to tell the publisher to correct the error. But we can be sure she finds time to cash the royalty checks.

Angela said her parents had participated in civil rights activities, and they probably had national or international contacts with red groups, although she only hints at this in her autobiography. Her brother Ben was on the Cleveland Browns football team for a time, which may or may not have some significance.

It is a fact that her family's background has not received the attention it deserves. She seems to have received a Red indoctrination starting at a very early age. Persons she knew in high school were involved in high profile terrorist crimes other than those Angela admitted to facilitating.

The Davis family was evidently in fairly good financial circumstances during her childhood. Her mother bought Angela a piano for her fifth birthday. As a childhood recreation, she and her friends would shout racial epithets at the poor white people in her neighborhood.

Her sex life was apparently quite full and varied, except when she was in jail. Then it was full, but not varied. However, there is no indication in her writings of a tendency toward homosexuality. Instead, she dwells lovingly on the "virile" or "beautiful" appearance of some of the moronic black thugs she helped to evade justice. She did not, however, discriminate on the basis of race. She mentions "seeing" a lot of a German, Manfred Clemenz, while she was at Brandeis University.

Davis was disturbed by the male chauvinism (she doesn't call it that) exhibited by the blacks she dealt with, and she was, in fact, admonished for her lack of subservience by some of her male (and female) friends. But, she passes this off as merely a lack of full development of the socialist spirit, which will be remedied when the red nation evolves to its final state of perfection. Stalin never saw it that way, and neither did Lenin.

Davis didn't like being in jail. She couldn't get coffee without milk, the fluorescent lighting "burned" her eyes, they only gave her one cigarette at a time (she is a chain smoker), the underwear they gave her was sometimes unsatisfactory (so she didn't wear it), and she couldn't get the proper implements to keep her Afro hairdo in top condition. And they call **this** a democracy!

In the autobiography, she quickly disposes of the assorted murders and other heinous crimes committed by her associates, and possibly participated in by her. She wrote a letter to one of her friends in prison in which appeared the comment: "For the black female, the solution is not to become less aggressive, not to lay down the gun, but to learn how to set the sights correctly, aim accurately, squeeze rather than jerk and not be overcome by the damage. We have to learn how to rejoice when pigs' [white people's] blood is spilled." In later reference to this passage, she implied it was merely a metaphor!

In recent years, this American-hating red witch has prospered mightily in spite of occasional setbacks. Although several of her friends have been killed by other "friends" or the police, although the nation for which she so loyally propagandized has fallen apart, although her sometime patron Castro is slowly sinking into the garbage pit of history, and although the philosophy on which she based all of her radical activities has been thoroughly discredited, she still gets more speaking invitations than she can fulfill and all the media space she cares to accept.

She travels extensively, appears at many events, and often receives awards, grants, honors, and most of the other goodies for which all academic celebrities strive. She has become a kind of Éminence Grise (you should pardon the expression) of the Communist Party.

As an afterword, we offer a quotation from Aleksandr Solzhenitsyn, the Russian dissident who risked his life many times to combat tyranny in the Soviet Russia that Angela Davis looked upon as her promised land (until she had spent some time there). The following passage is from a speech delivered by Solzhenitsyn at a convocation of labor organizations in New York City on July 9, 1975. He said, in part, "Although she didn't have a too difficult time in this country's [i.e., the US] jails, she came to recuperate in Soviet resorts. Some Soviet dissidents — but more important, a group of Czech dissidents — addressed an appeal to her: 'Comrade Davis, you were in prison. You know how unpleasant it is to sit in prison, especially when you consider yourself innocent. You have such great authority now. Could you help our Czech prisoners? Could you stand up for those people in Czechoslovakia who are being persecuted by the state?' Angela Davis answered: *'They deserve what they get. Let them remain in prison.'* [Solzhenitsyn continued] That is the face of Communism. That is the heart of Communism for you."

Yes. It was the response we would expect from a Red who has spent her lifetime toeing the party line and who knew how necessary it was to obey her white masters in the Kremlin.

Radical Rationalizations

In Sigmund Freud's essay entitled, "Some character types met with in psychoanalytic work," he describes persons whose rebelliousness and claims to privileged status are based on their belief that they have suffered injuries and humiliations which they have done nothing to deserve. Such people, among whom he specifically included Jews, often feel quite justified in harming others in retaliation.

This attitude is very obvious in the current literature, whether the statements are attributed to Jewish authors or otherwise, in which every excess, every terroristic act, of (for example) the Israeli government is justified by references to "the Holocaust," "two thousand years of oppression," "ghettoes," "pogroms," "The Pale of Settlement," "Kristallnacht," "Anne Frank," and the like. Furthermore, this special privilege is regarded as extending to individual Jews who may have led lives of luxury and arrogance since their infancy, and who have not undergone any kind of intentional deprivation whatsoever.

Sadism

Sadism is not an invariable accompaniment of a psychopath's emotional makeup. Often the psychopath is perfectly content to achieve his goals without harming anyone, if it is convenient for him to do so. Although he is totally indifferent as to whether or not he injures another person in his progress toward achieving his personal goals, he will not go out of his way to deliberately harm someone merely for the sake of the deed. His sexual enjoyments will often be achieved in ways which could be considered more or less normal. But, psychopathy does not *necessarily* exclude sexual perversions, and a particularly dangerous combination is found in the psychopath who is also a sadist.

Examples of sadistic behavior — It is instructive to review some incidents involving activists who were sadists *and* psychopaths. Each of the following examples show a combination of positive enjoyment of the injuries inflicted on others and the previously described suite of characteristics thought to be typical of psychopaths.

1. Bill Harris, of the Symbionese Liberation Army, was a member of the gang which included the person who shot Myrna Opsahl. Mrs Opsahl happened to be in a bank the gang was robbing in 1975. Patty Hearst, who had been kidnapped and brainwashed by the SLA, wrote that Bill Harris held up the brass base of a spent shotgun shell. He bragged that it was the murder round, and said "Good old Myrna, she took the buckshot." This is not merely callous behavior, it signifies a delight in inflicting pain and death — not only psychopathy but sadism as well. Bill's charming wife Emily, said Mrs. Opsahl's death didn't matter, because she was just a bourgeois pig anyway. In the bank robbery, a pregnant woman was kicked in the stomach, an act which must have been motivated by sadism, since there is no other conceivable cause for it, and it certainly could not have been an accident.

2. A second example can be found in a contemporary account of Bernardine Dohrn's remarks made at a convention of Students for a Democratic Society (Bugliosi and Gentry 1974). She was giving her

views on a particularly gruesome mass murder committed by followers of the cult leader cum assassin Charles Manson. "Offing those rich pigs with their own forks and knives, and then eating a meal in the same room, far out! The Weathermen dig Charles Manson."

3. In one of the Weatherman riots in Chicago, Richard Elrod, chief counsel of Chicago, suffered an injury which paralyzed him from the neck down. While he was hospitalized, hovering between life and death, a Weatherman spokesthing wrote (*New Left Notes* Oct. 21, 1969), "... Pig Daley's top legal oinker ... is now paralyzed — hopefully for life. He won't be so quick to play pig next time." A song was composed to celebrate the event: "Lay Elrod Lay." Among the lyrics were: "Stay Elrod stay, Stay in your iron lung, Play Elrod play, Play with your toes for awhile." See Schwarz (1972) for additional details.

Nothing could be clearer.

Examples of Soviet official torture — "Even at a time when the Soviet regime was fighting for its survival during the civil war, many of its own supporters were sickened by the scale of the Cheka's brutality. A number of Cheka interrogators, some only in their teens, employed tortures of scarcely believable barbarity. In Kharkhov the skin was peeled off victims' hands to produce gloves of human skin; in Voronezh naked prisoners were rolled around in barrels studded with nails; in Poltava priests were impaled; in Odessa, captured White officers were tied to planks and fed slowly into furnaces; in Kiev cages of rats were fixed to prisoners' bodies and heated until the rats gnawed their way into the victims' intestines" (Andrew and Mitrokhin 1999).

Envy

It has frequently been observed that some of the most violent and dedicated red terrorists/activists came from families of great wealth and excellent reputation. William Ayers comes to mind immediately. Here was a youth whose father was president of Commonwealth Edison. He was undoubtedly surrounded by luxury and attention during his childhood, and his future success was ready for the grasping. Why did he choose to become a scruffy bum consorting with the scum of the earth: whores, murderers, thieves, arsonists, druggers, terrorists, and the like? Why did he support organizations which were traitorous, violent, and without any cultural appeal? Nostalgie de boue certainly, psychopathy probably, sadism maybe — but could there be another reason forcing him to reject every positive aspect of his background? Consider envy.

Helmut Schoeck was at one time the director of the Institute of Sociology at the University of Mainz (Germany). He has studied and written extensively on the subject of "Envy," which he regards as an important motivating factor in human behavior. Some of his comments (Schoeck 1966) bear directly or indirectly on the topic being discussed in this chapter, and will be referred to in the following paragraphs.

" . . . envy involves: the consuming desire that no one should have anything, the destruction of pleasure in and for others, without deriving any advantage from this."

"The reproach of envy has been levelled at the socialist by Wilhelm Roscher and Joseph Schumpeter, by Jacob Burckhardt and Nietzsche, by Max Scheler, Oswald Spengler and Justice Oliver Wendell Holmes. But he [the socialist], usually so ready of tongue and so well versed in dialectics, has rarely tried to defend himself against the accusation, and has, indeed, carefully avoided controversy on the subject."

Schoeck believes, "This peculiar inverse coupling of socially relevant truth (or authenticity) with the welfare of the majority [i.e., the poorer the person is, the more astute he is] — a main proposition in Western social criticism since the early fifties — probably represents nothing but a revival of a much older ideological suspicion of purely Marxian origin . . . [i.e.] Only the proletarian, the worker, or at least his mouth-piece the intellectual, who shunned the upper or middle class from which he often stemmed, was possessed of genuine social truth."

Schoeck (1966) writes of children from wealthy homes who "attach themselves to a proletarian revolutionary movement but also adapt the frugal way of life . . . " Although he does not say so, I suggest this is due to their envy of their parents, which eventually turns into hatred.

Your present author suggests that envy does indeed play a major role in the decision of the jeunesse dorée to take the low road to personal gratification and social exaltation — perhaps we could call it "boue chic."

The envy felt by terrorists having upperclass origins is not solely, or perhaps not even mainly, due to the parents' possession of greater wealth or more material possessions of any kind. It results from the subject's envy of their parents' achievements and position, indeed, of their parents' learning, skills, and honors, which the offspring thinks (usually, quite correctly) he could never attain no matter how much effort he put into the attempt.

Neither socialism nor any other kind of "ism" can ever eliminate envy, because a person can always find something about other persons to envy regardless of the overall impoverishment of their combined milieu. One would imagine there are few environments more egalitarian than an army barracks, where the clothing is exactly alike and the food is exactly the same for everyone, living conditions are exactly the same, the social status is (presumably) perfectly uniform, and the method of personnel selection and training tends to blur any behavioral differences. Yet the author can testify there is much envy among the troops.

Envy is a common human response, but the behavior it elicits varies widely from person to person and has little to do with the objective magnitude of the triggering factor. For persons to whom actions based on envy are an integral part of the behavioral pattern, the slightest difference in skills, appearance, or health can serve as a trigger for the development of envy and even hatred. Differences in material possessions are not essential precipitating or contributory factors.

Further from Schoeck: "Envy is ineluctable, implacable and irreconciliable, is irritated by the slightest differences, is independent of the degree of inequality, appears in its worst form in social proximity, yet cannot of itself produce any kind of coherent revolutionary programs (Schoeck 1966)...A society, however, which raises the average envious man to the position of a censor or legislator is incapable of functioning for long, and is in any case very extravagant of resources."

It is interesting to speculate that envy may be a emotion based on genetically directed behavior which is present to some extent in all human beings. It may be a response of the human organism having the function of promoting survival by pressuring the envier to improve his living conditions. Perhaps it also encourages the envier to seek the destruction of the envied, thus increasing the envier's own chances of survival and reproduction in an environment having restricted opportunities to survive and reproduce.

Straight as an error — The motive behind all the Reds' piously described terroristic acts is the their fundamental and undeviating hatred of, and contempt for, "straights." Their emotions find expression in actions to attack and destroy all humans different from themselves (which in fine comes down to all humans *except* themselves). This motivation is a perversion of the inherent and usually beneficial human urge to better oneself by finding new and better ways to do things, to excel, and to improve status by making beneficial contributions to society.

It is this complex of envy and complete self-absorption which causes the enviers to reject all normally accepted codes of conduct, and to denigrate them. By completely devaluing these standards, they proclaim that their own failure to attain success through normal channels (which they recognize is impossible because of their own limited talents and extreme character defects) is not only of no consequence but is, in fact, a great achievement, greater than anything their parents have accomplished.

Envy in politics — Schoeck (1966) contrasts the use of envy by socialists as compared to its use by other kinds of politicians: "The decisive difference is this: the non-socialist politicians will always direct the voter's envy or indignation against certain excesses ... of individual politicians, but he will not pretend, either to himself or to his followers that, as soon as he is in power his aim will be a society in which everyone will be more or less equal, and that there will be no more envy." Further, "If a politician ... wishes to make use of the impulse of envy among those electors who may support him, he will find it particularly expedient to devise a plank in his platform that can ostensibly solve a host of problems by one simple legislative act. If this also happens to involve a complex matter upon which not even experts are agreed, nearly every advantage lies with the assailant."

Schoeck (1966) tells us, " ... the envious man does not so much want to have what is possessed by others as yearn for a state of affairs in which no one would enjoy the coveted ... style of life ... to put to shame those more highly placed than themselves." If this is correct, and it seems to be a precise description of some reds of public notoriety, it explains why there is so much destruction, vandalism, and pillage accompanying most of the red demonstrations. It tends to explain why these people live in squalor often exceeding that of welfare recipients, even though they have family resources sufficient to pay for a luxurious lifestyle.

Crosland (1957) presented his readers with the following opinion, " ... one of the rare cases in which a socialist discusses explicitly why his party invariably chooses for leverage the envy of the lower classes, even when these have long been comparatively prosperous ... [He] attributes the envy of Labour's financially emancipated protégés to the residual inequality between the highly educated products of schools for the elite and those with only average education."

A Psychotherapist's Viewpoint

Schoeck (1966), in a section entitled *Love for the distant as an alibi for lack of relation*, "A number of leading figures have ... explained their abstract social idealism and their struggle for social justice and radical reform movements as a result of their inability to establish uncomplicated, natural and relaxed contact with their neighbour. This ... lack of contact — a legitimate problem in psychotherapy — probably leads to distant and generalized human love in many intellectuals . . . Perhaps some who seek to establish overseas philanthropy as an institution know at bottom how much the patron and philanthropist is generally hated when his protégés are at close quarters. Can it be that distant love is an endeavour to escape from the practice of neighbourly philanthropy?"

Yes, it can be. The wealthy philanthropist does not want a crowd of dirty indigents swarming around him to give him thanks — that was not the reason he sent in the check. Nor does he want to know how many African peasants he has saved from starvation — so far as the donor is concerned, they can all die, and good riddance! He wants the charitable organization's management to give a banquet with his colleagues as paying participants and himself sitting at the head table as the guest of honor. He wants to see newspaper and magazine articles about his wealth and generosity. He wants his opinions solicited in interviews on public service television or radio. He may want an honorary Ph.D. degree. But, what he emphatically does *not* want is the bothersome, socially worthless, gratitude of the canaille.

Above all, he wants to spread the word that he has outspent his friends and associates, and so has proven himself to be superior to them.

Egalitarianism Never Was a Bolshevik Goal

"Egalitarianism has its noble side . . . but it is very easily perverted to envy, and socialistic propaganda has lost no opportunity of so perverting it" (Brogan 1948).

" . . . André Gide's autobiographical confession in which he tells how he was cured of his prejudice in favor of communism in the Soviet Union, when, on his journey there in 1936, he did not find the hoped-for equality but discovered how extreme was the discrepancy between the comforts and pleasures enjoyed by the elite and the circumstances of the simple people." It is absolutely amazing that anyone with access to public documents, or even to conservative news reporters, or to defectors from Russia, could have been deceived about the discrepancy of which Gide spoke. Yet, such people do not want to believe what is contrary to their ingrained value system. It is to Gide's credit that he was finally able to grasp some part of the truth.

"The income figures for top [Soviet] officials (and their expense accounts) are kept secret, but it is known from Soviet sources that in 1959 more than two-thirds of all workers and employees earned an average monthly wage of about 60 new roubles, whereas in 1960 an academic could earn up to 1,500, an opera singer up to 2,000, a plant manager up to 1,000. Even assuming that in 1965 the average monthly wage had risen to 95 roubles, a cautious estimate of the effective income of a top official would be 4,000 roubles, the income differential between the lowest class and the Soviet elite thus probably being 1:40; fifteen years ago it was still 1:100" (Schoeck 1966).

The very percipient Arthur Koestler described why he became antagonistic to the rich at an early age. "Well aware of the family crisis, and torn by pity for my father ... I suffered a pang of guilt whenever they bought me books or toys. This continued later on, when every suit I bought for myself meant so much less to send home. Simultaneously, I developed a strong dislike of the obviously rich, not because they could afford to buy things (envy plays a much smaller part in social conflict than is generally assumed) but because they were able to do so without a guilty conscience. Thus I projected a personal predicament onto the structure of society at large." Koestler did not realize that the attitude he described was also a form of envy.

Schoeck describes the agonizing of Beatrice Webb over the fact that Sidney Webb (both Bea and Sid were prominent English Reds) was going to get a government job paying a very good salary. Her attempts to rationalize this behind a strict egalitarian facade are laughable and ridiculous. They kept the money, of course.

"For the utopia of the egalitarians is invalidated in the first instance by the age-determined hierarchy existing in any society. Tensions and resentments between minors and adults in regard to ownership and discretionary powers are considerable ... "

"The overprivileged youngsters, from California to West Berlin, from Stockholm to Rome, strike out in senseless acts of vandalism as a result of their vague envy of a world of affluence they did not create but enjoyed with a sense of guilt as a matter of course. For years they were urged to compare guiltily their lot with that of the underprivileged abroad and at home. Since the poor will not vanish fast enough for their intense guilt to subside, they can ease their tensions only by symbolic acts of aggression against all that is thought dear and important to the envied elders."

Some Defining Traits of Reds

Within our present society, specimens of the behavioral race, *red*, can be distinguished from other human phenotypes by their exhibition of certain combinations of traits, which are sometimes visible through the distortion applied by the news and entertainment media but at other times are very difficult to ascertain because of the establishment's smoke screen of disinformation. Some touchstones useful for practical, everyday diagnosis by non-professionals are the following observable characteristics.

1. They support abortion on demand, the killing of innocent babies at the whim of a woman who finds it inconvenient to remain pregnant or to bear the baby she is carrying, but they are opposed to the death penalty for *any* crime. Generally, this opposition is universal in scope, regardless of the heinous nature of a crime or the number of victims, though some reds might be willing to allow death sentences if the person being tried has shown insufficient solicitude for the Jews, or abortionists, or blacks.

2. They react with rage (pretended or actual) to any adverse comments about sexual perversions, but they make disparaging, hateful remarks about families with children, especially if there is more than one child in the family, and they consider the traditional family (father, mother, and children) as obsolete or square or even as an abomination.

3. They denigrate and ridicule religious observances, except (sometimes) for those of Judaists, earth worshippers, Wiccans, Black Muslims, Quakers, etc. They are particularly contemptuous of

conservative Christians and consider their beliefs to be unworthy of respect or even of tolerance.

4. They tend toward homosexuality, or in a few cases bisexuality, and pederasty is not considered to be a deviation of any importance, unless it is committed by Catholic prelates. They often have a strong attachment to their mothers, an intense love which may show up in their writing. The homosexual reds are, as often as not, married — a marriage of convenience — and the spouses of male homosexuals may have a child. They consider the treatment of AIDS victims to be one of the most (if not *the* most) important responsibilities of government, with "free" treatment (however much it may cost the taxpayer) for every sufferer, even though the "victim" may have recklessly exposed himself to the disease during hundreds of unprotected sexual contacts and may refuse to consider changing his sexual practices either during treatment or subsequent to successful treatment. They think the government should give top priority to the development of a *vaccine* to prevent the transmission of AIDS, and they would give these projects precedence over all other health research, including, for example, investigations of means for preventing birth defects or rehabilitating paraplegics.

5. Many of them are zoophilists, often to such an extent they are willing to admit that, in a contest for survival, they would always favor animals over mankind, and it appears that some of them would even give a similar preference to the vegetable kingdom if push came to shove. The homosexual's totemic poodle or teddy bear is, of course, a cliché.

6. Most of them approve of the unfettered use of any kind of "recreational drug" at any time, in any quantity, by any person regardless of age or physical condition. They often profess to believe that the solution to the drug problem is for the government to supply everyone with all the drugs and drug application instruments they ask for — beginning with the furnishing of free hypodermic needles. Generally, however, they consider tobacco usage to be unacceptable, and alcoholic beverages to be laughably square. Not only do they wish to have drugs supplied free to all applicants, but they are in favor of using

public funds to support the recovery and rehabilitation treatments necessary to correct the damage done to the bodies of addicts by the free drugs they have consumed.

Conclusion

Psychopathy, envy, and sadism are three suites of characteristics that often can be found in Reds. All possible combinations can be seen in the behavior of various prominent activists. The traits may be genetically determined, but are undoubtedly modified in their expression by environmental pressures and internal dissonances. A predisposition to exhibit a particular combination of these behaviorisms may be present at birth. It is likely that none of the syndromes can be "cured," by any treatment known at present.

chapter twenty-two

COUNTERING TERRORISM

The material presented in the previous chapters strongly suggests that there exists in most, if not all, cultural and ethnic segments of significant size a certain percentage of individuals who have (and who will have throughout their lives) an instinctive hatred of their fellow human beings. We have called these persons, "reds," and pointed out they have been responsible for horrendous crimes against civilization.

It is the author's contention that the type of behavior exhibited by the mobs which played such a prominent role in the French Revolution, in the Bolshevik Revolution, and in many other less dramatic periods of chaos and destruction, is characteristic of a subset of humanity which is always present (at varying levels) in any population of substantial size. Persons of this type remain more or less quiescent when the forces of law and order are efficient, but they inevitably coalesce and perform violent and destructive acts when the population is released from all (or nearly all) restraint. These outbreaks will occur repeatedly when conditions provide an opportunity for the potential reds to operate without hindrance, and they will increase in severity with each repetition.

We have found strong support for our hypothesis in the activities of those persons who designate themselves, "Communists." Various offshoots of this philosophy are composed of individuals who call themselves anarchists, nihilists, and Bolsheviks, but they exhibit very few differences in their actual behavior, no matter how much the printed and spoken tenets of their faiths may differ. For convenience, we have called adherents to these (and similar) philosophies, "Reds."

The Causative Agent

The author contends that humans of the "red" phenotype differ from constructive members of civilization because their conduct is driven by a deeply maliferous suite of genetically controlled traits. All "races" include some persons exhibiting this type of behavior, but it is possible that the percentages of the genotype vary in different ethnic groups. It is conceivable that certain racial characteristics will be found to be closely linked to the genotype in question.

Traits causing this type of destructive behavior may have contributed survival value at sometime during the evolving of mankind. They might still be of value if coupled to an ability to excel in constructive endeavors. The real danger to humanity occurs when the urge to excel, the desire to be superior to one's fellow man, is not accompanied by the ability to perform constructive acts or is not tempered by a willingness to wait for a considerable time until an opportunity to excel occurs.

For those who cannot wait — the reds — excellence is thought to be achieved by degrading all competitors. They believe they become superior by lowering the level of competition, by destroying and killing those who are successful or even those who might, in some fashion, interfere with the rather simplistic rewards being sought by the reds.

It is characteristic of the red that he wants it all, he wants it now, and he is absolutely sure he deserves anything he can get. His desires are crude, even juvenile, and can easily result in destructive actions even when a few moments thought would show the value of patience. He is suggestible because he has great faith in his own ability (or "luck") and cannot apply ordinary standards of evaluation to the proposals of controllers who are as evil as he is but who are much more sophisticated in their methods of operation.

Furthermore, we have suggested that humans of this type, "reds," will continually increase in number relative to the number of normal individuals if preventative measures are not taken.

This increase will occur because of the reds' inhibitory influences on the reproductive rates of normal individuals, and their harmful (often lethal) effects on existing examples of the productive phenotype. If culturally and biologically productive persons wish to survive unharmed until they can bring their children through these perils to maturity, it is imperative that measures be taken to neutralize and isolate the reds. This will not be an easy task, and it will may require some tactics which are not politically correct.

Because the Red programs — whatever their names or professed goals — are inherently nonproductive and parasitical, they cannot prosper, or even exist, without a host civilization to feed on. Over a period of time, the host is inevitably destroyed and the Reds are left without means of support, at which time they return to their semi-civilized resting phase (we could call it the spore stage of the disease), feeding on weaker members of their own phenotype or on isolated remnants of the advanced culture they have destroyed. Eventually, the pitiful remnants of the destroyed cultures, mutated to give resistant forms, may be able to put up green shoots through the ruins, flowering into a productive and healthful society that is destined, as before, to contribute its life blood to the red fungus.

Making the Diagnosis

The same type of compulsion that motivated the demonstrators carrying posters of Ho Chi Minh, Stalin, and Marx a few decades ago is still alive and well on the campuses of IHE, in the alleys of San Francisco, and on the lush estates of Silicon Valley plutocrats.

We can see motivations such as the desire to gain excitement (sexual, drugs, etc.), to gain notoriety and/or social status by attracting media attention, and to gain wealth by looting. But at the base of it all (never acknowledged and seldom recognized) is plain vanilla, old-as-the-world, sadism — a hatred that seeks expression in maiming, killing, and degrading someone else, anyone else. Associated with the latter syndrome is the joy the red obtains from the destruction of property, totally absent of any financial gain or status enhancement.

Since we have reached the conclusion that there exists within the human community a cohort of individuals bearing a engrained suite of behaviorisms that can result, if sufficient opportunities develop, in the murder of millions of human beings and the enslavement of hundreds of millions, we are justified in recommending extreme measures to correct the disease.

There are certain characteristics of the environment/culture that can be manipulated so as to reduce the numbers of, and moderate the baneful influence of, the reds. These can be temporary or long lasting; some can be applied locally, while others have a systemic effect. A few examples will be discussed, but it should be obvious that all possibilities could not be dealt with, even if the author was prepared to fill a volume many times the size of this one, but a few possible approaches will be described.

A Serious Case

The Bolshevik-orchestrated plague that began to infect the world about 1918, and which is still operative, is a mutation of the previously described cultural "fungus" or disease which had its origin in the earliest forms of the human species. It has existed continuously throughout history, but it assumed various forms in different ages. It is frequently represented by more than one strain in the same place at the same time.

It would be unduly sanguine of the author to imagine that any single action or program recommended by him, or by anyone, would terminate or even substantially reduce the deteriorative effects on civilization of this cultural disease. Instead of providing a quick cure, the author will be satisfied if he can convince some of his readers to take measures which will: (1) protect themselves and their families from most of the maleficent influences of Reds, and (2) assist (inosfar as it is in their power) other persons and groups who want to institute programs for destroying Red organizations and inactivating Red agitators.

A Brief Remission

A false sense of security has been generated by the collapse of the Soviet Union. We must realize Reds are still very much with us. A foolish complacency would be fatal. We must use the tools which proved to be successful in neutralizing the Soviet menace as weapons for combatting the constantly re-plenished destructive forces pouring out of our colleges and universities. It appears to the author that recent international developments have provided openings for red activity that could not have been predicted ten years ago — not foreseen, that is, except by those at the center of the world conspiracy.

Amputation and Cauterization

Reds perform many illegal actions which would lead to long prison sentences or in some cases execution, for ordinary (non-protected) criminals. Members of the Weatherman and the Symbionese Liberation Army (discussed in a preceding chapter) committed just about every heinous crime one could imagine, yet few of them ever served a lengthy prison term and none of them, so far as the record shows, was ever executed. The most unlucky, or least useful, members of the group may have been assessed a small fine or spent a few months in jail.

They were protected in various ways. Perhaps the judges and prosecuting attorneys had a fellow feeling for these lawbreakers — the sympathy one crook feels for another. More likely, they received protection, if not encouragement, from the many reds in the political arena. After all, they could call on the Castro sympathizers, the Mao agents, and the remnants of the Soviet apparatus for help, and these movements still have their agents at high levels in the state and federal governments, in the media, and (especially) in academia.

This type of privilege for anarchist/communist lawbreakers must be brought to an end. One step in the corrective program should be to increase the penalties for treasonous activities, and for actions which disrupt the lives and harm the bodies or the property of productive, law abiding citizens.

Severe ills require strong medicine. Not an aspirin — amputation and cauterization are suitable remedies for the red infection. The death sentence, with prompt execution thereafter, will teach the remaining would-be murderers a very valuable lesson. This requires some rethinking of objections that have been made to the death penalty.

The death penalty — Executing a criminal has one unquestionably beneficial result: the subject never again commits any crime. We could perhaps add another: he can never, by his mere presence, freely moving among the living after committing some horrible crime, suggest to potential criminals that they, too, may commit such crimes without suffering the extreme penalty. And, make no mistake about it, death is a fate much more dreaded than a so-called life sentence, no matter what a Dr. Goody Two-shoes has to say about it on the TV talk shows.

Among the many bromides used by those arguing for abolition of the death penalty is: "How many innocent people are you willing to see executed?" — or, sometimes "What degree of failure are you willing to accept?" The correct answer is: "Whatever it takes to save hundreds of innocent future victims." Another answer might be: "How many dead Islamics, innocent of *any* crime, are you willing to see killed to protect the boundaries of Zionist Israel?"

Perhaps the answer to the latter will be: "Oh, but that's a war, that's different." To which non-answer, we might respond, "Then, you were willing to accept as many dead Vietnamese as possible in order that the US might win that war?" Their clever repartee, will be, as usual, "You are antisemitic and a denier of the holocaust!"

The risk of collateral deaths of innocent persons is accepted as a matter of course when legislation is being considered for environmental projects or for legitimatizing "recreational pleasures." Examples are:

1. Homosexuality, performance aspects of which are the principal facilitators of AIDS and several other fatal diseases are legitimatized and even encouraged by persons and organizations at the highest level. In fact, homosexuality seems to be the lifestyle of choice, if we accept the dicta of the establishment media. Yet this plague — potentially the most deadly in history — is building up because absolutelly no publicity discourages the actions which lead to infection.

2. Tobacco use is known to confer a high risk of premature death, yet federal, state, and local governments accept tobacco use in order to garner taxes, the money then being spent for purposes totally

unconnected with health.

3. As a result of poor tactics by weak, lazy, or venal prosecutors, persons with unquestionable criminal tendencies, violent and dishonest from their earliest childhood, remain unconfined (in every sense of that word) to prey upon weak, innocent, and gullible persons. There is a risk, which is not small, additional murders being committed by released prisoners, or by charged persons who are released on bail, etc. Yet many do-gooders promote early release, and other kinds of amnesty programs. Many collateral deaths occur from these practices, as well as from the release of multiple killers because of technicalities in their trials.

4. Mandatory vaccination/immunization for all sorts of diseases, some of them rare or virtually non-existent, always lead to a certain number of deaths or permanent damage because of allergic reactions, or actual infections with the disease (when live virus types of vaccines are used). Yet, very few people suggest that vaccinations should cease because of these collateral deaths. Producers of the vaccines know how to promote their product, and they are able to prevent any substantive discussion of the dangers involved in the widespread use of their products.

5. Everyone who drives a car takes the risk of causing accidents which will kill or maim one or more people. And, cautious driving will not prevent all of these deaths, some of which are due simply to being in the wrong place at the wrong time. Yet, no one suggests that motor vehicles should be outlawed because of these collateral deaths of innocent people.

6. Virtually all auto safety measures — seat belts, exploding bags, child car seats, etc. — lead to a certain amount of collateral deaths because of inappropriate use, or accidents of types which turn the safety feature into a death trap. Still, we have state laws mandating the use of these devices, and few if any of the affected persons complain. Activists and politicians ignore these collateral deaths, partly because of the large amounts of money coming to them from manufacturers of the products and from patent licensors.

Many other examples of the willing acceptance of collateral deaths by those who oppose all executions could be given. We are entitled to assume that it is not really the thought of the possible execution of an "innocent" person which concerns these activists. They act because they mindlessly accept the preaching of a leader who is being paid by a foundation which receives money from international criminal networks or from persons who wish to destabilize the community), or because they are victims of self-righteous delusions, perhaps based on spiritual tenets having no scientific validity. Some of the usual publicity hounds will also be found among the placard bearers, the slogan chanters, and candle lighters. In addition, we may find sadistic psychopaths who wish to expose as many persons as possible to the ravages of criminal killers, because the thought of others suffering gives them satisfaction.

Supposed examples of wrongful convictions — Activists who oppose the death penalty usually supply themselves with lists of people who have been "erroneously" convicted of capital murder. Typically, some of their exemplars will have been put to death before their "innocence" was "proven." Evidence for a wrongful guilty verdict may appear in the following versions (which do not exhaust all the possibilities):

1. Another person confesses that he is the guilty person after the conviction of someone else. This situation can result from one of the following scenarios.

1.1. The confessor has been suborned by someone acting for the convicted party. A shyster whose client is obviously guilty of a capital crime locates a convict serving multiple life terms, or perhaps a convict having a terminal illness, and convinces him to confess to the crime. The attorney provides all the information the convict needs to support a credible confession, and may plant evidence confirming the confession. The confessor will usually be someone who is already serving multiple life terms and who has no hope of parole unless he receives outside assistance. He will be promised money for himself or members of his family, and possibly guaranteed legal representation on other charges. Perhaps the confessor is already under death sentence and has lost hope of reprieve, and is willing to save another (guilty) person as a revenge on society.

1.2. The confessor finds imprisonment intolerable and looks upon execution as a method of committing suicide.

1.3. Many people are driven by some inner demon to confess to all sorts of crimes. It has been said that the more heinous the crime, the more persons will confess to it. The desire to attract attention is part of the motive, but there is in some cases a masochistic urge which will only be satisfied by extreme self-degradation and humiliation.

2. Persons executed for murdering someone who later appears (or is alleged to have appeared) among the living. In modern times, this is must be extremely rare, if it happens at all. Convicting a person in the absence of identified human remains as evidence of death of the victim must be next to impossible.

3. Legal maneuverings tending to show that the executed person was convicted on evidence that was faked or misinterpreted, or perjured testimony, or as a result of inadequate legal representation. Often these cases are reopened after years or even decades of inactivity, when witnesses are no longer available, evidence has disappeared or become damaged, etc. In these cases, the new claims must be examined with the greatest rigor to detect substitution and perjury. It must be remembered that claims of poor jury performance long after conviction must be weighed against the jury's opinions at the time of conviction. If data are missing, they must be assumed to have been as originally claimed. Few, if any capital murder verdicts should be reversed as a result of claims of jury malfeasance or misfeasance.

4. Claims that the executed person was prosecuted by a biased attorney, convicted by a biased jury, or sentenced by a biased judge. These claims are mere propaganda and have nothing to do with guilt or innocence.

Evidence that executions reduce murders — There are many studies from reputable sources that show executions of murderers reduce the murder rates in subsequent periods, within the state affected.

In a brief summary of work done by scientists at the U of Houston,

Cloninger and Marchesini (2002) say: "... all reveal statistical evidence that is consistent with the deterrent hypothesis ... Our study suggests two further conclusions that are supported by evidence: 1. An execution moratorium may result in more-than-expected homicides over the affected period and 2. Executions have a deterrent effect over and above that of life sentences. Depending upon the variant of our model used, the number of additional (unexpected) homicides that occurred over the approximate 12 month de facto moratorium in TX ranged from 150 to 250. The court-ordered hiatus deferred the scheduled executions of 14 death row inmates. Simple math suggests that anywhere from 11 to 18 unexpected homicides occurred for each deferred execution ... To date, the scientific studies that find evidence of a deterrent effect of executions have gone largely unreported by the media. Readers of the nation's periodicals would be well-served if they were provided with a dose of scientific evidence along with the steady diet of often uninformed journalistic and personal opinion."

David McCarthy (2002) points out that "Most of the arguments about the efficacy of death penalties are concerned only with 'general deterrence' — whether or not the imposition of capital punishment on a convicted murderer will deter others from committing murder. Capital punishment serves another, and in my mind more compelling purpose: 'specific deterrence' — when a convicted murderer is executed, he or she will never kill again. I maintain a file of convicted murderers who either parole and kill again, escape and kill again or kill other inmates or prison guards. The file, sadly, is very, very thick. I maintain that had those convicted murderers been executed when they should have been, that is after obligatory appeals had been exhausted, those victims would in all likelihood be alive today. We as a society have an obligation to protect the citizenry from the depredations of those who would murder in cold blood."

Gow (1995) recalls that C.S. Lewis said that persons who make excuses for vicious criminals are denying that criminals are rational beings who possess the inherent capacity to make free choices and judgements. They are, instead, saying that human beings are no better than animals, that human beings are victims of their environments or biological appetites.

A Catholic cleric and scholar, Malachi Martin, wrote that strict justice demands that we execute someone who has committed premeditated murder. "Punishment, if it is to be just, must be proportionate to the crime committed . . . St. Thomas Aquinas made it clear that the only fair and proportionate punishment for murder is the death penalty" (Gow 1995).

There is plenty of money flowing into the anti-capital punishment campaigns. Some of it comes from tax-advantaged foundations such as Open Society Foundation, an organization run by George Soros, an immigrant from Hungary who has developed mutual funds with hundreds of millions of dollars in assets in spite of having no acknowledged connections, education, or experience in this kind of operation. There are those who believe that Soros' funds, or some of them, are essentially money laundering operations benefitting international narcotics traffickers. If that is true, there are obvious reasons why Open Society Foundation would want to protect its enforcers from possible death penalties.

A study conducted by a commission showed that the vast majority of death-penalty reversals result from procedural mistakes made during sentencing, long after guilt has been determined, and have nothing to do with guilt or innocence. More than 95% of these error claims are made about sentencing procedures — which took effect after the guilt of the defendant had been settled. In some cases, the Supreme Court issues a ruling that is applied retroactively, thus nullifying a death sentence. This study effectively negates all of the death-penalty opponents' propaganda about the danger of executing innocent persons because of mistaken verdicts.

Furthermore, the increased sophistication of forensic procedures, such as identification based on DNA, increase the certainty that only the guilty will be convicted and face the possibility of a death sentence.

It is important to remember that re-trying a case because of a technical error of perhaps insignificant degree, means that both evidence and witnesses may be lost, or lose their certainty due to the passage of time, and the guilty person may be released to kill again, strictly because of a technicality discovered by a clever and unscrupulous lawyer.

Life without parole? — A sentence of "life without parole" never means "life without chance of parole." Many persons who have been sentenced to "life without parole" are walking the streets today. The verdict, the sentence, and every other aspect of the trial can be re-examined and reversed on a technicality.

We will not at this time discuss the terrible burden on the taxpayer of supporting these murderers and financing their numerous appeals assisted by tax-advantaged lawyers.

For some reason, criminals of the most debased and evil kind, are often allowed to continue their lives in protected environments called prisons, but (for them) more like country clubs, with unlimited sex and drugs for those who can pay for them. When the furor over their actions has died down, they can be released on parole or as the result of an appeal.

It is obvious that many such persons are being protected by very high officials who have the clout to cause these things to happen. Carreyrou (2001) mentions the case of "Carlos The Jackal," whose real name may or may not be Ilich Ramirez Sanchez. This Venezuelan, who committed many murders, has, ostensibly, been in a Paris prison since 1994. While in this prison, he had many visits (Carreyrou says, three times a week) from his lawyer, a woman named Isabelle Coutant-Peyre. Love blossomed, and they plan to get married. A slight impediment to their plans exists in that both of them are already married. Mrs. Coutant-Peyre says The Jackal's killings don't bother her because she believes in the same causes he does, namely in the communist ideal.

Dealing with Hostage Situations

Terrorists have learned to expect a bargaining period when they take hostages, this gives them a tremendous advantage when negotiating with law enforcement authorities. They get intense media attention, sometimes for days on end, gaining what is for them more important than meat and drink, while they lose nothing since on any given day they can bargain for their freedom on the same or better terms than they could have had the day before. Similarly, they can kill some hostages without feeling they have closed the door to freedom, even though their perception may not be entirely correct.

The strategy that should be put into effect by counter-terrorist troops when hostages are taken, is to surround the place of imprisonment, gradually close in (under cover, of course), and when and if the terrorists start to kill prisoners, charge the fortress and kill every terrorist found inside, man or woman, young or old, wounded or whole, repentant or not.

This will prove a very salutary lesson to those romantics in the terrorist ranks who feel they have nothing to lose. Seeing a few blasted and burned terrorists in the news videos, and having no live heroes emerging from the fray, will give the publicity hounds in the terrorist ranks an opportunity to rethink the risk-and-rewards balance of their position. They are willing to give all to their cause — but, maybe, on second thought, not *quite* all. A mangled corpse is not a very romantic role model.

An even more convincing tactic, but probably one that has no chance of being implemented in these days in which statesmen have been replaced by human marshmallows and violets, is to bring imprisoned and recalcitrant members of the mob to the scene, and shoot them one by one on an announced timetable as soon as any hostage has been killed or wounded by the terrorists. When all captive terrorists have been killed, and no surrender has occurred, proceed to storm the citadel.

Inoculate Against Further Infection

Although the sources of infection, i.e., the genotype that may exist in every population of significant size, are so numerous and widespread that a complete extirpation of them is impossible, there are some protective measures that might be helpful in reducing their opportunities to further infect civilization.

The business of rioting — All riots are organized to some extent, even though on-paper planning may have been non-existent. It is unlikely that a collection of juvenile thugs could be induced to spend their own time and money traveling to a distant point on the promise of a pre- or post-demonstration orgy (which they can find nearer home with the expenditure of much less time and money)

The collecting of suggestible workers who'll work cheap, the organizing of them into groups, and the selecting of disposable platoon leaders, argues the existence of a plan and a director of that plan, plus a considerable amount of funding and/or provisioning. The corporals leading the frenzied mob may or may not be receiving cash compensation. There must be provisions for legal representation of arrested conspirators, media liaison, and the like. In many larger or more violent demonstrations there are intermediate leaders who must be compensated in a material way for their work. The top layer of management, which may consist of a single person, is often relatively expensive, though sometimes he or she is on a salaried basis.

Generating riots is, in fact, a business in many ways like other businesses, and there are people who work at it full time. Their cover is almost always a type of "charity" or non-profit foundation, so in every riot you can see your tax dollars at work.

Stopping the non-profits' subsidy — Some of these organizations are registered as nonprofits, i.e., charitable organizations. This format allows them certain tax benefits which ultimately must be compensated for by increases in the payments made by law-abiding taxpayers. In addition, contributions to such organizations will normally be deductible from taxable income, shifting still more government expenses on to the good guys. What is still more obnoxious, is that many of these organizations are housed in campus buildings, provided campus services, and staffed by persons at least partially paid by institutions of higher education, all of this supported by grants and other money transfers that were never intended to support public enemies.

There can be little doubt that many of the placard-wavers, slogan shouters, and brick throwers we see at major demonstrations are indigent persons receiving unemployment benefits, disability payments, student grants, free medical treatment, social security money, and free transportation, all of which funds come out of the public purse. It is possible that some of these persons have temporary release permits from jails and mental institutions, to which they return after their public service activities. It may indeed be possible that some of these people are using computers in their jail cells to conduct their nonprofit business and spread their inflammatory propaganda.

The public should at the very minimum be able to learn the names, addresses, and affiliations of these blatant outlaws, but such information is unobtainable, even for persons who have been arrested (unless the crime is major). Some of the demonstrators no doubt use their youth as a defense against criminal prosecution — it is essential that their parents or other custodial persons be held responsible for their charges' actions and, in addition, they should be prosecuted for child endangerment if they fail to keep their children under control.

There are many avenues to pursue in bringing the organizers to justice and to mulct the financial backers (including nonprofit organizations and colleges) of both the actual costs for property damage and a calculated amount for the police activities. In addition, we should hold all persons and organizations who gave services, drugs, transportation, shelter, food, and placards and the like fully responsible for losses due to the actions of their protégés.

There seems to be a real potential for the use of RICO in recovering treble damages from persons in the background of these actions, even though many of the controllers have their offices, or their homes, in foreign countries. I foresee the possibility of applying criminal charges — including murder — against persons who assist in demonstrations and other activites which lead to the death from any cause of persons participating in the demonstrations, or who combat the rioters, or even of bystanders who were killed by ancillary events.

Other Sources of Infection

The red community includes numerous phantom clubs and wanna-be organizations that exist only in the minds of their originators. The Internet enables hopeless misfits to pretend to have, if not a following, at least a few comrades, and to probe for publicity and human contact by placing their febrile gibberish on public display. It is roughly the same urge which causes some men and women to webcast nude photos of themselves. In either case the result is both repulsive and sad. Although such persons do not deserve our sympathy, they are unlikely to cause much damage.

There are, however, a few anarchist organizations that appear to have the potential for gaining the support of enough dedicated accomplices to complete projects that may result in the death or injury of numerous persons and the destruction of large amounts of property. Protective and punitive measures should be taken against such groups. There are several legal actions that concerned citizens may use to put these potential criminals out of business, but space is insufficient to describe them in detail here.

Eliminate campuses — Campus-based institutions of higher education are the buboes of the plague that threatens to destroy civilization, the source of the infection that is killing America's spirit — that is, in fact, enslaving and degrading the world.

From the earliest examples, colleges and universities have sought to form isolated and self-governing enclaves, protected from interference by civil authorities. Their prototype was the medieval monastery or nunnery, where laws and regulations affecting ordinary citizens were inoperative, or at least held in abeyance. The justification for these special privileges was, first, that the academy had a divine right to exist, and secondly, that the learning imparted to the students had a beneficial effect on the nation — that IHE were needed to train future leaders. As civilizations became more technologically oriented, the IHE assumed the role of research institutes and arrogated to themselves the status of fons et origo of scientific truth.

Such critical conditions require heroic remedies. For starters, we might try the following steps.

1. Eliminate the current system of campus-based institutions of higher education. Even if we leave philosophical matters at one side, surely, even the most obtuse individual can see the economic inadequacies of academia.

Current colleges and universities are the most inefficient systems one could possibly imagine. Replace the existing institutions with a world-wide, fully accredited, distance teaching network available to all, teaching every subject for which there is a demand, with classes available day and night, at a fee of a few dollars per *course* (not, per class session). Such systems were described in the books, *Twilight of the Universities* and *The Virtual Campus* by F X Foulke-ffeinberg.

Many commentators have written about the many deficiencies and inefficiencies of our system of higher education. Some of them have suggested remedies for these problems. It is characteristic of most of these solutions that they concentrate on superficial details or on local or isolated phenomena. They seek to treat the symptoms, not the disease.

The first step in devising a permanent cure is to recognize that the central problem is the university itself, not a ridiculous course at Yale, the suppression of a student newspaper at Dartmouth, a treasonous professor at Amherst, or a perverted chancellor at Oxford. Diffusing our energies by attacking small, localized, and possibly irremediable behavior leaves the focus of the infection in place, and it is only a matter of time (and, usually, a very short period of time) before the remnants regroup and multiply the original offense many times over.

This octopus has ten thousand tentacles, cutting off one or a dozen will not seriously discommode it — we must find a potion that stops the circulation. Money is the lifeblood of academia. Money pours into the university from many sources: taxes of a hundred different kinds, donations, fees, and earnings from tax-protected real estate and businesses owned by the institutions. And, always there is a cry for increased funding — more is never enough. Vast sums are spent in supporting a mostly idle, often incompetent, and usually vicious group of employees and in promoting a group of causes that few taxpayers would ratify separately, if they knew what they were paying for. Much of the income is simply lost or stolen, going to recipients that no auditor will ever be able to identify.

The number of actual votes available to the academies in an open election involving large segments of the population is rather small. Most members of the general public do not benefit from *any* of the higher education measures submitted to popular vote, and, if this can be brought to their attention, they will vote against them. But, by far the greater amount of money moving into the hands of the academy is several steps removed from any vote of the public or even of elected officials.

The influence of the academy upon politics in this country, and in most countries, is very great. Attempting to reform academia by political methods is likely to be ineffective, market-based measures — economic pressures — are available to the populace and might be effective. The author has advocated for several years the replacement of campus-based higher education with distant teaching methods (basically, use of the Internet) to replace all classroom, campus-located, colleges and universities. Complete details can be found in the books by F X Foulke-ffeinberg: *Twilight of the Universities* and *The Virtual Campus*. If the general public would use the methods described in these books, and would encourage private industry to enter the education marketplace, much of the current campus-based activities would become too expensive to continue in operation. If the customer base of academia is significantly reduced, their demands upon politicians will eventually become too great for the latter to countenance, and without a political base, academia will shrivel away. Politicians should realize that the effect of universities on votes cast is much smaller than the institutions try to claim. The IHE make a lot of noise, but their actual force is almost negligible.

Result: The elimination of protected enclaves within which the professors and administrators of the current higher education system can congregate and hide from examination by potential students and their sponsors, and from oversight by government agencies and citizen oversight groups, will bring to light many of the existing abuses and inefficiencies. This information will soon bring calls from the populace to close down the campus and, as a result, greatly reduce the pool of talent which the reds can use to increase their ranks of leaders and followers.

2. Legislators and courts must be imbued with the sense that the most important purpose of the law, the spirit (or philosophy) which underlies both the Declaration of Independence and the original Constitution of the United States, is the protection of the persons and properties of citizens, all citizens equally and that cultural architects working under a red system of values, or any system of values, are enemies of the people.

This move will remove the protection of the laws (laws respected by useful citizens and ignored by reds) from the existing cohort of reds.

3. The removal of harmful members of society by whatever methods are necessary, perhaps exile, imprisonment, or other means.

Breaking laws for a cause — Many persons believe they are entitled to defy laws that they consider unjust. One result of this misapprehension is that speeding fines cover a large part of the operating expenses of some small towns. Certain environmental activists have the same philosophy, but they often get away with just about everything short of murder ... maybe even murder. Their excuse is, they are saving the planet — or some such asinity.

Chaker (2001) describes a group, Rainforest Action Network, whose Executive Director (Christopher Hatch) said, "We believe that when laws are unjust they can be broken in a symbolic way." As a result, they have attempted to prevent a ship from leaving port and blocking the entrance to the San Francisco offices of Mitsubishi Bank. Although the IRS apparently knew of these illegal activities, it recently approved the organization's tax-exempt status. The IRS says, that, to determine which groups qualify, it examines the methods the organizations use to develop and present their views. "Groups must present a factual foundation for their positions, and their presentations should avoid 'substantial use' of disparaging and inflammatory terms."

In a 1975 ruling, the IRS disqualified groups whose primary activities was sponsoring demonstrations at which participants were encouraged to block vehicles or pedestrians, prevent the movement of supplies or disrupt the work of government. The IRS has subsequently granted charity status to a group that boycotted companies selling infant formula in developing countries. In other words, destroying a company's business is OK, if it's for a good cause. "During the Clinton administration, the nonpartisan [sic] Americans United for Separation of Church and State complained about the political activities of certain churches." The IRS investigated 25 organizations, and as a result it denied charitable status to Branch Ministries, a Christian organization which had run newspaper ads encouraging voters to reject Clinton. It is not stated whether any Jewish organizations were investigated, but, if they were, everything was OK — of course.

Creating a Healthy Life Style

The virtue of democracy is that, in the best cases, it enables a constant trade-off of power between the general populace and elected authorities. Of course, this is an idealized concept, always much corrupted in the realization, but even flawed attempts to approach such a goal yield results that are superior in terms of human values when compared to the deliberate abandonment of any possibility of influencing the larger matters. People are imperfect by nature — neither banding them together in large units nor isolating them in smaller units will make them perfect. There is no way to extract perfection from a conglomeration of imperfect examples.

It would perhaps be accurate, but extremely offensive to the delicate flowers of peace among our readers, to answer the question, "How can we defeat the terrorists among us," by the biverbal prescription, "Kill them." In the long run such a process would result in a net saving of lives and property, and might save our republic, but the application of such strong medicine is always delayed until the terminal stages of the disease, and sometimes the patient does not survive. Vide France before 1789 and Russia before 1916.

PROSIT

GLOSSARY

Most of the non-specialized terms used in this book conform to definitions found in Webster's New International Dictionary, Second Edition, Unabridged, published in 1961 by G. & C. Merriam & Co.

The jargon of historians in general and of students of international intrigue in particular, like that of most specialists, includes words and phrases differing in their meanings from the way they are intended to be understood in the speech and written communications of most other people. Some of these specialized terms are defined in this glossary to avoid misunderstandings of the quoted authors' intentions.

For the convenience of readers, some terms which are either uncommon or used in a specialized sense are defined here. Acronyms of recent coinage and names of certain organizations are also included.

In general, quotations from books, journals, and other printed materials and from articles found on the Internet have been kept as they appeared in the original publications, and, if their authors adjusted their terminology to make their words politically correct, your guess as to their meaning is as good as mine.

In a few matters of rhetoric, the author's practice differs slightly from common usage and/or from the conventions recommended by many supposedly authoritative reference works. Among these differences are:

• In running lists of nouns, etc., in which items are normally separated by commas but with no comma after the penultimate item, the author chooses to add a comma after the penultimate item.

• In plurals of items identified by numbers or capital letters, conventionally formed by adding an apostrophe followed by an s, the author chooses to add only an s, e.g., 1980s, NCOs.

• In quotations where the present author chooses to emphasize a passage not emphasized by the original author, the material is differentiated by bolding or italicizing the words and is followed by "emphasis added" in square brackets.

• The official abbreviations for names of the States are used instead of the full form, thus: "WA" for Washington state. The letter U is used instead of University for the names of these institutions: thus, "U MD" means the University of Maryland. In quoted passages, however, the style used by the source is usually maintained.

accepted — This evolutionary theory involves the concept that species are not unchanging but have developed and are developing from pre-existing and different species. As a corollary, the ultimate ancestor of a species in many cases may not be definable in charcteristics or time and place. More or less superseded by Darwinism.

active measures — In Soviet terminology, the term means clandestine operations designed to extend Red influence and power around the world. Such measures include psychological warfare, informal penetration, covert action, "dirty tricks," etc. Reds do not recognize sharp distinctions between propaganda and action, political operations and military actions, or overt and covert actions.

analogue — *Biol* 1. An organ similar in function to an organ of another animal or plant, but different in structure and origin. 2. A species in one group corresponding in some particular characters with a member of another group. 3. A species or genus in one country closely related to a species of the same genus, or a genus of the same group, in another country.

animism — (n) The belief that all objects possess a natural life or vitality or are endowed with indwelling souls. The term usually denotes the most primitive and superstitious forms of religion.

anomic — Avoiding meaningful interrelationships with other people; the absence of significant personal ties to other people; a senses of loneliness and alienation. A category of sociology. Antonym is cachetic.

asymptote — *Math.* A line that is the limiting position which the tangent to a curve approaches, as the point of contact recedes indefinitely along an infinite branch of the curve.[two other math. defs. not particularly applicable]

Balkanize — (vt) To separate into hostile units — refers to the inharmonious conditions prevailing in the Balkan States . . . esp. at the time of the Balkan Wars (1912-1913)

beard — In "gay" lingo, an escort or companion of the opposite sex whose presence is intended to conceal a person's homosexual lifestyle, or as bait to attract bisexuals or potential converts to homosexuality.

Bentham, Jeremy — An eccentric English jurist and philosopher (1748-1832), who wrote *Introduction to the Principles of Morals and Legislation.* This 1780 book includes a short section which seems to argue that animals have rights because they are sentient beings who can feel pain. For some reason, animal liberation fanatics feel Bentham's drivel authenticates their own fantasies.

Berserkeley — Refers to the nihilistic attitudes frequently displayed by activist students at Univ. of Calif. Berkeley.

biota — (n) *Biol.* The animal and plant life of a region; flora and fauna, collectively.

Bolshevik, bolshevik — In Russian politics, a member or adherent of the radical wing (the Bolsheviki) of the Social Democratic party, which favored immediate full introduction of the Marxian socialist program, using for this purpose "a dictatorship of the proletariat." This group formed the Third International. Since 1918, the Bolsheviki have called their party, the "Communist" party.

Bolshevism — [capitalized and uncapitalized] Doctrines, tactics, or practices of, or like those of the Bolsheviki; Bolshevist form of government.

cargo cult — describes the behavior of certain Pacific Islanders who, trying to duplicate their favorable experiences during World War II, place crude replicas of airplanes and landing strips near beaches, in the hope they will attract Westerners bearing riches. This behavior been described in the literature as "religions" though there do not appear to be supernatural aspects of the practices.

carnage — 1. Flesh of slain animals or men; a collection of carcasses. 2. Great destruction of life, as in battle; great bloodshed; slaughter; butchery; massacre.

Cheka — the first Soviet organization of the KGB type; in existence from about 1917 until 1922; in full, the name was All-Russian Extraordinary Commission for Combatting Counter-revolution and Sabotage.

CIA — the United States Central Intelligence Agency, a government organization having covert responsibilities; regarded by the Establishment media as the principal culprit in all foreign and most domestic shenanigans that could lead, or have led, to scandalous or disastrous results. They are probably only about half right, but the organization itself is not at all Right.

climate — relates exclusively to long-term weather patterns, as in a given location.

Comintern — The Third International, the principal Soviet organization created to facilitate the spread of communism throughout the world; it was in operation during the period of about 1919 to 1943.

communalism — A system in which communes or other small political units have large powers, as compared with both the individual and the central government; it shades into communism.

Communist International — see *Third International.*

conspiracy — (n) 1. Combination of men for an evil purpose; an agreement between two or more persons to commit a crime (e.g., treason) in concert; a plot. 2. Combination of persons for a single end; a concurrence of general tendency, as of circumstances, to one event; harmonious action. 3. *Law* An agreement, manifesting itself in words or deeds, by which two or more persons confederate to do an unlawful act, or to use unlawful means to do an act which is lawful.

deification — 1 ... exaltation to divine honors. 2. *Mysticism* The causing of one to become a part of the deity; absorption, as of the soul into deity.

Delphian, *or* **Delphic Oracle** — *Greek Religion* The most famous oracle of the ancient world. Originally, it was an oracle of Gaea, the earth.

disinformation — 1. The dissemination of deliberately falsified information, especially when it is supplied by a government or its agent to a foreign power or to the media, with the intention of influencing the policies or opinions of those who receive it; also, the information so supplied. 2. Propaganda designed to distract attention from a program that must be protected from disclosure or inspection.

doyen (*fem* doyenne) — A dean,; the senior member of a body or group, as of a diplomatic corps.

eisegesis Faulty interpretation of a text, as of the Bible, by reading into it one's own ideas.

eminence gris — [if not capitalized] a confidential agent, esp. one exercising unofficial power. [capitalized] A specific historical personage.

enlandisement — Tying a religious tradition to a particular place; treating Judaism as the religion of a particular land, first and foremost.

entomology — the subdivision of zoology that treats of insects; also, a treatise on this subject.

Eretz Yisrael — The Land of Israel, the Holy Land, in contradistinction to everywhere else. Jews tend to avoid referring to the Holy Land as Palestine, and prefer to speak of The Land. In Hebrew, a reference to "our Land," can mean only the Land of Israel.

ethnos — (n) *Sociol.* 1. A group of kindred in clan and tribal organization — contrasted with *demos*. 2. The most primitive natural or kindred group

exegesis — exposition; esp. a critical explanation of a text or portion of Scripture; also, an explanatory note.

experientialism — *Philos* The doctrine that experience is the source of all knowledge. [and the entry indicates *experientalist* is a word].

facultative homosexual — a person who willingly has sexual relations with both males and females.

fallacy of accident — the fallacy which consists in arguing from some accidental character as if it were essential or necessary. Thus: "the food you buy, you eat. You buy raw meat. Therefore you eat raw meat."

fallacy of composition — The fallacy of arguing from premises in which a term is used distributively to a conclusion in which it is used collectively, or of assuming that what is true of each (member of a class, part of a whole, etc.) will be true of all together, as "If my money bought more goods, I should be better off, therefore we should all benefit if prices were lower."

fallacy of division — A fallacy in which a term taken collectively is used as if taken distributively.

First International — the successor organization to *The International Working Men's Association*, a group founded in London in 1864 and dissolved in Philadelphia in 1876. The doctrines of Karl Marx were the basis of its goals.

Gaia/Gaea — In Greek mythology, the earth as a goddess; according to Hesiod, Gaia was the eldest-born of Chaos, and mother of Uranus and the Titans. She was the object of many local cults.

genocide — The systematic destruction of an ethnic group by killing off all its individuals.

genotype — 1. *Biol. & Zool.* The type species of a genus. 2. *Biol.* a The genetic makeup (the genes collectively) of an organism. b Sometimes, a class or group of individuals having a common genetic constitution.

goy — (n) *plural* = goyim. A non-Jew; an animal that, in some superficial aspects, resembles a human.

Green International — an international organization of the peasants of Central European countries united for (ostensibly) social and economic purposes.

homeosis — change of something into the likeness of something else.

homosexual — person who has sexual relations with persons of his or her own gender. See *facultative* homosexual and *obligate* homosexual.

hormone — *Physiol.* A substance, esp. a specific organic product of the cells of one part, as secretin. Transported in the body fluid or the sap of an organism and producing a specific effect on the activity of cells remote from its source; an internal secretion; an autacoid; strictly, one which is excitory, as disting. from *chalone.*

Humanism — [capitalized] A contemporary cult or belief calling itself religious but substituting faith in man for faith in God.

hysteria — 1. *Med.* A psychoneurosis characterized by emotional excitability and often by a great variety of other symptoms. 2. Any outbreak of wild emotionalism, as war hysteria.

IHE — institutions of higher education; i.e., campus-based colleges and universities.

illuminati — (n pl) (singular, illuminatus) 1. Persons in the early church who had received baptism. 2. (cap) 1. Alumbrados. 2 Members of a French sect which arose from the foregoing in 1623, under the name of the *Illuminés*; — known also as *Guerinet* after the adherence of Guérin (1634). 3. Members of a sect (Illuminés) in the south of France, 1722 to 1794. 4. Members of a secret, rationalistic, anti-clerical sect founded in 1776 by Adam Weishaupt, professor of canon law at Ingolstadt; called also, *Perfectibilists.*

INO — the foreign intelligence department of Cheka and successor organizations from about 1920 to 1941; succeeded by INU.

insect powder — A powder for the extermination of insects. Specif., the dried powdered flowers of a Dalmatian herb.

instinct — (n) 1. A tendency to actions which lead to the attainment of some goal natural to the species; natural and unreasoning prompting to action as the web-building instinct of spiders ... not dependent on the individual's previous experience ... distinguished from emotion it is a tendency to an external act affecting the environment, [more complex than a reflex] and [instinct] may involve a conscious impulse to activity. 2. The native or hereditary factor in behavior.

intellectualism — (n) 1. Exclusive devotion to the exercise of intellect or intellectual pursuits. 2. The doctrine that knowledge is derived from pure reason; also, the doctrine that the ultimate principle of reality is reason.

intergrade — (n) An intermediate or transitional form. (vi) To merge gradually one with another through a continuous series of intermediate forms or types.

Jacobin — One of a society of radical democrats in France during the revolution of 1789. The society (originally a loose organization known as the "Club Breton" and meeting at Versailles) was called by its members the "Society of Friends of the Constitution," but by its adversaries its members were called *Jacobins*, from their meeting place, an old Jacobin convent. The society came to be controlled by violent agitators, and, under the leadership of Robespierre, conducted the Reign of Terror. With his fall, their power was broken.

Jewish — Of or pert. to Jews or Hebrews; characteristic of, or resembling, Jews or their customs; Israelitish.

Jewish Agency — a group recognized by the British Mandate in Palestine as representative of Jewish and Zionist interests in Palestine.

jihad (also, jehad) — (n) *Moham.* A religious war against infidels or Mohammedan heretics; also, any bitter war or crusade for a principle or belief.

Judaism — (n) 1. The religious doctrines and rites of the Jews; the Jewish religious system or polity. The chief doctrine of Judaism is the belief in one God and in the mission of the Jews to teach the fatherhood of God, as revealed in the Hebrew scriptures. 2. Conformity to the Jewish rites and ceremonies.

Judaist — (n) One who believes in, or practices, Judaism; a Judaizer; specif., a Jew of the apostolic age who became a Christian but clung to the Jewish ritual, etc.

KGB — "Committee for State Security." The principal Soviet counterintelligence and espionage service.

landgod — a name given by the author to the diffuse and poorly defined god worshipped by persons who regard "land" qua "Land" as a kind of deity, to be fawned upon by preserving it (whatever "it" is) undefiled by human activity, except for recreational use by enlightened persons such as adherents to this philosophy.

Lepidoptera — the order of insects consisting of butterflies and moths.

liberation theology — described by one critic as a "Roman Catholic movement dedicated to correct the social abuses originally caused by the Roman Catholic Church." This definition seems unsatisfactory, however, because the main impetus nowadays is not from rogue RC priests, but from lay people of many denominations. Liberation technology came to mean, or was invented to describe, the inciting by allegedly religious leaders of poor people to use terroristic methods to kill, steal from, and destroy the property of, their more fortunate neighbors.

locative — Emphasizing a particular place, e.g., land, in which what happens is important because it happens in that particular place. The antonym is utopian, that is, noplace, stressing what happens and is relevant everywhere.

logo — in the lingo of commercial packaging designers, this generally refers to the visual impact of the brand name, or company name, as it is embellished by the artist to create a unique piece of selling graphics.

Magnificent Five — The five Cambridge graduates, Anthony Blunt, Guy Burgess, John Cairncross, Donald Maclean, and Kim Philby, who were recruited by Arnold Deutsch (an Austrian Jew) as spies for Russia.

media — (n) In the sense in which the word is used in this volume, it signifies the organizations (including persons and physical plants) which distribute news, information, entertainment, and propaganda to the masses — including (as examples) newspapers, magazines, radio and television broadcasts, and organized entertainments of all kinds (theatrical performances whether live or recorded, sports events, lectures, etc.).

merozoite — (n) A form of spore produced by segmentation of the schizonts of the malarial parasite, and by some other Sporozoa.

metaphor — (n) Use of a word or a phrase literally denoting one kind of object or idea in place of another by way of suggesting a likeness or analogy between them (the ship plows the sea; a volley of oaths). A metaphor may be regarded as a compressed simile, the comparison implied in the form (a marble brow) being explicit in the latter (a brow white like marble).

Middle Ages — the historical period between ancient times and modern times, usually considered to be from about 400 AD to about 1400 AD; also stated as beginning with the fall of the Roman Empire and the "revival of letters."

mindset – (n) The flow or current of one's mind or thoughts; esp., a strong current of the mind in one direction or toward a fixed conclusion; also, a fixed or firm state of the mind.

misdirection — Describes the technique used by a conjurer, swindler, propagandist, etc., whereby the victim's attention is drawn by some stratagem (not necessarily blatantly) to a trivial thing or idea which prevents him from observing an action which his victimizer wishes to conceal.

moral sense — the feeling of the rightness or wrongness of an action or the power of having such feelings.

Mosaic — (adj) Of or pertaining to Moses, the leader of the Israelites, or the institutions or writings attributed to him.

Mossad — Israel's Institute for Intelligence and Special Operations. It gathers information by all necessary methods, legal and illegal, and performs many kinds of clandestine activities, including, it is said, assassinations of persons perceived as being Israel's enemies. Their slogan is, "By way of deception, thou shalt do war."

MVD — this term originally referred to the Russian "Ministry of Internal Affairs," but after mid-1962, "Ministries for the Preservation of Public Order and Safety." The intention (or claim) was that each Soviet "republic" would have its own MVD. In any case, some of the overt functions of these organizations were civil law enforcement and administration of prisons and forced labor camps.

myth — A story, the origin of which is forgotten, that ostensibly relates historical events, which are usually of such character as to serve to explain some practice, belief, institution, or natural phenomenon.

naturalism — *Philos.* The doctrine which expands conceptions drawn from the natural sciences into a world view, denying that anything in reality has a supernatural or other than natural significance, specif. the doctrine that cause-and-effect laws, such as those of physics and chemistry, are adequate to account for all phenomena, and that teleological conceptions of nature are invalid.

naturism — 1. Naturalism. 2. Theory that the earliest religion was nature worship.

one-time pad — a tablet of paper sheets, each sheet of which bears a set of randomly chosen numbers; it is the characterizing tool of a complex cryptographic system much used by Soviet spies.

pellitory of Spain — *Anacyclus pyrethrum,* a southern European plant resembling yarrow. In pharamacology, the root of this plant, used as a sialagogue, etc. The name has also been applied to other plants.

People's Party — In US politics, the term denotes a party formed in 1891, to advocate increasing the stock of money, free coinage of silver, public operation of railroads, telegraphs, etc., an income tax, limitation in ownership of land, etc.

phenotype — *Biol.* 1. A type determined by the visible characters common to a group, as distinguished from their hereditary characters. 2 A group of organisms belonging to such a type.

plaintiff — (n) *Law* 1. One who commences a personal action or suit to obtain a remedy for an injury to his rights — opposed to *defendant.* 2 In recent usage, the complaining party in any litigation.

Populist — (n) In US politics, a member of the People's Party. Also, sometimes used (not cap.) to mean a politician who favors middle class aims.

praxis — (n) 1. action; practice; specif.: *a* Exercise or practice of an art, science, or technical occupation (as opposed to *theory*). *b.* Habit; custom; conventional conduct. 2. An example or form of exercise, or a collection of such examples, for practice, as in grammar; a practical example or model.

primitivism — (n) Belief in the superiority of primitive life, Christianity, etc.; specif., the doctrine, or the practice of the doctrine, that man should return to nature.

propositional revelation — the belief that God has given to mankind factual information in the Bible (i.e., propositions) about Himself; the view that God's special revelation in Scripture has been given in propositional statements.

psychopathy — 1. Mental disorder in general. 2. More commonly, a mental disorder not amounting to insanity or taking the specific form of a psychoneurosis, but characterized by defect of character or personality, eccentricity, emotional instability, inadequacy or perversity of conduct, undue conceit and suspiciousness, or lack of common sense, social feeling, self-control, truthfulness, or persistence. Different psychopathic individuals show different combinations of these traits.

pyrethrin — 1. Either of two physiologically active liquid esters obtained from Dalmatian insect powder; also, any similar artificial ester. 2. A resinous substance obtained from the root of the pellitory of Spain.

Quaker — a member of a religious sect (The Society of Friends) founded in England about 1650. Some present-day branches engage in left wing and internationalist work, and the Society has been a haven for persons who do not care to be associated with a more restrictive religion but wish to be able to believe (or pretend) they are "spiritual" — in this respect it is sort of a poor man's version of the Episcopalian Church. It has long been a congenial haven for draft dodgers and other freeloaders. Alger Hiss and some other spies were Quakers.

race — *Biol.* 1. A group of organisms exhibiting general similarities but not sufficiently distinct from other forms to constitute a species. The distinguishing characteristics are practically constant, and are transmissible to the progeny. As generally understood, the term race is used to include many varieties, but it may also be applied, restrictedly, to a strain within a variety. 2. Sometimes, such a group constituted by individuals of a particular geographical area; — in this sense, equivalent to a geographical subspecies. 3. A group of individuals differing from other members of a species, as in some physiological character, or in adaptability to a type of environment, or the like. *Ethnol,* A division of mankind possessing constant traits, transmissible by descent, sufficient to characterize it as a distinct human type; a permanent variety of the genus

reactionary — (adj) Of, pertaining to, characterized by, or favoring reaction, or return to the older order; as reactionary movements, influences, or legislators. (n) One who favors reaction, esp., one who seeks to undo political changes.

Red — (n) as used in this book, the word as capitalized means a member of, or an adherent to, the Bolshevik/Soviet political system, even though the person may not have been formally enrolled in any Soviet-sponsored organization or subjected to individual supervision by Soviet officials.

red — (n) as used in this book, the non-capitalized word means a person dedicated to, or working for, the destruction of the government to which he owes allegiance, whether or not that person recognizes this result as his goal. Violence is an accepted strategy, but not a necessary tactic in all cases.

Reign of Terror — A period of anarchy, bloodshed, and confiscation in the French Revolution, during which the country was under the sway of an overpowering fear inspired by the ferocious measures of its temporary rulers. It began in the spring of 1793 and practically ended with the fall of Robespierre, July 27, 1794.

religious — (n, singular & pl.) Person(s) bound by monastic vows, or sequestered from secular concerns, and devoted to a life of piety and religion; a monk or friar; a nun.

sanction — (n) *Law* The detriment loss of reward, or other coercive intervention annexed to a violation of a law as a means of enforcing the law. This may consist in the direct infliction of injury or inconvenience, as in the punishment of crime (punitive sanctions) or in mere coercion, restitution or undoing of what was wrongly accomplished, as in the judgments of civil actions (civil sanctions), [etc].

sectarian — an ardent, often narrow-minded adherent of a sect.

sentient — (adj) 1. Capable of sensation and of at least rudimentary consciousness. 2. Serving as the physical correlative of consciousness; sensitive. 3. Subject to the play of sensation.

shabbes goy — also given as shabbos goy, and also shabbot/shabbas. "Someone doing the dirty work for others. — (Lit., gentile doing work for a jew on Sabbath)."

shibboleth — The criterion, test, or watchword of something, as: **a.** A word or saying distinguishing the adherents of a party or sect; as, the shibboleths of democracy; a party cry or pet phrase.

solipsism — *Philos* The theory, assumption, or belief that: *a* The self knows and can know nothing but its own modifications and states. *b* That the self is the only existent thing, or, inaccurately, that all reality is subjective. Except as inaccurately applied by opponents to certain forms of idealism, 'solipsism' represents only a hypothetical position incidentally used in metaphysical reasonings.

soviet — A council; specifically, [often capitalized] either one of two governing bodies in the USSR established as a result of the Russian revolution of 1917 and the constitution of the Republic of July 1918, and later by the constitution of the Union, July 1923. "Soviets" were the primary elements of a government based on the principle of communism. They were the supreme local authorities, and sent deputies to the higher soviet congresses.

species — (ns & np) *Biol.* A category of classification lower than a genus or subgenus and above a subspecies or variety; a group of biota which possess in common one or more characters distinguishing them from similar groups, and do or may interbreed and reproduce their characters in their offspring, exhibiting between each other only minor differences bridged over by intermediate forms (as, subspecies) and differences ascribable to age, sex, polymorphism, individual peculiarity or accident, or to selective breeding by man; a distinct kind of living organism. With the abandonment of the doctrine of separate creation of species, the term *species* lost much theoretical importance. In the case of closely allied groups, common practice is to recognize those as distinct species whose members are not known to, or are assumed not to, intergrade with some other species, even if the characters distinguishing them are very slight. Groups which intergrade are regarded as subspecies.

statistics — (n) 1. (Construed as singular) The science of the collection and classification of relative numbers or occurrences as a ground for induction; systematic compilation of instances for the inference of general truths; the doctrine of frequency distributions. 2. (Construed as plural) Classified facts respecting the condition in various respects of people in a state, or respecting any particular class or interest; esp., facts which can be stated in numbers, or in tables of numbers.

strategy — As used by the author, the word means a generalized plan for achieving a relatively large and previously defined objective over a period of time, as opposed to actions and decisions developed during, or immediately before and after, the course of a campaign.

substantive — (adj) Having the character or status of, or referring to that which is real rather than apparent; firm; solid.

suspicional — (adj) Of, or pertaining to suspicion, esp., the morbid, suspicions marking incipient insanity.

swamp — (n) Wet, spongy, land; soft, low ground that is saturated, but not usually covered, with water; specif., *Ecol.* such a tract, sometimes inundated, and characteristically dominated by trees and shrubs. It differs from a bog in not having an acid substratum.

teleology — (n) The fact or the character of being directed toward an end or shaped by a purpose; said esp. of natural processes, or of nature as a whole, conceived as determined by final causes, or by the design of a divine Providence, and opposed to purely mechanical determinism or causation exclusively by what is temporally antecedent, esp. the doctrine that processes of life are not exclusively determined by mechanical causes, but are directed toward the realization of certain normal, wholes or entelechies; opposed to mechanism. 2. The philosophical study of evidence of design in nature.

theology — (n) 1. The ideational element in religion; religious knowledge or belief; esp. when methodically formulated. 2. More loosely, theological science; the scientifically critical, historical, and psychological study of religion and religious ideas; specif., of the Bible and historical and contemporary Christianity.

Third International — a group or movement that has also been called *Communist International* or *Red International*. It was formed in Moscow in March 1919, under the leadership of the Russian Communist party, and was composed of affiliated national Communist parties, which called upon the world's proletariat to overthrow all existing capitalistic governments. Officially disbanded at Moscow in May 23, 1943, but it was revived in a limited form in 1947 as the Cominform or Communist Information Bureau, with its center originally in Belgrade but later (1948) moved to Bucharest.

trait-complex — *Anthropol.* A group of functionally related traits in a culture of a people as distinguished from a single trait, as a complex including all the observances, property rights, and processes associated in the making of pottery.

treason — (n) in general, the offense of attempting by overt acts to overthrow the government of the state to which the offender owes allegiance. According to the United States Constitution (Article III, Section 3.1.): "Treason against the United States shall consist in levying war against them, or in adhering to their enemies, giving them aid and comfort. No person shall be convicted of treason unless on the testimony of two witnesses to the same overt act, or on confession in open court." And, (Article III, Section 3.2.) "The Congress shall have power to declare the punishment of treason, but no attainder of treason shall work corruption of blood, or forfeiture except during the life of the person attained." It seems any state can punish treason, since Article IV, Section 2, states, in part: "A person charged in any State with treason . . . "

type — (n) 1. *Anthropology* The pattern or average of the characteristics which define the inbreeding division of man (as a tribe or nation) or of the fundamental characteristics which define the race, or of the characteristics of a homogenous group as determined by measurements on the skeleton or the body, the average and range of variability considered as defining the type for the group. 2. (*Biol. and Physiol.*) A group classified according to the physiological and morphological characters of the individuals and to their specific interreaction; as a blood "type."

Utopia — 1. The title of a book by Thomas More, published about 1516, describing an imaginary land having a high degree of desirable features. 2. Hence, any place or state of ideal perfection, esp., in laws, government, and social conditions; also, an impracticable scheme of social regeneraton.

WASP — "White-Anglo Saxon-Protestant." A derogatory or derisive term apparently invented by E. Digby Baltzell in about 1964, and widely used, especially by Jews, to incite and justify prejudice against Christians in general, and white Christians especially.

wolf — (n) Any of certain large doglike carnivorous mammals of the genus *Canis*; especially, the European *C. lupis* or allied species. It is crafty, rapacious, and very destructive to game and cattle. It is usually cowardly, but sometimes attacks men. Wolves sometimes breed with dogs, especially Eskimo dogs.

Abbreviations: (adj) = adjective; (adv) = adverb; (n) = noun; (np) = noun, plural form; (ns) = noun, singular form; (v) = verb; (vi) intransitive verb; (vt) transitive verb.

bibliography

What rage for fame attends both great and small!
Better be damned than mentioned not at all.
To the Royal Academicians
John Wolcott (1738-1819)

Adalja, A. 1998. Capitalist radical, not an anarchist. WSJ *102*, No. 20,

Allen, M., et al. 2001. Uncertainty in the IPCC's Third Assessment Report. Sci. *293*, 430.

Al-Olayan, E., et al. 2002. Complete development of mosquito . . . . Sci. *295*, 204.

Alverson, K., et al. 2001. A global paleoclimate observing system. Sci. *293*, 47

Anderson, C., and Bushman, B. 2002. Effects of media violence . . . . Sci. *295*, 2377.

Angulo, A. 2001. An infamous campaign against human rights. WSJ *237*, No. 124, A-15.

Anon. 1970A. Communism and the New Left. US News & World Report, Washington DC

Anon. 1970B. The Human Cost of Soviet Communism. US Senate Internal Security.

Anon. 1988A. Communists congregate. Campus Report *3*, No. 7, 1

Anon. 1988B. Squeaky chalk. Campus Report *3*, No. 4, 2

Anon. 1988C. Stanford: Equal time for Marx. Campus Report *3*, 4.

Anon. 1992A. Dr. Marx's therapy. WSJ (5 May 1992) p.A10

Anon. 1992B. Notable and quotable. WSJ 7-24-92, p. 10.

Anon. 1994. Reductio ad absurdum. Operation Phoenix. Heterodoxy *2*, No. 11, 3.

Anon. 1999. Anarchist group is blamed for vandalism in Seattle. WSJ *104*, No.

Anon. 2001A. Bush proposes $500 million in AIDS fight. WSJ *239*, no. 190, D4.

Anon. 2001B. CAFE's true cost. WSJ *238*, No. 14, A-10.

Anon. 2001C. Emissions impossible? WSJ *238*, No. 15, A-14.

Anon. 2001D. George's cross. WSJ *238*, No. 25, A-12.

Anon. 2001E. Going coastal. WSJ *238*, No. 9, A-10.

Anon. 2001F. Hamster alert! Software Strategies *6*, No. 10, 10.

Anon. 2001G. Hold the granola. HE *57*, No. 27, 24.

Anon. 2001H. Lean, green recession machine. WSJ *238*, No. 8, A-10

Anon. 2001I. NRDC sues over arsenic standard for . . . water. C&EN *79*, No. 28, 30.

Anon. 2001J. Professor Weatherman. WSJ *238*. No. 84, A-22.

Anon. 2001K. Senate sides with suckers. WSJ *238*, No. 10, A-22.

Anon. 2001L. The earth rebalanced. WSJ *238*, No. 6, A-18.

Anon. 2001M. Tony & tacky: Grin and bear it. WSJ *238*, No. 39, W-13.

Anon. 2001N. Transgenic mice: Leading to "Green" Pigs? TCAW *10*, No. 6, 12.

Anon. 2002A. Arrested development. WSJ *239*, No. 13, W13 A-15

Anon. 2002B. Endangering the Beltway. WSJ *239*, No. 7, A12

Anon. 2002B. More hot air on Kyoto. WSJ *239*, No. 109, A18.

Anon. 2002C. The law of the jungle. WSJ *239*, No. 174, A-18.

Armey, D. 1992. Socialism on campus. WSJ 19 Aug 92, A8.

Arnold, R. 1982. At the Eye of the Storm. Regnery Gateway, Chicago.

Auerbach, A.J. 1992. The galls of academe. Barrons (14 Sep 1992) p. 8

Ayers, R.D. 2001. It's what you don't say. Sci. *180*, 211

Ball, J. 2001. GM report asserts . . . rules mean more deaths. WSJ *238*, No. 9, B-7.

Bank, D. 2002. All species great and small. WSJ *239*, No. 15, B1.

Barrett, D.V. 1996. Sects, Cults, and Alternative Religions. Cassell, London

Bartley, R.L. 2000. The press pack: news by stereotype. WSJ *236*, No. 49, A45.

Beatty, R.G. 1973. The DDT Myth: Triumph of the Amateurs. The John Day Co., NYC

Beck, R. 1993. Roadmap for a queer church. Heterodoxy *1*. No. 12, 13.

Ben-Yehuda, N. (1993). Political Assassination by Jews. State U of NY Press, Albany NY

Bernstein, R. 1994. Dictatorship of Virtue. Knopf, NYC

Billingsley, K.L. 1993. PC goes to church. Heterodoxy *1*. No. 12, 1.

Bittman, L. 1985. The KGB and Soviet Disinformation. Pergamon-Brassey's, NYC

Block, R. 2001. Saving dogs . . . Bailey is finding people . . . . WSJ *238*, No. 5, 1A.

Blum, D. 1994. The Monkey Wars. Oxford U Press, NYC

Bozell, L.B., III 1999. Marxist rage against the machine: HE *55*, No. 48, 16.

Bozell, L.B., III 2001. John Stossel's silly censors. HE *57*, No. 26, 13.

Brogan, C. 1948. Our New Masters. London,

Bromwich, D. 1992. Politics by Other Means. Yale U Press, New Haven CT

Brooks, P. 1971. The Pursuit of Wilderness. Houghton-Mifflin, Boston MA

Brown, D. 2001. Civil liberties groups to fight snooping. Inter@ctive *8*, No. 37, 13.

Brownfeld, A.C. 1999. Fundamentalists and the Millennium: WROMEA June 1999, 82.

Bugliosi, V., and Gentry, C. 1974. Helter Skelter. W.W. Norton & Co., NYC

Burg, D.L. 2001. Kyoto ill-conceived. WSJ *238*, No. 20, A-19.

Burtchaell, J.T. 1988. How authentically Christian . . . Review of Politics *50*, 264.

Campbell, K.J. 1994. Moscow's Words, Western Voices. AIM, Washington DC

Carens, A. 2002. US rise in HIV catches the least aware. WSJ *240*, No. 5, A-17.

Carlton, J. 2001A. A quiet truce in the Green wars. WSJ *238*, No. 97, B1.

Carlton, J. 2001B. Studying pollution's impact on genetic level. WSJ *238*, No. 21, B-1.

Carlton, J. 2002. The howl you hear may . . . be Mr. Haber. WSJ *239*, No. 3, A1.

Carlton, J., and Murray, M. 2001. Scientists dispute benefits. WSJ *238*, No. 23, A-4.

Carreyrou, J. 2001. Carlos the Jackal . . . to marry lawyer. WSJ *238*. No. 90, A 1.

Carson, R. 1962. Silent Spring. Houghton Mifflin, NYC

Carstairs, G.M. 1958. The Twice-Born. Indiana U Press, Bloomington IN

Chaker, A.M. 2001. Conservatives seek IRS inquiry . . . . WSJ *237*, No. 121, B-1.

Chase, A. 1995. In a Dark Wood. Houghton Mifflin, NYC

Cho, A. 2002. Transgenic moths on the make. Sci. *295*, 619.

Cleckley, H. 1964. The Mask of Sanity, 4th ed. The C.V. Mosby Co., St. Louis MO

Cloninger, D. et al. 2002. Scientific data support executions. WSJ *239*, No. 125, A21.

Cohen, J., et al. 2001 . . . transmission of American tryposomiasis. Sci. *293*, 694.

Colvin, R.A. 2002. Will Robert Altman ever say goodbye? WSJ *239*, No. 36, A19.

Conquest, R. 1971. The human cost of Soviet communism. US Senate Doc. *92-36*. US Govt. Printing Office, Washington DC

Conquest, R. 1990. The Great Terror: A Reassessment. Oxford U Press, NYC

Conquest, R. 1992. Getting Communism wrong. WSJ 9-15-1992.

Courtois, S. (ed) 1999. The Black Book of Communism. Harvard U Press, Cambridge MA.

Crandall, R., and Smith, F. 2001. Carbon dioxide controls . . . . WSJ *238*, No. 21, A-18.

Creque, S. 2001. The deranged war against 'bad things.' WSJ *238*. No. 124, A-1.

Crosland, C.A.R. 1957. The Future of Socialism. Macmillan, NYC

Crowder, H.S. 2002. Clap if you believe ethanol will solve . . . WSJ *239*, No. 102, A13.

Dalrymple, T. 2001. Life at the Bottom. Ivan R. Dee, NYC

Davis, A. 1974. Angela Davis: With My Mind on Freedom. Bantam Books, NYC

Del Genio, A.D. 2002. The dust settles on water vapor feedback. Sci. *296*, 665.

Desowitz, R.S. 1993. The Malaria Capers. WW Norton & Co.

Donovan, J. 1962. Red Machete. Bobbs-Merrill, Indianapolis IN

Dreazen, Y.J. 2001. Cellular towers get static . . . . WSJ *238*, No. 15, B-1.

Dziak, R., and Johnson, H. 2002. Stirring the ocean incubator. Sci. *296*, 1406.

Easterbrook, G. 2001. Free speech doesn't come without cost. WSJ *238*. No. 89, A20.

Efron, E. 1972. The News Twisters. Manor Books, NYC

Ehrlich, P., and Ehrlich, A. 1973. The Population Explosion. Simon and Schuster, NYC

Ehrlich, P., et al. 1973. Human Ecology. W. H. Freeman & Co., San Francisco

Ellenson, D. 2001. A Jewish legal authority addresses Jewish-Christian dialogue. Am. Jewish Archives J. (Sept.) 113.

Endlich, L. 1999. Goldman Sachs: The Culture of Success. Alfred A. Knopf, NYC.

Essien-Udom, E.U. 1962. Black Nationalism. U Chicago Press.

Evans, M.S. 2000. Media myths and Joe McCarthy. HE *56*, No. 37, 12.

Fahlman, B.D. 2001. The apparent energy shortage. TCAW *10*, No. 7, 57.

Fainsod, M. 1953. How Russia is Ruled. Harvard U Press, Cambridge MA

Feder, D. 2001. Sierra Club Democrats vs. National Security. HE *57*, No. 43, 18.

Fedder, D. 2001. Eco-clerics Biblically off-base. HE *57*, No. 27, 16,

Fenchel, T. 2001. Marine bugs and carbon flow. Sci. *292*, 2444.

Ferguson, T. 1988. The battle against liberal bias. WSJ (4-8-1988) p. 9

Fialka, J.J. 2001. Talks on climate-change . . . hit . . . snags. WSJ *238*, No. 15, A-16.

Fialka, J.J. 2002. EPA investigates emissions of ethanol plants. WSJ *239*, No. 89, A2.

Finsen, L., et al. 1994. The Animal Rights Movement in America. Twayne, NYC

Fontaine, P., et al. In Courtois, S., et al. The Black Book of Communism: crimes, terror, repression. Harvard U Press, Cambridge MA.

Foulke-ffeinberg, F. 1995. Twilight of the Universities. Pan-Tech Internat'l, McAllen TX

Foulke-ffeinberg, F. 1998. The Virtual Campus. Pan-Tech International, McAllen TX

Fountain, C. 2002. Clap if you believe ethanol will solve . . . . WSJ *239*, No. 102, A13.

Fournier, R. 2001. President unveils climate initiatives. SA Daily News (AP) WSJ *136*, No. 284, 12-B.

Fox, M.A. 1986. The Case for Animal Experimentation. U of CA Press, Berkeley CA

Fox, M.W. 1991. Animals Have Rights, Too. Continuum, NYC

Francione, G.L. Rain Without Thunder: The Ideology of the Animal Rights Movement. Temple U Press, Philadelphia PA

Fukuda-Parr, S. 2001. Politically incorrect UN. WSJ *238*, No. 8, A-16.

Fumento, M. 1993. Science Under Siege. Quill/William Morrow, NYC

Galbreath, R.L. 2001. Ah, for the days when discourse was ripe. WSJ *238*. No. 85, A23

Giraudi, C. 2001. Bush's energy policy. C&EN *79*, No. 29, 6.

Goldberg, B. 2001. Bias: A CBS insider exposes how media distorts . . . Regnery.

Goldenberg, S., et al. 2001. Recent increase in Atlantic hurricane activity. Sci. *293*, 474.

Goodman, J., and Walsh, V. 2001. The Story of Taxol. Cambridge U Press

Gore, A. 1992. Earth in the Balance. Houghton Mifflin Co., NYC

Gow, H.B. 1995. Not applying the death penalty is cruel . . . . HE *52*, No. 45, 22.

Graham, F. 1970. Since Silent Spring. Houghton-Mifflin, Boston

Green, S.K. 2001. Green chemistry. C&EN *79*, No. 29, 27.

Grossman, R. 2001. Anarchists. What are they for? (AP) McA Monitor *3*, No. 39, 1D.

Gutierrez, G. 1973. A Theology of Liberation. Orbis, Maryknoll NY

Gutierrez, G. 1983. The Power of the Poor in History. Orbis, Maryknoll NY

Halevi, Y.K. 1995. Stranger at Home. Memoirs of a Jewish Extremist. Story. Little, Brown & Co., NYC

Hammond, K.A., et al. (Editors). Sourcebook on the Environment: A Guide to the Literature. U of Chicago Press, Chicago

Harnack, A. (ed.) 1996. Animal Rights: Opposing Viewpoints. Greenhaven Press, San Diego

Hartwright, C. 1999. The JFK Assassination. Pan-Tech International, McAllen TX

Hayden, T. (ed.) 2002. The Zapatista Reader. Thunder's Mouth Press.

Herbert, T., et al. 2001. Collapse of the California current . . . Sci. *293*, 71,

Herrick, T. 2002. BT will drop MTBE for ethanol. . . WSJ *239*, No. 87, A4

Hill, C. 1972. The World Turned Upside Down. Maurice Temple Smith, London UK

Hoffheiser, C. 2001. Previous hot theory was global cooling. WSJ *237*, No. 119, A-23

Hoover, J.E. 1958. Masters of Deceit. Holt, Rinehart, and Winston, NYC

Howard, P.K. 1994. The Death of Common Sense. Random House, NYC

Huang, J., et al. 2002. Plant biotechnology in China. Sci. *295*, 674.

Hurley, J.A. 1999. Animal Rights. Greenhaven Press, San Diego CA ..

Irvine, R. (Ed.) 1994. Smithsonian plot thwarted. AIM Report *23*, No. 21, 1

Jasper, J.M., and Nelkin, D. 1992. The Animal Rights Crusade: The Growth of a Moral Protest. Free Press, NYC

Jenkins, H.W., Jr. 2001. How to be agreeable about global warming. *WSJ*, No. 17, A-7.

Johnson, G.J., et al. 2002. Television viewing and aggressive behavior . . . Science *295*, 2469.

Jones, P. 1991. The 1848 Revolutions, 2nd ed. Longman, NYC

Kaiser, J. 2001. Recreated wetlands no match for original. Sci. *239*, 25

Karatnycky, A. 2000. Modern martyrs. WSJ *237*, No. 127, W-17

Kellen, K. 1990. Ideology and rebellion. *In* Origins of Terrorism. Woodrow Wilson Center Press, Washington DC.

Kennedy, D. 2002. Good news on a tropical disease. Sci. *296*, 1365.

Kimball, R. 1992. "Heterotextuality" and other literary matters. WSJ *90*, No. 122, A6

Kingston, D.G.I. 2001. A blockbuster drug that almost wasn't. C&EN *79*, No. 35, 64.

Kingston, G. 2001. Wetlands owners seek top dollar. WSJ *238*, No. 17, A-17.

Klick, C. 2001. Emissions appeasement. WSJ *238*, No. 20, A-19.

Koestler, A. 1976. The Thirteenth Tribe: The Khazar Empire and Its Heritage. Random House, NYC

Kolber et al. (2001) Science *292*, 2492

Kraus, R. 2001. Bible forbids Jews marrying gentiles. WSJ *238*, No. 3, A-13.

Kuntz, P. 2001. Left-wing conspiracy? WSJ *238*, No. 34, A-1.

Landsburg, S.E. 2001. The imperialism of compassion. *WSJ*, No. 15, A-14.

Lea, D.W. 2001. Ice ages, the California current, and Devil's Hole. Sci. *293*, 59.

Leaming, B. 2001. The "unmasking" of Liberation Technology. Internet — www.n4gix.8m.com/Catholic Pages/liberation_theology

Lee, H.B., Jr. 2001. On global warming, cooler heads prevail. WSJ *238*, No. 39, A-9.

Leo, J. 1994. Two Steps Ahead of the Thought Police. Simon & Shuster, NYC

Lewis, A. 2001. TV: A documentary dispels an urban legend. WSJ *257*, No. 125, A-17.

Lichter, S., et al. 1986. The Media Elite. Adler & Adler, Bethesda MD

Lipschultz, D. 2002. Bosses from abroad. Chief Executive, No. 174, 18.

Liroff, R.A. 2001. Alternatives to DDT can control malaria. WSJ *238*, No. 13, A-23.

Lovel, H.M.S. 2001. Butterfly rebuttal. Sci. News *160*, 275.

Lutherer, L.O., and Simon, M.S. 1992. The Anatomy of an Animal Rights Attack. U of OK Press, Norman OK

Luzzatto, L., and Notaro, R. 2001. Protecting against bad air. Sci. *293*, 442.

MacDonald, H. 2001. Will the excuse empire return? WSJ *238*, No. 127, A8.

Maher, K. 2002. Foundation fishes for operating chief. WSJ *239*, No. 108, B-14.

Malia, M. 1999. Foreword: The uses of atrocity. In Courtois, S., et al. The Black Book of Communism. Harvard U Press, Cambridge MA.

Margolin, J-L., and Rigoulot, P. 1999. In Courtois, S., et al. The Black Book of Communism.. Harvard U Press, Cambridge MA.

Martin, J.J. 1970. Men Against the State. Ralph Myles Publisher, Colorado Springs CO

Mason, J. 1993. An Unnatural Order: Uncovering the Roots of Our Domination of Nature and Each Other. Simon & Schuster, NYC

McCarthy, D. 2002. Scientific data support executions' effect. WSJ *239*, No. 125, A21.

McCourt, F. 2002. A call to action for Irish to seek their roots. SAXN *137*, No. 158, 7H

McGovern, A., et al. 1988. Updating Liberation Theology. America *159*, No. 2, 33.

McGowan, W. 1994. The fall of city college. WSJ *94*, No. 66, A16

McKinney, Ian. 2001. Why Jews are communists. www.jeffsarchive.com

McNear, D.J. 2001. Home for aging rads: The campus, of course. WSJ *238*, No. 89, A21.

Meehan, W., III. 1994. Leo's new book keeps PC crowd hopping. Campus Rept. *9*, No.9, 6.

Mencken, H.L. 1920. *Introduction* to Mencken's English translation of Nietzsche's *The Antichrist*. Alfred A. Knopf, NYC

Mendoza, F., et al. 2000. Risk factors associated with malaria ... Trans. R. Soc. Trop. Med. Hyg. *94*, no. 4, 367

Mendoza, P.A. 2001. How Colombia's rebels use 'Human rights' as a weapon. WSJ *237*, No. 117, A-15.

Midgely, M. 1978. Beast and Man. Cornell U Press, Ithaca NY

Milius, S. 2002. Better mosquito. Sci. News *161*, 324.

Miller, H.I. 2001. Science and the UN's Luddites. WSJ *238*, No. 20, A-19.

Miller, J. J. 2002. How do you say 'extinct'? WSJ *239*, No. 47, W13.

Moreno, J.G. 2001. An infamous campaign against ... rights. WSJ *237*, No. 124, A-15.

Muggeridge, M. 1972. Chronicles of Wasted Time. Regnery Publishing, Washington DC

Naik, G. 2001. Deadly mutant strain of malaria appears to have reached Africa. WSJ *238*, No. 18, B-1.

Naik, G. 2002. Agency to unveil a joint assault on TB and HIV. WSJ *240*, No. 6, D4.

Neusner, J. 1981. Stranger at Home: "The Holocaust," Zionism, and American Judaism. U of Chicago Press, Chicago IL

Nietzsche, F. 1920. The Antichrist [Mencken's English translation]. Knopf, NYC)

Niven, C.D. 1967. History of the Humane Movement. Johnson, London UK

O'Grady, M.A. 2001. What about Colombia's terrorists. WSJ *238*, No. 68, A-15.

Olasky, M. 2000. Zeus bless America. Brill's Content *3*, No. 4, 68.

Oman, C. 1968. The Great Revolt of 1381. Haskell House Publ., NYC

Orlans, F.B. 1993. In the Name of Science: Isues in Responsible Animal Experimentation. Oxford U Press, NYC

Orlov, A. 1953. The Secret History of Stalin's Crimes. Random House, NYC

Ostrovsky, V. 1994. The Other Side of Deception: A rogue agent exposes the Mossad's secret agenda. Harper-Collins Publ., NYC

Ostrovsky, V., and Hoy, C, 1990. By Way of Deception: The making and unmaking of a Mossad officer. St. Martin's Press, NYC

Paczkowski, A., and Bartosek, K. 1999. The other Europe. In The Black Book of Communism. Harvard U Press, Cambridge MA.

Pauken, T. 1995. The Thirty Years War. Jameson Books, Ottawa IL

Pease, T.C. 1965. The Leveller Movement. Peter Smith, Gloucester MA

Pennisi, E. 2001A. Malaria's beginnings on the heels of hoes. Sci. *293*, 417.

Pennisi, E. 2001B. Sequences reveal borrowed genes. Sci. *294*, 1705.

Perkins, S. 2001A. Amazon forest could disappear, soon. Sci. News *160*, 24

Perkins, S. 2001B. Atlanta leaves big chemical footprint. Sci. News *160*, 24

Perkins, S. 2001C. Earth science. Sci. News, *153*, 6

Perkins, S. 2001D. For past climate clues, ask a stalag-mite [sic]. Sci News, *160*. 55.

Perkins, S. 2001E. New type of hydrothermal vent looms large. Sci. News *160*, 21.

Prell, R-E. 1999. Fighting to Become Americans: Assimilation and the Trouble between Jewish Women and Jewish Men. Beacon Press, Boston MA

Pryce-Jones, D. 2001. Evil empire. The Communist 'hot, smart book of the moment.' Nat. Rev. *53*, No. 18, 72.

Queary, P. 2001. Falling into a trap. Ban leads to too much wildlife. SA Express News *137*, No. 11, 25-A.

Radosh, R., et al. (Ed.) 2000. Spain Betrayed. Yale U Press, New Haven CT

Raloff, J. 2001. A foamy threat to ozone. Sci. News *160*, 9

Raloff, J. 2001. Climate accord reached. Sci. News *160*, 54.

Ramirez, A.L. 2001. Peasants caught in the middle of war. WSJ *238*, No. 11, A-18.

Ray, D.L., and Guzzo, L. 1993. Environmental Overkill: Whatever Happened to Common Sense? Regnery Gateway, Washington.

Reavis, D.J. 2001. Ex-Weatherman in a new climate. San Antonio Express News *137*, No. 60, 6H.

Reavis, D.J. 2002. The power and the story. SAXN *137*, No. 158, 7H

Reese, R.M. 2001. Australia fights methane. C&EN *79*, No. 23, 194.

Regan, T. 1987. Struggle for Animal Rights. Intl. Soc. Animal Rights, Clarks Summit PA

Regan, T., and Singer, P. (eds.) 1989. Animal Rights and Human Obligations. Prentice-Hall, NJ

Reich, W. (ed) 1990. Origins of Terrorism: Psychologies, ideologies, theologies, states of mind. Woodrow Wilson Ctr. Press, Wash. DC

Revel, J.F. 1991. (C. Cate, trans.) The Flight from Truth. Random House, NYC

Rich, F.C. 2001. Greens go to market. WSJ *238*, No. 23, A-15

Rind, D. 2002. The sun's role in climate variations. Sci. *296*, 673

Risen, J., and Johnston, D. 2001. Hanssen's wife says she knew. SA Express News (ex NY Times) *136*, No. 256, 15-A.

Ritter, S.K. 2001. Accepting the Green challenge. C&EN *79*, No. 27, 24.

Ritvo,, H. 1987. The Animal Estate. Harvard U, Cambridge MA

Roberts, D.R., et al. 2000. DDT . . . spraying and . . . malaria. Lancet *356*, 330.

Roberts, P.C. 2001. Academia and media remain hostile to America. Human Events *57*, No. 41, 4.

Roberts, S. 2001. The Brother. Random House, NYC

Roleff, T.L. and Hurley, J.A. (eds.) 1999. The Rights of Animals. Greenhaven Press, San Diego CA

Ross, G. 2002. Sacrificed on altar of genetic purity. WSJ *239*, No. 42, A-15

Ross, P.E. 1999. Safety may be hazardous to your health. [prob. Forbes, late in the year]

Rosseaux, C. 2001. Ambiguity . . . approach to global warming. HE *57*, No. 26, 13.

Rubinkam, M. 2001. Fugitive "Unicorn" returns to US 22 years later. McAllen Monitor (AP release) *93*, No. 384, 3A.

Rusher, W.A. 1988. The Coming Battle for the Media Elite. Morrow.

Ryan, V. 2000. No free speech for the right-minded. Spotlight *26*, No. 48, 16.

Ryder, R.D. 1989. Animal Revolution. Basil Blackwell, Oxford UK

Ryskind, A.H. 2002. Hollywood celebrates Reds — again. HE *58*, No. 11, 11.

Salt, H.S. 1980. Animals' Rights (Reprint 1892 ed.) Soc. for Animal Rights, Clarks Summit PA

Schafly, P. 1994. Flawed heroes of cultural trends. Campus Report *9*, No. 9, 7.

Schoeck, H. 1966. Envy. Liberty Press, Indianapolis IN

Schoofs, M., and Zimmerman, R. 2002. Sexual politics drive AIDS. WSJ *240*, No. 6, D4.

Schubert, C. 2001. Global warming debate gets hotter. Sci. News *159*, 372. 381.

Schwarz, F. 1972. The Three Faces of Revolution. Capitol Hill Press, Falls Church VA.

Seltzer, W. 1991. Deconstructionism's founder deconstructed. WSJ *87*, Mar. 15, A10

Seppa, N. 2001. Synthetic protein may yield malaria vaccine. Sci. News *160*, 54.

Shafarevich, I. 1980. The Socialist Phenomenon (trans. W. Tjalsma) Harper & Row, NYC

Shafran, A. 2001. Bible forbids Jews marrying gentiles. WSJ *238*, No. 3, A-13.

Shelef, M. 2002. Clap if you believe ethanol will solve anything. WSJ *239*, No. 102, A13.

Shriver, L. 2001. A conference of victims. WSJ *238*, No. 22, A-14.

Simpson, R.D. 1999. The price of biodiversity. Issues in Science and Technology Online.

Singer, I.B. 1970. [name of article not given]. The New Yorker (March 21, 1970)

Singer, P. 1975. Animal Liberation: A New Ethics . . . . Avon Books, NYC

Singer, P. 1990. Animal Liberation. NY Review of Books, NYC

Smith, R. 2001. That's the way it isn't, truth vs. network news. WSJ *238*, No. 116, A14.

Soden, B.J., et al. 2002. Global cooling after the eruption of Mount Pinatubo: A test of climate feedback by water vapor. Sci. *296*, 727.

Sokolov, R. 2002. A surprise attack . . . you stupid Yanks! WSJ *239*, No. 37, W-13.

Somkin, F. 1990. Commentary on Schlesinger's views. WSJ *85*, May 24, A15

Specht, E.E. 2002. Disciples of Jesus, not the Greens. WSJ *239*, No. 64, A-21

Starkman, D. 2001. More courts . . . misapply eminent domain. WSJ *238*, No. 15, B-1.

Sterba, J.P. 2002. As forest reclaims . . . East, it's man vs. beast. WSJ *239*, No. 99, A1.

Stern, S. 1975. With the Weatherman. Doubleday, Garden City NY

Stern, A. 2001. Risk vs. effect. Sci. News *160*, 51.

Strassel, K.A. 2001. Rural cleansing. WSJ *238*, No. 18, A-14.

Strassel, K.A. 2002. Hug a logger, not a tree. WSJ *239*, No. 101, A16.

Strobach, M. 2001. Hot topic. Sci. News *160*, 51.

Sturua, M. 1991. How a tyrant made us believe in him. Parade Mag. 28 July, p. 4.

Sullivan, A. 2001. The agony of the Left. WSJ *238*, No. 67, A-22.

Swanson, S. 2001. Ex-radicals . . . rile alumni . . . Chi. Trib. (11/4/2001 Sec. 1, p. 17).

Swires, L. 2001. Marxist rebels thrive on Colombian weakness. WSJ *238*. No. 18, A15

Tam, P-W. 2001. Turning videocams into weapons. WSJ *238*, No. 50, B1.

Taylor, M.T. 2001. Butterfly rebuttal. Sci. News *160*, 275.

Terzian, P. 2002. Idle, addicted, violent — and self-pitying. WSJ *239*, No. 36,

Thompson, D., and Wallace, J. 2001. Regional climate impacts of the Northern Hemisphere annular mode. Sci. *233*, 85

Thurow, R. 2001. Choice of evils. WSJ *238*, No. 18, A-1.

Timmons, B. 1990. That's no Okie, thats my torts professor. WSJ *85*, Apr. 3, A20

Toman, M. 2001. On emissions: No pain, no gain. WSJ *238*, No. 26, A-15.

Tooley, M. 2001. Liberal clergy rally against land mines. HE *57*, No. 29, 12.

Trenberth, K.E. 2001. Climate variability and global warming. Sci. *293*, 48.

Turk, D., et al. 2001. Remotely sensed biological production . . . Pacific. Sci. *293*, 472.

Undeland, J.R. 2002. Bridge project protects our eagle neighbors. WSJ *239*, No. 25, A19.

Vasilieva, L. 1992. Kremlin Wives (translated by C. Porter). Arcade Publishing, NYC

Vogel, G., et al. 2002. Science scope. Science *296*, 1381.

Waldman, D. 1994. Dissembling at Yale. WSJ *94*, No. 124, A17.

Waldman, P. 2001. While deploring . . . radicals fear crackdown. WSJ *238*, No. 52, A4.

Watkins, K. 2001. Ethanol's sunny day. C&EN *79*, No. 30, 21

Watkins, K. 2002. Company sues EPA over pesticide. C&EN *March 18*, p. 10.

Webb, J. 2002. Is Hollywood pro-military now? WSJ *239*, No. 58, A18.

Weiss, H., and Bradley, R. 2001. What drives societal collapse? Science *291*, 609.

Werth, N. 1999. A state against its people. *In* The Black Book of Communism. Harvard U Press, Cambridge MA.

Windham, C. 2001. Measures to cut auto emissions . . . . WSJ *238*, No. 13, A-14.

Wormser, R.A. 1958. Foundations: Their Power and Influence. Devin-Adair, NYC

Ybarra, M.J. 2001. A civil war and the comrades who joined in. WSJ *237*, No. 7, A-15.

Young, W.H. 2002. Disciples of Jesus, not the Greens. WSJ *239*, No. 64, A-21

Zachary, G. 2001. Environmentalists . . . soldiers of fortune. WSJ *237*, NO. 119, A-1.

Zimmer, C. 2001. Inconceivable bugs eat methane on the ocean floor. Sci. *293*, 418.

Zimmerman, R., and Schoofs, M. 2002. World AIDS experts debate treatment vs. prevention. WSJ *240*, No. 3, B1.

Notes:

(1) In alphabetizing titles, the articles THE, A, and AN are considered functional parts of the titles.

(2) States of the Union are *usually* indicated by their postal abbreviation, e.g., GA = Georgia. (3) Some titles of articles were truncated to save space.

Abbreviations of journal titles and other sources:

C&EN = Chemical and Engineering News

JAMA = Journal of the American Medical Association

MDD = Modern Drug Discovery

Sci. = Science

Sci. News = Science News

TCAW = Today's Chemist at Work

WSJ = Wall Street Journal

AP = Associated Press

Internet = most Internet addresses are printed in the text at the end of the discussion of them. However, a few of the more elaborate ones are included in this Bibliography.

INDEX

Printed in the United States
86280LV00007B/1/A